CW00446526

CONFRONTING SCALE IN ARCHAEOLOGY

Issues of Theory and Practice

CONFRONTING SCALE IN ARCHAEOLOGY
Issues of Theory and Practice

Edited by

Gary Lock
University of Oxford
Oxford, United Kingdom

and

Brian Leigh Molyneaux
University of South Dakota
Vermillion, South Dakota, USA

 Springer

Gary Lock
Institute of Archaeology
University of Oxford
36 Beaumont Street
Oxford OX1 2PG
UK
gary.lock@arch.ox.ac.uk

Brian Leigh Molyneaux
University of South Dakota
414 East Clark Street
Vermillion, South Dakota 57069
USA
moly@usd.edu

Library of Congress Control Number: 2006921906

ISBN-10: 0-387-32772-X
ISBN-13: 978-0387-32772-3

©2006 Springer Science+Business Media, LLC
All rights reserved. This work may not be translated or copied in whole or in part without the written
permission of the publisher (Springer Science+Business Media, LLC, 233 Spring Street, New York,
NY 10013, USA), except for brief excerpts in connection with reviews or scholarly analysis. Use in
connection with any form of information storage and retrieval, electronic adaptation, computer software, or
by similar or dissimilar methodology now known or hereafter developed is forbidden. The use in this
publication of trade names, trademarks, service marks and similar terms, even if they are not identified as
such, is not to be taken as an expression of opinion as to whether or not they are subject to proprietary rights.

Printed in the United States of America (SPI/IBT)

9 8 7 6 5 4 3 2 1

springer.com

He form'd a line and a plummet
To divide the Abyss beneath;
He form'd a dividing rule;
He formed scales to weigh,
He formed massy weights;
He formed a brazen quadrant;
He formed golden compasses,
And began to explore the Abyss;
And he planted a garden of fruits.

William Blake, The First Book of Urizen (1794), Chapter VII, Verses 7–8.

Contributors

Joe Alan Artz
Office of the State Archaeologist, University of Iowa, USA

William E. Banks
Institut de Prehistoire et de Geologie du Quaternaire, France

Andrew Bevan
Institute of Archaeology, University College London, UK

Oskar Burger
Department of Anthropology, University of New Mexico, USA

James Conolly
Department of Anthropology, Trent University, Canada

Alan Costall
Department of Psychology, University of Portsmouth, UK

Graham Fairclough
English Heritage, UK

Richard A. Fox
Department of Anthropology and Sociology, University of South Dakota, USA

Chris Gosden
Institute of Archaeology, University of Oxford, UK

Trevor Harris
Department of Geology and Geography, West Virginia University, USA

Gill Hey
Oxford Archaeology, Oxford, UK

Simon Holdaway
Department of Anthropology, University of Auckland, New Zealand

Karola Kirsanow
Department of Anthropology, University of Cambridge, UK

Malcolm Ridges
Department of Environment and Conservation, New South Wales, Australia

Lawrence C. Todd
Department of Anthropology, Colorado State University, USA

Vuk Trifković
Institute of Archaeology, University of Oxford, UK

LuAnn Wandsnider
Department of Anthropology and Geography, University of Nebraska-Lincoln, USA

H. Martin Wobst
Department of Anthropology, University of Massachusetts, USA

Thomas Yarrow
Department of Social Anthropology, University of Cambridge, UK

Larry J. Zimmerman
Department of Anthropology, Indiana University-Purdue University Indianapolis, USA

Acknowledgements

This collection of papers is loosely based on a session at TAG 2000 (Theoretical Archaeology Group) at Oxford University. We would like to thank all of the contributors for their patience and understanding during the gestation and production of this volume. We hope the final result has been worth the wait. We would also like to thank Teresa Krauss of Springer for her support and encouragement.

Preface

Archaeological analysis operates on a continuum of scale from the microscopic analysis of a single artifact to regional interpretations of cultural adaptations over thousands of years. A common assumption is that shifting from one scale to another in space and time is a seamless process. Scale in this sense is invisible, a mere mathematical abstraction. Yet, issues of scale exist at the fundamental level of archaeological interpretation. The traditional analytical debate in archaeology – between advocates of the so-called ''processual'' and ''postprocessual'' approaches – ranges around the question of scales of reasoning. At the one extreme, remote observation and the ability to interpret events and processes over vast reaches of time and space are possible, because the analysis concerns the hoped-for elucidation of general cultural processes; at the other, they are not, as both analyst and subject are isolated in their own subjectivities. Analysts occupying the middle ground often advocate a ''multidimensional'' or ''holistic'' approach, which involves multiple scales of analysis and interpretation.

As the battleground tends to be the degree to which specific datasets and analytical processes justify the interpretations put forth, archaeologists rarely address issues relating to the profound shifts in the scale of visualization necessary in all approaches to the past. And why should they? Ignoring scale is the concession archaeology makes to interpretation. After all, is it not ludicrous to imagine that we can understand actual cultural life from rubbish and ruins? This problem is exacerbated by the rise of computer-based visualization and analysis technologies such as remote sensing, geographical information systems (GIS) and virtual reality (VR). Researchers are now able to resolve and interpret their data at multiple scales almost effortlessly – a seduction so persuasive that the entire issue of scale is simply, and commonly, ignored.

However, scale has a direct impact on archaeology's vision of the past. The common experience of scale by both the subjects of archaeological research and archaeologists relates to space, time and social position. As humans in the lived-in world, we are middle-sized objects and develop our knowledge up and down through the cosmos from this position. By nature, we oversee things and relationships that are smaller than us and use imaginative and technological means to encompass the larger-scale world that we cannot see directly. As for time, the essential problem is that time simply passes, and past time only exists for all practical purposes in the material traces (data) of its action. We are left with the profound problem of recognizing, and reconstituting, masses of data as portions of time (as if time occupies space). Finally, scale as a human phenomenon is culturally constructed. This is simply to recognize that the positions we adopt in life relate to our positions within a society and culture. This clearly affects our perceptions of things and situations and the way we act on, with or through these phenomena. We can therefore interpret cultural production – whether artifacts or archaeological studies – as acts within social (political) discourse at scales related to cultural, rather than natural, dynamics.

To complicate the question further, archaeological analysis has two general referents: the culture of production and the culture of interpretation. The challenge of the archaeologist is to understand the dynamics of scale that entered into production and to account for these in interpretation.

The goal of *Confronting Scale in Archaeology* is to illustrate the workings of scale in the production of culture and its analysis. Befitting its scope, the book brings together scholars from Europe and North America to express their own opinions about this seminal issue. Mindful of the diverse cultural and intellectual traditions represented, we have retained the spellings and word usages consistent with each contributor's cultural milieu. We asked each author to address key questions crucial to multidimensional research into the past for all archaeologists, whether they work with conventional analytical techniques or with computer-based visualization tools:

- How does scale influence our perception of space and time?
- Is an understanding of scale socially, or culturally, constructed? If so, how can we recognize and decipher past meaningful scales of living through the present material record?
- What are the problems and implications of moving between scales? Are scales of meaning different to scales of data and how do we make connections? Are the claims for seamless transitions between scales justified?
- If the production and analysis of material culture have different scales of reference, or even multiple scales of reference, how can we integrate data into the broader interpretive form of a landscape?

By facing the issues of scale head-on in an explicit theoretical discourse, the authors gathered here explore processes of understanding data, the design, conduct and interpretation of surface surveys and excavations, and the nature of past and present human perceptions and uses of the environment. We hope that their insights will enhance archaeology's ceaseless exploration of space, time and culture.

Gary Lock
Brian Molyneaux

Contents

Introduction:
Confronting Scale

Gary Lock and Brian L. Molyneaux

Scale is a slippery concept, one that is sometimes easy to define but often difficult
to grasp. In the practice of archaeology, there is much equivocation about scale, as it
is at the same time a concept, a lived experience and an analytical framework. If
they think about it at all, archaeologists most often treat scale as a sort of geomet-
rical given that they can manipulate at will and without cost in analysis and
interpretation. This is unfortunate. In taking scale for granted, archaeologists rarely
expose its complexities and therefore overlook its crucial role in the process of
representing the past.

The dictionary definition of scale includes terms such as "a graduated series",
"a system of relative values or correspondences" and "a ratio of representation or
relative extent". The sense here is one of scale being relational, of only making
sense as a measure of proportion among other assumably more concrete phenomena. Most explorations of scale in archaeology, with some converging interests in
the disciplines of geography and ecology, have focused on scale as a quantification
issue, or at least an issue concerning things that are in some way quantifiable. This
understanding of scale as "analytical scale" (Mathieu and Scott, 2004a) is obviously important as it feeds into the process of archaeology's basic tasks: collection,
classification and interpretation. Yet, there is much more to scale than this. Archaeology is not a remote laboratory pastime – it is a human task responding to a
seemingly innate curiosity about history and a human construction of past events,
meanings and processes from the traces that are left. Archaeologists deal implicitly
with this qualitative and phenomenological aspect of scale every time they ponder
the passing of time and the transformation of space.

The essence of the problem of scale relates to the human desire to overcome
the perceptual limitations of our middle-sized world. In Chapter 1 of this book, Alan
Costall explores the importance of us understanding the material world in relation to
our "body-scale". His emphasis is on affordances, the action-possibilities of
objects that can only make sense in relation to an agent. Since our physical and
conceptual systems have developed at this bodily scale, there is no guarantee that
we can understand relationships in the larger and smaller worlds that these days

Gary Lock • University of Oxford   Brian L. Molyneaux • University of South Dakota

technology allows us to visit or construct (see Cherniak, 1986). We may lack the physiological capacity and experience to understand these alien worlds, seeing them more as isolated forms than as analogous environments with their own dynamic networks of relations.

This is not simply a practical issue. Every shift from ordinary human experience requires a leap of faith. Ancient hunters pursuing game or navigating through unfamiliar territory seized the opportunity to climb hills and mountains in order to see a greater expanse, prospects that many of their societies also associated with the sacred. This duality of perception and belief suggests that the visualization of the cosmos, the apprehension of the world beyond human space and time that underpins and validates religions, is also, rather humbly, an issue of scale. Indeed, while Galileo Galilei (AD1564–1642) perfected the telescope in 1609 in part so that the military could "discover at a much greater distance than usual the hulls and sails of the enemy" (extract of a letter, in Van Helden, 1989), he soon fell foul of the Catholic Church and was eventually imprisoned after promoting astronomical discoveries that supported the Copernican heliocentric view of the universe. The ability to transcend the limitations of human scale seemed too close to the omniscience of God.

Those landscapes beyond direct sight, aided or unaided, and those we cannot grasp in a single view, require imaginative styles of visualization. Traditionally, people relied mainly on what geographers describe as cognitive or mental maps – spatial schema that all humans use to navigate through cultural and natural landscapes. Today we have a range of additional aids, from old-fashioned paper maps to computer-based geographical information systems (GIS). The problem is that no representation, however detailed, captures an appropriately scaled "reality". This is not simply an issue of the nature and density of information crammed into a frame and flattened into two dimensions: early in the twentieth century, artists such as Picasso, Braque and Duchamps explored the problem of pictorial representation, which, in essence, is the mapping of very small scale moments into spatial constructs that are frozen in time. In the past, such static, map-like transformations of reality very likely contributed to the development of archaeology's concepts of site and culture, which similarly represent diffuse, dynamic and multi-dimensional phenomena as bounded constructs (Molyneaux, 1991).

Turning to archaeology, the essence of the scale issue is the confrontation between the archaeologist and the array of information identified as archaeological, from material objects encountered directly to the host of representations in different media at different degrees of removal from the physical environment. Consider, for example, the difference in engagement between artifacts capable of being held in the hand and those too large or too small. We obviously find it difficult to conceive of these outsized things *as* artifacts: we give the larger ones different names, such as features or structures, and we treat the smaller ones, tiny flake residue from tool manufacture, for example, as subjects of somewhat arcane specialties. Similarly, we have a better understanding of local environments – the places we can explore in an hour or two – than regions that may require a lifetime to cover.

The movement from material information to processed data to knowledge requires an enormous scalar compression, in time and space, leading first to texts and ultimately to the most extreme departure from actuality: the timeline. This oddly compelling heuristic allows us to avoid the fact that while we may have little to say about vast reaches of human history we can represent its existence in a seemingly authoritative way through the piecing together of bits of evidence at different scales. If we compressed space to the same extent, maps of the earth would be limited to views of a bluish globe in the solar system! Temporal scales are generally less considered and discussed than spatial scale and in Chapter 2, Chris Gosden and Karola Kirsanow show why that is so. Archaeological evidence contains within it complex "nested durations" that range from the detailed intimate moments of an individual's life, such as eating a meal or breaking a pot, to the global discussions of issues such as the origins of hunting. Using a series of case-studies they illustrate the qualitative and quantitative dimensions of time which are brought into contention through the range of analytical techniques now available including the chemical analysis of human remains, scientific dating and traditional artifact studies. Well preserved remains, such as the Ötztal ice-man, provide biographical information about the first and final few years of his life through teeth and bone isotopic analysis, his final meal through intestinal contents, as well as positioning him in the wider flux of temporal developments established through radiocarbon dating and artifact typologies. These are nested durations, from moments to millennia.

The lure of perceptual overviews is their greater scope, which seems to facilitate understanding, as one is extending, rather than supplanting, vision and experience. Yet, even these have issues of scale. The Cree use of scapulimancy exemplifies this subtle problem. The Cree, hunters and gatherers in the boreal forests of central and eastern Canada, have a recurring dilemma when they set out to hunt: where in their vast territory is the game? A traditional Cree solution is divination: a hunter scrapes the flesh from the shoulder blade of a moose, caribou or other animal and holds it in the fire, which causes it to craze or crack, and then reads the patterns as a map directing the group to its quarry. In modern times, would he not be better served if he had a map that marked the highest potential areas or, even better, if he could fly over the hunting grounds and spot the game from the air? He would certainly be more successful. By using scapulimancy over time, however, Cree hunters carry out a random form of resource exploitation that decreases the chance of overhunting any one place.

This process has some troubling implications in matters of scale. First, the fact that we think we may know a better way to find game – because of our access to larger scales of view – makes no difference to the Cree, as their magic works; and second, given the evident success of Cree hunting techniques in maintaining stable game populations, our ability to perceive a large territory from the sky and maximize our potential for hunting success may not be as good a solution on the ground as reading cracks in a burnt bone! Indeed, the divinatory solution for the Cree may be a pragmatic approach that emerged through long practical experience – a good instance of magic and religion as useful tools. The lesson is this: we may be pleased and intrigued by the knowledge we gain in the overview, but it may not be particularly useful in practice.

Transforming scale makes a difference in getting facts right, but of course there are no absolute facts, only facts in certain contexts and situations that are mutable and endlessly variable. We can deal with the facts at hand more easily because we can deal with them directly. For everything else the connections that make up our perception and understanding of worlds at other scales are tentative, speculative – and subject to the vicissitudes of the imagination!

CONSIDERATIONS OF SCALE

The explicit discussion, and by implication the theorization, of scale is not recent in archaeology. One of the early doyens of quantitative archaeology, Albert Spaulding, equated scale with "dimensions" and proposed the triad of time, space and form that is still generally accepted today (Spaulding, 1960). Here Spaulding was referring to analytical scale and to material form, whether the tiny attributes of a ceramic thin section seen through the microscope or the regional extent of a "culture" as represented by the distribution map of artefact assemblages. Spaulding's discussion raised issues of lasting interest despite being couched in the language of emerging quantification that characterized the time – the idea of correlation along two or more dimensions. Do large forms (e.g., settlement patterns) automatically fit with large spaces and long time periods, do small forms (e.g., a particular type of pot) always correlate with a small area and short time span? The conclusion at the time was that no necessary correlation existed between these dimensions, no 1:1 relationship, and this emphasis on the complexity and subtlety of trying to understand scale continues today.

In one of the most recent discussions of analytical scale, social form appears as a fourth dimension, shifting interest to whether the context of study involves an individual, group, community or "society" (Mathieu and Scott, 2004b:2). Not surprisingly, geographers have been actively interested in matters of scale for a long time, and their theoretical concerns are equally relevant to archaeology (Sheppard and McMaster, 2004). In a seminal paper, Haggett (1965) identifies the three scale "problems" that challenge geographical (and archaeological) research. The first problem, scale coverage, arises because the potential scope of geography, the surface of the earth, is so large that recording and understanding its variability is an enormous task. Second, geographical studies, including fieldwork, are restricted to relatively small areas, so linking them can be difficult. Indeed, to what extent is it possible to extrapolate interpretations at one scale to other scales or understand large areas from sets of small-scale data? Finally, there is the issue of standardization, which is concerned with the merging and integration of various types of geographical data from a range of environments into a coherent form.

Trevor Harris, a geographer, explores these and other issues in Chapter 3 and shows their continuing relevance to both geography and archaeology. The problems of moving between scales are highlighted through the exposition of ecological fallacy and, in particular, through the Modifiable Areal Unit Problem (MAUP). This is concerned with "the imposition of artificial units of spatial reporting on contiguous geographical phenomena" and is of obvious interest to archaeologists as we go about our normal business of categorizing space into "sites". As Harris points out it is now forty years since Haggett raised these issues and accused many geographers of "working in happy or perverse oblivion to the problems that scale brings". How many archaeologists, we wonder, give consideration to the MAUP when carrying out spatial analysis of any kind?

Essential to any constructive discussion of scale is terminology, an area of some confusion at the analytical level that geographers, but few archaeologists, have taken up vigorously. There is a somewhat tense semantic standoff between the two disciplines. Geographers focus on the ratio or "representative fraction" of a scale, and so maintain that "small-scale" refers to a large area (the fraction is a smaller number) and "large-scale" to small areas (the fraction is a larger number). On the contrary, archaeologists tend to take the common view that "small-scale" refers to relatively small things and "large-scale" to relatively large things. These oppositions are further complicated by the use of terms derived from the optical measure of resolution, such as "coarse" and "fine" grain or scale, and areal categories such as "small-" and "broad-scale". Underlying such terms are notions of relative correspondence (Quattrochi, 1993) and, as indicated above, the important analytical elements of extent and resolution (Mathieu and Scott, 2004b). Spatial and temporal extent is the size of the area or the span of time under study whereas resolution is the smallest unit or object of study within that range. These definitions are relatively straightforward, especially in digital visualization technologies such as GIS and remote sensing where an image has a maximum extent and resolution relates to the density of pixels. In fact, with more and more archaeology becoming GIS-based, and focused at the regional scale, extent and resolution are becoming routine issues of quantification, subsumed within the technicalities of the application and somewhat automated. There is a danger that through this soft technological determinism archaeologists are losing sight of scale as a fundamental concept with a theoretical basis that has implications for interpretation.

The real challenge is trying to expose the connections between the relational scales inherent in past behaviour and the relational scales structured into the analytical and interpretative procedures that attempt to understand that behaviour – for example, in the analysis of the breaking of a pot and its placement in the fill of a pit, which was a common practice in the British Iron Age. The person carrying out that action would have made a series of temporal and spatial connections, perhaps consciously and sub-consciously, a mixture of secular and ritual traditions and practices linked to a network of other individuals and groups both near and far in time and space, both known and known-about. We archaeologists attempt to expose and understand the multi-scalar relations and transformations inherent in that act through analytical scale. By structuring and collecting data within analytical and interpretative frameworks we attempt to identify and explain the multi-scalar patterns implicated in that single action – sherds within a pit, pits within a settlement, settlements within a landscape, the relationship between individual and regional religious and ritual practices in the Iron Age (Daly and Lock, 2004).

Crucially, as we carry out these tasks, scale also mediates our labour, depending on the circumstances of our choosing to select, analyse and interpret a particular phenomenon within the institution defined as "archaeology". The impact of our intervention is an important aspect of scale as it is used here, as an emotional, intellectual, analytical, mystical, cultural tool. As H. Martin Wobst emphasizes in Chapter 4, we need to understand that scale is not a benign phenomenon but an active instrument in the making and changing of a society in which, as he says, "the people, the scales, and the discourses about and among them are forever in flux and unresolved".

This blurring of boundaries between the "concept of scale" and the "methodology of scale" as played out in an archaeological context through the "scale of then as lived" and the "scale of now as worked", is the central theme of this introduction and of this collection of papers. We are not removed from variations of scale, viewing our pots and projectile points as networks of relations in social and environmental settings; we define and are defined by this scalar relationship as we manipulate our point of view, actually and symbolically, to achieve our own desired ends. In Chapter 5, Brian L. Molyneaux explores the relationship between the physical and perceptual experiences of scale shared across time, space and culture between ancient hunter–gatherers and a modern-day archaeologist at Devils Tower, Wyoming, in the United States. The sheer fact that on the evidence of material cultural and literary and oral traditions, humans may have similar reactions to large-scale physical landmarks such as Devils Tower and use these features in similar ways, strongly suggests that we may gain access to otherwise impenetrable ideological realms by analysing the physical landscape in terms of the perceptions and actions it affords. The implication is that the study of mutuality in environmental experience brings us closer to a multi-dimensional archaeological approach grounded in traditional empirical analysis.

While an understanding of spatial scale and its effects is crucial, it does not then follow that scalar approaches are exercises in the management of spatial perspectives. Simon Holdaway and LuAnn Wandsnider write in Chapter 12 about the "remarkably under-theorized" concepts of time and temporal scales in archaeology, which fail to deal with the often-overlooked fact that archaeological deposits are poly-temporal in nature and require analytical methods commensurate with what are highly complex artifact palimpsests formed by cultural activity at varying scales.

The complexities of scalar relationships discussed above suggest that we need to rethink the methodological procedures involved in the most fundamental archaeological activity – fieldwork. At the operational and organizational levels, fieldwork is multi-scalar, ranging from the excavation of small exploratory trenches which invite questions of individual past actions to the regional surveying of landscapes which are concerned with questions of social organization and relations. Yet, even the most taken for granted mechanics of fieldwork have implications for scale, as shown in Chapter 8 where Gill Hey discusses the impact of evaluation strategies on evidence and interpretation. The results are worrying and suggest not only that we devise evaluation strategies to find more evidence of what we already know about, but also that there is a distinct lack of connection between the interpretative scale of landscape and the data-collecting scale of excavation. Thomas Yarrow takes an anthropological view of excavation in Chapter 6 and explores the relationship between scale and perspective. By following the excavation of flint number 68176 he interrogates the practices and processes that generate the sense of shifting scale as different perspectives are "brought into vision". As we move from the flint in the ground to its representation as one of many points on a site plan so the "same" object moves through different scales of interpretation and invites different questions to be asked of it. Will Banks exploits an even wider range of archaeological scales in Chapter 7, as he discusses use–wear on the microscopic landscapes of Upper Palaeolithic tools in order to interpret regional sequences of resource exploitation at the site of Solutré, in hills along the Saône River valley in south-central France. Given the potential contribution of use-wear analysis in the interpretation of regional cultural adaptations, does its persistence as a specialized sideline outside the archaeological mainstream relate to the fact that ordinary archaeology operates at the scale of things within human grasp?

The influence of familiar scale in archaeological theory and practice becomes even more problematic when we use the shape- and scale-shifting technology, GIS. As GIS is a profoundly spatial discipline, its rapid adoption and adaptation to meet a range of archaeological needs is not surprising, and while the focus of this volume is not on GIS, many of the papers incorporate GIS in view of its significance as an inherently scale-based technology. In Chapter 3, Trevor Harris details the scale implications of GIS use as a technical and interpretative device, noting some spatial problems that pre-date GIS but are inherent within its use. One of the perceived strengths of GIS is that it is "multi-scalar" although, as Trevor points out, being able to easily move between scales of data and interpretation does not necessarily mean that the implications of doing this are always understood.

In Chapter 9, Larry Zimmerman and Joe Artz caution against the uncritical adoption of GIS to solve archaeological problems because of its ability to characterize landforms with a scale and precision heretofore impossible. In a comparison of settlement behaviour at a complex of Central Plains earthlodges in western Iowa in the United States with a much more sophisticated GIS model constructed 25 years later, they found that modelling at an increasingly finer scale (nearly 1:1) with precise landform variables including elevation, slope and aspect did not accomplish any more in terms of understanding cultural processes than the earlier, coarser-grained approach. More significantly, the GIS was not able to address the cultural meanings of the landscape to its inhabitants, an issue that marks the schism between modern and post-modern archaeology.

Malcolm Ridges presents an example in Chapter 10 of how GIS-based multi-scalar analysis can be integrated within interpretative understandings when such issues of scale are made explicit. Looking at two different aspects of Aboriginal interactions with landscape, rock-art and trading routes, Malcolm compares the results from a region and two sub-regions within it. The complexity and subtlety of the differences in spatial patterns suggest different levels of social behaviour and relations.

Scales of spatial patterning and their interpretation is also the focus of the work of Andrew Bevan and James Connolly presented in Chapter 14. Here the emphasis is on the methodology and spatial statistics in particular, with the demonstration of Ripley's K function as a tool designed to be multi-scalar. Andrew and James emphasize the importance of a "reflexive approach" to spatial statistics to move us beyond the rigidity of traditional methods such as Nearest Neighbour Analysis. Also at the regional scale but not concerned with point patterning at all is Graham Fairclough's contribution, Chapter 13. Historic Landscape Characterization (HLC), as Graham describes, is, in fact, intentionally devoid of points and focuses on polygons of land that conjoin to create regional representations of land-use. Underlying this approach is a complex web of scalar understandings, including spatial, temporal, perceptual and social, that feeds into the concept of "landscape". Some of these define the HLC methodology while another group of scale-issues arise from HLC projects, these include selectivity, detail/generalization, interpretation, applications, affordances and management. The interaction between the qualitative scales of perception and the quantitative scales of measurement and recording ensures that HLC is not a mechanical and objective application of GIS technology.

Several of the papers in this volume refer to the distinction between "absolute scale" and "relative scale" (Quattrochi, 1993). The accepted difference is that between an actual distance, shape or other phenomenon defined within a Euclidean-based system and a relative scale based on some form of functional and meaningful relationship. This parallels our distinction between analytical scale, which is more likely to be based within a framework of absolute co-ordinates, distances and differences, and lived scale, which is inherently relational. Humans are situated in the material world: places, features and things are in front or behind, near or far, reachable within an hour's walk or not. The quantified framework as imposed by an absolute scale is limited in range, heavily reduced in the density of information, and artificial – except as an environment that the analyst occupies (Molyneaux, 1991, 1997). Another term sometimes used in geography is "characteristic scale", the spatial and temporal intervals at which an analyst can best detect and understand the processes and patterns under study. This is similar to Crumley's (1995) "effective scale" at which patterns are best identified and meaning inferred. Again, these terms and concepts relate to analytical scale, attempts by observers to structure their analysis according to what they conceive as the most effective and efficient way.

Of course, analysts have not focused entirely on scale as a fixed entity, as any meaningful linkage to the world requires a fluid concept of a kind that warrants terms such as "multi-scalar" and "multiple-scaled spatio-temporal" phenomena. Indeed, while Haggett (1965) invokes the problems of scale-linkage and standardization mentioned above, he accepts that geographers (and archaeologists) collect and analyse data at a range of different scales. How we conduct such multi-scalar research is at the heart of understanding and working with scale and raises several issues that many of the papers within this volume address.

In the geographical and ecological literature, analysts often use concepts of "hierarchy", and even a formal Hierarchy Theory, in conjunction with considerations of scale (Turner et al., 2001). For analytical scale in archaeological analysis, this can be a useful device, although it resonates rather too closely with a systems-based approach to sit comfortably within current postmodernist (in archaeology, post-processual) thinking. The conception of phenomena in a hierarchy of levels of organization imposes a particular and rather remote kind of order on worldly chaos. To understand a complex multi-scalar situation, the analyst must identify individual phenomena at a particular time-space scale and investigate how they relate to each other and combine to influence phenomena at lower and higher scales. A crucial, and very problematic, aspect of this approach is the assumption that phenomena at a higher level are the background against which lower-level phenomena operate – analysts typically describe this higher level as the "context" of the lower-level phenomena. Returning to our example of Iron Age pot breaking, sherds within an individual pit, in this view, occur within the regional patterning of ritual deposition. Viewed another way, as the phenomenon at one scale (regional patterning) is a logical description, or "consequence", of numerous instances of a phenomenon at a lower level (the placing of a shattered pot in a pit), one understands the individual act in terms of the phenomenon at the higher scale.

Carrying out data collection with the dynamics of scale in mind requires new approaches, in order to overcome the constraints of traditional hierarchical methods. For Oskar Burger and Lawrence C. Todd, in Chapter 15, the challenge of a research design and sampling strategy is to identify at what scale individual phenomena best resolve, and what kind of data collection is appropriate, given that spatial and temporal phenomena are scale-dependent. Their solution is a multi-scale model derived from landscape ecology that takes the scalar variability of archaeological deposits and processes into account, and so better adapts the essential task of data collection to real world situations.

More recent considerations of similar issues centre on the concept of agency and the relationship between individuals, groups and "society" – agency being a recent term applied to a long-standing approach in various fields that focuses on the situational analysis of individuals in natural and cultural environments. These approaches depart substantially from observer-based studies using an analytical scale as they treat the "hierarchy" of social life as relational. Life exists in situations, rather than processes, and in situations, individuals assess group intentions and develop strategies that eventuate social goals (Molyneaux, 1991). Dobres (2000) identifies "analytical scale" as the purview of research, the recognition and analysis of patterns, and "conceptual or phenomenological scale" as the world of human interactions in daily life. The micro-scale dynamics of the everyday contribute to macro-scale phenomena, such as social reproduction and cultural change, that we are interested in as analysts. According to Dobres (2000:133) conceptual scale is made up of "tangible and intangible structures that create the fluid parameters within which agents live"; this merges the material world and the social world as passed on through social norms, culture and tradition. Both of these realms are infinitely multi-scalar and also in a recursive relationship with individuals, so that people are created through their material and social worlds while at the same time creating those worlds. In this human-centred view there is a constant transformation between social structure (society) and the individual, but it is the material world and material things that enable us as individuals and social groups to create this cultural theatre and ensure its persistence, and effect, at temporal scales longer than is humanly possible (Gosden, 1994).

In Chapter 16, Vuk Trifkovic critiques these "archaeologies of practice" and offers a novel approach to the integration of excavation data and landscape theory by "situating individuals and their bodies within the wider flux of landscape and meaning''. Again, it is the technology of GIS that underlies this work, enabling him to apply the theoretical concepts of taskscape and distributed persons. For Vuk, the classic post-modern tension between a ''boundless global world and the body as an irreducible basis for understanding'' is a question of scale or perspective. His macro-scale understandings derive from ''quality of vision'' relating to landmarks at the landscape scale, while at the micro-scale he ''explodes the biography of an individual onto the landscape''. He achieves these results through the detailed analysis of skeletal remains including the positioning and orientation of graves in relation to landscape characteristics.

Issues of scale in archaeology ultimately find their way into publication and critical exegesis. Richard Fox in Chapter 11 provides a detailed examination of the sequence of events that make up one of the most famous incidents in the history of the United States: the ''Last Stand'' of General George Armstrong Custer and his 7th Cavalry at the Battle of the Little Bighorn in eastern Montana Territory in 1876. Using empirical evidence to complement eyewitness accounts (derived from a painstaking archaeological survey of the battlefield, which included mapping the position and articulation of each surviving cartridge case and bullet), he takes to task participants in the thriving literary mythology of the battle. While some legendary versions, fueled more by patriotism than by material evidence, feed off their own generalized discourse, Fox walks us across the short-grass prairie hills overlooking the Little Bighorn River that specifically and precisely led Custer and his men to their deaths.

As these papers all show, there are a series of tensions outlined in this introduction that overlap and merge within the flux of archaeological practice: that between phenomenological scale as lived and analytical scale as observed; that between method and theory; and that between detail and generalization in interpretation. The first section of this book explores these in a series of papers that lay the foundations for the following papers, which are more focused on specific problem areas and applications that bring issues of scale to the fore. While we are not claiming that this volume will provide a ''manual'' for understanding and working with scale, if such a thing is possible, we do hope that it goes some way to raising issues and lifting the ''happy or perverse oblivion'' that pervades much archaeological understanding of scale.

REFERENCES

Cherniak, C., 1986, *Minimal Rationality*. The MIT Press, Cambridge.
Crumley, C., 1995, Heterarchy and the Analysis of Complex Societies. In *Heterarchy and the Analysis of Complex Societies*, edited by R.M. Ehrenreich, C.L. Crumley, and J.E. Levy, pp. 1–5. Archaeological Papers of the American Anthropological Association No. 6, Arlington.
Daly, P., and Lock, G., 2004, Time, Space and Archaeological Landscapes: Establishing Connections in the First Millennium BC. In *Spatially Integrated Social Science*, edited by M.F. Goodchild and D.G. Janelle, pp. 349–365. Oxford University Press, Oxford.
Dobres, M-A., 2000, *Technology and Social Agency*. Blackwell, Oxford.
Gosden, C.,1994, *Social Being and Time*. Blackwell, Oxford.
Haggett, P.,1965, *Locational Analysis in Human Geography*. Edward Arnold, London.

Mathieu, J.R., and Scott, R.E., editors, 2004a, *Exploring the Role of Analytical Scale in Archaeological Interpretation.* BAR International Series 1261, Oxford.

Mathieu, J.R., and Scott, R.E., 2004b, Introduction: Exploring the Role of Analytical Scale in Archaeological Interpretation. In *Exploring the Role of Analytical Scale in Archaeological Interpretation,* edited by J.R. Mathieu and R.E. Scott, pp. 1–9. BAR International Series 1261, Oxford.

Molyneaux, B.L., 1997, Representation and Reality in Private Tombs of the Late Eighteenth Dynasty, Egypt: an Approach to the Study of the Shape of Meaning. In *The Cultural Life of Images: Visual Representation in Archaeology,* edited by B.L. Molyneaux, pp. 108–129. Routledge, London.

Molyneaux, B.L., 1991, *Perception and Situation in the Analysis of Representations.* Unpublished PhD Disseration, Department of Archaeology, University of Southampton, England.

Quattrochi, D.A , 1993, The Need for a Lexicon of Scale Terms in Integrating Remote Sensing Data with Geographic Information Systems. *Journal of Geography* 92 (5):206–212.

Spaulding, A.,1960, The Dimensions of Archaeology. In *Essays in the Science of Culture,* edited by G.E. Dole and R.L. Carneiro, pp. 437–456. Cromwell, New York.

Turner, M.G., Gardner, R.H., and O'Neil, R.V., 2001, *Landscape Ecology in Theory and Practice: Pattern and Process.* Springer-Verlag, New York.

Van Helden, Albert, 1989, Introduction. In *Sidereus Nuncius, or The Sidereal Messenger,* by Galileo Galilei. Translated by Albert Van Helden. University of Chicago Press, Chicago and London.

INTRODUCING SCALE: SPACE, TIME AND SIZE IN THE PAST AND THE PRESENT

CHAPTER 1

On Being the Right Size: Affordances and the Meaning of Scale

ALAN COSTALL

The world can be analyzed at many levels, from atomic through terrestrial to cosmic. There is physical structure on the scale of millimicrons at one extreme and on the scale of light years at another. But surely the appropriate scale for animals is the intermediate one of millimeters to kilometers, and it is appropriate *because the world and the animal are then comparable* (Gibson, 1968:22; emphasis added).

In the course of a long career, the American psychologist, James Gibson (1904–1979) attempted to develop an "ecological approach" to psychology and related human sciences that would undermine the many dualisms that have traditionally defined these disciplines and the awkward boundaries between them. These dualisms include: mind vs. body, mind vs. world, individual vs. society, and nature vs. culture.

From the 1950s, Gibson often wrote as though "finding the right scale" would, in itself, be the *solution*. However, with his later introduction of the concept of "affordances" (Gibson, 1977, 1979, 1982), the issue of scale – *though still critical* – became subordinated to a new approach to the meanings of things, and to the relation of ourselves and other animals to our worlds.

It is not easy, however, to appreciate the point of Gibson's proposed solutions. Not only does he take our recognition of the problems largely for granted, but also the solutions he presents often seem much too *easy*. He goes to great lengths to inform us about the blindingly obvious – for example, that there is a sky above us and a ground beneath us, that we can see ourselves (e.g., our hands, arms, and legs) *in* the world, and that, to live in that world, we need to act in and upon it (Gibson, 1979). Like the deeply unsatisfying answer of "Forty-two" to the ultimate question of Life, the Universe, and Everything (Adams, 1984:128), Gibson's homely observations hardly sound like answers to serious problems.

So, first, I need to explain why these problems really are serious, and how they keep *blinding* us to the "blindingly" obvious.

ALAN COSTALL ● University of Portsmouth

THE BIFURCATION OF NATURE

The ambitious project of traditional physical science – to explain *everything* on the basis of a definite set of methods and principles – seemed to be largely achieved at a remarkably early stage. By the seventeenth century, the new science had not only extended beyond the limits of our terrestrial world to the previously quite separate realm of the "heavens" but also to the intimacy of own bodies, now to be understood in terms of levers, tubes, pumps, and valves. Yet this awesome success was acquired at a serious cost to the human sciences (and indeed the entire western tradition): the radical exclusion of *ourselves* – now disembodied – from the realm of science.

The supposed inclusiveness of the scheme of physical science was achieved through a rhetorical trick, the claim that the new science covers everything, and so anything it fails to include must, evidently, fall beyond the scientific realm of things. Anything resistant to the methods of the new science could not, therefore, be truly "real," and hence, had to, instead, be purely *subjective*. This subjective realm of the *un*scientific has come to include "secondary qualities" such as colour and warmth, "tertiary qualities" such as meaning and expression, and, in the end, ourselves, the very sanctuary for all of these banished qualities (Lewis, 1964:215).

The exclusion of *us* from the "physical world" (i.e., the world as described by physics) gave rise to *psychophysical* dualism, the assumption that mind and matter are "mutually exclusive and utterly antithetic" (Lovejoy, 1929:3). This exclusion of us from the natural order of things gave rise, in turn, to the *epistemological* dualism of knower and known, and it is this derivative dualism that has been taken to be the pressing problem within Western thought. This secondary problem has been "solved", to the satisfaction of a surprisingly large number of thoughtful people, through the supposition that "ideas" or some other subjective mediators "forever interpose themselves between the knower and the objects which he would know" (Lovejoy, 1929:3). This line of theorizing persists as the dominant and seemingly inevitable theoretical option within cognitivist psychology and many other human sciences, in the form of the modern "representationalist theory of mind."

In this chapter, I will be concerned with just two of the many big problems that arise from psychophysical dualism.

1. *The alienation of the material.* If the material really has to fall on the "far" side of a psychophysical divide, then it is difficult to see how *materiality* could be seriously included within psychological and social theory. While the disciplines of psychology and sociology, through their unworldliness, have largely "shelved" this problem, archaeologists, given their very method, are surely required to take things more seriously. Admittedly, their engagement with material evidence has not entirely protected them, however, from also opting for representationalism, and this perhaps is because of the second serious problem.

2. *The subjectification of culture.* Psychophysical dualism also presents serious problems about how to theorize "culture". Given the dualistic exclusion of *us* from the natural order of things, where can we "locate" *culture* other than ultimately on the *mental* side of the psychophysical

divide? Culture, through guilt by association with us, has to be banished from the "real" world, and subjectivized; it has to be located within a realm of individual or social *re-presentations*.

THE REVOLTS AGAINST DUALISM

There have been some serious challenges to the dualistic framework of science over many years. Towards the end of the nineteenth century, psychologists such as William James and John Dewey were emphasizing the importance of Darwinian theory as a distinctly different *kind* of science, one which returned "the mental" to the natural order of things, "mind and world" evolving in mutual relation (James, 1892:4). Radical developments within physical theory, such as relativity theory and quantum theory, have also been cause for searching examination and criticism of "the metaphysics of modern physical science" (Burtt, 1967 [1924]; Koyré, 1965; Whitehead, 1926). As a philosopher, Arthur Bentley, engagingly put it:

> Since the "mental" as we have known it in the past was a squeeze-out from Newtonian space, the physicist may be asked to ponder how it can still remain a squeeze-out when the space out of which it was squeezed is no longer there to squeeze it out. (Bentley, 1938:165)

Nevertheless, the separation of the mental and physical, of meaning and materiality, of the world and *us*, still structures a good deal of current theory in the human sciences, especially within that last outpost of scientism and individualism, modern cognitivist theory. As one of its proponents proudly proclaimed, cognitivism provides us with "a science of structure and function *divorced from material substance*" (Pylyshyn, 1986:68, emphasis added).

Yet, even when the human sciences, as in social constructivism and postmodernism, try to go their own way, they often manage to retain these traditional dualisms through a failure to engage seriously in an examination of all this seemingly old-fashioned metaphysics. Thus, we find an anthropologist, Roy Ellen (1996:31), having argued for a discursive view of nature to replace a scientistic one – in a book devoted precisely to "redefining nature" – coming to the remarkable traditional conclusion that "Culture emerges from nature as the symbolic representation of the latter". And we have a social constructivist, Stuart Hall, insisting that meaning is confined to the representational realm of *symbols*:

> ...we must not confuse the material world, where things and people exist, and the symbolic practices and processes through which representation, meaning and language operate. Constructivists do not deny the existence of the material world. However, it is not the material world which conveys meaning: it is the language system or whatever system we are using to represent our concepts. (Hall, 1997:25)

JAMES GIBSON'S "ECOLOGICAL
APPROACH"

Let us now look more closely at Gibson's revolt against dualism. To begin to make sense of his project, we need to be clear that his real target was not epistemological dualism but the more fundamental dualism of matter and mind that it presupposes. Many critics of Gibson's "ecological approach" have complained about his dogmatic denial of *any* role for representations in the explanation of human thought and conduct. Yet Gibson was intensely interested in the question of the historical and material bases of the diverse human practices of representation (Reed, 1991). His objection was to *representationalism*, and the inherent incapacity of this theoretical approach to address the basic problem of how representations can possibly represent – if we are indeed all entirely enclosed within a realm of representations. As he saw it, the big problem with representationalism is that it simply takes *representation* for granted, and then pretends to "solve" the profound epistemological problem posed by traditional dualism. Representationalism can be no solution, since, given its assumption of *psychophysical* dualism, there is no way it could account for how representations represent. How could our mental representations ever connect to the world, if *we* are always excluded from it?

In fact, Richard Gregory, the psychologist, has somehow managed to make a scientific career out of promoting representationalism while at the same time (for the more astute) giving the whole silly game away:

> It used to be thought that perceptions, by vision and touch and so on, can give direct knowledge of objective reality.... But, largely through the physiological study of the senses over the last two hundred years, this has become ever more difficult to defend...ultimately we cannot know directly what is illusion, any more than truth – for we cannot step outside perception to compare experience with objective reality. (Gregory, 1989:94)

Hint: If we are *all* (including, of course, important scientists, such as Richard Gregory) trapped in a realm of representations and "cognitive assumptions," where is all this hard *objective* evidence, apparently supporting this radically *subjectivist* conclusion, coming from?!

Affordances and the Scale of Meaning

James Gibson, in contrast to most other psychologists, preferred to dissolve, rather than solve, the seemingly intractable problems posed by dualism. Although his concept of affordances was just part of his wider project to undermine the various dualisms of traditional psychological and social theory, this concept is, in my view, his most fundamental contribution to a *non*dualistic approach to both materiality and culture.

Gibson was seeking to develop alternative descriptions of animals and their environments that would capture their interdependence or "mutuality."

> The words animal and environment make an inseparable pair. Each term implies the other. No animal could exist without an environment surrounding it. Equally, although not so obvious, an environment implies an animal (or at least an organism) to be surrounded. ...The mutuality of animal and environment is not [however] implied by the physical sciences. (Gibson, 1979:8)

Gibson's initial attempts to find a way to describe the world in such a way that it is appears compatible with, rather than alien to, the existence of animals focused upon *scale*.

> The world of man and animals consists of matter in the solid, liquid, or gaseous state, organized as an array of surfaces or interfaces between matter in these different states. It is the habitat of an animal. In some respects it is the world studied by ecology.... Present day physical science is of little help, since it jumps from crystals to planets and shows no interest in the entities of the world which we can see and feel with our unaided sense organs.... (Gibson, 1959:469–470)

Although there are hints of the idea of affordances in his earlier writings, it is only in Gibson's later work that this concept takes a prominent position (Gibson, 1977, 1979; cf. Gibson, 1950, Ch. 11). Affordances are the meanings of things for our actions, but these meanings are not something we "mentally project" onto objects. They concern the *relation* between agent and the world.

> The *affordances* of the environment are what it *offers* the animal, what it *provides* or *furnishes*, either for good or ill. The verb to afford is found in the dictionary, but the noun affordance is not.... I mean by it something that refers to both the environment and the animal in a way that no existing term does. It implies the complementarity of the animal and the environment. (Gibson, 1979:127)

Now scale continues to figure as an important issue within Gibson's treatment of affordances, since – along with a host of other factors – it is critically important to what things can *mean*. What matters, however, is not scale in an absolute and abstracted sense, but scale in relation to the *animal*. So let us, after all of this talk of history and metaphysics, descend to two concrete examples, such as going up and down stairs, and grasping things.

Clearly, the dimensions of both the risers and treads of the stairs matter critically. Beyond a certain critical point, the stair no longer affords climbing. To ascend a staircase, we need to be able to reach the next step with our foot, and, furthermore, then be able to lift our body so that its weight is centered on that step. Going down stairs is more precarious, since we also need to check that we do not overdo things and end up in a painful fall.

Normally, young children do have serious problems going up and down stairs. In fact, one can find age "norms" in the textbooks on motor development and developmental psychology, where the failure or success to achieve that norm is taken to reflect the intrinsic developmental condition of the child (Gesell et al., 1977). There are striking differences in the age norms for going down as opposed to going up stairs, and also for alternating the feet between steps as opposed to moving one foot forward and then gingerly following through but putting the other foot onto that same step. With the *normal* staircases that children *normally* encounter, it is not until they are around the late age of four and a half years that they begin to risk alternating their feet when descending.

However, although the climbability of a staircase is a function of *its* dimensions, it also depends upon the size of the person in question. People do not come in standard sizes, and, in particular, young children are generally much smaller than adults. Yet these age norms have been based on "normal" sized staircases – stairs, in other words, designed for adults, *not* children.

It is very curious that in our schools, for example, there are child-sized chairs and tables, but not child-sized stairs. In an inspired study, Josep Roca and his colleagues simply checked to see how children would cope with a scaled-down staircase where the steps were just 10 cm high and 20 cm deep (Roca et al., 1986).

The children coped remarkably well. The mean age at which they could climb either up or down the staircase was about *twelve months*, and alternating the feet between steps was achieved only slightly later at around eighteen months.

Even this study did not make allowances for the fact that some of the participants were smaller than others, not least because of their different ages. Yet it is the precise relation between the dimensions of the stair and of *the individual user* that is crucial. For example, according to Warren (1995), when the ratio of height of a step to leg length is greater than .88, it is simply no longer possible to step up onto it, and one must then resort to climbing with ones hands and knees. There is also a definite optimum ratio where energy expenditure in climbing is least, and this, again, is a conjoint function of both the stair and the user. Under the specific conditions used in Warren's research, where the diagonal distance between successive stairs was held constant at 14 in., the optimum ratio of riser height to leg length was .26.

Let us take just one more example. The ways in which young children (and indeed other primates) are able to grasp objects has been of great interest to developmental psychologists, paediatricians, and primatologists, especially the precision grip where the object is held between thumb and forefinger. Presumably in the sake of the serious pursuit of "scientific control," in many of the main studies on grasping, the target object has been of a single, "normal" size, one more appropriate, once again, to the body size of a human adult (Halverson, 1931; Connolly and Elliott, 1972). Primates, however, including children and indeed even human adults, do not come in a *standard* size, and the graspability of the object surely depends on the *relation* between the object and the agent.

Karl Newell and his colleagues presented both young children and adults with a range of cubes of different sizes and recorded the different kinds of ways they picked them up, e.g., between the flat of the palms, within the palm of one hand with all of the fingers grasping the object, and the prestigious precision grip (Newell et al., 1989). When these investigators related the frequency of these various grip patterns, not to the absolute size of the cubes, but body-scaled to the individual participants, the transitions between different kinds of grip corresponded to definite ratios common to both the children and adults. Indeed, it was the bodily-scaled dimensions of the cubes, rather than age, that accounted for most of the variability between the different grip patterns. Although the children in this study were older than the age at which children have been recorded as first being able to use the precision grip, the results suggest we need to be wary about age norms that make no reference to the child's *relation* to the test situation.

There are critical points concerning scale, therefore, that define the limits within which we can act upon something in a particular way – and beyond which we simply cannot at all. *Scale really does matter*. But not in isolation. For example, whether – and how – we might grasp an object depends upon a host of its other characteristics: its fragility, its slipperiness, its mass and also the distribution of its mass, its monetary value, and so on. And what "holds" scale together with all of these other characteristics together and gives them *meaning* is the animal or person in question, though not as a "perceiver" (cf. Gibson, 1979:137; Heft, 2001:132; Ingold, 2000:168) but, much more fundamentally, as an *agent*.

> [Affordances] have unity relative to the *posture* and *behavior* of the animal being considered. So
> an affordance cannot be measured as we measure in physics. (Gibson, 1979:127–128; emphasis
> added)

This, then, is how the concept of affordances is supposed to help undermine, rather than merely "bridge", the old psychophysical dualism. Affordances constitute the material resources for action but they do not fall on the far side of the material-mental divide. They are, as Gibson put it, *both* physical and mental, because they already implicate the needs and purposes of an agent, who, in turn, is envisaged as existing *within* – rather than *beyond* – the natural order of things (Heft, 1989).

Affordances and the Dualism of Materiality and Culture

Gibson's concept of affordances was meant to help undermine not only the dualism of the material and mental, but also that of *materiality* vs. *culture*. However, even commentators attracted to Gibson's emphasis upon materiality, and also embodiment (see Costall, In Press), have failed to see how his ecological approach could possibly "take on" culture. George Lakoff, for example, though generally sympathetic to the thrust of the ecological approach, has complained that "the Gibsonian environment is monolithic and self-consistent and the same for all people," and that his approach "cannot make sense of experiential or cultural categories" (Lakoff, 1987:216; see also Ben Ze'ev (1993:72).

It is certainly true that Gibson did not adequately develop an account of affordances that connects them to the wider collectivity and the historical process. The entire treatment of affordances is, frankly, sketchy. Despite, or maybe because of this, Gibson manages to set up two nasty traps that would lead the unwary to suppose that the concept of affordances is essentially individualistic, and biologically reductionistic and universalistic!

THE "DIRECT PERCEPTION" OF AFFORDANCES

The first trap concerns Gibson's claim that affordances can be "directly perceived." According to Michaels and Carello (1981), "affordances write perception into the language of action," yet, unfortunately, the reverse has largely happened in the subsequent research. Action has been "written" in the language of perception. The main studies on affordances have (though for perfectly good reasons of their own) usually involved asking people merely to look at objects and make verbal reports about them, rather than act upon them. Furthermore, Gibson's own research over many years had focused upon perception, and it was the *perception* of affordances, he claimed, that was primary:

> The *central question* for the theory of affordances *is not whether they exist and are real* but
> whether information is available in the ambient light for perceiving them (Gibson, 1979:140;
> emphasis added).

Gibson (1950:xiv; 1968:156; 1979:232) often quoted, approvingly, Bishop Berkeley's claim that vision enables animals "to *foresee* the damage or benefit which is like to ensue upon the application of their own bodies to this or that body which is at a distance'' (see Berkeley, 1975 [1707]:24). There is now a substantial body of research with adults and children showing that we can be very effective in ''foreseeing'' affordances, for example, whether a staircase is climbable and even the optimum riser height for one's own height, whether one can walk through a gap either with or without turning one's shoulders, or ducking one's head, and so on (e.g., Mark, 1987; Warren, 1984; Warren and Whang, 1987). And we typically do this *not* by first visually ''measuring'' the object and only then comparing it our own body. Rather, we experience the object *in relation to ourselves*: As Gibson himself put it, ''The awareness of the world and one's complementary relations to the world are not separable'' (Gibson, 1979:141).

This is obviously the case, for example, when we are about to pick up an object. We do not just see the object nor just our hands, but the object and our hands in relation to one another. The relation of the object to our bodies is also specified in more subtle ways. Thus our eye-height is specified by the ''visible horizon'' (Gibson, 1979:162–164). Objects extending beyond the horizon are higher than our own eye-level, and the proportion in which it intersects the horizon corresponds to the height of that object relative to one's eye-height. Like the critical ratios for stepping on stairs and picking up cubes, these horizon relations relative to the height of the point of observation lack an objective metric, they are dimensionless and body-scaled. They directly relate to *us*, and are all the better for that:

> ...the ''knowledge'' of his height that comes to the observer simply from living in his body is both more fundamental and more meaningful to him than the knowledge communicated to him by a statement such as ''X is Y feet long.'' (Sedgwick, 1973:47)[1]

Complementarily, we develop, and continually update, a relatively stable sense of the limits and capacities of own bodies – *in relation to the world* – in the very course of our activities (Stins, Kadar, and Costall, 2001). Interestingly (if not surprisingly), this sense of our own bodies can be disrupted during periods of rapid growth (Heffernan and Thomson, 1999).

Now, to the extent that we are able reliably to see what an object affords, there must be *something* about it that specifically distinguishes it *visually* from other objects that do *not* have that affordance. For example, if a doorway does *not* extend above my eye level, I had better duck when passing through it. If *this* is all that Gibson means by the claim that ''information is available in the ambient light'' for perceiving affordances, then it is surely hardly contentious (Gibson, 1979:140). But his claim that affordances can be *directly* perceived seems to imply much more than that: an appeal to a universal and innate kind of ''immaculate perception'' that immediately reveals the meanings of things – that *just* by peering at things we can foresee precisely what they might afford.

Gibson's cavalier use of the term ''direct perception'' is the source of the trouble here. He used the term direct perception to make a whole range of contrasts with many quite different senses of *indirect* perception, but he failed properly to

---

[1] The variety of ''anthropocentric'' measurements of length is remarkable: (Klein, 1975; Connor, 1987) – based on the size of the hand, the length or width of the fingers, the thumbnail, the fist and outstretched thumb, the foot, the pace of the legs, and so on.

distinguish among them. In the end, therefore, "direct perception" seemed to preclude any kind of experience of the world that was historically situated or socially mediated in any way (Costall, 1989).

Yet, there can be no doubt that Gibson intended "affordances" to include the culturally specific, as in his much discussed example of a postbox, which "affords letter-mailing to a letter-writing human in a community with a postal system" (Gibson, 1979:139). Community is usually supposed to crowd out materiality. But, when you think about it, even though a postal system constitutes a highly specific human practice, its *materiality* still matters. Postboxes, for example, as part of this system, have to perform the function of accepting and temporarily storing letters, but they also need to be distinguishable visually from litter bins and other kinds of things. And, of course, we do not discover what postboxes *mean* just by peering at them! It is through being a member of a community in which postboxes are actually *used* that we come to understand what they are *supposed* to afford, including being instructed by other people about how to use them, seeing other people using them, and, if all else fails, consulting a manual on how to use them. Indeed, if, as in the case of autism, we are somehow excluded from "connecting" with other people, the normal use of objects can be seriously disrupted (Williams, Costall, and Reddy, 1999).

THE OBJECTIFICATION OF AFFORDANCES

There is another serious trap that Gibson sets for us in his account of affordances, and this one involves not just an imprecise use of terms, but a blatant contradiction. From an early point in his career, as we have seen, Gibson put great emphasis on the need to find an appropriate *spatial* scale for making the animal and its world "comparable" (Gibson, 1968:22). However, as I shall now try to explain, it is also essential to find the right scale in two other senses.

Gibson defined the concept of affordances relative to the posture and behavior of the animal (Gibson, 1979:127–128), and as such affordances are "anchored in human beings at one pole and in things at the other" (Gibson, 1975:320). And it is precisely because they are relationally defined that affordances serve to undermine the traditional dualism of the objective and subjective[2]. Yet, he then went on to insist upon their *independence* – not *inter*dependence – of *us*: "The organism depends on its environment for its life, but the environment does not depend on the organism for its existence" (Gibson, 1979:129).

Gibson certainly had long-standing misgivings about the ethical and political implications of cultural relativism (Costall and Still, 1989). But his retreat into a notion of affordances as independent of *us* was itself "afforded" by restricting his analysis primarily to a very local *scale* of analysis: an individual dealing with things in the immediate "here and now." And with such a specific focus, one can conveniently lose sight not just of the wider social context but also of *historical process*.

---

[2] As Aaron Ben Ze'ev (1993:73) has put it, "The relational nature of the perceptual environment is a price one has to pay for the meaningfulness of that environment."

Any object or situation we encounter has a *limitless* number of affordances (although this does not mean that we can do *anything* with *anything*). Yet many of the objects in our environment are nevertheless meant to have just one "intended" affordance – they have been designed for a specific use, and/or have come to be identified with a particular activity: postboxes, chairs, pencils, apples, sunny sandy beaches, or whatever. In such cases, it makes sense to ask the question – what is this thing *really* for? Clearly, the proper use of the object, its "canonical affordance" (Costall, 1995, 1997), is not dependent on any individual in particular – on any one of us. It is impersonal. *One* sits on a chair; *one* is supposed to post letters not bombs in a postbox; *one* does this, not that, with this particular object. Yet this social process of impersonalization, this *objectification* of affordances, most emphatically, involves *us*. And it is not, in most cases, just a question of "designating" privileged, impersonal meanings to things. The actual objects involved, along with their distinctive affordances, cannot, from this wider historical perspective, be regarded as the "independent" preconditions of the human practice in which they exist. They themselves came into being and took shape in relation to that very practice. Chairs are constructed within a whole tradition of such construction, and of people sitting down on such things. To suppose that affordances even of this kind are independent of *us* would be to commit what John Dewey, that wonderfully insightful psychologist and philosopher, deemed to be the ultimate "psychological fallacy":

> ... the increasing control over the environment is not as if the environment were something fixed and the organism responded at this point and that, adapting itself by fitting itself in, in a plaster-like way. The psychological or historical fallacy is likely to come in here ... [when] we conceive the environment, which is really the outcome of the process of development, which has gone on developing along with the organism, as if it was something which had been there from the start, and the whole problem had been for the organism to accommodate itself to that set of given surroundings. (Dewey, 1976 [1898]:283–284)

If I have been largely critical in this chapter – about mainstream cognitive psychology, about the human sciences more generally, about Gibson's critics, and, indeed, about Gibson himself – it is because I am convinced Gibson provided us with some important theoretical resources for going beyond dualism, not least with his concept of "affordance." As the anthropologist, François Sigaut, has recently observed, if "it is only a word, it is a very useful one" (Sigaut, 1996:432). First of all, it reminds us that the human sciences are faced with a fundamental problem, the exclusion of us from the natural order of things, the problem of *psycholophysical* dualism.

Representationalist theory is an attempt to deal with the derivative problem of *epistemological* dualism, and if it really is "the only game in town" we are talking about a very small town, and, in any case, the game is hardly worth playing. Properly handled, the concept of affordances promises to undermine not only the dualism of matter and mind, but also that of materiality and culture. But it is not enough to have a good sense of a *spatial* scale that will relate the individual animal to its world. That animal and its world need also to be seen within the more comprehensive scales of sociality and history.

REFERENCES

Adams, D., 1984, *The Hitch Hiker's Guide to the Galaxy: A Trilogy in Four Parts.* Heinemann, London.

Ben Ze'ev, A., 1993, *The Perceptual System: A Philosophical and Psychological Perspective.* Peter Lang, New York.

Bentley, A.F., 1938, Physicists and Fairies. *Philosophy of Science* 5:132–165.

Berkeley, G., 1975 [1709], *Philosophical Works Including the Works on Vision.* [Introduction and Notes by M.R. Ayers.] Dent, London.

Burtt, E.A., 1967 [1924], *The Metaphysical Foundations of Modern Physical Science: A Historical and Critical Essay.* Routledge and Kegan Paul, London.

Connolly, K.J., and Elliott, J.M., 1978, Evolution and Ontogeny of Hand Function. In *Ethological Studies of Child Behavior*, edited by N. Blurton-Jones, pp. 329–383. Cambridge University Press, London.

Connor, R.D., 1987, *The Weights and Measures of England.* Her Majesty's Stationery Office (Science Museum), London.

Costall, A., and Still, A.W., 1989, Gibson's Theory of Direct Perception and the Problem of Cultural Relativism. *Journal for the Theory of Social Behavior* 19:433–441.

Costall, A., 1989, A Closer Look at 'Direct Perception'. In *Cognition and Social Worlds*, edited by A. Gellatly, D. Rogers, and J.A. Sloboda, pp. 10–21. Clarendon Press, Oxford.

Costall, A., 1995, Socializing Affordances. *Theory and Psychology* 5:467–481.

Costall, A., 1997, The Meaning of Things. *Social Analysis* 41(1):76–86.

Costall, A., In Press, The Missing Body in Psychological Theory – and its Return in Ecological Psychology. In *Body, Language and Mind: Vol. 1: Embodiment*, edited by T. Ziemke, J. Zlatev, R. Frank Mouton. De Gruyter, Berlin.

Dewey, J., 1976 [1884], The New Psychology. *Andover Review* 2:278–289.

Ellen, R., 1996, Introduction. In *Redefining Nature: Ecology, Culture and Domestication*, edited by Roy Ellen and Katsuyoshi Fukui, pp. 1–36. Berg, Oxford.

Gesell, A., Ilg, F., and Ames, L.B., 1977, *The Child from Five to Ten.* Harper and Row, New York.

Gibson, J.J., 1950, *The Perception of the Visual World.* Houghton-Mifflin, Boston.

Gibson, J.J., 1959, Perception as a Function of Stimulation. In *Psychology: A Study of a Science. Vol. 1*, edited by S. Koch, pp. 456–501. McGraw-Hill, New York.

Gibson, J.J., 1968, *The Senses Considered as Perceptual Systems.* George Allen and Unwin, London.

Gibson, J.J., 1975, Pickford and the Failure of Experimental Esthetics. *Leonardo* 8:319–21.

Gibson, J.J., 1977, The Theory of Affordances. In *Perceiving, Acting and Knowing: Toward an Ecological Psychology*, edited by R. Shaw and J. Bransford, pp. 67–88. Erlbaum, Hillsdale, New Jersey.

Gibson, J.J., 1979, The Ecological Approach to Visual Perception. Erlbaum, Hillsdale, New Jersey.

Gibson, J.J., 1982, Notes on Affordances. In *Reasons for Realism*, edited by E. Reed and R. Jones, pp. 401–418. Erlbaum, Hillsdale, New Jersey.

Gregory, R.L., 1989, Touching Truth. In *Dismantling Truth: Reality in the Post-modern World*, edited by H. Lawson and L. Appignanesi, pp. 93–100. Weidenfeld and Nicolson, London.

Hall, S., editor, 1997, *Representation: Cultural Representations and Signifying Practices.* Sage, London.

Halverson, H.M., 1931, An Experimental Study of Prehension in Infants by Means of Systematic Methods. *Genetic Psychology Monographs* 10:107–283.

Heffernan, D., and Thomson, J.A., 1999, Gone Fishin': Perceiving What is Reachable with Rods During a Period of Rapid Growth. In *Studies in Perception and Action V*, edited by M.A. Grealy and J.A. Thomson, pp. 223–228. Erlbaum, Mahwah, New Jersey.

Heft, H., 1989, Affordances and the Body: An Intentional Analysis of Gibson's Ecological Approach to Visual Perception. *Journal for the Theory of Social Behaviour* 19(1):1–30.

Heft, H., 2001, *Ecological Psychology in Context: James Gibson, Roger Barker, and the Legacy of William James's Radical Empiricism.* Erlbaum, Mahwah, New Jersey.

Ingold, T., 2000, *The Perception of the Environment: Essays in Livelihood, Dwelling and Skill.* Routledge, London.

James, W., 1892, *Psychology: The Briefer Course.* Henry Holt, New York.

Klein, H.A., 1975, *The World of Measurements*. George Allen and Unwin, London.

Koyré, A., 1965, *Newtonian Studies*. Chapman and Hall, London.

Lakoff, G., 1987, *Women, Fire, and Dangerous Things: What Categories Reveal about the Mind*. University of Chicago Press, Chicago.

Lewis, C.S., 1964, *The Discarded Image: An Introduction to Medieval and Renaissance Literature*. Cambridge University Press, Cambridge.

Lovejoy, A.O., 1929, *The Revolt against Dualism: An Inquiry Concerning the Existence of Ideas*. Open Court, LaSalle, Illinois.

Mark, L.S., 1987, Eyeheight-scaled Information about Affordances: A Study of Sitting and Stair Climbing. *Journal of Experimental Psychology: Human Perception and Performance* 13:361–370.

Michaels, C., and Carello, C., 1981, *Direct Perception*. Prentice-Hall, Englewood Cliffs, New Jersey.

Newell, K.M., Scully, D.M., Tenenbaum, F., and Hardiman, S., 1989, Body Scale and the Development of Prehension. *Developmental Psychobiology* 22:1–13.

Pylyshyn, Z., 1986, *Computation and Cognition*. MIT Press, Cambridge, Massachusetts.

Reed, E. S., 1991, James Gibson's Ecological Approach to Cognition. In *Against Cognitivism*, edited by A. Still and A.Costall, pp. 171–197. Harvester Press, Hemel Hempstead.

Roca, J., Martinez, M., Lizandra, M., Fabregas, A., and Cordoner, A., 1986, Registres Evolutius Motors: Una Observació Crítica. *Apunts* 6:61–64.

Sedgwick, H.A., 1973, The Visible Horizon: A Potential Source of Visual Information for the Perception of Size and Distance. Unpublished Doctoral Dissertation, Cornell University.

Sigaut, F., 1996, Crops, Techniques, and Affordances. In *Redefining Nature: Ecology, Culture and Domestication*, edited by Roy Ellen and Katsuyoshi Fukui, pp. 417–436. Berg, Oxford.

Stins, J., Kadar, E., and Costall, A., 2001, A Kinematic Analysis of Hand Selection in a Reaching Task. *Laterality* 6:347–367.

Warren, W.H., Jr., 1984, Perceiving Affordances: Visual Guidance of Stair Climbing. *Journal of Experimental Psychology: Human Perception and Performance* 10:683–703.

Warren, W.H., 1995, Constructing an Econiche. In *Global Perspectives on the Ecology of Human-machine Systems, Vol. 1*, edited by J. Flach, P. Hancock, J. Caird, and K. Vicente, pp. 210–237. Erlbaum, Hillsdale, New Jersey.

Warren, W.H., and Whang, S., 1987, Visual Guidance of Walking Through Apertures: Body-scaled Information for Affordance. *Journal of Experimental Psychology: Human Perception and Performance* 13:371–383.

Whitehead, A.N., 1926, *Science and the Modern World: Lowell Lectures, 1925*. Cambridge University Press, Cambridge.

Williams, E., Costall, A., and Reddy, V., 1999, Children with Autism Experience Problems with both Objects and People. *Journal of Autism and Developmental Disorders* 29:367–378.

CHAPTER 2

Timescales

CHRIS GOSDEN AND KAROLA KIRSANOW

Archaeology prides itself on its long timescales. Despite the disadvantages of missing, fragmentary and dispersed evidence, archaeology has the one great advantage of looking at the longest of all *longue durée*, potentially spanning the last six million years. However, as we well know scale is context dependent – nothing is inherently big or small, but only by comparison to something else. Lying behind archaeology's claim to long timescales is an implicit and unexamined set of assumptions concerning what constitutes a general view of duration in other disciplines, which, when compared with archaeology, makes our timescales look big. What we might call short duration disciplines, such as anthropology or sociology, investigate sets of events or take a biographical view spanning a person's life time. History explores a range of timescales, overlapping at the micro end of the scale with anthropology, to the long durations of Braudel as people's relationships with land and sea unfolded over centuries and even millennia. By any of these standards, archaeological timescales appear generous, although of course we cannot compete with the geologists or palaeontologists, even though neither of these is worried about humans and their effects. Of the disciplines concerned with human action the span of millennia and millions of years available to archaeology dwarfs all others, allowing us to pose the big questions of what it means to be human, to get lost in the vastness of time at our disposal or dive into minute details of people's lives where these are preserved.

However, size is not everything, or rather is not one single thing. Here is the key point of our chapter – temporal scales are hard to make easy sense of, being not one thing but many; each set of archaeological evidence contains nested within it a number of different forms of duration and means of measurement. Archaeological interpretation involves shuttling backwards and forwards between different spans and durations of time in a manner that is not straightforward. To look at the inherent complexity of timescales, let us compare the temporal and the spatial, as spatial scales, we would argue, are more intuitively easy to understand than temporal ones. Metaphors used to understand time are often spatial: we feel that the future is in front of us and the past behind (a spatial positioning famously reversed in Maori thought where the past, more visible than the future, is thought to be in front of us – in either case a spatial metaphor is used). We talk of the distant past or the near

CHRIS GOSDEN ● University of Oxford
KAROLA KIRSANOW ● University of Cambridge

future and hope to take things forward (see Lakoff and Johnson, 1980, 1999). The use of spatial metaphors in dealing with time is comforting, but ultimately misleading, as space can be understood through three dimensions, but time is of a greater complexity, less easy to translate into a fixed number of dimensions. Our argument is that as a discipline embraces longer stretches of human time its workers encounter not so much a larger scale, but a greater complexity of scales, made up of a variety of times hard to harmonize into a single picture. In order to explore this key point let us look a little more at the contrast between spatial and temporal scale.

SPATIAL SCALE AND TEMPORAL SCALE

In order to understand, replicate or simulate past sets of spatial scales, it is necessary to start with an averagely sized human body and place it in a landscape or some form of terrain model. Distance, areas of visibility or feelings of enclosure can then all be judged against an average human body and its general capabilities. The same is also true for human constructions in the landscape: forms of boundaries, field systems or buildings can all be subject to estimates as to the labour time involved in their construction and maintenance, and their effects on human and animal patterns of movement or forms of perception can be judged.

In contrast, there is not one temporal scale, but many and it is not entirely clear what standards we should judge our various measurements of duration against. The obvious point of comparison with which to start is the average human life span. However, such spans vary considerably over time and across a single population. According to the latest Human Development Report (Human Development Report Office, 2003) the world average life expectancy is 67 years, with Japanese women having the best life expectancy at 85 years. Shockingly, although predictably, some contemporary African countries have a life expectancy of half that due to a combination of Aids, famine and, sometimes, war. However, the picture within all countries is variable, with class, gender and ethnicity being responsible for considerable differences. Aboriginal people in Australia have life expectancy more in line with those of the Third World than the rest of Australia, which supports one of the longest-lived of the world's populations with an overall life expectancy of 79 years. Such variability is certain to have occurred in the past – slaves and free citizens of fourth century Athens would have had quite different life expectancies. A single yardstick of comparison is elusive.

The term 'life expectancy' can be used in a more philosophical sense. Western cultures at present attempt to hold death at arm's length, constructing the projects of our lives as if death is not imminent. We do not expect to die before extreme old age and feel cheated if this is not the case. At the age of forty most of us are still planning for a long-term future. Many cultures live with a more ready acknowledgement of death and personal finitude. This is not just because life spans were shorter, but also because the emphasis on an individual and their deeds through life was less marked. Ironically, our emphasis on personal longevity might have cut us off from the long-term elements in human life caused by generational succession and being part of the overall flow of life. We are now becoming aware that prehistoric and early historic groups in Britain orientated themselves on a long term past in order to create their life in the present (Bradley, 2002; Gosden and Lock, 1998), an awareness now slow in coming as we do not feel personally part of a succession of generations that leave marks of their activities all round us. Such feelings of succession are currently displaced onto broader groups – nations, towns or institutions have long-term histories, but individuals and kin groups are less likely to partake in them, despite the current popularity for reconstructing family histories. Consequently, we can see that time has a qualitative dimension, as much as a quantitative one – what people feel about the duration of their lives and how this fits in with lengths of time beyond the individual life spans are crucial to the nature of individual and group projects.

Variability in individual life spans within and between societies is not the major complicating factor in working with time archaeologically. The greater problem is that individuals and groups do not present themselves in a straightforward sense archaeologically. Let us start with a single human body. If we assume an average prehistoric lifespan of some forty years then the application of radiocarbon dating, generally with a minimum period of plus or minus fifty years, will provide a determination with a range longer than the life of the person whose bones can be dated. People cannot be placed in time using absolute methods at a timescale commensurable with the spans of their lives. If we focus in on events and processes occurring within the life of a person, then complexity increases. When looking at diet we can sample bones in which isotopic values depend on the food eaten in the last decade of life. In order to understand human movement, we can sample for strontium and compare the values for the adult teeth, laid down in the few years in which the teeth were grown, with the values for the bones created in the last few years of life. Differences between teeth and bones might indicate movement, but provide us with two snapshots of a whole human biography. The times of the body thus vary and are difficult to fix. We cannot reconstruct a whole human biography, but can gain brief flashes of insight into people's histories. These individual flashes start to make some sense when a large enough sample is gained of human individuals, from which broader patterns can be discerned. But it must be remembered that these broader patterns are dependent on individual instances and structured by these.

It is even more difficult to connect people to their products. A hand axe or a pot might take a few hours each to produce, with each individual step of production taking seconds or minutes. Objects might be used and immediately discarded, or curated and used for many hundreds or thousands of years, an ultimate instance of which is the display of handaxes in Roman temples, or indeed the recovery of long-buried materials through excavation. The total biography of an object in production and use might either be much shorter or much longer than an individual life span, only occasionally approximating it (these are the truly biographical objects that people have carried for much of their lives, accruing the significance of their lives – Hoskins, 1998). As Chapman (2000) reminds us, some things were made to be broken and deposited, others to be kept and curated. The treatment of artefacts can give us vital clues as to the cultural forces at work in creating groups and individuals. Artefacts have their own longer temporal rhythms, so that changes in style can be described by battleship curves, as styles wax and wane over periods more or less than a human life span. In many cases different classes of materials, for instance pottery and metalwork in Britain from the Bronze Age onwards, have their own separate histories. A chronology for metalwork is hard to tie to that for pottery; and it is harder to link the history of settlements with metals as most metal is in cemeteries or hoards, whereas pottery is crucial for the dating of settlements.

The nature of the archaeological evidence is generated through a series of timescales, from a single event, such as knapping, to palimpsests of material that may build up very slowly over centuries and millennia through a complex combination of human and natural factors. There is no one single temporal landscape, as our understanding of time is made up of many forms of evidence, each with their own influences and biases. A useful analogy is the contrast between perspectival painting and Cubism. Constable's *The Hay Wain* depicts a bucolic English landscape at a human scale, complete with buildings, human figures and the hay wain itself as comforting reference points. The paintings of Picasso's Cubist period are much harder to assimilate, precisely because they introduce the temporal dimension of human experience to explore what an object looks like when the various angles from which it can be seen are rendered in two dimensions. Archaeological time necessitates a Cubist form of reconstruction in which various measures and qualities of time intersect in ways that do not always make immediate sense. Scale is not a strong quality of Cubist painting and in the same way timescales in archaeology are hard to judge due to their internal complexity.

In order to develop and elaborate these points we will look at a number of sites and case studies each with their own complexity of timescales and problems of combining long timescales with short-term events and processes. The contrast between long and the short come out most clearly with Palaeolithic sites, so that we will start with the famous British site of Boxgrove.

BOXGROVE

The Lower Palaeolithic calcareous silts of Boxgrove in West Sussex have preserved an extensive archaeological landscape, including a human tibia and associated stone tools believed to date to approximately 500,000 years ago (Roberts et al., 1994:311). The site also contains evidence for butchery and possible large-game hunting (Roberts and Parfitt, 1999:415).

As Clive Gamble notes, "the Boxgrove landscape vividly records a series of brief activities, maybe as little as 15 minutes each, that took place 500,000 years ago on a beach in southern England" (Gamble, 1994:275). Boxgrove contrasts the minute temporal scale of everyday activities such as flint-knapping and carcass processing with larger-scale questions such as the timing of the earliest human colonization of Europe.

Boxgrove also poses important questions about the most fruitful applications of stratigraphic and radiometric dating techniques. Because of the site's great antiquity, relative dating techniques with real temporal depth, such as biostratigraphy, have been crucial to dating efforts. The vole clock – the evolutionary change from rooted molar dentition of *Mimomys savini* to the unrooted molars of the extant *Arvicola terrestris* – is the key element around which much of the Boxgrove chronology has been constructed, and occurred shortly before the Boxgrove site was formed (Roberts et al., 1994:312). The artifact-bearing silts at Boxgrove have been dated by mammalian biostratigraphy to a temperate stage immediately preceding the Anglian glaciation (Roberts and Parfitt, 1999:307). Correlative biostratigraphy, combined with geomorphological evidence from fluvial gravels, points to a date in oxygen isotope stage 13 (OIS 13), between 524,000 and 478,000 years ago (Roberts et al., 1994:312).

These dates are controversial. Other researchers have pointed out that inter-site biostratigraphic comparisons are not securely underpinned by independent physical-chemical dating, and that the dating argument based on fluvial gravels is not unambiguous (Bowen and Sykes, 1994:751). Indeed, chemical and radiometric methods have been generally unsuccessful at Boxgrove, producing dates ranging from OIS 6 to OIS 13 (Roberts and Parfitt, 1999). Most of the scientific methods produced later dates that the biostratigraphic estimates: Electron Spin Resonance (ESR) and Uranium series results suggested a date in OIS 7 (245,000 years ago), and aminostratigraphic results support a date in OIS 11, 423,000–362,000 years ago (ibid:303). Optically Stimulated Luminescence (OSL) dating supports the OIS 13 date, but an OIS 11 date is within one standard deviation of the OSL age estimate, so the dating is not unquestionable (McNabb, 2000:440).

Boxgrove raises the difficulties of reconciling long and short elements of dating. One the one hand are the things of ultimate interest – hominid activity at a very early point in the hominid occupation of Britain, in this case flint knapping and animal butchery. These are faithfully recorded in high resolution by the Boxgrove palaeosurfaces, due to the suddenness of burial. They are also well-recorded through high-quality excavation. On the other hand, there is the overall uncertainty about which oxygen isotope stage Boxgrove should fall into. A key element of the Boxgrove evidence is a strong indication that hunting was taking place. The origins of hunting, an activity which takes considerable social coordination, as well as technical expertize, has been much debated, with many feeling that true hunting may not occur prior to the Upper Palaeolithic, some 40,000 years ago. The combination of the comparatively instantaneous activities of knapping and butchery at Boxgrove, and the uncertainty about placing the site in time makes the temporal situation of Boxgrove complicated and hard to evaluate.

POUNDBURY

The case of Poundbury, a site in Dorchester in southern England, illustrates the different degrees of temporal resolution provided by both different materials and investigative methods. Poundbury comprises a settlement with occupational phases beginning in the Neolithic and continuing to the post-Medieval era associated with a series of cemeteries from which over 1,400 inhumations have been recovered

(Farwell and Molleson, 1993:ix). The earliest evidence for burials occurs in the Middle Bronze Age, and the latest securely-assigned burials appear to be associated with the Late Roman period (1993:xii). The Iron Age and Roman phases at Poundbury are particularly interesting because one can attempt to trace the development of the cemetery and settlement together through time. Fifty-nine burials derive from the late Iron Age and early Roman periods and 1114 graves were associated with the late Roman period (4th century BC). Diachronic change in architecture, artifacts, and even skeletal form can be observed in a long-lived settlement such as Poundbury, especially given the sample sizes available.

Both radiocarbon and artefactual dating were employed in order to untangle the complex stratigraphy encountered in many of the phases of the site, especially in trying to relate the constructional phases in each complex to the overall site chronology (Sparey-Green, 1987:91). Spatial scale was intimately related to temporal scale at Poundbury: most of the dating was accomplished through artefact typology and stratigraphic and proximal association. Radiocarbon dating was applied to several phases of the settlement, and the dates obtained span from the 15th century BC to the 5th century AD (1987:141).

Radiocarbon and artefactual dating were important at Poundbury as part of efforts to understand the physical development of a non-living entity – the site itself – and to trace the evolution of lifeways at the settlement. A different sort of resolution is provided by stable isotope analysis performed on skeletons from the Iron Age to post-Roman eras, which illuminated the social scales and scales of migration in operation during this period, along with variations in diet through time. Isotopic analysis of individual remains illuminated differences in diet corresponding to inferred variations in social status within a population, variations in diet between the populations of different periods, and dietary differences between Poundbury natives and possible immigrants from a warmer clime (Richards et al., 1998:1251). The late Iron Age and early Roman period skeletons show that most people had a similar diet, with meat and vegetables but no marine foods. In the late Roman period people buried in more elaborate graves, with lead coffins or mausolea ate more animal protein than those in poorer graves and some immigrants were picked out by variations in bone chemistry related both to the foods making up the diet and geological substrates on which food had been grown.

Poundbury provides us with a mix of chronological perspectives, which it is possible to enter at different scales depending upon interest. A single human biography may be discerned from bone isotopes or more general and longer-term trends may be seen. The artefacts in the graves and the forms of the graves themselves respond to long-term trends, many of which emanate from outside the region, through influences flowing through the Roman Empire more broadly. A single grave may represent a compound of longer term changes in material culture, with evidence from a human body personal to the individual concerned and this later bodily information may have been laid down at a variety of times, from childhood to the last few years of life, depending on whether bones or teeth were being sampled. Such complexity within an individual is found in even greater measure on those rare occasions when tissues and hair are preserved – one much discussed case being Ötzi, the Iceman.

ÖTZTAL

The Ötztal iceman was discovered by a pair of hikers in 1991 on the Italian side of the Ötztal Alps, near the Austrian border (Kutschera and Rom, 2000:13). The Ötztal case represents a reversal of the Poundbury scenario, where artefactual dating based on a well-known regional typology sequence produced a finer degree of temporal resolution than scientific methods. Here, radiocarbon and stable isotopes provide information on Ötzi's position within a worldwide radiocarbon chronology and movements through the region during his lifetime.

Prehistorians initially dated the extraordinarily well-preserved remains to around 2000 BC on the basis of the flanged axe in the Iceman's kit, an artifact characteristic of the Early Bronze Age in the northern Alps (Barfield, 1994:20). However, radiocarbon determinations produced even earlier dates. AMS radiocarbon measurements on tissue, bone, equipment, and grass from the Iceman assemblage produced an (averaged) radiocarbon age of $4{,}550 \pm 19$ BP indicating that the Iceman lived in the Late Neolithic, between 3370 and 3100 BC (Bonani et al., 1994, Kutschera and Rom, 2003:709), in contrast to the Early Bronze Age date suggested by the artefactual evidence. Further investigation into the stylistic chronology of the region was conducted in order to reconcile this discrepancy, and a possible correlation of the axe from Ötzi's kit with another early instance of the flanged axe form in the greater region may have resolved the disagreement between the artefactual and radiocarbon age estimates (Barfield, 1994:22).

The intimate connection between spatial and temporal scales is illustrated by the investigation of Ötzi's origin and movements through isotopic analysis of different body tissues representing different developmental stages (Kutschera and Rom, 2003; Holden, 2003). A combination of radiogenic (Sr, Pb, Nd) and stable (O, C, N) isotopes were measured in order to investigate different aspects of the Iceman's prehistoric movements. The heavy radiogenic isotopes enable the reconstruction of movement relative to the local geological substrate, while the lighter stable isotopes track changes in palaeodiet (C and N) and altitude and position relative to a watershed (O) (2003:715). Argon dating was performed on ingested mica samples from the Iceman's intestine in order to determine their provenance from among local lithologies of different geological ages (Müller et al., 2003:865).

Different lithological units have different isotopic compositions, and these differences are preserved in the vegetation and fauna of each geological region. Human hard tissues such as bone and tooth enamel mineralize at different developmental stages and incorporate radiogenic isotopes bearing the signature of their geological environment during each ontogenetic stage. The enamel of the permanent dentition mineralizes in early childhood and remains compositionally unaltered thereafter, while bones are continually re-mineralizing throughout an individual's lifetime. The isotopic composition of bone reflects the last 10 or so years of life, with spongy bone turning over more rapidly than cortical bone (Sealy et al., 1995).

Strontium and lead ratios from Ötzi's tooth enamel were significantly different from ratios from spongy and cortical bone samples, indicating that the region in which the Iceman was an adult was geologically distinct from that of his childhood. Analysis of oxygen isotope ratios indicated a southerly origin for the Iceman, and

Sr and Pb ratios pointed to the region within 60 km south of the find site (Kutschera and Rom, 2003:718). Investigators also noted the possibility that the Sr and $\delta^{18}O$ isotope values observed in the Iceman reflect a pattern of seasonal migration between low altitude settlements in the south and summer grazing areas above the timberline in the north, around southern Ötztal (Müller et al., 2003:865).

So for Ötzi, isotopic analysis of dental enamel zooms in to the third to fifth years of his life, analysis of bone describes the last 10–20 years, his kit attests to the demands of his final days, and the ingested mica in his intestine reflects his last hours. Because of the unusual preservation of tissue, stomach contents and artefacts, Ötzi highlights how complex the temporality surrounding an individual can be. Any person represents a point of intersection of varying temporal scales. For Ötzi there is the biography of his life – his origin lies some 60 km south of where he died. The movement between place of birth and death may be something accidental to him or reflect broader patterns of movement – which possibility pertains, we do not know. The same goes for his diet, over which there is considerable controversy, particularly in the comparison between stomach contents revealing his last meal and analyses of his hair, which grew over a longer period. It seems most likely that he ate a mixed diet of meat, bread and vegetable matter, totally unsurprisingly, and each component of this reflects long histories of domestication and local knowledge vital for procurement. One of the most intriguing features of the Iceman find is the presence of a suite of equipment and clothing representing the kit of one person at a particular point in time. These artefacts have not gone through a post-mortem selection process, and so more accurately represent a certain moment within the Iceman's lifetime, a moment primarily concerned with survival in the mountainous terrain of the Alps (Barfield, 1994:12). The material culture found with the body, such as the bows, copper axe, a backpack, and birch bark containers demonstrate that 18 different sorts of woods were used, each presumably chosen for its properties being suitable to the object being made. Such knowledge was not individual to Ötzi, but the product of long traditions of working in the mountains and Alpine valleys. The birchbark containers, backpack, and bows were specific instances of broader assemblages of material originally found in large numbers at the very end of the Neolithic, most of which perished long ago.

DISCUSSION

Absolute methods provide a global scale, so that a site, landscape or assemblage of material can be placed within a set of chronological schemes that can ultimately span the globe. Thus, Boxgrove is of interest globally, feeding into debates about human ancestral capabilities, especially to do with hunting from periods when evidence is sparse anywhere in the world. The Boxgrove finds excited much British interest, but again because it put Britain on a larger map. *The Times* famously described the find of a human tibia at Boxgrove as evidence of the ''first European'' (a phrase replete with temporal confusions, Europe being a very recent category and having little utility in describing the identity of hominids living so long ago, and also factually incorrect, there being a number of older sites within the territory of present day Europe). It is the scale of discussions and consideration that is crucial to people's views of dating evidence. Ötzi is known and discussed globally due to the unusual nature of preservation and the evidence, but the artefactual assemblages and more detailed pattern of actions are of great interest to local prehistorians, as well as to the world community. Poundbury is of somewhat more local interest, but the evidence is again a compound of varying sets of scales among individuals buried and the complex of evidence from the site more generally.

Time and timescales can only be understood through metaphor – long time-scales, the deep past and so on – rather than directly. This being so we need to think more about the range of metaphors we employ and their internal compatibility. In addition to the spatial metaphors used to understand time, which are deeply engrained in our thought and will obviously continue in use, we can see that there are also discursive effects on our conception of time, although here again the scope of discussions are often influenced spatially. Boxgrove is a site most immediately thought of in a larger ambit – whether hominids were in Britain 500,000 years ago tells us something about the pulses of populations across the continent of Europe and beyond, as does whether Britain was only occupied in warmer climatic or during cold ones as well. Even the short-term evidence of killing, knapping and butchery are best thought of broadly, once we have got over that amazing preservation and degree of detail from a site of this age. The Iceman again commands headlines due to the nature of his preservation, but ultimately there is a surprisingly local story being told here based on considerable geological variability expressed in the various isotopic values in tissue, hair, teeth and bone. The objects found with him also tell of a fine knowledge of the local region and its resources. People living near to Boxgrove might be excited that such an amazing find lies in their vicinity, if they think about the matter at all, but it tells them little about the use of the local region. Ötzi is globally known and discussed, but the evidence derived from his body and artefacts fit directly into local knowledge and feel for the varying altitudinal zones, their plants and animals, that still exists in the region today. Poundbury's story can be entered at different temporal levels, ranging from the long-term coming into being of a single place in use from the Neolithic to the medieval period and beyond; it informs on the nature of diet and movement in the Iron Age and Roman periods that specialists of both periods can relate to and discuss in terms of the histories of artefacts and of human bodies.

Time excites a range of reactions in us all. Even the hardened professional gains a sense of wonder from a knapping episode perfectly preserved from half a million years ago, or from a single person and his equipment from 5,000 years ago. Once this sense of wonder has diminished, more pragmatic, analytical concerns set in arising from what one can say about evidence of this type and how to place it within a broader narrative of long term trends and changes. The pinpoint nature of events that first excite attention, become part of an analytical problem of how to fit rich short-term elements of evidence within a longer, thinner record from which so much has been lost. If all our evidence was as rich as that surrounding Ötzi we would quickly become overwhelmed in detail and our ability to see long-term trends would be lost, but this is not a great fear, faced as we are with the opposite problem.

Understanding time and timescales is a complex business. Complexity is not something to be dissolved or disaggregated into simpler forms. Almost any piece of archaeological evidence mixes longer and shorter times within it and can appeal to varying sets of discussion of local or more global significance. We do need to be aware of the complex nature of our temporal evidence and think how we can use this. The radiocarbon revolution (and subsequent advances in absolute dating) have taken some of the worry out of chronology, in that many sites can be placed in a scheme of ultimately global scope, with determinations also very helpful in creating internal sequences within sites. Placing sites in some measurable scale creates confidence, culturally inclined as we are to see time as measurement in our daily lives. But radiocarbon determinations bring us up against events that happened so quickly (such as an individual lifespan) that they cannot be placed within timescales deriving from absolute dating methods. Rather than seeing temporal complexity and a lack of a single timescale as a problem, we can use this as a spur to reflect on the fact that time is a quality as much as a quantity – some minutes or hours fly by and others drag on interminably. Most of the minutes and hours have vanished from our evidence, but some are still there and how to bring these together with years, decades, centuries and millennia is still a key issue for archaeology, which needs to be more clearly recognized than it has to date.

REFERENCES

Barfield, L., 1994, The Iceman Reviewed. *Antiquity* 68:10–26.
Bradley, R., 2002, *The Past in Prehistoric Societies*. Routledge, London.
Bonani, G., Ivy, S.D., Hajdas, I., Niklaus, T.R., and Suter, M., 1994, AMS 14C age Determinations of Tissue, Bone, and Grass Samples from the Otztal Ice Man. *Radiocarbon* 36 (2):247–250.
Bowen, D.Q., and Sykes, G.A., 1994, How Old is Boxgrove man? *Nature* 371:751.
Chapman, J., 2000, *Fragmentation in Archaeology: People, Places and Broken Objects in the Prehistory of Southeast Europe*. Routledge, London.
Farwell, D.E., and Molleson, T.L., 1993, *Excavations at Poundbury, 1968–80. Volume II: The Cemeteries*. Dorset Natural History and Archaeological Society Monograph Series No. 11.
Gamble. C., 1994, Time for Boxgrove Man. *Nature* 369:275.
Gosden, C., and Lock, G., 1998, Prehistoric Histories. *World Archaeology* 30:2–12.
Holden, C., 2003, Isotopic Data Pinpoint Iceman's Origins. *Science* 302:759–760.
Hoskins, J., 1998, *Biographical Objects: How Things Tell the Story of People's Lives*. Routledge, London.
Human Development Report Office, 2003, *Human Development Report 2003. Millennium Development Goals: A compact among nations to end human poverty*. Online: http://www.undp.org/hdr2003/ (accessed 6th December 2004).
Kutschera, W., and Rom, W., 2000, Ötzi the Prehistoric Iceman. *Nuclear Instruments and Methods in Physics Research B* 164–165:12–22.
Kutschera, W., and Rom, W., 2003, "Isotope Language" of the Alpine Iceman Investigated with AMS and MS. *Nuclear Instruments and Methods in Physics Research B* 204:705–719.
Lakoff, G., and Johnson, M., 1980, *Metaphors We Live By*. University of Chicago Press, Chicago.
Lakoff, G., and Johnson, M., 1999, *Philosophy in the Flesh. The Embodied Mind and its Challenge to Western Thought*. Basic Books, New York.
McNabb, J., 2000, Boxgrove. *Antiquity* 74:439–441.
Müller, W., Fricke, H., Halliday, A.N., McCulloch, M.T., and Wartho, J., 2003, Origin and Migration of the Alpine Iceman. *Science* 302:862–866.

Richards, M.P., Hedges, R.E.M., Molleson, T.I., and Vogel, J.C., 1998, Stable Isotope Analysis Reveals Variations in Human Diet at the Poundbury Camp Site. *Journal of Archaeological Science* 25:1247–1252.

Roberts, M.B., and Parfitt, S.A., 1999, *Boxgrove: A Middle Pleistocene Hominid Site at Eartham Quarry, Boxgrove, West Sussex*. English Heritage Archaeological Report 17.

Roberts, M.B., Stringer, C.B., and Parfitt, S.A., 1994, A Hominid Tibia from Middle Pleistocene Sediments at Boxgrove, UK. *Nature* 369:311–312.

Sealy, J., Armstrong, R., and Schrire, C., 1995, Beyond Lifetime Averages: Tracing Life Histories through Isotopic Analysis of Different Calcified Tissues from Archaeological Human Skeletons. *Antiquity* 69:290–300.

Sparey-Green, C, 1987, *Excavations of Poundbury, Dorchester, Dorset, 1966–1982. Vol. I: The Settlements*. Dorset Natural History and Archaeological Society Monograph Series No. 7.

CHAPTER 3

Scale as Artifact: GIS, Ecological Fallacy, and Archaeological Analysis

TREVOR M. HARRIS

INTRODUCTION

The concept of scale is confusing, frustrating, little understood, and yet . . . intriguing. Geography, as the discipline with spatial pattern and relationships as its core focus, has traditionally embraced and confronted the meaning, interpretation, explanatory power, and some would suggest, intractability, that scale brings to studies. There are many other spatially related disciplines such as archaeology that share with geography the need to operate across a scale continuum ranging from the local to the regional, national, and international levels. Indeed, as Mcmaster and Sheppard (2004) point out, it is difficult to identify a completely "scaleless" discipline. Our understanding of geographical and archaeological patterns, societal processes, and spatial heterogeneity, are highly dependent on scale. Because of the extent and complexity of the Earth's surface, researchers must invariably sample, generalize, or aggregate in order to comprehend reality. Identifying an appropriate scale of data capture and analysis to use in a study, and managing the trade-offs that must occur in matching resources with data capture, have long been acknowledged. But while scale is readily associated with the level of detail involved with geographical description, what is missing from most studies is any discussion of how representative that scale of analysis is, given that there are no standard measures of uncertainty related to particular scales of analysis (Tate and Atkinson 2001). Indeed, Meentemeyer (1989) suggests that it seems that study scales are selected unconsciously and therefore may seem to be completely arbitrary. Watson (1978) observes that we tend to work at one analytical level exclusively and implicitly, without considering other alternatives, almost as an act of faith. Scale issues associated with line generalization, scale of data capture and data display, and with the even less well-known issues of ecological fallacy and its derivative, the Modifiable Areal Unit Problem, are only rarely acknowledged.

TREVOR M. HARRIS ● West Virginia University

Geographic Information Systems, GIS, facilitate an almost effortless integration and display of multi-scale data and aggregation of areal units. Generating data for GIS analysis invariably requires extensive effort and introduces a slew of issues associated with data capture, data accuracy, data resolution, error estimation, metadata, data structure, storage and compression, and data sharing to name but a few. The problem of identifying an appropriate scale of study when using GIS is compounded by the need to utilize, wherever possible, data created by others in order to reduce data duplication and replication and to minimize the cost of populating the GIS database. As a result, additional problems arise because of the need to work with digital data inherited from elsewhere and over which an investigator had very little, if any, control in its creation. The ease of digital data use in GIS thus raises concern not only about how scale issues are handled *explicitly* in disciplinary studies but *implicitly* through data acquisition and the application of a range of methods and tools.

The identification of an optimal scale, the sampling and generalization of reality that underpins "data scale", multi-scalar data issues, and the desire to "jump" scale from local to global and the interconnections that lie between them, is methodologically highly problematic. In the face of these many scale-based issues, Gregory (1994:545) contends that "one might expect a renewed and conjoint interest in both the technical and the theoretical issues raised by the question of scale...." Given the multiple meanings of the term scale, this chapter explores the conjoint implications and meanings of scale by focusing on spatial scale, and the implications arising from aggregation issues and inferences that contribute to the fundamental problem of ecological fallacy. If, as Bird (1989:22) suggests, different scales of approach may eventuate in different results and study outcomes, then it is important to understand scale not solely as a "mechanism" or scalar measure of data accuracy or cartographic display, but as a conceptual *primateur* in the production and reproduction of space. This paper focuses on the theoretical link between data scale and the inferences that can be drawn from scale-conditioned studies.

DEFINING SCALE

The term scale has acquired multiple connotations and some ambiguity because of its several meanings and abstract complexities. By far the most commonly recognized and widespread use of the term is that it represents a level of spatial representation, as commonly used in cartography, and defines the relationship between distance on a map image and the corresponding difference in reality. Some authors perceive scale more broadly as a level of spatio-temporal representation, experience, or organization of events and processes (Gregory, 1994:543; Smith, 2000:724). Scale is certainly used in the context of regional scale and, more recently, has centered on the causal mechanisms derived from the globalization of capitalism and modernity (Gregory, 1994:544). These latter questions on the theorization and representation of scale and the political economy of scale clearly extend the meaning of scale well beyond more traditional notions of its usage in spatial science and analytical method (1994:544).

Beyond these very broad definitions of scale, a number of authors have sought to provide greater specificity of its varied meanings (Dungan et al., 2002; Meentemeyer, 1989). Gregory (1994:544) draws on the work of Haggett (1965) and Harvey (1969) to identify three basic questions of scale. Scale *coverage* refers to the need to study the world at all relevant scales using exploration, resurvey, and sampling procedures. Scale *standardization* refers to the need to aggregate and weight areal procedures in order to obtain the necessary data for analysis. Finally, scale *linkage* applies to the need to link scaled studies at a comparative "same-level" relation, as a contextual relation, high to low levels, or as an aggregative relation, low to high levels. As Gregory rightly points out, the linkage of scales between high to low and low to high levels brings about concerns for ecological fallacy because "generalizations about patterns and processes at one level of scale may not hold true at another level" (1994:544).

Smith (2000:724) also identifies three discernible meanings of scale: *cartographic* scale, *methodological* scale, and *geographical* scale. Cartographic scale, as its name suggests, refers to the level of abstraction at which a map is constructed and its relative correspondence to reality. Methodological scale refers to the scale selected by a researcher in order to garner the information necessary to pursue a research problem. Smith suggests cartographic scale and methodological scale relate more to issues of specific processes in the human and physical landscape and are therefore distinct from the conceptual abstraction implied by geographical scale. In contrast to these two conceptualizations, Smith (2000:725) suggests the third meaning of scale, *geographical* scale, which represents an overarching conceptual abstraction lain over these scaled landscapes. Methodological and geographical scale, he suggests, were not significantly separated in the minds of researchers until the 1980s and have only come to the fore more recently in the wake of social theory, Marxist Geography, and a focus on the ways in which space is produced, reproduced, and redifferentiated into places, groups of places, and social units (Smith, 2000:725). Smith (2000:725; and see McMaster and Sheppard, 2004) also suggests that geographical scale is not natural or given but provides

> a central organizing principle according to which geographical differentiation takes place. It is a metric of spatial differentiation: it arbitrates and organizes the kinds of spatial differentiation that frames the landscape. As such, it is the production of geographical scale rather than scale per se that is the appropriate research focus.

This moves the discussion of scale a considerable distance from the early interpretations of scale in geographic enquiry as a level of detail ranging from the local to the global and the interaction between these scales – what Bird (1989) refers to as micro-scale, mesoscale, and macroscale. Geographical scale, as defined by Smith, even moves beyond Gregory's focus on how space and scale articulates and influences the examination of substantive processes (Gregory, 1994). Hierarchy theory draws on ecological approaches to scale that involves a system of vertical and horizontal structures of levels wherein subsystems operate at spatial and temporal scales that are nested series within a hierarchical system (Levin, 1992; McMaster and Sheppard, 2004). Interactions are stronger within these structures or "holons" than between them and analysis is facilitated because it is assumed that spatial and temporal scales covary simultaneously (McMaster and Sheppard, 2004).

These meanings and interpretations are applicable, if not central, to most disciplines, but especially archaeology, geography and ecology, where studies tend to be predominantly scale dependent.

While these multiple meanings and complex abstractions of scale have provided opportunity for rethinking notions of scale, invariably they have contributed more to a growing confusion about scale, and how scale impacts studies. Several authors writing on scale issues have referred to the multiple meanings of the term and to the many interpretations that accompany these definitions (Goodchild and Quattrachi, 1996; Mcmaster and Sheppard, 2004; Tate and Atkinson, 2001). Indeed, Goodchild and Quattrachi (1996) refer to the over half column in Webster's dictionary dedicated to defining scale. To complicate matters still further, they suggest that scale also has different meanings in different disciplines. The landscape ecologist, for example, focuses on "grain" as a measure of the size of patch or discrete habitat in the landscape. To a GIS user, scale can refer to the geographical extent of a study and to the degree of detail or content exhibited. At a 1:2,400 scale, archaeological sites may well be represented in a GIS as polygonal units whereas at a 1:50,000 scale these same sites could be represented as point data. In the latter, scale is inferred to represent accuracy, or conversely is an assessment of error.

Scale can also be used to infer a level of representation. Scholars in different disciplines often use small-scale and large-scale in seemingly opposing senses meaning coarse scale, large area – small scale, and fine scale, small area – large scale, or as "large" areal extent or "small" areal extent (Goodchild and Quattrachi, 1996). The latter reflects another use of the term scale in representing the areal extent of a study. Scale and resolution are also interrelated in that resolution defines the smallest object or feature that is discernible in the data. Scale and resolution are related because there is a lower limit to the size of an object that can be usefully distinguished, sampled, or represented. As scale becomes coarser, so resolution diminishes. In this respect scale is the basic dimension of generalization that, by definition, must introduce uncertainty into the representation of the real phenomenon. Here, the larger the scale, the less the generalization and the greater the apparent detail (Goodchild and Quattrachi, 1996). However, generalization should not simply be equated with less information, for generalization could add information rather than reduce it simply by the ability to display more features for a larger areal unit. Scale is thus intertwined with issues of data measurement, data accuracy, and data resolution. Absolute and relative scale of course are not synonymous, for while absolute scale is tied to Euclidian space and is underpinned by measured space, relative distance can be based on more than measured distance (Meentemeyer, 1989). Social distance and relative access are not based on a Euclidian construct but suggest different ways of understanding space and scale. Spatio-temporal scaling is a further conceptual and methodological problem that applies to almost all social sciences, though GIS is increasingly exacerbating the issues because of its ability to move beyond the restrictions previously imposed by the static and controlled environment of the paper map. Representations of the real world are based on spatial and temporal data usually captured at a limited range of scales and scale issues plague data collection efforts as well as subsequent analyses. Data at "sub-optimal" scales are sometimes all that is available and GIS users must be very conscious of this constraint on the validity and quality of results. The dramatic diffusion of GIScience, GISci (Geographical Information Science), forces disciplines, even those long acquainted with the use of geographical information, to reconsider and reflect on the changes that this technology brings. Scale issues certainly come to the fore in matters of GIS and GISci.

Finally, while the definitions outlined above do not deliberately set out to portray a linear conceptualization of scale, a perception of linear scale certainly predominates based on an assumed scale linkage extending from the local to the global, or even a metaphysical scale that continues beyond the earth (Ferber and Harris, 2005). Smith (2000:725) proposes a loose nested hierarchical schema of geographical scales from the body, home, and community through to the local, regional, national and global and suggests that the production of scale is not arbitrary or even voluntary but is ordered and contested. It is also appropriate, however, to consider scale as a non-hierarchical relation. In this regard, Ferber (2005) suggests that in addition to the ontological complexities of scale given by Smith and Gregory that a hermeneutical perspective might also apply. Thus Herod and Wright (2002) refer to scalar metaphors that also frame the discussion of scale. Herod suggests four scale metaphors that comprise the *ladder*, the more traditional linear perception of scale with the local at the base and the global at the top of the ladder, as well as the *circle*, the *Matryoshka doll*, and the *network*. The Matryoshka doll scale metaphor suggests that each level of scale can be larger or smaller than another but is not necessarily hierarchical or linear in the sense of being above or below the other as in the scale ladder metaphor. The circle metaphor suggests a scale linkage in which scale relations surround one another. The network metaphor suggests that places can be either local or global and are not constrained by traditional notions of Euclidian space. Thus earthworm type tunnels could connect one scaled place to another but one scale is neither above, below, or surrounding the other; rather each scale level is positioned beside the other. This perhaps comes closest to Smith's (2000:726) suggestion of the simultaneity of scales.

SPATIAL DATA AND SCALE IN GIS

Because our understanding of scale largely originates from the historical use of the traditional non-dynamic paper map, the flexibility and dynamism of digital GIS represents new and significant challenges to the understanding of scale issues. On the paper map, the scale of display remains fixed because it is the scale of the output map product. The ability of a user to alter or change that ratio in traditional paper-based maps is severely limited. However, digital mapping allows the user to vary this fixed constant, and provides unfortunate opportunities for the misuse of display scale. Many will have probably heard or experienced the horror stories of those who, in their search for supposedly "larger scale" data, photocopied and enlarged paper maps thinking they were changing the scale of the map. Of course, while the ratio between map units and real world units had changed, the *original* scale at which the data had been captured remained the same. The distinction between scale of data capture and the scale of data display is critical to understand in GIS usage. The ease with which GIS enables the important ratio of scale to be changed, demands that care and attention must be exercised regarding its use.

GIS studies are often undertaken by researchers using spatial data created by others, and over which the researcher has little control and, despite metadata, possibly only limited understanding about the limitations, purpose, or ontology of that data (Gahegan, 2005). Decisions or interpretations are often made based on geographic scales and units determined by other groups and which are invariably aligned with areal units defined by bureaucratic or political purposes. Thus, the scale of data used in a GIS is often outside the control of the geographer or archaeologist and is determined or inherited from data collection efforts or activities designed for different purposes. Given the substantial cost of obtaining GIS data this trend will likely continue. Archaeologists are unlikely to be able to control the entire process of project data collection, compilation, management, analysis and modeling. It is entirely possible then, that the digital spatial data available for many GIS-archaeological projects will not match the scales at which processes are actually operating. Science in this respect will become complex, more interpretive, and highly scale dependent. What are required, of course, are analytical techniques that will work at different scales of analysis or at scales that are not considered ideal (Goodchild and Quattrochi, 1996).

One of the powerful functional features of GIS is its capacity to integrate multi-scale data captured at a variety of scales. This implies, however, that the implications of utilizing data captured at different scales are fully understood. Given that scale represents the extent of detail in the digital representation of real world features, the issue of generalization has significant impact on the integration and use of multi-scale data. A well-known question posed to geography students studying the fractal nature of landscape is to ask them to estimate the length of a specified coastline. The subsequent discussion on the fractal nature of lines reveals that such a distance is infinite, for the length of a coastline is a property of the scale at which the information is collected (Mandelbrot, 1977). From space, the length of the measured coastline will reflect the need to severely generalize the coast's sampling points; much more so than if the coast were measured from a lower altitude. If the line sampling were to shift to a sampling measure based on walking the coastline then the line will be considerably more complex and "wiggly". Although Mandelbrot discovered that the fractal nature of landscape was relatively constant across a range of scales, nonetheless, the actual line lengths will vary depending on the sampling density and line generalization. Ultimately, one could go the extent of measuring around every boulder or even grains of sand to calculate the length of a coastline – the coastline length thus depends on the level of scale and the resultant effect of coordinate point sampling on the line generalization. The measurement of shore length is thus a function of the density of sample points and the scale used to describe it. This continuum of scales enforces the generalization or simplification of features, or the densification of such features, as one transitions from the macro to the micro-scale and vice versa.

Overlaying data captured at different scales creates similar issues as to how line features are captured or depicted – whether at coarser or finer scale. Scale in this respect reflects the generalized geometry at which the feature was defined (see Figure 3.1). Overlaying feature data captured at one scale onto another feature captured at a different scale is prone to produce scale artifacts and significant error if appropriate care is not exercised. In the hypothetical schematic Figure 3.1, two data sets representing road and stream features were ostensibly captured at a 1:24,000 scale and represent a comparable level of sampling and line generalization. If a data coverage of one of these features was captured at 1:100,000 scale then the line representation is further generalized with fewer coordinates to describe the feature geometry. Overlaying features captured at different scales thus has the potential to produce spurious errors, as in this example where the overlay of features captured at two different scales generates several crossing points of the stream whereas at a more appropriate scale no such crossings are portrayed.

Scale then has a significant impact on the results of a GIS analysis. Consider an extrapolation of the mixed scale example in Figure 3.1 to an application to calculate the time taken to transport patients from several townships to a trauma hospital using network analysis in which road conditions and speeds, turning directions, and traffic directions were included in the calculation. Significantly, and irrespective of

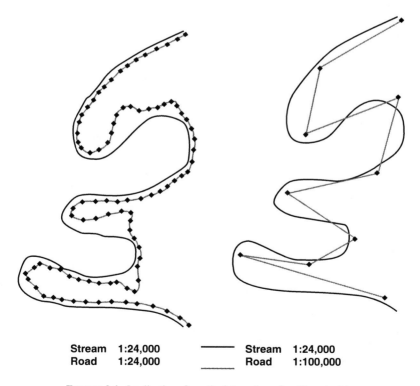

| Stream | 1:24,000 | —————— | Stream | 1:24,000 |
| Road | 1:24,000 | ————— | Road | 1:100,000 |

FIGURE 3-1. Implications from the integration of multi-scale data.

the sophistication of the network algorithm, the distance and time taken to cover the respective distances between township and trauma hospital will vary markedly as the scale of the road network line representation is changed. Based on student studies of this problem, we found that as the road network becomes less generalized and the sampling points more dense to represent greater detail in the sinuosity of the road, so the "length" of the road "increased", by as much as one third when performing analysis at 1:100,000 and 1:24,000 scales. This is not dissimilar to the inference made by Mandelbrot and his wiggly lines. Appreciating the impact of data scale on analytical outcomes is a critical part in the appropriate use of GIS technology.

Ecological Fallacy

The advent and rapid diffusion of GIS then has intruded scale into the frontline of spatial analysis and a multiplicity of users must now grapple with spatial data and scale issues. The utility and appropriateness of spatial data is invariably related to the scale of geographic representation in the form of the attribution, accuracy, and resolution of the spatial geometry used to describe the spatial primitives of point, line, polygon, and pixel. In addition to the issues of data scale and data representation discussed above, this paper also focuses on the deeper underlying implications arising from scale. While the issues of line generalization, scale of data capture and display, are problematic, the influence of scale inference as conceptualized in ecological fallacy and in the aggregation effects of the Modifiable Areal Unit Problem are even less well known but equally problematic.

Haggett suggests that scale obtrudes into geographical studies because of the problem of linking results obtained at one scale of analysis to those obtained at another (Haggett, 1965:164). In particular, he proposed that scale is problematic because of: (a) the variety of studies undertaken at differing areal extents – the scale-coverage problem; (b) the desire to link results obtained at one scale to those obtained at another – the scale-linkage problem; and (c) the problems of standardizing data that are captured at a variety of fixed scales – the scale-standardization problem. Invariably scale is a factor in most analyses simply because of the need to change scale in order to comprehend the enormity of the area covered. In the context of the scale standardization problem Haggett suggested that differing statistical results could be obtained by changing the boundaries of the areal units for which the data was first captured (Haggett, 1965:179). If differing outcomes can be obtained by aggregating areal units in differing ways then this issue is highly problematic for researchers. This concern lies at the heart of what became known as the Modifiable Areal Unit Problem, MAUP, which bedevils much of areal unit based GIS analysis. In the context of the scale-linkage problem, Haggett also identified a concern that is now known by the term ecological fallacy.

Robinson first highlighted the potential concerns about ecological fallacy in 1950, and Alker (1969), advanced and extended Robinson's revolutionary ideas by outlining several forms of ecological fallacy. Reduced to its essential elements, ecological fallacy occurs in several forms. *Individualistic fallacy* occurs when attempts are made to impute macrolevel, aggregate, relationships from micro-level, individual, relationships. *Cross-level fallacy* occurs when one makes inferences from one sub-population to another sub-population at the same level of analysis. *Ecological fallacy* is the opposite of individualistic fallacy in that it involves making inferences from higher to lower levels of analysis, from coarse to fine. A derivative of ecological fallacy is to be found in the modifiable areal unit problem that questions the assumption that relationships observed at one level of population aggregation are a universal feature of that population (Alker 1969).

Ecological fallacy represents a little known but continuing and unresolved issue in the analysis and interpretation of geographical and archaeological phenomenon. As the name suggests, the fallacy is especially prominent in the field of ecology where data scale ranges from the individual plant to forest ecosystems (Levin, 1992; Dungan et al., 2002; Turner et al., 1989; Wiens et al., 1993). In essence, ecological fallacy suggests that scale underpins the patterns that we see and our ability to understand the processes that we cannot see. Perhaps here a simple rhetorical question positions the quandary well. Can the operation of a forest ecosystem be determined if the problem were studied at the scale of a leaf? Equally, can one understand the physiology of a leaf if the problem were examined at the scale of the forest? As early as 1956 Mccarty et al. (1956, quoted in Haggett, 1965:170) provided insight into the implications of pursuing analysis at different scales and he concisely captures the tenor of ecological fallacy.

> In geographic investigation it is apparent that conclusions derived from studies made at one scale should not be expected to apply to problems whose data are expressed at other scales. Every change in scale will bring about the statement of a new problem, and there is no basis for assessing that associations existing at one scale will also exist at another.

Bird (1956), for example, discovered in a comparative study of Cornwall and Brittany that at a small scale of analysis he determined the areas to have similar characteristics. However, when viewed at a large scale he found the areas to be essentially dissimilar. Delcourt et al., (1983) study of the influence of scale on ecology reinforces this. He found that each major process operating on a landscape occurred over a limited range of characteristic scales. Thus, the process of secondary succession operated over a particular range of both time and space, and this differed from the process of speciation extinction which process was observable and interpretable at a coarser spatial and temporal scale. Importantly, Delcourt noted that temporal and spatial scales in ecology are usually linked and co-vary because of the influence of the transportation mechanism in ecology. This study, undertaken over 40 years ago, should be instrumental to GIS practitioners in archaeology and unless this is explicitly recognized, many results derived from spatial analytical studies may be meaningless. The implications of ecological fallacy for archaeologists are significant for if conclusions derived at one scale of analysis should not be expected to apply to problems expressed at other scales, then it is unclear whether the patterns and understanding of an archaeological phenomenon are in fact an artifact of scale dependency.

Given the range of scale used in archaeological analysis, from intra-site to intersite, such cautionary warnings are poignant. No single mechanism can explain patterns at all scales, and these mechanisms typically operate at different scales than the scales at which the patterns are observed (Levin, 1992; Gardner et al., 1989; Addicott et al., 1987; Dale et al., 1989; Schwartz, 1994). Some geographic patterns only become apparent at a certain scale and when "viewed" at a certain distance. As studies move progressively from fine scale to coarse scale, it is unknown whether patterns and processes change smoothly and gradually, or abruptly. To move from the individual micro-organism to the macro-scale it is crucial to understand how information becomes discernible as scale changes from fine to coarse scales (Jarvis and McNaughton, 1986). The key to understanding how information is transferred across scales is to determine what information is preserved and what information is lost as one moves from one scale to the other (Levin, 1992). The effects of moving from one scale to another has received some discussion (Haggett, 1965; Harvey, 1968; Hudson, 1992) but central to the concern about scale change is the extent to which our understanding of patterns and processes obtained at one scale level may be valid or invalid at another level. This is the basis of ecological fallacy.

THE MODIFIABLE AREAL UNIT PROBLEM

The Modifiable Areal Unit Problem, MAUP, is probably one of the most widely recognized forms of ecological fallacy. The MAUP is related to the extent to which the choice of areal unit impacts the results of analysis. In the MAUP, ecological fallacy arises when findings obtained from the analysis of grouped data aggregated into areal units of one specific type are then inferred as applying to all the individuals who formed that group (Openshaw, 1984:8). Heywood et al. (2002:8) defines the MAUP as "a problem arising from the imposition of artificial units of spatial reporting on continuous geographical phenomenon resulting in the generation of artificial spatial patterns." The MAUP is endemic to all analyses involving areal data and although the MAUP is generally well known by geographers, it is questionable to what extent the problem is understood by the broader GIS community or related spatial disciplines (Openshaw and Johnston, 1981; Openshaw and Taylor, 1979; Openshaw and Alvandies, 1999). Whether the problem is acknowledged or not, it is often, as with other aspects of scale, just ignored or assumed away as being insoluble.

One of the best concise studies laying out the case explaining the MAUP and detailing the severity and implications of the problem is a monograph by Openshaw (1983; see also Openshaw and Taylor, 1979). According to Openshaw (1983:8) the MAUP is comprised of three separate but very related problems:

1. a scale problem in which there are questions as to the number of zonal units needed for a study and the significant variation in results that can arise as data is progressively aggregated into fewer and larger units of analysis;
2. an aggregation problem that raises questions about how data are to be aggregated and the variation in results that may arise due to the use of possible alternative aggregation schemes at equal or similar scales; and
3. the impact of ecological fallacy in instances where spatially aggregated data are used to infer similar characteristics on those individuals who populated the aggregated zones.

In many geographical and archaeological studies, individual data are often assigned to areal units that form the base spatial units for the study of some phenomenon. In many instances, these units are themselves subsequently aggregated into larger units. Openshaw indicates that these units are invariably modifiable and could take many forms, but that no fixed rules exist as to how the units are first generated. "Quite simply, the areal units ... used in many geographical studies are arbitrary, modifiable, and subject to the whims and fancies of whoever is doing, or did, the aggregating" (Openshaw 1983:3).

The census enumeration unit is a good example of a modifiable zone that is "designed" such that an enumerator may reasonably take a census of a number of non-modifiable households (Cleave et al., 1995; Tranmer and Steel, 1998). The enumeration units may have some geographical basis but in many instances, they may simply be determined to meet the operational requirements of the census taker or government administration. Many geographic data refer to similar points in space that are, in turn, aggregated into larger spatial units that are arbitrary and modifiable. As a result, the units have no intrinsic geographical meaning (Openshaw, 1983). This factor is what Openshaw sees as the crux of the MAUP problem. There are many modifiable, arbitrarily defined units used in spatial analysis but few non-modifiable units. If most areal units are arbitrary and modifiable then so too might be the results of any spatial analysis, which could be heavily dependent on the defined modifiable units, employed (Openshaw, 1983:4). Furthermore, if different rules of aggregation were applied to generate an almost infinite number of modifiable units then the resulting patterns may too vary markedly and be artifacts not of the underlying geography or archaeology, but of the modifiable units and the unit aggregation procedures applied. The lack of established rules or standards contribute to the lack of verifiable practice and the understanding of replicable error.

The MAUP is clearly a factor when defining electoral boundaries and the lack of established rules are well illustrated by the term "gerrymandering" where the outcome of the electoral districting is distinctly influenced by the modifiable unit employed. Irrespective of outright gerrymandering, Johnston and Rossiter (1982), indicate that the relative success of political parties in the United Kingdom is substantially influenced by the specific aggregation procedure used to combine contiguous electoral wards into parliamentary constituencies. Dummer found that different results could be generated from analyses of stillbirth deaths depending on whether he used wards or postcode sectors as the base zonal unit (Dummer, 2002:37). In addition to being wary of inferring that individuals in each area share the same attributes, the ecological fallacy, Dummer also identified the MAUP as the root cause of the varying interpretation of areal results and concluded that the choice of areal unit and the data aggregation process influenced the observed pattern. Krieger et al. (2002) in an analysis of area-based socio-economic measures for monitoring population health found inconsistent results between findings using census and tract block and zip codes. As Openshaw (1983:5), found ".... different aggregations yield different results but without any systematic trends emerging that can be used for prediction or correction purposes." Openshaw (1983, 1984), for example, found that because of the scale effect of ecological fallacy, the larger the unit of aggregation the larger on average is the correlation between two variables. Furthermore, Openshaw and Taylor (1979, 1981) found that because of the aggregation effect that a very large number of possible zonal aggregations generates a distribution curve of possible correlation values between two variables which, although leptokurtic, may cover the full range from −1.0 to +1.0. Openshaw saw this conundrum as an opportunity to move away from rigid and aspatial statistics to new techniques that cater to the needs that geographical analysis brings (Openshaw 1983:6).

CONCLUSION

An understanding of scale is central to recording and interpreting archaeological patterns and process in the landscape. Scale and the analysis and interpretation of spatial pattern and process are interwoven. In looking to the future, several lines of inquiry for handling multi-scale data are discernible. Core questions relate to identifying an appropriate scale of analysis and determining that a chosen scale is appropriate to the study in hand and whether the results can be extrapolated from one scale to another. These questions also extend to identifying and understanding scale effects on geographical analysis. Goodchild (2001) in his discussion of the science of scale posed several tasks and questions for further investigation. These questions include: identifying what human or physical systems are invariant to the influence of scale; identifying the possibilities for transforming between scales; recognizing the impact of scale change on information loss and how an understanding of process is manifested or impacted by changes in scale; exploring the role of scale in the parameterization of process models and how models are affected by the use of data at inappropriate scales; and pursuing the implementation and integration of multi-scale data and databases.

Central to any resolution of ecological fallacy is to recognize that the problem exists and to be sensitive to analyses that involve the potential for fallacy. Ecological fallacy and the inability to distinguish between the spatial associations of aggregated data from the real associations of the non-modifiable individual data prior to aggregation is endemic to all analyses of areal data and spatially aggregated zones (Openshaw, 1983). Openshaw (1983) and Goodchild (2001) suggest that the MAUP and the question of scale is not only a fundamental and universal geographical problem but probably the most important unresolved problem left in spatial analysis. Openshaw (1983) suggests that several options exist for handling the MAUP. One option is to ignore the problem and the potential impact on study results as long as such results are plausible. Such a decision need not be based solely on ignorance but a conscious one that assumes that the zoning systems are independent of the geography and that aggregation procedures have little impact on the results. Given the lack of discussion in many studies of ecological fallacy or the MAUP, Openshaw considers this option to be implicitly the accepted case. A second option is to accept that the MAUP is an insoluble problem, that researchers have little control over the zonal system anyway, though they do in cases of re-aggregation, and that no solutions are known. A further option is that understanding the MAUP provides an opportunity for a geographical and not just a statistical solution such that a variety of zoning systems might be tested for the same data at multiple scales or zonal aggregations. The MAUP is particularly problematic because the effects are not consistent and is it not easy to determine how differing modifiable spatial units impact differing non-modifiable data. There is thus a need to search for techniques that are frame independent and avoid aggregation bias (Kousser, 2001; Tobler, 1989) where the method is independent of scale and the geographical unit (Cleave et al, 1995; Holt et al., 1996; King, 1997; Tranmer and Steel, 1998; Johnston and Pattie, 2001; Usery, 2000; Openshaw and Alvanides, 1999; Mennis, 2002; Fotheringham et al, 2001; Nakaya, 2000; Tate and Wood, 2001; Withers, 2001). Larger spatial units may create greater stability in the results but may also mask important geographical variation that might be found at smaller units of aggregation. As Goodchild and Quattrochi (1996:5) write, ''As science becomes more complex, data-dependent, and multidisciplinary, it is more and more important that we develop the tools and techniques needed to operate at multiple scales, to work with data whose scales are not necessarily ideal, and to produce results that can be aggregated or disaggregated in ways that suit the decision-making process''.

In 1965, Haggett suggested that while scale problems were a traditional problem in geography, at that time he considered that scale was becoming more acutely recognized and provided a very real challenge to Geography. Optimistically one might assume that practitioners now generally recognize the importance of scale though Cao and Lam (1996) refer to the ignorance of many geographers, let alone the broader community, to these very same issues of scale, ecological fallacy, and the MAUP. The advent of GIS and its broad acceptance into mainstream information technology use will only increase the likelihood of scale misunderstanding and misuse. While Bird (1989:19) suggested that geographer's eyes light up at the mention of scale, Haggett (1965:183) equally suggested that many continue to work in ''happy or perverse oblivion to the problems'' that scale brings. Given the fundamental importance of space and scale in archaeology it is critical that archaeologists acknowledge and struggle with these concepts and refuse to work in perverse oblivion to the problems of scale.

REFERENCES

Addicott, J. F., Aho, J. M., Antolin, M. F., Padilla, D. K., Richardson, J. S., and Soluk, D. A., 1987, Ecological Neighborhoods: Scaling Environmental Patterns. *OIKOS* 49:340–346.

Alker, H. R., 1969, A Typology of Ecological Fallacies. In *Quantitative Ecological Analysis in the Social Sciences*, edited by M. Dogan and S. Rokkan, pp. 69–86. The MIT Press, Cambridge.

Bird, J., 1956, Scale in Regional Study: Illustrated by Brief Comparisons Between the Western Peninsulas of England and France. *Geography* 41:25–38.

Bird, J. H., 1989, *The Changing Worlds of Geography: A Critical Guide to Concepts and Methods.* [See especially Chapter 2: Problems of Scale, 19–43]. Oxford University Press, New York.

Cao, C., and Lam, N. S.-N., 1996, Understanding the Scale and Resolution Effects in Remote Sensing and GIS. In *Scale in Remote Sensing and GIS*, edited by D.A. Quattrochi and M.F. Goodchild, pp. 57–72. Lewis Publications, Boca Raton, FL.

Cleave, N., Brown, P. J., and Payne, C. D., 1995, Evaluation of Methods for Ecological Inference. *Journal of the Royal Statistical Society, Series A* 158(1):55–72.

Dale, V. H., Gardner, R. H., and Turner, M. G., 1989, Predicting Across Scales. *Landscape Ecology* 3(3–4):147–151.

Delcourt, H. R., Delcourt, P. A. and Webb, T., 1983, Dynamic plant ecology: the spectrum of vegetational change in space and time, *Quatenary Science Reviews*, 1:153–175.

Dummer, T., 2002, GIS, Mapping and Health: A Study of Stillbirth Rates in Cumbria. *Bulletin of the Society of Cartographers* 36(2):31–38.

Dungan, J. L., Perry, J. N., Dale, M. R. T., Legendre, P., Citron-Pousty, S., Fortin, M.-J., Jakoumulska, A., Miriti, M., and Rosenberg, M. S., 2002, A Balanced View of Scale in Spatial Statistical Analysis. *Ecography* 25:626–640.

Ferber, M., 2005, *Questioning Ontological and Epistemological Issues of Scale in the Geography of Religion*, PhD Proposal, West Virginia University.

Ferber, M., and Harris, T. M., 2005, *A Leap of Faith: Scale in the Geography of Religions and Belief Systems*. Presentation at the Annual Meeting of the Association of American Geographers, Denver, April.

Fotheringham, A. S., Brunsdon, C., and Charlton, M., 2001, Scale Issues and Geographically Weighted Regression. In *Modelling Scale in Geographical Information Science*, edited by N. J. Tate and P. M. Atkinson, pp. 123–140. Wiley, New York.

Gahegan, M., 2005, Personal Communication.

Gardner, R. H., O'Neill, R. V., Turner, M. G., and Dale, V. H., 1989, Quantifying Scale-Dependent Effects of Animal Movement With Simple Percolation Models. *Landscape Ecology* 3(3–4):217–227.

Goodchild, M. F., 2001, Models of Scale and Scales of Modeling. In *Modelling Scale in Geographical Information Science*, edited by N. J. Tate and P.M. Atkinson, pp. 3–10. Wiley, New York.

Goodchild, M. F., and Quattrachi, D. A., 1996, Introduction: Scale, Multiscaling, Remote Sensing, and GIS. In *Scale in Remote Sensing and GIS*, edited by D. A. Quattrachi and M. F. Goodchild, pp. 1–11. Lewis Publishers, Boca Raton, FL.

Gregory, D., 1994. Scale. In *The Dictionary of Human Geography*, edited by R. J. Johnston, D. Gregory, and D. M. Smith, p. 543. Third Edition. Blackwell, Oxford.

Haggett, P., 1965, Scale Components in Geographical Problems. In *Frontiers in Geographical Teaching*, edited by R. J. Chorley and P. Haggett, pp. 164–185. Methuen, London.

Harvey, D. W., 1968, Pattern, Process and the Scale Problem in Geographical Research. *Transactions of the Institute of British Geographers* 45:71–78.

Harvey, D., 1969, *Explanation in Geography*. Edward Arnold, London.

Herod, A., and Wright, M., 2002, *Geographies of Power: Placing Scale*. Blackwell, Oxford.

Heywood, I., Cornelius, S. and Carver. S., 2002, *An Introduction to Geographical Information Systems*, Prentice Hall, New York.

Holt, D., Steel, D. G., Tranmer, M., and Wrigley, N., 1996, Aggregation and Ecological Effects in Geographically Based Data. *Geographical Analysis* 28(3):244–261.

Hudson, J., 1992, Scale in space and time. In *Geography's inner worlds: pervasive themes in contemporary American geography*, edited by R. F. Abler, M. G. Marcus and J. M. Olsen, pp. 280–297. Rutgers University Press, New Brunswick.

Jarvis, P. G. and McNaughton, K. G., 1986, Stomatal control of transpiration: Scaling up from leaf to region, *Advances in Ecological Research*, 15:1–49.

Johnston, R. J., and Pattie, C., 2001, On Geographers and Ecological Inference. *Annals of the Association of American Geographers* 91(2):281–282.

Johnston, R. J., and Rossiter, D. J., 1982, Constituency Building, Political Representation and Electoral Bias in Urban England. In *Geography and Urban Environment: Progress in Research and Applications*, Volume 5, edited by D. T. Herbert and R. J. Johnston, pp. 113–155. Wiley, New York.

King, G., 1997, *A Solution to the Ecological Inference Problem: Reconstructing individual Behavior From Aggregate Data*. Princeton University Press, Princeton.

Kousser, J. M., 2001, Ecological Inference from Goodman to King. *Historical Methods* 34(3):101–115.

Krieger, N., Chen, J. T., Waterman, P. D., Soobader, M-J., Subramanian, S. V., and Carson, R., 2002, Geocoding and Monitoring of US Socioeconomic inequalities in Mortality and Cancer incidence: Does the Choice of Area-Based Measure and Geographic Level Matter? *American Journal of Epidemiology* 156(5):471–482.

Levin, S. A., 1992, The Problem of Pattern and Scale in Ecology. *Ecology* 73(6):1943–1967.

Mandelbrot, B. B., 1977, *Fractal: Form, Chance, and Dimension*. Freeman, San Francisco.

Mccarty, H. H., Hook, J. C., and Knos, D. S., 1956, The Measurement of Association in Industrial Geography. *University of Iowa Department of Geography Report* 1.

Mcmaster, R. B., and Sheppard, E., editors, 2004, *Scale and Geographic Inquiry: Nature, Society, and Method*. Blackwell, Bodmin, Cornwall.

Meentemeyer, V., 1989, Geographical Perspectives of Space, Time, and Scale. *Landscape Ecology* 3(3–4):163–173.

Mennis, J., 2002, Using Geographic information Systems to Create and Analyze Statistical Surfaces of Population and Risk for Environmental Justice Analysis. *Social Science Quarterly* 83(1):281–297.

Nakaya, T., 2000, An Information Statistical Approach to the Modifiable Areal Unit Problem in Incidence Rate Maps. *Environment and Planning A* 32:91–109.

Openshaw, S., 1983, The Modifiable Areal Unit Problem. *Concepts and Techniques in Modern Geography* 38. Norwich, Geo Books.

Openshaw, S., 1984, Ecological Fallacies and the Analysis of Areal Census Data, *Environment and Planning A* 6:17–31.

Openshaw S., and Alvandies, S., 1999, Applying Geocomputation to the Analysis of Spatial Distributions. In *Geographic Information Systems: Principles and Technical Issues, Volume 1*, edited by P. Longley, M. Goodchild, D. Maguire, and D. Rhind, pp. 267–282. Second Edition. Wiley, New York.

Openshaw, S., and Taylor, P. J., 1979, A Million or So Correlation Coefficients: Three Experiments on the Modifiable Areal Unit Problem. In *Statistical Methods in the Spatial Sciences*, edited by R. J. Bennett, N. J. Thrift, and N. Wrigley, pp. 127–144. Pion, London.

Openshaw, S., and Taylor, P. J., 1981, The Modifiable Areal Unit Problem. In *Quantitative Geography: A British View*, edited by N. Wrigley and R. J. Bennet, pp. 60–70. Routledge and Kegan Paul, London.

Robinson, W. S., 1950, Ecological Correlations and the Behavior of Individuals. *American Sociological Review* 15(3):351–357.

Schwartz, S., 1994, The Fallacy of the Ecological Fallacy: the Potential Misuse of a Concept and the Consequences. *American Journal of Public Health* 84(5):819–824.

Smith, N., 2000, Scale. In T*he Dictionary of Human Geography*, edited by R. J. Johnston, D. Gregory, G. Pratt, and M.Watts. Fourth Edition, Blackwell, Oxford.

Tate, N. J., and Atkinson, P. M., editors, 2001, *Modelling Scale in Geographical Information Science*. Wiley, New York.

Tate, N. J., and Wood, J., 2001, Fractals and Scale Dependencies in Topography. In *Modelling Scale in Geographical Information Science*, edited by N. J. Tate and P.M. Atkinson, pp. 35–51. Wiley, New York.

Tranmer, M., and Steel, D. G., 1998, Using Census Data to Investigate the Causes of the Ecological Fallacy. *Environment and Planning A* 30:817–831.

Tobler, W. R., 1989, Frame independent spatial analysis. In *Accuracy of spatial databases*, edited by M. F. Goodchild and S. Gopal, pp. 115–122, Taylor and Francis, London.

Turner, M. G., O'Neill, R. V., Gardner, R. H., and Milne, B. T., 1989, Effects of Changing Spatial Scale on the Analysis of Landscape Pattern. *Landscape Ecology* 3(3–4):153–162.

Usery, E. L., 2000, Raster Data Pixels as Modifiable Areal Units. Online: http://www.geog.umd.edu /gis/ literature/conferences /GIScience2000/papers/ [Accessed November 2005].

Watson, M. K., 1978, The Scale Problem in Human Geography. *Geografiska Annaler* 60B:36–47.

Wiens, J. A., Stenseth, N. C., Van Horne, B., and Ims, R. A., 1993, Ecological Mechanisms and Landscape Ecology. *OIKOS* 66:369–380.

Withers, S. D., 2001, Quantitative Methods: Advancement in Ecological inference, *Progress in Human Geography*, 25(1):87–96.

CHAPTER 4

Artifacts as Social Interference: The Politics of Spatial Scale

H. Martin Wobst

INTRODUCTION

This is an article on the theory of method in archaeology. Often spatial method structures the archaeological record quite contrary to the goals of archaeologists. Even before archaeologists have posed their questions, defined their problems, or spelled out their research designs, spatial method may have structured their data already. Such a pre-given data structure might make it difficult, if not impossible, to reach certain kinds of conclusions, while making other conclusions virtually inescapable. My article argues that theory needs to instruct spatial method at any point of archaeological practice lest archaeologists lose theoretical control over their research. There are four parts to my argument. I lay out some basic assumptions, caricature normal archaeological practice, lay out a theoretical critique of that practice, and develop some alternatives to present practice.

SOME BASIC ASSUMPTIONS

One must assume that archaeological data, the material products and precedents of human behavior, are continuously distributed across space (see, for example, Wobst, 1979, 1983). If one plotted them as counts of artifacts, or as intensity of observable human material impact, the archaeological record would form a globe-encircling envelope. This envelope would have some steep peaks (our "sites"), as well as large areas of low values and vast stretches of virtually zero readings. Archaeologists, and social scientists, usually allocate their data to socio-spatial units, that is, cohesive, bounded nonoverlapping spatial entities, for describing, analyzing, and theorizing. In theory, these socio-spatial units range from points (a point reading of human material impact, an artifact or a grouping of artifacts) as the smallest possible unit

H. Martin Wobst ● University of Massachusetts, Amherst

size, to one continuous entity (the entire archaeological record, discovered and as yet undiscovered) at the largest possible unit size, with an infinity of potential spatial unit sizes in between. At each unit size, one would learn something different about human behavior. Presumably, at the smallest sizes, counts or differential intensity readings would heavily depend on local variables such as earthworms; at the largest ones, earthworms would not have much impact on the observations, their place being taken by global processes such as colonialism or world systems, with regional and interregional variables gaining in archaeological visibility in the middle ranges of unit sizes.

Like the archaeological record, the human population surface is continuous around the world. Per geographic unit in which it is measured, it has a few steep peaks (cities, rock concerts), and many areas of intermediate (the *oikoumene*) and low counts (deserts, oceans). Modern humans have shown that they can organize themselves into units of any size, from living the life of a hermit to organizing a world government, with an infinite number of socio-spatial unit sizes in between. The same individual can subscribe to membership in a multitude of spatial entities of different geographic inclusiveness (for example, nation, county, and township). Socio-spatial entities of the same kind or size may overlap in space or personnel, with people having multiple, often competing allegiances (e.g., Kurds in Turkey, Iraq, Iran, and Syria). Such socio-spatial entities are not essential attributes of humans, but are constructed, shored up, and maintained by cultural process. They need to compete for allegiance and membership, and a given member may alternatively champion, resist, or sabotage them. Socio-spatial units are never complete, but forever in a process of construction. Membership is never resolved, but in a field of tension between fusion and fission, voluntary subscription, recruitment and resistance. Socio-spatial entities are thus forever in motion.

Artifacts, the material products and precedents of human behavior, including of the behavior to form and disband socio-spatial bonds, should sensitively track this motion. Certain socio-spatial entities, particularly toward the more inclusive sizes, are even unthinkable without certain kinds of artifacts (such as flags and boundary markers, record keeping, uniforms, or currency). How has archaeological practice dealt with all of this motion?

NORMAL ARCHAEOLOGICAL PRACTICE

There should be an infinity of potential unit sizes through which one could look at human performance on this globe today and in the archaeological record. From this potential infinity, archaeologists select a very few. Archaeological space is usually surveyed, excavated, reported, and theorized only with a very small sample of preferred spatial unit sizes. Cultural research management practice, method and textbooks, archaeological field schools, and introductory archaeology classes center on these grid sizes. Going from smallest to largest, archaeologists usually talk about behavior in the spatial units of artifact, feature, household, community, region, culture, country, and continent. It is my sense that most archaeologists would tend to view these entities as "natural" ones. They are often juxtaposed to the arbitrary square grid sizes for fieldwork units, the likes of 5×5 or 10×10 square feet or square meters, or the larger field survey tracks (even though these grid sizes are obviously arbitrary, their size is often justified to be large enough so that they may reliably intercept the afore-mentioned "natural" socio-spatial entities) (cf., Dincauze et al., 1981).

Short of artifacts that are points, features are the next inclusive unit of analysis, description and explanation. Conceptualized as disturbances of the background matrix in the field, features such as fireplaces or storage pits serve to situate activities; and activities thus located are thought to be, in part, explained by that association. "Structures," while they are technically also features, are usually the next stepping point on the march of archaeologists from smallest to largest unit in tying down human behavior in space, the likes of tent circles or house foundations – modifications of the ground suitable for dwellers, or functionally related to dwelling. Behavior in and around such structures is thought as having been anchored in this material evidence of residence and dwelling. In social terms, structures are usually related to "households," that is, to coresident and cooperating groups of closest relatives.

If we increase our spatial inclusiveness beyond households, we are looking for communities next (which are thought to generate our commonsensical "sites" or "settlements," although, of course, even a single artifact could be called a site). We imagine communities composed of clustered "households" when we see cohesive, dense and intensive materiality. Intense marking at their periphery (e.g., walls and moats) or at their center (e.g., church spires), helps us to infer the presence of these entities. We often envision such remains to have been the product, the outflow, and the material reflection of community. Thus, "the Leverett Community" in Massachusetts (where I live) has as its artifact "the Town of Leverett," with its not yet archaeological but quite material "correlates" of a town hall, a Congregational Church, a garbage dump, and an elementary school. This community contrasts with the "Amherst community" (where I work) from which it is separated by fields and woods. That community has its own material "correlates," in its own town hall, garbage dump, and schools. The artifacts that mark these spaces as separate and different are seen as attributes of the assumed communities.

Regions, cultures, or societies are about as inclusive as habitual units of archaeological integration get: groups of communities, similar in attributes, surrounded by contrastive materiality or by empty space as in valley or island cultures. We assume the people in such entities to share characteristics and values, thus generating *similarity* within, in the materials they generate and leave behind, in *difference* to the material products of other such entities. Thus, when we hear "the Germans," "the Connecticut Valley," or "Maine," we imagine households grouped into communities grouped into regional cultures, each with material characteristics that are internally homogeneous, and different from "the French," "the Hudson Valley," and "Vermont" in this example. The theory behind such "archaeological cultures" or "archaeological regions" has been criticized for a long time already in archaeology (see, for example, Barth, 1969). Beyond this size, textbooks, museums, courses, and grand syntheses may contrast spatial unit sizes larger than the region, as in interaction spheres (Caldwell, 1965), technocomplexes (Clark, 1968), and various other culture area formulations.

From an infinity of potential sizes for socio-spatial units, archaeologists tend to select only four or five, thought to represent natural and pan-human ways of subdividing society. Of course, these habitual types of units, of individuals, households, communities, and cultures, are European and Euro-American common sense. Archaeologists will look for the evidence in their archaeological data to be similarly constituted. If they find archaeological data that map onto these modern social units, they assume that society must have been organized along these same scales. Once they have that match, they will feel comfortable to map past behavior onto households, communities, or cultures. The preferred unit sizes are thought to be associated with, and to generate, *archaeological correlates*, that is, material traces of their essential qualities. When such correlates are found, archaeologists infer the presence of that scale, and interpret archaeological finds in reference to these arenas for spatial behavior.

In the sixties and seventies, archaeologists often formalized this methodology. Thus, Chang (1967) theorized for a "settlement archaeology" to help expose "communities"; Trigger (1968:55–60) argued that "individual structures" should be archaeology's most basic units, and the principal components of communities; and David Clarke (1968) systematized the region, and differentiated a microlevel (within structures), from a semi-microlevel (within sites), and a macrolevel (between sites) (Clarke, 1977) – very much in cahoots with the locational geography of the day (such as the widely read Haggett, 1965, or Chorley and Haggett, 1967). For Binford (see, for example, 1964 or Binford et al., 1970), hunter–gatherer remains were naturally organized into artifact, feature, site, and cultural system in the same way that Flannery (1976) had Mesoamerican agriculturalists adapt in households, villages, and "all the villages in a single valley."

THE SOCIAL DIMENSIONS OF ARTIFACTS

If "social" units were actually human universals, and if people's artifacts would actually settle into the archaeological record reflecting these units, archaeological method would be straightforward, and reconstituting the societal matrix from archaeological traces would be easy. Looking from the top down, "obvious" cultural markers such as church towers would guide us to communities, and house-walls would locate households. From the bottom up, we could systematically search for those grid sizes, where chance was least to blame for the observed distributions, that is, where the action of the social units of the day would have been most marked (for an early application of this logic, see Whallon, 1973). These two logics form the mainstay of spatial method in archaeology today.

Both logics take artifacts as *products* of human behavior. If a given social entity had been present, it must have generated products – if we find its products, the given social entity *must have been a reality*. From the top down, a house-wall, as material product, is seen as a natural outflow of the resolved existence of a household: a house-wall is there, thus, a household must have existed; a town wall signals the unquestionable existence of a community. From the bottom up, we infer social entities when we have located the grid sizes at which factors other than chance are most forcefully expressed: social units of that size must have generated the sharp contrasts between clusters and sterile spaces.

Whether top-down or bottom-up, that approach treats artifacts as (unthinking and obvious) fallout of real and resolved entities. Since at least 1982, with *Symbols in Action* (Hodder, 1982), we should know that that is highly problematic. To users, artifacts are devices to bring about something that would not otherwise exist or happen; that is, they are designs to change aspects of the social world that are considered objectionable, or to keep aspects from changing that are considered agreeable. Thus, artifacts rarely if ever talk about uncontested or incontestable aspects of the social world. If they did, they would waste matter, energy, or information. If things were indeed incontestable or uncontested, why address them at all, much less address them by producing, acquiring, using or discarding *artifacts* (with their cost in energy and matter)?

To explain why people would shoulder artifactual costs, we need to think about what they were thinking of changing! In terms of socio-spatial units and how people materially modify their visual scapes, artifacts do not communicate that the dimensions of social space are, indeed, uncontested or incontestable dimensions of social space. They are designs to construct something that is different from what would be if things were left alone, that is, without artifactual interference.

If artifacts are designs to shape the future, they will not *describe* the present. Instead, artifacts are interventions designed to change that present, whether to preserve it as it is (since it is thought that it would change otherwise) or to change it (because it is thought to be unpleasantly stationary otherwise) (see Wobst, 2000). They are designed as interferences in the anticipated trajectory of society. A given social context, in its artifactual traces, is an amalgam of such interferences. To gain access to social process, we need to feel our way to the competing plans with which artifact users approach social contexts to affect their own futures and the future of the given context. For socio-spatial units, this has immediate implications. Our artifacts that talk about the scale of social process do not talk about scale as it once was, but about scales to be achieved in the future. They are contributions to a conversation about social scale, not reflections of it. They are instruments to bring about or evade scales of social process, not mirrors of their existence.

AN INFINITY OF SCALES FOR ACTION

Social contexts are pushed and pulled by their participants toward, or away from, a number of different social scales simultaneously. The people, the scales, and the discourses about and among them are forever in flux and unresolved. In the recent human past, artifacts have been a very active, if not essential part of that discourse. They do not reflect a given socio-spatial order. Instead, they reflect attempts to bring it about, to maintain it, to change it, or to resist it.

Let us look at individuals in the US as an example. Their individuality is forever in contest. On one hand, people are under the constant material bombardment of social security cards, passports, birth and death records, credit cards, beds, personal dining and silverware, chairs, toilet seats, diaries, etc., to constitute themselves as independent agents, and to imagine that they are possessing free will. On the other hand, advertising continuously tries to make them unhappy with that individuation, to construct improved versions via the consumption of commodities. The destabilization of the free-willed agent, self-empowerment via consumption, and the affiliation with desirable and disaffiliation with undesirable groups that implies, keep individuals and their materiality forever in flux. Artifacts chronicle that flux; that is, they are a discourse about the unit "free-willed individual," not its resolved presence. Ironically, the material conversation about individuals should be strongest where the "individuality" is most contested.

Similarly, households are not generated by gravity or nature. Artifacts that map onto that entity do not record its existence. Rather, they attempt to interfere in society to bring it about, to strengthen it, or to resist it. The state envisions households with artifacts such as census forms, tax returns, zoning regulations, building codes, inheritance laws, and the like. Household members shoot in the same direction with family plots, bibles, dining tables, and mail boxes; house-walls, drive-ways, and swimming pools; gardens and fences; and integrated heating-, sound-, or vacuum systems. The principal counterstrategy is social fission. There is a discourse about households, and that discourse eats up significant "household" resources.

Whose agency is fossilized in "household" artifacts? Who gains or loses with or without those artifacts? The corporate entity "household" does not envision or generate "household" artifacts, these come from a constellation of individual household members (whose agendas often contradict each other). Such artifacts make some members more powerful, disempower others, or raise their thresholds to fission. If we blindly treat archaeological traces as attesting to households as resolved, we merely empower some sectarian interests, and disempower other ones. Given that our state considers households as natural constituents of its social contract, we also thereby empower the state.

Community is a concept with a very positive meaning in the US. Communities do not exist, they are in process. States make laws about, and tax, zone, and regulate, communities. "Communities" are associated in our minds with administrative centers and communal institutions, moats and walls, and symbolic markers such as church towers, statuary, and communal cemeteries. Such artifacts are easy to see, and would be obvious to the average archaeologist. But these artifacts are not evidence of community, but of efforts to bring about community. They do not attest to strong community bonding or to a resolved understanding that community was a normal and natural entity. Rather, they interfere in the discourse about community in order to shore up that concept and the entity "community," and to make fission from it harder to think and do. The most glaring "community" artifacts should go with places where doubt about community is strongest.

The same argument should apply to regions and states. Artifacts that map on to them are not "natural" outflows of an internally homogeneous membership, but attempts to make members more homogeneous. Anthems, flags, and border markers are material interferences to bring about a bounded entity. They should be more intense, where doubt about borders is greatest, and where, internally, membership is least homogeneous. They are sectarian interventions to portray that entity as bounded by reference to external others, to generate more homogeneity where little existed before, and to decrease the ability and ease of fission. If archaeologists organize their data blindly into resolved agreed-to states, they merely foster those sectarian interests. They have made the state easier to think.

WHAT TO DO ABOUT IT?

How then should we deal with socio-spatial units in the archaeological record? Obviously, we have to pay closer attention to contexts and their history. Artifacts designed to interfere on the social axes of fission and fusion can help us in feeling our way into that discourse. Massive household walls made it harder to see one's continuity into the next household, and raised the start-up costs for members who wanted to fission. It must have been in somebody's interest (not necessarily at the household level) to keep people's feet nailed to the ground. Resistance to that interest, unfortunately, does not leave equally obvious remains. The most obvious reaction would simply be social fission, a strategy that does not leave obtrusive artifacts in situ. Mechanical inference that merely interprets the most obvious artifacts will always exaggerate the resolvedness of social spaces and entities.

To take the pulse of this discourse, we can report with ease on the variation in time, space, and medium in the sectarian measures designed to bring about social units of certain kinds. We have to develop ways to measure the varying intensity of these interferences, because that would speak to the importance of countervailing forces. We also have to peel our eyeballs to instances of shirking and sabotage, as well as discourses that otherwise subvert with artifacts the raw power of materiality. Frequencies of dissolution, collapse, and abandonment of social entities should sensitively track this discourse. This is actually a very accessible variable, since it is what frees archaeological space for excavation. In those places that were left behind by their former populations, the previous rules and material processes that held the socio-spatial entities together have proved insufficient. Thus, these cases illuminate the forces in context (and provide glimpses of the fissioning end of the conversation about spatial entities winning and thus help to balance the habitual bias for the other side of the contest to a certain degree).

Fine-grained analysis of contexts through time needs to be given more weight. It gives me a considerable sense of optimism that even jails (as some of the most powerful artifacts for suppressing spatial agency) do not prevent the weak from expressing themselves materially. As shown in the archaeological analysis of the 19th century Rhode Island State Penitentiary by James Garman (Garman, 2005), or Alejandro Haber's (2004, personal communication) research into the materiality of political prisoners during the Argentinean junta, even prisoners are not exhaustively predicted by their jailer's materiality, and leave material evidence of their resistance as well as their humanity that is not predicted by or predicated on the socio-spatial designs of their jailers.

   In this reporting, the central tendencies of materiality, the means, the modes, and the medians will not be half as important in reading the content of the conversation as the shape of that variation. Equally important is how that shape, for a given variable, changes through time and over space, and what happens to the spread or range of measures over time and space (see also Wobst, 1999). It is those distributions and their changes that chronicle the discourse about spatial unit size. In that game, the central tendency that results when such measures are grouped in time or space may not have been in the perception of the contemporaneous players at all and, at best, is only one of many aspects of that distribution that had been in the visual scape of the artifact makers users or discarders, in reference to which they placed their own material artifacts into the context or modified the ones that were there already.

   Archaeologists rarely if ever operationalize this conversation about spatial unit size. Though his goals differ from the ones championed here, Ronald Fletcher has been one of the path-breaking exceptions here, in his work on settlement patterns in a wide variety of different contexts. He has always been very generous in presenting the shape of variation for measurements of socio-spatial variables. Particularly intriguing is an article about a 13th century Mongol hillfort in Anatolia. The time trajectory of the distribution of measurements, relative to spatial scale, chronicles how administratively given standard spatial measures were locally subverted. In the end, the broadening spreads around the administratively given measures document the eventual demise of centralized administration, at least in terms of local socio-spatial entities (Fletcher, 1984).

   On the other hand, if only the central tendency had been recorded, one might not have been able to notice *any* change through time, or, since the modes in this case did not have any behavioral relevance, any changes noticed would most likely appear as random from generation to generation. Both of those conclusions would have been interpreted, in "normal" archaeology, as reflections of the "normal" output of the resolved and uncontested existence of these spatial entities.

SOME CONCLUSIONS

If we do not sensitively report on the spatial contest between those who want to materially establish or shore up socio-spatial entities and those who want to materially resist them or evade them altogether, our results merely aggrandize some sectarian interests at the cost of others. Most likely, our silence about socio-spatial entities in process and in contest helps people to cocoon themselves into bounded, nonoverlapping socio-spatial entities. It makes households, communities, regions, and countries (or cultures) look more natural rather than cultural, more resolved rather than in process, and more agreed on than in contest. In terms of the specific socio-spatial units naturalized by archaeologists in the archaeological record, we have been handmaidens of the state, making our own society easier to think!

   To break that bondage does not require more work. The central tendencies with which archaeologists usually report on spatial organization require the same number and kinds of individual measurements as graphs of the shapes of measurement distributions do. Rather, they require that spatial method is specified and applied only after its context of application is theoretically thought through. This will assure that our method tracks human actions sensitively, so that we can learn from our observations about the human condition and its alternatives, rather than accidentally destroying our data accidentally, or forever reinforcing our unevaluated biases and prejudices.

ACKNOWLEDGEMENTS   Many of the thoughts in this paper gained from interactions with graduate students in my theory and method courses at the University of Massachusetts in Amherst. Greg, Natalia, and Jude let me hide in my study longer than I wanted, to get this paper done, and Brian was kind, mellow, patient, and insistent with me while I was trying to find excuses for not completing this paper. But when all is said and done, I cannot blame anybody but myself for the shortcomings of this paper.

REFERENCES

Barth, F., editor, 1969, *Ethnic Groups* and *Boundaries*. Little, Brown and Co., Boston.

Binford, L.R., 1964, A Consideration of Archaeological Research Design. *American Antiquity* 29:425–441.

Binford, Lewis R., Binford, S.R., Whallon, R., and Hardin, M.A., 1970, Archaeology at Hatchery West. *Memoirs of the Society for American Archaeology* 24.

Caldwell, J.R., 1965, Interaction Spheres in Prehistory. In *Hopewellian Studies*, edited by J.R. Caldwell and R.L. Hall, pp. 133–143. Illinois State Museum Scientific Papers. Vol. 12. Springfield, Illinois.

Chang, K.C., 1967, *Rethinking Archaeology*. Random House, New York.

Chorley, R.J., and Haggett, P., editors, 1967, *Models in Geography*. Methuen, London.

Clarke, D.L., 1968, *Analytical Archaeology*. Methuen, London.

Clarke, D.L., editor, 1977, *Spatial Archaeology*. Academic Press, London.

Dincauze, D.F., Hasenstab, R., Lacy, D., and Wobst, H.M., 1981, *Retrospective Assessment of Archaeological Survey Contracts in Massachusetts*. Three Volumes. Massachusetts Historical Commission, Boston.

Flannery, K.V., editor, 1976, *The Early Mesoamerican Village*. Academic Press, New York.

Fletcher, R., 1984, Identifying Spatial Disorder: A Case Study of a Mongol Fort. In *Intra-Site Spatial Analysis in Archaeology*, edited by Harold Hietala, pp. 196–223. Cambridge University Press, Cambridge.

Garman, J., 2005, *Detention Castles of Stone and Steel: Landscape, Labor, and The Urban Penitentiary*. University of Tennessee Press, Knoxville.

Haber, A., 2004, Personal Communication (about his research on Argentinean jails during the Junta). Adelaide, South Australia, Australia.

Haggett, P., 1965, *Locational Analysis in Human Geography*. Arnold, London.

Hodder, I., 1982, *Symbols in Action*. Cambridge University Press, Cambridge.

Trigger, B.G., 1968, *The Methods of Prehistory*. Holt, Rinehart and Winston, New York.

Whallon, R. Jr., 1973, Spatial Analysis of Occupation Floors. I. Application of Dimensional Analysis of Variance. *American Antiquity* 39:16–34.

Wobst, H.M., 1979, Computers and Coordinates: Strategies for the Analysis of Paleolithic Stratigraphy. In *Statistical Cartographic Applications to Spatial Analysis in Archaeological Contexts*, edited by S. Upham and G.A. Clark, pp. 61–67. Arizona State University, Tempe.

Wobst, H.M., 1983, We Can't See the Forest for the Trees: Sampling and the Shapes of Archaeological Distributions. In *Archaeological Hammers and Theories*, edited by J.A. Moore and A.S. Keene, pp. 37–85. Academic Press, New York City.

Wobst, H.M., 1999, Style in Archaeology, or Archaeologists in Style. In *Material Meanings: Critical Approaches to the Interpretation of Material Culture*, edited by Elizabeth S. Chilton, pp. 118–132, University of Utah Press, Salt Lake City.
Wobst, H.M., 2000, Agency in (Spite of) Material Culture. In *Agency in Archaeology*, edited by Marcia-Anne Dobres and John Robb, pp. 40–50. Routledge, London.

CONSTRUCTING SCALE: IDENTIFYING PROBLEMS

Topographical Scale as Ideological and Practical Affordance: The Case of Devils Tower

Brian Leigh Molyneaux

INTRODUCTION: SCALE AS A BODILY RELATION

The issue of scale is not a geometric matter, resolved by machine, but a problem of perceptual engagement at the core of knowledge and understanding. While theoretical discussion tends to focus on the fit between the scale of analysis of archaeological phenomena and the scale of the cultural life that produced them, the crucial relation is our own, materially and socially, to the information we retrieve. The typical analytical environment consists of artifacts at least twice removed from their original contexts and most often from utterly different cultures than our own, imagined against an arid background of maps and images that substitutes for the real world. This combination of remoteness and alienation, which passes for objective distance, effectively removes us from the environment of use values and relations that is cultural reality. Constructing a figurative archaeological past from these traces may be fairly simple, but the profound discontinuity between the situations of production and interpretation makes it difficult to understand the circumstances that once gave them life. We need access to ideological resources in order to view material objects as cultural things (see, for example, Saunders' recent (2001) investigation of the cultural transmutation of obsidian from material to cosmological substance in Mesoamerica).

While the relativity of use relations and values in material culture may hamper the potential for interpretation, however, we all participate in the theatre of human action. We may not be able to get into the heads of others, but we do share the physical aspects of human experience that underlie ideology. The powerful have

BRIAN LEIGH MOLYNEAUX ● University of South Dakota

most obviously taken advantage of this through the aggrandizements of monumental architecture and larger-than-life imagery. By elevating their subjects above ordinary humanity, actually and symbolically, they diminish those who can only bear witness. Of course power is relative: even a humble graveyard may have larger stones promoting some special dead. No matter what the absolute scale is, such hyperbolic fictions convey information about power and status across time, space and culture. Indeed, we may be equally struck, or cowed, by Abu Simbel and the Statue of Liberty, even if we know little of their meanings, because we recognize the sort of message that outsized scale conveys.

Is the power of scale to influence perception and interpretation something innate, or part of the politics of vision? In the following discussion, I take this issue into the landscape, to explore ways of identifying past uses of scale as an instrument in perception, action, and understanding.

LANDMARKS

Large-scale landmarks command particular attention because they have conspicuous physical attributes that set them apart from their surroundings. While meaning can transform an inconspicuous object or locality into a significant place, landmarks assert themselves so dramatically that they transcend the specificities of culture. Because of this salience, landmarks act as anchors or nodes in the cognitive maps that enable people to find their way through the environment. But a landmark is more than a navigational guide: it may be an organizing concept for a society (Golledge, 1999:16) with a social description that may encompass origins, significance, and function. A landmark becomes a meaningful cultural object through the education of attention to this description and thus a focus for worship, respect, admiration, or awe. It therefore affords social beliefs and actions, and becomes a powerful means of ideological reinforcement.

While the language of a landmark description is symbolic, it needs to refer to physical form to ensure common understanding. With the symbolic content grounded in the material world, the knowledge of the landmark can pass across social and cultural boundaries. A striking example is Sri Pada ("Holy Footprint"), in Sri Lanka, known in the west since medieval times as Adam's Peak. Since it rises near the edge of the ocean and is visible from a great distance, this distinctive, pyramidal mountain has been a navigational landmark for centuries. As it is an isolated peak, it also seems extraordinarily high. The missionary Giovanni De' Marignolli (b. ca. AD1290), who traveled to China between 1342 and 1346, wrote that it was "perhaps after Paradise the highest mountain on the face of the earth" (extract from Recollections of Travel in the East, manuscript translated and published by Sir Henry Yule, 1866:358), and Fra Mauro (d. AD1460), a Camaldulian monk from near Venice, thought it significant enough to include on his Mappamundi, the most detailed map of the world to that time (AD1457–1459).

Although the peak's large scale attracted the attention of navigators, a small-scale feature fired the imaginations of several great cultures and religions. Near its summit is a natural hollow, just under two meters long, that resembles a giant footprint. Buddhist writings before 300BC described it as the footprint of the Buddha; Chinese writers described it as the mark of a god or of their first ancestor; in a Muslim legend it is the footprint that Adam left where he landed after his fall from Paradise, the place where he stood on one foot for a thousand years in penance; Portuguese traders in the 16th century saw it as the footprint of St. Thomas; and Hindus see it as the footprint of the god Shiva. It is even depicted on Fra Mauro's great map. With this profound attention, Adam's Peak has been an important wayplace for centuries, visited by Marco Polo (AD1254–1324), Ibn Batuta (AD1304–1368) and many other explorers, missionaries and pilgrims. Among other amazing features associated with the mountain are heavy chains that help climbers along the steepest part of the route to the summit – in one account, put there by Alexander the Great (Giovanni De' Marignolli, in Yule, 1866:345).

The presence of a common physical feature in diverse descriptions of a landmark suggests that it is possible to conduct a cross-cultural study of the relationship between perception, ideology and expression in the environment. As topographical descriptions embody meaning and function, they provide an ideological veneer over the landscape that may inform and complement the archaeological record. Crucially, the physical features tend to remain intact over the millennia, providing archaeologists with the opportunity to explore first-hand the effects of dramatic changes in scale on meaning and understanding.

We can make the connection between past and present landscapes because the environment presents a limited range of possibilities for perception and action. In the radical approach to perception advocated by the psychologist James J. Gibson (e.g., 1976), we perceive the features of the environment directly, rather than through programmes that resolve imagery in the brain, and so exist in a complementary relationship with our surroundings. As part of this complementarity, we perceive environmental features in terms of *affordances*, the possibilities for action that they present (see also Costall's 1995 interpretation). With its striking form, mass and great height, Adam's Peak clearly presents a common situation to spectators, asserting itself in consciousness and provoking action and interpretation – as its notoriety shows. Indeed, we can interpret a landmark description as a cumulation of endlessly repeated individual perceptions that in their contents share aspects of the physical attributes of the landform despite the normal relativity of cultural content. This phenomenon helps account for the common features in interpretations of the anomaly on Adam's Peak despite the great religious differences. At the scale of the *longue durée*, some of a landmark's cultural functions may change as cultures and technologies change. Indeed, the peak is no longer a key marker in regional navigation or, to even the most enthusiastic Christians, an entryway into Paradise, but it remains an important pilgrimage site and a magnet for tourists in the region. The survival of such intense affordance values into the modern world shows that prominent topographical features have an impact beyond the specificities of culture.

As the example of Adam's Peak suggests, nature and culture work together to intensify affordance values. Consider Stonehenge. It is undeniably an anomaly in the Wiltshire countryside, but its notoriety across the world makes it seem much bigger than the somewhat diminutive reality that some visitors perceive. What is surely massive is its description and the expectation that follows, the result of centuries of speculation about its origins and function, reinforced by enthusiastic accounts of the heaviness of the stones and the immense human effort required to transport and lift them. Such weighty significance has helped make it an icon of ancient monuments everywhere.

The visual and emotional impacts of monumental constructions repeat endlessly in culture, as they strive to be seen, to direct and educate the attention of inhabitants. Whether it is the many thousands of tons of stone devoted to Egyptian kings, or statues of Lenin, or honorific monuments to other leaders and governments, such displays use scale explicitly as a visual form of ideological reinforcement. South Dakota is the home of the *Shrine of Democracy* on Mount Rushmore, where the sculpted heads of four American presidents project from the face of the granite near the peak. Each head is about 60 ft high and set at a height that conforms to the scale of the man, so they are almost 500 ft above the base. The original intent was to inject money into the South Dakota economy by carving heroes of the Wild West, such as Buffalo Bill, General George Armstrong Custer, and Sitting Bull, but the lure of ideology was too great for an emerging industrial giant – as the sculptor, Gutson Borglum, related in 1924, in words now entombed in the partly completed Hall of Records near the sculptures:

> We believe the dimensions of national heartbeats are greater than village impulses, greater than city demands, greater than state dreams or ambitions. Therefore, we believe a nation's memorial should, like Washington, Jefferson, Lincoln, and Roosevelt, have a serenity, a nobility, a power that reflects the gods who inspired them and suggests the gods they have become.

It is not just the appearance of a great landmark against the horizon that draws us in; it is the dramatic shift in the scale of observation it promises. From its heights, a landmark is an instrument that increases the range of vision. Its use can be purely practical, as a navigational aid, or it can resonate within emotional, philosophical, or spiritual realms of culture, as the spectator hovers between a vast earth and sky. This dramatic contrast in perception is what makes a landmark so compelling. It dominates the landscape, urges spectators to it, and then permits them a point of view they cannot achieve in ordinary life – an illusory sense of mastery over the physical environment and a superior position in the social landscape. As Barthes (1979:17) says of the Eiffel Tower: "one can feel oneself cut off from the world and yet the owner of a world."

The psychological impact of perceiving at dramatically different scales suggests that we must interpret landmarks within a politics of vision. Consider Richard Bradley's distinction between stone circles and what he calls the "inward-looking world of the henge" (1998:145) in Britain. A monumental stone circle afforded a continuous relationship between the interior and the landscape beyond, as people outside could observe what was happening within, while those inside could relate its configuration to a wider world. Increasing social differentiation was incompatible with such perceptual and conceptual freedom, and so there followed a process of closure, supported by new religious ideologies that, in general, began to identify particular people with particular locations in the landscape.

Consider also church architecture, the extension of the ancient enclosed sacred space. Cathedrals and other religious monuments are often still the most dramatic monuments on the landscape. They were designed as much to be seen, to dominate the landscape, so as to draw the spectator in and then to shut the world out, save for the light from the heavens. Indeed, in a high vaulted Gothic church, the lure of the upward gaze is almost irresistible. But churches and religions change, and in modern religious architecture controversy surrounds new interior designs that go against this traditional order. In the Catholic Church, the problem is that new church interiors shift the gaze from the altar to the congregation:

> ... it is no mere accident that our churches are now designed (or remodeled as the case may well be) "in the round," placing congregants around the centralized focus of the altar table. We, the congregants, have in effect become a part of (or have become) the sanctuary while the Blessed Sacrament has been moved or removed from its traditional position as the focal point of the sanctuary (Rose, 1996:1).

This democratization of perception subverts the power of the cynosure, weakens the effect of the single, fixed focus. In essence, the looking away from the original, sacred source allows a social communion, which threatens to make society, rather than god, the subject and the object of worship.

Following these examples, we may also describe landmark studies in terms of a politics of scale – as variation in the scale of perception becomes a way of attracting, directing, and educating attention to meanings applied to the object itself. In an archaeological approach, we can look at the relationship between the patterns of speech and behaviour in landmark descriptions and the patterns of human activity at the landmark itself.

BEAR'S LODGE, OR DEVILS TOWER

One of the most important geological and religious sites in North America, a massive volcanic anomaly in northeastern Wyoming known to the many tribal groups who lived in the region as Bear's Lodge (or Bear Lodge) and to most Euroamerican people as Devils Tower, provides an appropriate case study.

In the rugged uplands west of the Black Hills, broken by deep river valleys and mesas, this strange object looks like the deeply furrowed stump of an enormous tree, long ago topped by the fierce prairie winds, or the core of a great buffalo horn (Figure 5.1). The Kiowa, who once lived to the west near the headwaters of the Yellowstone River until early in the 19th century, recall the giant tree in their name for this place, "Tso-aa" (tree rock). An actor in the film Close Encounters of the Third Kind, which features the Tower in its story of alien contacts, described it as "a mammoth rectangle that stands out against the blue Wyoming sky as if it has been drawn on with a fine line marker" (Balaban, 1978:14).

Such a place demands to be interpreted, and so it figures in the oral traditions of tribes who lived in the region before their dispersal and confinement in the late 19th century. In 1932, an aged Crow woman, Kills-Coming-to-the-Birds, said that it was "put there by the Great Spirit for a special reason, because it was different from

FIGURE 5-1. View of Devils Tower from the south.

other rocks'' (Gunderson, 1988:32). A modern telling of the Kiowa theory of its origin, by N. Scott Momaday (1996:8) who learned it from his grandmother, has the essential features:

> Eight children were there at play, seven sisters and their brother. Suddenly the boy was struck dumb; he trembled and began to run upon his hands and feet. His fingers became claws, and his body was covered with fur. Directly there was a bear where the boy had been. The sisters were terrified; they ran, and the bear [ran] after them. They came to the stump of a great tree, and the tree spoke to them. It bade them climb upon it, and as they did so it began to rise into the air. The bear came to kill them, but they were just beyond its reach. It reared against the tree and scored the bark all around with its claws. The seven sisters were borne into the sky, and they became the stars of the Big Dipper.

Other tribes formerly or presently in the region share the essence of the story, as shown by some of the other names for the Tower: ''Dabicha Asow'' (Bear's Home) for the Crow; ''Woox-niii-non'' (Bear's Tipi) for the Arapaho; ''Na Kovea'' (Bear's Lodge) for the Cheyenne; and ''Mato Tipi, or Tipila'' (Bear Lodge) for the Lakota Sioux.

When we strip these descriptions of their mythological contents, there is common ground here that relates to the ''shape of meaning'' (Molyneaux, 1991; 1997). Each text contains the fundamental material elements that all people see and respond to: a towering rock shaped like a giant tree trunk with deep scoring down its sides.

There is commonality as well in cultural behaviour at the site. Many American Indians come to the Tower to worship, as their ancestors did, some of them preparing vision quest or prayer sites in the privacy of the forest or tying small strips and bundles of cloth as votive offerings in the trees. There is also compelling archaeological evidence that their ancestors have been coming here for at least 10,000 years. While Americans of European descent may not share this religious tradition, they too recognize the special nature of this place. In 1906, it became the first National Monument in the United States, a measure designed to protect sites of unique historical and scientific interest.

The question here is this: can we decipher in the oral traditions and the archaeological evidence at Devils Tower something about "past meaningful scales of living" in the terms I have discussed here, the politics of scale and vision?

A landmark is partly significant because it gives people the ability to orient in space and to easily pass on a geographical description to others (Orians and Heerwagen, 1992:564). American Indian people undoubtedly visualized and communicated geographical knowledge about the Tower over a wide area, following the shifts in tribal territory – and forced relocation – after the coming of the white man. This is dramatically evident in the recollections of I-See-Many-Camp-Fire-Places, a Kiowa soldier at Fort Sill, Oklahoma, recorded in 1897 (General Scott's notes, Volume 1, p. 99, quoted in Stone, n.d.: 68):

> No Kiowa living has ever seen this rock, but the old men have told about it – it is very far north where the Kiowa used to live. It is a single rock with scratched sides, the marks of the bears' claws are there yet, rising straight up, very high. There is no other like it in the whole country, there are no trees on it, only grass on top. The Kiowa call this rock "Tso-aa," a tree rock, possibly because it grew tall like a tree.

This was also very likely the case in prehistoric times. Hunter–gatherers would have used this landmark in navigation and carried its description – probably expressed in analogical or metaphorical terms similar to the extant oral traditions – as they moved through the vast grasslands and drainages between the western mountains and the Great Plains and along the corridor between the front range of the Rocky Mountains and the Black Hills. It was an ideal anchor for cognitive maps, visible at a great distance and unmistakable, and as such, a focus of key oral traditions about the origins of land, people, and the cosmos. Indeed, in modern times, the high meadows around the Tower are sacrosanct for American Indians. But the archaeological evidence confounds those who might attribute the presence of these ancestral peoples to purely religious activity – as is the common practice today, here and at other sacred places. An archaeological survey commissioned by the National Park Service showed that the grounds below the Tower concealed a dense scatter of stone tools and manufacturing debris – the stuff of daily life–whereas, the meadows along the Belle Fourche River valley, close to the river resources, should have had abundant evidence of human activity, but they did not (Molyneaux et al., 2001).

Several environmental factors may account for this unusual situation: destruction of lower elevation sites by erosion; the lure of scattered outcrops of quartzite partly buried in the high meadows; and the sheltering effect of the Tower itself. One find suggests another important practical function. Eroding from a narrow bench in a very steep talus slope on the Tower flanks high above the meadows was the stem of a Late PaleoIndian point, perhaps 10,000 years old, along with several bifaces and a scatter of debitage. From this vantage point, the Belle Fourche River was a silver ribbon, winding through the valley and disappearing into the upland hills, while the dark mass of the northern Black Hills loomed against the eastern sky.

Other recorded recollections of American Indian people about the Tower contain crucial information related to ordinary activities. Sioux accounts that Stone (n.d.) records in the 1930s mention camping for solitary vision quests and rituals (Stone, n.d.: 50), camping by a band who went there to worship (Stone, n.d.: 51), and camping ''because the cold winds were kept out by the hills'' and because it was ''fine winter country...with all kinds of animals'' (Oscar One Bull, Hunkpapa, 1934 (translated by Luke Eagle Man) and recorded by Stone, n.d.: 52). An Arapaho account of the origin of the rock begins with a lodge camped at Bear's Tipi (Stone, n.d.: 58). In a Cheyenne version, the protagonists took their families and camped there while they worshiped (Stone, n.d.: 61), and in another account, they fire arrows at a bear trying to climb the rock (Stone, n.d.: 63B). Two Crow accounts mention the building of ''dream houses'' there (Stone, n.d.: 65A, 66), and another mentions that ''the Indians used to throw arrows up at the Bears House by [sic] that none could throw over it'' (Mrs. White Man Runs Him, ca. 1935, recorded by Stone, n.d.: 66). Finally, information offered by White Bull, a chief of the Minneconju, in 1934 (translated by George White Bull) to Dick Stone (n.d.:53–53A) is explicit about life at the Tower prior to the forced resettlement of Indian people:

> Sometimes, years ago, we would go to Bears Tipi and stay all winter, that is how the arrows and scraping knives came to be found there. When I was two years old [ca. 1852] I spent the winter there with the Minneconjui, Itazipco and Uncpapa bands, these bands all speak the same language. They hunted antelope, buffalo and deer, there was also black bears and grey wolves around there. When I was fourteen years old we wintered at this place and again when I was eighteen years old. We wintered in different places around this hill each time.

This evidence suggests that before white settlement in the area, Bear's Lodge served as both a place to live and a place to worship.

Perhaps the most satisfactory interpretation of what today seem like contradictory functions is that the line between the sacred and the secular, drawn so clearly now, was not so clear in prehistory. This more integrative understanding of the world enabled the original inhabitants to conduct their daily lives in the shadow of something they also held sacred. If we take this point of view, then the cultural landscape of Bear's Lodge becomes clear. Here, the highest meadows afforded the greatest number of benefits for daily life in prehistoric times. The Tower flanks provide commanding views of the Belle Fourche River valley and its resources. The meadows, nestled among talus boulders and sheltered by the great rock, provide level, well-drained habitation sites and work areas in all seasons. Springs and seeps attract game and give water. Good-quality lithic sources are near at hand. Upland resources, the broad lower meadows, river terraces and the river valley are a short distance away. Above all, the spiritual resources of the Tower are within reach.

This scenario can also help us understand why no physical evidence has yet surfaced relating to the time immediately before the removal of the original inhabitants and the establishment of cattle ranches around the Tower in the 1870s. With the introduction of the horse in the 18th century, and slightly later, European trade goods, the time-honored cultural landscape of Bear's Lodge no longer represented an ideal place to live. What people on foot achieved in days, people on horses took hours. There are better places from which to view the Belle Fourche valley, hills that a horse can quickly climb. And with the introduction of metal goods, the stone tool sources became obsolete. It seems likely, therefore, that as the fur trade period progressed, the original inhabitants largely abandoned the quiet, sheltered meadows high on the Tower for lands more amenable to a way of life by then fully adapted to travel by horseback. While this gave the Tower relief from the stress of settlement, it did nothing to lessen its primary impact as a landmark in topographical and spiritual landscapes.

In terms of scale, there has been a shift in emphasis over the 10,000 years of cultural life evident at Bear's Lodge. To hunter–gatherers who walked on foot, the strange towering rock was a key anchor point in the cultural landscape, most likely voiced and remembered in ways similar to later oral traditions. Its sight then, and now, is irresistible and unforgettable. Complementing this intense inward focus were the equally stunning viewsheds from the heights of the talus slopes that creep up the tower's neck, accessible from the high meadows below, and at this lofty elevation, the closeness of the sky. Then, sometime in the 18th century, the Euroamerican invasion disrupted traditional American Indian cultural life, at first indirectly, with horses and trade goods, and then, directly and cruelly, in genocidal conflicts that removed these original inhabitants to distant reservations. During this terrible period, the great rock lost its practical affordances and, despite tribal resistance, the primacy of its traditional names. Still, for the many people who hold it sacred, Bear's Lodge is a landmark remembered and possessed as a spiritual symbol, a monument gazed at with reverence that, long ago, their people also climbed to look out over the vast reaches of their homelands.

All monumental natural landmarks provoke reactions that are simultaneously behavioural and cultural. They attract and direct attention in the environment and in so doing, may become repositories for meaning, as cultural groups elaborate their descriptions in the processes of communication and memory. Monumental constructions more explicitly educate attention, as they carry messages about power and status within societies – and, most significantly, across cultures. Both afford ways of seeing that are impossible at ordinary ground level. Evidence of ideological behaviour associated with monumental features exists in the nature and distribution of material traces associated with perceptual affordances for navigation, overviews, and access to the heavens. Crucially, archaeologists can perceive these affordances directly and unequivocally and be confident about their associations, as they are universal attributes of scale at the level of daily cultural life.

REFERENCES

Balaban, Bob, 1978, *Close Encounters of the Third Kind Diary*. Sphere Books, New York.
Barthes, Roland, 1979, *The Eiffel Tower and Other Mythologies*. Farrar, Straus & Giroux, New York.
Bradley, Richard, 1998, *The Significance of Monuments: On the Shaping of Human Experience in Neolithic and Bronze Age Europe*. London, Routledge.
Costall, Alan, 1995, Socializing Affordances. *Theory and Psychology* 5:467–481.
Gibson, James J., 1976, *The Ecological Approach to Visual Perception*. Houghton Mifflin, Boston.

Gollege, Reginald G., 1999, Human Wayfinding and Cognitive Maps. In *Wayfinding Behavior: Cognitive Mapping and Other Spatial Processes,* edited by Reginald G. Golledge, pp. 5–45. The John Hopkins University Press, Baltimore and London.

Gunderson, Mary A., 1988, *Devils Tower: Stories in Stone.* High Plains Press, Glendo, Wyoming.

Molyneaux, Brian L., 1991, Perception and Situation in the Analysis of Representations. PhD thesis, Department of Archaeology, University of Southampton, England.

Molyneaux, Brian L., editor, 1997, *The Cultural Life of Images: Visual Representation in Archaeology.* Routledge, London.

Molyneaux, Brian L., Nancy J. Hodgson, and Rachel M. Hinton, 2001, *The Archaeological Survey and National Register Evaluation of Devils Tower National Monument, Crook County, Wyoming, 1997–1998.* National Park Service, Denver.

Momaday, N. Scott, 1996, *The Way to Rainy Mountain.* University of Arizona Press, Tucson.

Orians, Gordon H. and Udith Heerwagen, J. H. 1992, Evolved Responses to Landscapes. In *The Adapted Mind: Evolutionary Psychology and the Generation of Culture,* edited by Jerome H. Barkow, L. Cosmides and J. Tooby, pp. 555–578. Oxford University Press, New York.

Rose, Michael S., 1996, The Gothic Ideal and Modern Church Building. *St. Catherine Review* (November–December):1.

Saunders, Nicholas B., 2001, A Dark Light: Reflections on Obsidian in Mesoamerica. *World Archaeology* 33:220–236.

Stone, Dick, n.d., Untitled manuscript, #1701. Devils Tower National Monument Archives, Devils Tower, Wyoming.

Yule, Sir Henry (translator and editor), 1866, *Cathay and the Way Thither; Being a Collection of Medieval Notices of China.* Hakluyt Society, London.

CHAPTER 6

Perspective Matters: Traversing Scale through Archaeological Practice

THOMAS YARROW

SCALE AND PERSPECTIVE

Anthropology, Strathern (1991:xiii) notes, is concerned to demonstrate the complexity of social phenomena. But in the demonstration, phenomena must be simplified sufficiently to make this complexity visible. An exact scale-replica of the world, after all, would simply be a tautology, providing nothing in the way of insight or understanding; like the "obviate mirror", described by Roy Wagner, "that reflects so perfectly what appears in front of it that it provides no perspective of its own and might as well not be there" (2001: 248).[1] In looking at archaeological fieldwork from an anthropological perspective,[2] it is therefore necessary to simplify the relationships and practices observed. As the archaeologists that I have worked with simplified the phenomena that they encountered through fieldwork practices and conventions, I will foreground some aspects of the site as significant, relegating others to form the background against which these appear. However, in contrast to archaeological fieldwork (which simplifies the site through particular processes and practices), the simplification enacted in this account is brought about by a particular set of interests and theoretical concerns: the relationship between scale and perspective.

The first time I participated in excavation, I was struck by the contrast between the practices that I observed in fieldwork and the archaeological books, articles and site reports that I had read beforehand. It seemed to me strange that relations, patterns and connections that were evident in the texts were often invisible in the process of fieldwork. Paradoxically, it appeared that the closer I was to particular

THOMAS YARROW ● University of Cambridge

[1] Roy Wagner points to the necessarily partial nature of all perception, noting that "Total perception would burn away the world" (2001:123).

[2] Other ethnographies of archaeology include Abu El Haj (1998), Edgeworth (1990), Holtorf (2002), and Shankland (1996).

artefacts, the further away I was from understanding them. At the same time, however, as a number of the archaeologists on site pointed out to me, many of the relations and practices that occurred on site were completely missing in the accounts that were produced.

Archaeology is a "global" discipline (Hodder, 1997:693), connecting diverse ideas, and people from all over the world, and from this perspective one could see the site as just one local instance or example. But in the context of the various relationships and activities on site, archaeology seemed to be scaled differently. Where archaeology was just one discipline, people on site composed a social totality, and their conversations in this context often relativised archaeology as just one of many possible perspectives to take, or subjects to talk about. And while the site report selected only certain aspects of the site as being of significance, in fieldwork I was told, it was necessary to record everything, even if only potentially of importance. Moreover, people on site often pointed to the richness and complexity of what they were finding and to the corresponding paucity of theories to account for it.

Archaeology can therefore seem big or small, significant or insignificant, depending on how or from where one looks at it. Changing perspective in this way alters how it appears to be scaled. But we would not normally imagine that the relationships, ideas and practices of which it is composed are themselves altered by such shifts. This, of course, is true of the way in which westerners tend to think about the world more generally. We can switch perspective or change the position from which we look at the world and in doing so we see different things. Changing scale, in this way, changes the level of phenomena that we look at. Seen close-up, things may well appear different than they do from a distance, and indeed, different issues or questions might become interesting according to the scale at which one looks (cf. Hodder, 1997, 1999; Jones 2002; Strathern, 1991). But what does not change in this formulation is the essential nature of the phenomena themselves. Although people can change perspectives on the world, they do not regard the world itself as changing (Strathern, 1991; Vivieros De Castro, 1998).

The following account traces the processes and practices through which an artefact is recorded on an archaeological site, and in this sense it is a form of life history or artefact biography (cf. Kopytoff, 1986; N. Thomas, 1991; and, e.g., from an archaeological perspective, J. Thomas, 1996; Tilley, 1996; Gosden and Marshall, 1999). But as Holtorf (2002:54) notes, such approaches tend to assume, as westerners do in general, that whilst people are free to assign different meanings to artefacts, and re-negotiate them in different social circumstances, their material essence does not itself change. In contrast, here no such assumption is made. The intent is not to examine, how "the same" artefact appears from different perspectives or scales of interpretation. Rather the account seeks to interrogate the processes and practices that act to generate the sense of shifting scale. To this end, it looks at how new perspectives and scales are brought into vision, in part through changes that such practices make to the material world itself (cf. Latour, 1993, 1999; Law, 1994).

SWITCHING PERSPECTIVES, TRAVERSING SCALE

The artefact that this chapter traces is find number 68176, excavated from site SK, a Mesolithic site close to Star Carr in The Vale of Pickering, North Yorkshire, England.[3] This can be seen in Figure 6.1, which depicts the flint, as it emerged from the soil, excavated by Richard, one of the archaeologists on site. The particular flint in question is just one of many hundreds of artefacts excavated and recorded that day. However many more stones identified as "natural" were discarded on the spoil heap, along with most of the rest of the site (Johnson, 2001:76). The decision to leave this flint in the position that it was found was probably influenced by a number of factors. Scale (cf. Hodder, 1997; Holtorf 2002) was one of these, since the archaeologists left in place only pieces over 1cm in length. But not all flints over this length were kept. Also important, as the site "flint specialist" pointed out to me, were the kind of material from which they were manufactured and the presence of features such as the "bulb of percussion" or "striking platform", indicating that they were "worked".

FIGURE 6-1. The flint later to become "find number 68176" was excavated and identified as "an artefact" by its size, shape, and the material it was made from. Since not all that is excavated is retained, the artefact is already an abstraction relative to the site as a whole.

---

[3] The fieldwork which this article is based on was undertaken during consecutive seasons in 1999 and 2000, although subsequent work within developer funded archaeology also indirectly informs the account.

In this way, through carefully trowelling back of the earth in flat spits, selecting some things as being significant and discarding others, the archaeologists acted to reveal certain artefacts and features. The flint therefore became visible, precisely because the soil and "natural" stones that previously surrounded it were carefully cleared away; and it became "archaeological" because of the ways in which the conventions of trowelling and identification turned the site into an instance of its own method (cf. Lucas, 2001b). These artefacts were, in this way, revealed through the background that was created around them.

In relation to the site as a whole, then, this flint was already at this stage of the process an archaeological abstraction. Although it had been designated "an arte-fact", however, it remained disconnected from the other artefacts that had been found on site: from those that were excavated over the past twenty-five years of fieldwork by different people in different places; and from those yet to be found. It therefore remained too local, too particular and too material to reveal much of significance. On its own, it said nothing about the kinds of things that these archaeologists were interested in, such as how different sites relate to each other (Conneller, 2000), how technology was organised (Conneller and Schadla-Hall, 2003), the nature of the seasonal round (Rowley-Conwy, 1994) or how people interacted with the landscape (Lane and Schadla Hall, forthcoming). These kinds of processes, I was informed, "are not really visible at this scale".

Archaeology, as many of the volunteers on site told me, is not so much about finding things as about the relations between the things that are found. These relations are often referred to as "context" and it is an assumption of much archaeological theory that this context exists prior to the act of excavation (Lucas 2001b; Holtorf, 2002:55); archaeologists simply "discover", "record", or "repre-sent" relationships that are already there. But until the artefact is actually recorded, can this really be said to be true? Holtorf suggests that it cannot, arguing that "*all* the properties and characteristics, including its material identity and age, are ascribed to the thing some time after the moment of its discovery" (2002:55). Before recording, artefacts do undoubtedly have *a* context, insofar as they exist in relation to all sorts of other people and things on and around the site. But this is not the same as an archaeological context. Although there is a physical proximity between the various people and things that become intimately enmeshed with one another through fieldwork, these were not all considered relevant and neither would it be archaeologically meaningful to compare them with one another.

Indeed at this stage of excavation, the problem is rather that the very material form of the site prevented important comparisons and relationships from being made. Attached to the spot that it was found, it was impossible to remove it for analysis elsewhere by other archaeologists and specialists and it was impossible to relate it to other artefacts on site. When asked what they were finding, those excavating often replied that "it's too early to tell" or that "you never really know at this stage". The flint therefore needed to be abstracted from certain aspects of the context that surrounded it on site, whilst retaining other aspects seen as "archaeologically significant".

This apparently complex problem was resolved through a relatively simple procedure, using an equally simple technology. A tag with the "find number" on it was carefully nailed to the position previously occupied by the flint, whilst the find itself was placed in a small plastic "finds bag", and labelled with the same number. In this way, the find and its context were detached from one another. But critically, the use of the individual find number 68176 meant that so long as the find remained in the bag and the tag remained nailed to its context, the find and its context nonetheless remained connected to one another, despite the loss of physical proximity. Immediately after excavation, the flint was placed in a bucket, mixed up with all the others that had been found in that area, and later it was taken to the barn where it joined finds from other sites, to be sorted and recorded. The flint became incorporated into a new context and in this sense it was "sheared" (Jones 2002:73) from its original location. But is this disconnection responsible for the movement beyond "the framework of human observation" (2002) that Andrew Jones suggests is associated with such transformations?

If we look at Figure 6.2, the usefulness of this process of abstraction becomes more evident. The finds themselves were attached precariously to their context by gravity alone. But the numbered tags that substituted for them were nailed securely in place. This meant that it was possible for archaeologists to continue trowelling and identifying artefacts without dislodging those that had earlier been found.

FIGURE 6-2. The numbered tags that substitute for the flints make it possible to view a number of these artefacts simultaneously. They therefore reveal relationships that were not previously visible.

Consequently it became possible to view the results of an hour or so of work simultaneously in a single glance. The relatively more abstract perspective that the tags made visible revealed relationships that remained hidden at earlier stages of the process, so that whilst the particularity of the individual artefacts was lost along with most of the site, greater "comparability and compatibility" (Latour, 1999:51) was gained amongst what were previously disparate elements. By losing most of its original context, the find in fact gained more of an archaeological context: as such, it could be related to more artefacts, all simultaneously visible *within the framework of human observation* (*pace* Jones, 2002). The simplification entailed in the substitution of artefacts for tags therefore generated relationships and complexities previously hidden.

Looking at the area, the site flint specialist was intrigued by the number of finds. From the relatively large number of artefacts emerging in this area, she was able to tell that Mesolithic people were once active in this spot. However, she was unable to infer much more than this. This area, she said, was too small to be of much significance and it would therefore have to be looked at in relation to other sites. To find out more it was therefore necessary to relate the flints depicted, to ones which were in that instance invisible: to those that were still hidden in the soil; and to those out of sight or in storage from past years. Though the tags abstracted no more than the position of the artefacts, they were still too particular to reveal much of archaeological significance. Nailed literally to their spot, they were still too material to allow Richard to excavate further and too local to allow the flint specialist to compare them to other sites.

As with the flint, the archaeologists needed to be able to remove the tags and hence more of the context. And yet as with the process through which artefacts were replaced by tags, they also needed to be able to retain aspects of this context in a modified and simplified form. The tags were not themselves interesting to these archaeologists and neither was the soil that surrounded them. What they regarded as crucial, however, were the relationships that they had materialised and made visible. Indeed they saw these as so important that in instances where the "context" became detached from their artefacts, as when flints were discovered on the spoil heap, they regarded them in the words of one volunteer as "more or less useless".

In order to remove these relationships from the particularity and materiality of the already simplified site, the archaeologists used a total station. The literalness of this translation is more difficult to grasp, since so long as the machine worked as it was intended to, it obscured the complexity and conventions materialised in its circuitry. The objectivity of the find was ensured by the excavator's careful adherence to archaeological conventions (Yarrow, 2003). But by contrast, the total station objectified the conventions and knowledge of specialist disciplines including, I was told, trigonometry, physics and computer science. These enabled it, when operated by somebody, as I was told, "in the correct way", to represent the physical, three-dimensional context of the flint in the two dimensions of the total station screen. However, although the person operating the machine needed to be able to correctly manage its inputs and outputs, they need not know anything of the conventions by which the machine itself worked. In this sense, the total station acted to background or "black box" (Latour, 1987) complexity and knowledge, obscuring the technical and scientific practices that enabled it to work.[4]

Even converted into binary code, the context still had a physical presence, in the machine. But crucially this kind of presence is far easier to transport through space and time and is therefore much more mobile. As with previous translations, the total station therefore enabled a more tangible, more particular, more material presence to be substituted for one which is more abstract, simpler and, because of this, more "superimposable and combinable" (Latour, 1999:306) with other archaeological data.

That evening in the finds' room the data from the total station was downloaded onto a laptop. Looking at column upon column of numbers, it appeared as though the site had disappeared entirely. The rows of co-ordinates abstracted only the tiniest part of the reality of the finds' tags. But the mathematical convention that allowed for this reduction made the finds' relative positions invisible through its own complexity (cf. Bateson, 1972; Wagner, 2001). The numbers, as with earlier translations, therefore obscured aspects of the relationships that they materialised.

To make these relationships visible again, a computer program simplified each three-dimensional co-ordinate to a single dot on a two-dimensional map. As with the total station, the conventions through which this was achieved were not visible or even known by those operating the programme. But so long as the computer worked as it was intended, all that was needed was somebody who knew how to enter the data correctly from the total station. As a result of the simplification that the computer enabled, it became possible to view the site, as the specialist put it, "as a whole" (Figure 6.3).

As seen earlier, the tags made it possible to view only those finds that had been excavated over the period of an hour or so. Converted into binary code, it was barely possible to conceive of one of these many artefacts. But through this map, all points become comparable and compatible with one another, as never before (cf. Latour, 1999:51). Thus in one glance (still very much within the framework of human observation) it is possible for the flint specialist to view the results of a dozen or so peoples' work, over more than a fortnight. Bound by the site's physicality, she was unsure what she was looking at. But sitting in the finds' room, poring over the site maps, relationships began to emerge that were previously invisible: "The site represents a very dense area of intense activity – much denser than the area to the east" she declared. It would seem that a broad range of activities occurred on site SK. And she thinks, "it is evident from the large percentage of spalls that most of the tools were manufactured on the site". As with other translations, then, simplification of phenomena allows for greater compatibility and comparability with other phenomena, which in turn brings into

---

[4] Gregory Bateson draws attention to the necessity of such black-boxing (although not in these terms) through the following hypothetical example: "consider the impossibility of constructing a television set which would report upon its screen all the workings of its component parts, including especially those parts concerned in this reporting" (1972:136).

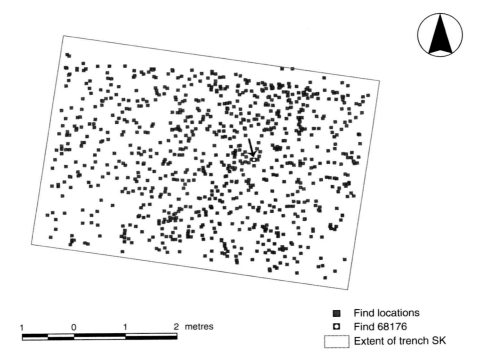

FIGURE 6-3. The plan of SK, through which all artefacts excavated on site over a number of weeks are made comparable and compatible with one another. In this way it becomes possible to view the site "as a whole".

view new relationships and hence new forms of complexity. The map therefore makes tangible a part of reality, concealed by the particularity of any single find. It makes these new relationships concrete precisely because it abstracts only a part of this reality, making it possible to see relationships, connections and patterns between phenomena that were previously disparate and unconnected.

PERSPECTIVE MATTERS

As we have seen, at every stage of translation, there is a literal correspondence between the more and the less abstract form. As the flint is substituted for the tag, the tag for the total station co-ordinate, and, finally, the co-ordinate for the map, certain aspects of the artefact and its context are kept constant. Consequently, the process is objective, in the sense that it retains particular elements regardless of the scale (cf. Latour, 1999: Chapter 2). Indeed, it is *only* because these attributes are kept constant that archaeologists are able to occupy different perspectives in relation to them, or to look at "the same" phenomena in the context of different interpretative or analytical scales.

But recall the flint depicted at the beginning, and it becomes obvious that while there are literal continuities through different stages of translation, there is no sense in which its material essence remains the same (cf. Holtorf, 2002; Lucas, 2001a); and hence no sense in which there is a "concrete reality" beyond which all else is fabrication or abstraction. At every stage of translation there is a loss in terms of matter and therefore in terms of particular kinds of complexity.[5] The map reveals nothing about such things as the way in which the flint was manufactured, or the type of use it was put to. To answer these questions, it would be necessary to return to the relationships concretised in the flint itself and therefore to undertake a different scale of analysis.[6] Although the map reveals as much as it does because it hides things, it nonetheless hides as much as it reveals.

There is no sense, therefore, in which the various perspectives could be added to one another to produce a more complete whole, and no sense in which the map (or any representation for that matter) could be said to provide a complete description of the phenomena for which it substitutes (cf. Strathern, 1991). Rather, in the switching of perspectives, creating more (for example in terms of greater comparability amongst elements) always creates less in others (such as a loss of detail in terms of any one of the elements combined). As Strathern succinctly observes, '...at every level, complexity replicates itself in scale of detail' (1991:xvi). It follows from this that similar intellectual operations have to be performed, whatever the scale of analysis or interpretation.[7]

Of course, relationships and interpretations do not simply emerge of their own accord; the site and the material that it yields have to be thought about by those excavating and interpreting it. But as the preceding account demonstrates, neither do these interpretations or perspectives come only from the mental operations performed by the various archaeologists involved in the process of recording and interpretation. Rather, I suggest that different perspectives and hence different scales of understanding are brought into view through the ways in which people on site order, organise and "materialise" (Lucas, 2001b: 42) the phenomena they encounter. In this sense archaeologists on site never simply occupy a perspective on the world. Rather they are always moving to new ones through the application of tools and techniques, re-ordering the world so as to bring into view different kinds and scales of comparison and relationship and, in this way, re-ordering their own

---

[5] In this account I have tended to focus on the gains that are derived through the loss of particular kinds of detail and so on the ways in which peoples' perceptual capacities may be extended, enhanced or changed through fieldwork practices. However, there are also political dimensions to these practices, insofar as they enable some peoples' vision to be privileged over that of others, or make visible the work or interpretation of some at the expense of others. These issues of invisibility were highlighted in a joint project in a Bronze Age ring-ditch in Cambridgeshire and posed in the following very visceral way: "In terms of the excavation work that we carry out, we cannot find the words, and this is literally speaking, to describe to you how painful the process of cutting ourselves out of an archaeological imagination is. Or describe what a dangerous shattering of subjectivity there is in drawing and interpreting where you and others made something, but without you" (McFadyen et al. 1997).

[6] For example, extensive re-fitting was often done within or between sites at the Vale of Pickering; micro-wear analysis and raw material characterisation were also done.

[7] Although in the light of earlier observations (footnote 4), it should be noted that some peoples' intellectual operations will tend to be regarded as more "intellectual" than others.

thoughts and extending their perceptual faculties (cf. Haraway, 1988). If people are able to move through scales, to shift perspective on the world and so bring new phenomena into vision, then perspective also in this sense moves people.

ACKNOWLEDGEMENTS   A number of people have read and commented on earlier versions of this chapter and I would like to acknowledge in this regard the help and insight of the following: Chantal Conneller, Duncan Garrow, Cornelius Holtorf, Mark Knight, Gavin Lucas, Lesley McFadyen and Marilyn Strathern. I would also like to thank those I excavated with at the Vale of Pickering and in particular Tim Schadla-Hall for his tolerance and generosity, intellectually and otherwise. I am grateful to Corpus Christi College, Cambridge, for funding the fieldwork on which this chapter is based.

REFERENCES

Abu-El-Haj, N., 1998, Translating Truths: Nationalism, the Practice of Archaeology and the remaking of Past and Present in Contemporary Jerusalem. *American Ethnologist* 25:166–188.

Bateson, G., 1972, *Steps to an Ecology of Mind*. University of Chicago Press, Chicago.

Conneller, C., 2000, *Space, Time and Technology: the Early Mesolithic in the Vale of Pickering, North Yorkshire*. Unpublished PhD Thesis, University of Cambridge.

Conneller, C., and Schadla-Hall, T., 2003, Beyond Star Carr: The Vale of Pickering in the 10th Millenium BP. *Proceedings of the Prehistoric Society* 69:85–105.

Edgeworth, M., 1990, Analogy as Practical Reason: the Perception of Objects in Excavation Practice. *Archaeological Review from Cambridge* 9(2):2243–2252.

Gosden, C., and Marshall, Y., editors, 1999, The Cultural Biography of Objects. *World Archaeology* 31(2).

Haraway, D., 1988, Situated Knowledges: The Science Question in Feminism and the Privilege of Partial Perspective. *Feminist Studies* 14:575–599.

Hodder, I., 1997, "Always Momentary, Fluid and Flexible": Towards a Reflexive Excavation Methodology. *Antiquity* 71:691–700.

Hodder, I., 1999, *The Archaeological Process: an Introduction*. Routledge, London.

Holtorf, C., 2002, Notes on the Life History of a Pot Sherd. *Journal of Material Culture* 7:49–71.

Johnson, M., 2001, Renovating Hue (Vietnam): Authenticating, Destruction, Reconstructing Authenticity. In *Destruction and Conservation of Cultural Property*, edited by R. Layton, P. Stone, and J. Thomas, pp. 75–92. Routledge, London and New York.

Jones, A., 2002, *Archaeological Theory and Scientific Practice*. Cambridge University Press, Cambridge.

Kopytoff, I., 1986, The Cultural Biography of Things: Commoditization as Process. In *The Social Life of Things: Commodities in Cultural Perspective*, edited by A. Appadurai, pp. 64–91. Cambridge University Press, Cambridge.

Lane P.J., and Schadla-Hall R.T., Forthcoming, *Hunter Gatherers in the Landscape: Archaeological and Palaeoenvironmental Investigations in the Vale of Pickering, North Yorkshire, 1976–1997*. McDonald Institute Monographs, Cambridge.

Latour, B., 1987, *Science in Action: How to Follow Scientists and Engineers through Society*. Open University Press, Milton Keynes.

Latour, B., 1993, *We Have Never Been Modern*. Harvard University Press, Cambridge.

Latour, B., 1999, *Pandora's Hope: Essays on the Reality of Science Studies*. Harvard University Press, Cambridge.

Law, J., 1994, *Organising Modernity*. Blackwells, Oxford.

Lucas, G., 2001a, Destruction and the Rhetoric of Excavation. *Norwegian Archaeological Review* 30(1):35–46.

Lucas, G., 2001b, *Critical Approaches to Fieldwork: Contemporary and Historical Archaeological Practice*. Routledge, London and New York.

McFadyen, L., Lewis, H., Challands, N., Challands, A., Garrow, D., Poole, S., Knight, M., Dodwell, N., Mackay, D., Denny, L.,Whitaker, P., Breach, P., Lloyd-Smith, L., Gibson, D., and White, P., n.d., *Gossiping on Peoples' Bodies*. Unpublished paper presented at TAG (Theoretical Archaeology Group), 1997, Bournemouth.

Rowley-Conwy, P., 1994, Mesolithic Settlement Patterns: New Zooarchaeological Evidence from the Vale of Pickering, Yorkshire. *Archaeological Reports (University of Durham and Newcastle upon Tyne)* 1994:1–7.

Shankland, D., 1996, Çatalhöyük: The Anthroplogy of an Archaeological Presence. In *On the Surface: Çatalhöyük 1993–1995*, edited by I. Hodder, pp. 349–358. McDonald Institute Monographs, Cambridge.

Strathern, M., 1991, *Partial Connections*. Rowman and Littlefield Publishers, Maryland.

Thomas, J., 1996, *Time, Culture and Identity: An Interpretative Archaeology*. Routledge, London and New York.

Thomas, N., 1991, *Entangled Objects: Exchange, Material Culture and Colonialism in the Pacific*. Harvard University Press, Harvard.

Tilley, C., 1996, *An Ethnography of the Early Neolithic: Early Prehistoric Societies in Southern Scandinavia*. Cambridge University Press, Cambridge.

Vivieros De Castro, E., 1998, Cosmological Deixis and Amerindian Perspectivism. *Journal of the Royal Anthropological Institute* 4:469–488.

Wagner, R., 2001, *An Anthropology of the Subject: Holographic Worldview in New Guinea and its Meaning and Significance for the World of Anthropology*. University of California Press, Berkeley, Los Angeles and London.

Yarrow, T., 2003, Artefactual Persons: the Relational Capacities of Persons and Things in the Practice of Excavation. *Norwegian Archaeological Review* 36(1):65–73.

CHAPTER 7

Artifacts as Landscapes: A Use-Wear Case Study of Upper Paleolithic Assemblages at the Solutré Kill Site, France

WILLIAM E. BANKS

INTRODUCTION

The concepts of landscape and scale vary considerably during archaeological analysis. Landscape typically invokes ideas of site distribution studies and analyses of site function variability across localities, regions, or continents. Rarely, though, is the landscape concept consciously applied to the analysis of individual artifacts.

When looking at human activity patterning across a landscape, it is important to understand what took place at individual sites, i.e., site function. One prominent and important source of information is the stone tool assemblage, especially at sites where little else is preserved. Researchers often infer the different activities from formal tool types: hunting from projectile points or armatures, butchery and other processing from scrapers, and work with hard contact materials, such as bone or antler, from burins. In addition, they use the frequencies of formal types in an assemblage or archaeological component to estimate the relative importance of such activities. As tools can serve a variety of purposes, however, inferences of site function based on the morphology and composition of a lithic tool assemblage are insufficient. Only high-power use-wear methodologies can reveal the nature and extent of individual tool use and, hence, the pattern of activity at a site.

At issue here is the need to understand a toolkit's structure and flexibility in order to make the analytical leap to the recognition of secondary site activities and temporal variability between components. Schlanger (1990:20) points out that the real existence of a tool is when it is in action or animated by gestures. A tool loses its technological meaning as soon as it moves from its behavioral

---

WILLIAM E. BANKS ● Institut de Prehistoire et de Geologíe du Quaternaire

context. Use-wear analysis allows one to witness a tool in action and the gestures of its user indirectly, through the use-wear signatures visible within the landscape of the tool at a microscopic scale, and then project this behavior within the context of site activities at a human scale. Lithic analyses focused on metrics and reduction sequence attributes provide only a partial description of the productive sequence.

The landscape concept may seem inappropriate for use-wear analysis, but it emphasizes that the study of human behavior is not confined to the scale of the lived-in environment that we perceive. The locations of wear traces indicate which specific portions of a tool were in contact with a worked material, as well as which portions of a tool were contained within a haft element or held in the user's hand, and the patterning of the recognized wear features across the landscape of the artifact suggest tool use and tool function. Use-wear analysis therefore allows researchers to understand the nuances of tool use and human behavior at specific places and, after this process is complete, enables them to consider the evidence at increasingly larger scales, moving from site function to an understanding of the scope and complexity of human activity across a larger landscape.

This chapter summarizes the results of a high-resolution use-wear analysis of lithic artifacts from the cultural components at the Upper Paleolithic kill site of Solutré (Saône-et-Loire), France (Banks, 2004). The analysis employed a binocular differential-interference microscope with polarized reflected-light and Nomarski optics (Hoffman and Gross, 1970) at intermediate range magnifications ($100\times-400\times$) for use-wear determination and various statistical methods for interpretation. I will show that this use-wear analysis is an effective and necessary first step in understanding human activity in east-central France during the Upper Paleolithic, accomplished by building upon a multi-scalar foundation that begins with the treatment of individual artifacts as landscapes.

THE SOLUTRÉ SITE

The site of Solutré is located just west of the city of Mâcon in the hills alongside the Saône River valley, between the uplands of the Massif Central and the Saône River floodplain. (Figure 7.1). The archaeological deposits are in a talus slope below "La Roche de Solutré," a small uplift of Jurassic limestone that forms a southerly facing cliff, next to a small stream drainage between the southern side of Solutré and the northern terminus of the Mont de Pouilly, another uplift of Jurassic limestone. This drainage creates a prominent corridor between the two uplifts that served as a natural funnel constricting the movement of large game animal herds during the Upper Paleolithic.

Solutré contains components that represent each major Upper Paleolithic cultural complex, however not each site area contains the complete Upper Paleolithic sequence. Also, sediment deposition was so slow during the periods of time that the site was used that it is virtually impossible to recognize specific or

FIGURE 7-1. Map of France and general site location.

individual occupational/kill events. Therefore, each of the cultural components (Aurignacian, Gravettian, Solutrean, and Magdalenian) is viewed as a whole. Combier and Montet-White (2002) and Banks (2004) provide more detailed descriptions of the site's stratigraphy and cultural sequence.

The use-wear samples from excavations here, sorted by time period and artifact class, are contained in Table 7.1, and Figure 7.2 is a map of the site and the modern excavation grid. The sample sizes are not equal, for several reasons. The frequencies of lithic artifacts in these assemblages vary greatly, ranging from relatively sparse samples in the Aurignacian and Solutréan assemblages to extensive collections in the Gravettian and Magdalenian assemblages. In addition, heavily carbonated and patinated artifacts were left out because it was likely that any wear traces on such specimens had been compromised. Finally, the prohibitive cost of casting every artifact led to the selection of complete or nearly complete specimens. The subject of casting artifacts for microscopic

TABLE 7-1. Artifact Composition of Use-Wear Samples

Type	Aurignacian	Gravettian	Solutrean	Magdalenian	Total
Formal tools	14	4	12	25	55
Blades	25	38	5	23	91
Flakes	1	2	8	7	18
Total	40	44	25	55	164

examination is beyond the scope of this chapter, but detailed discussions of the reasons for and methods of casting are provided by Banks (2004) and Banks and Kay (2003).

While the sample sizes vary, each time period's inventory consists of a wide range of tool types and is assumed to represent the distribution in the recovered assemblages. The Solutrean sample is smaller because relatively narrow "windows" were excavated into deposits of this age during recent times. Also, the Magdalenian sample seems small when viewed against the large number of lithics in the total assemblage until one notes that many specimens recovered from Magdalenian levels were broken pieces and reduction waste materials (Montet-White, 2002).

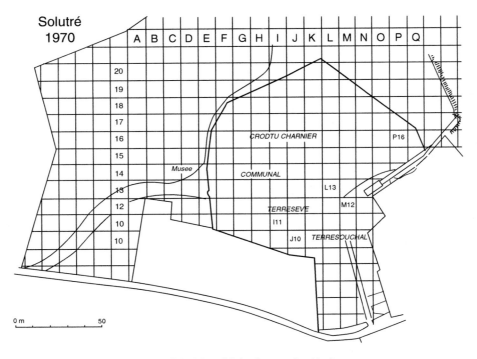

FIGURE 7-2. Map of Solutré excavation blocks.

ANALYSIS

The dense bonebeds at Solutré, the presence of hunting weaponry, and the evidence of butchery on many recovered faunal elements all demonstrate that people used this place to intercept and dispatch large game animals during the Upper Paleolithic. Despite these commonalities, there are differences in the composition of the lithic assemblages recovered from the different cultural levels. The Aurignacian assemblages are relatively lithic poor, blades dominate the Gravettian components, the Solutrean has a wide variety of specialized and general-purpose tools, and the Magdalenian toolkit is diverse and typologically specialized. This variability hints at possible differences in secondary site activities between the time periods and potential differences in how Solutré figured in settlement systems and resource acquisition schedules through time.

Chi-Square Comparisons

The chi-square statistic is necessary because the determinations of tool action and worked material are not continuous variables; it determines if the observed variability between the assemblages is significant. Thomas (1986:283) quotes Leslie A. White, "A device that explains everything explains nothing," to suggest that while chi-square tests can be informative, they are often misused in the anthropological literature and are difficult to interpret. While this is true, one can understand which cells in the contingency table influence a statistically significant result by considering the value of each cell's contribution to the final chi-square statistic, along with graphical plots of the data.

TOOL MOTION OR USE ACTION

The first chi-square statistic is the comparison of use action (the types of movements adopted by the tool user) across the time periods represented by Aurignacian, Gravettian, Solutrean and Magdalenian toolkit assemblages. To suit the demands of an analysis based on tool actions rather than tool form, this comparison focuses on the employable unit (EU) – the portion of the tool used for a given action – rather than the whole artifact. Working at this scale, one can account for the complete range of tool actions for each time period (see Table 7.2).

TABLE 7-2. General Use Action Counts for Employable Units

Time period	Butchery	Scraping	Burin	Total
Aurignacian	11	23	4	38
Gravettian	44	7	3	54
Solutrean	10	13	2	25
Magdalenian	7	18	9	34
Total	72	61	18	151

$X^2_{\alpha=0.05,\,6} = 45.57; p < 0.001$

The resulting chi-square statistic calculated for this contingency table
($X^2 = 45.57$, d.f. $= 6$, $\alpha = 0.05$, $p < 0.001$) is significant, allowing the null hypothesis of no difference to be rejected. The primary contributors to this significant result are the high observed frequency of butchery activities and low frequency of scraping and planing actions in relation to the expected frequency in the Gravettian assemblage (Figure 7.3). The Gravettian occupations therefore appear to be focused on butchery and related processing activities. The secondary contributors are the low frequency of butchery activities and high frequency of burin type actions in the Magdalenian assemblage, while the frequencies associated with butchery and

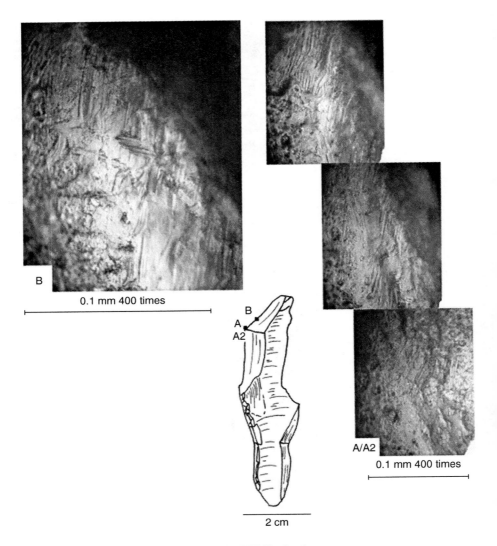

FIGURE 7-3. L13k WEB18 – butchery wear.

scraping activities in the Aurignacian assemblage – a slightly lower than expected frequency of butchery activities, and a slightly higher than expected frequency of scraping activities – are possible but distant contributors. The Solutrean assemblage's observed and expected frequencies show almost no difference for each broad category of use action and do not contribute to the significant chi-square result.

A plot of the percentages of each use action with respect to each time period's total EU sample provides a visual depiction of this significant use action variability (Figure 7.4). While percentages of use action are not the same as the observed frequencies, calculating percentages allows the observed frequencies to be roughly normalized, and the graphic results mirror the statistical results detailed above.

The results of this use action comparison fit well with the observed morphological characteristics of the recovered lithic assemblages. The Gravettian is dominated by retouched and unretouched blades and has relatively few formal tools compared to the other time periods – a composition expected in an assemblage geared towards butchery and initial carcass processing. On the contrary, the wide variety of formal tool types in the Magdalenian tool assemblage suggests that many use actions are not directly related to butchery or carcass processing. This is also the case for the Aurignacian assemblage. While it tends to be lithic poor, and less dominated by formal tools than the Magdalenian, the Aurignacian sample has more formal tool types than the Gravettian assemblage, indicating processing activities beyond primary butchery and carcass processing.

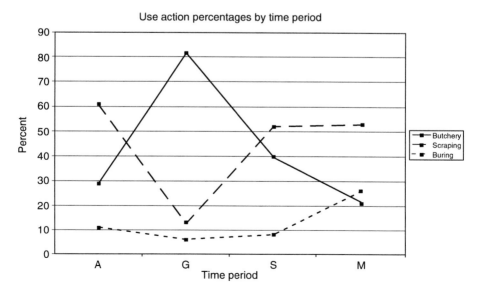

FIGURE 7-4. Use action percentages by time period.

WORKED MATERIAL

The next chi-square test evaluates the frequencies of worked material hardness at
the level of the employable unit (Table 7.3). The resulting chi-square statistic
($X^2 = 31.07$, d.f = 6, $\alpha = 0.05$, $p < 0.001$) for this contingency table is significant. A review of the contributing chi-square contributions from each cell of the
contingency table indicates the hardness category and time period cells that cause
this significant result. In contrast to the previous comparison, the Magdalenian
assemblage accounts for much of the significant variability (ca. 33%). The primary
Magdalenian contributors are the high observed frequency of hard contact materials
and the low frequency of soft contact materials in relation to the expected frequency
in the assemblage. This correlates with lower than expected butchery use action
frequencies and higher than expected frequencies of burin and grooving actions in
the sample. Again, as with the use action statistical comparison, the Gravettian
assemblage accounts for much of significant variability between observed and
expected frequencies: a high frequency of soft contact materials (butchery) and
a low frequency of hard contact materials (burin related actions). The minor
contributors to this significant chi-square statistics are the lower than expected
frequency of soft contact materials in the Aurignacian assemblage and the lower
than expected frequency of hard contact materials in the Solutrean assemblage.
However, these calculations are so low that they most likely do not contribute to the
significant result. As expected, the worked material patterns closely resemble the
use action patterns discussed previously.

The worked material hardness counts were converted to percentages and
graphed. The line graph (Figure 7.5) illustrates the significant results with only
one erroneous graphic placement: the soft category for the Solutréan assemblage.
While it appears to be significant when the percentages are viewed graphically, the
statistical calculations demonstrate that this is not the case.

HAFTING/PREHENSION

The frequencies of microwear traces from hafting and prehension (holding or
grasping in the hand) are evaluated to reveal any significant variability between
the cultural components (see Table 7.4). Unlike the previous comparisons, conducted at the level of the EU, this statistic uses the whole artifact as the basis of
comparison.

TABLE 7-3. Worked material hardness counts for employable units

Time period	Soft	Medium	Hard	Total
Aurignacien	16	17	14	47
Gravettian	40	14	5	59
Solutrean	24	10	3	37
Magdalenian	12	15	18	45
Total	92	56	40	188

$X^2_{\alpha=0.05,\,6} = 31.07$; $p < 0.001$

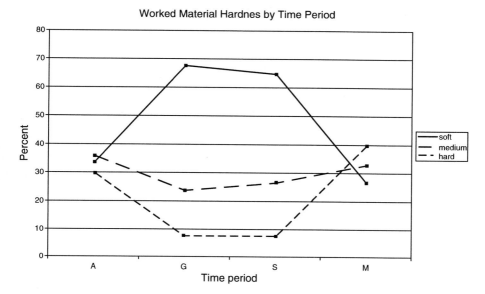

FIGURE 7-5. Hardness percentages by time period.

The calculated chi-square statistic ($X^2 = 18.51$, d.f = 3, $\alpha = 0.05$, $p < 0.001$) is significant. The greatest contributors to this result are the higher than expected frequency of Aurignacian hafted tools and the lower than expected frequency of Gravettian hafted tools in the samples. The secondary contributors are the higher than expected frequencies of Gravettian hand-held and Magdalenian hafted tools. While the frequency of Aurignacian hand-held tools is lower than expected, there is only one tool in the sample with identifiable traces of prehension.

Figure 7.6 graphically depicts the percentages calculated for this contingency table, and the patterns closely parallel the calculated statistical results. The hafted tool samples are small, and one might question the comparisons between the Aurignacian sample and the other time periods, but the Aurignacian components are relatively lithic poor, so the Aurignacian computation may be accurate.

EDGE ROUNDING

The final chi-square statistic comparison concerns the degree of edge rounding. Pronounced edge wear in an assemblage suggests that the tools were kept and used

TABLE 7-4. Hafting and Prehension Wear for Employable Units

	Aurignacian	Gravettian	Solutrean	Magdalenian	Total
Hand	1	30	18	6	55
Haft	7	7	13	11	38
Total	8	37	31	17	93

$X^2_{\alpha=0.05,\ 3} = 18.51$; $p < 0.001$

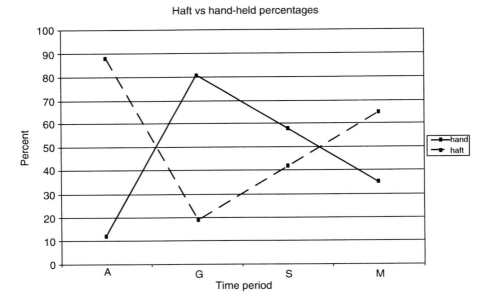

FIGURE 7-6. Hafting and prehension percentages by time period.

frequently (curated) rather than used and discarded. As with hafting and prehension, this analysis uses the whole artifact for comparison (see Table 7.5).

The resulting chi-square statistic ($X^2 = 9.415$, d.f $= 6$, $\alpha = 0.05$, $0.10 < p < 0.25$) is not significant; the null hypothesis is accepted. While not statistically significant, the two principal contributors to the calculated statistic are the higher than expected frequency of minor edge rounding and the lower than expected frequency of moderate rounding in the Aurignacian assemblage. The other cells in the contingency table have only minor variations between the observed and expected rounding frequencies. Therefore, the chi-square comparison of edge rounding does not point to one cultural assemblage being used more intensively.

ANOVA RESULTS

Standard metric attributes for each artifact and the associated edge angle for each EU are recorded in order to identify any possible differences in tool use over time.

TABLE 7-5. Degree of edge rounding counts for employable units

Time period	Minor	Moderate	Well	Total
Aurignacian	15	7	6	28
Gravettian	12	20	12	44
Solutrean	5	12	3	20
Magdalenian	10	16	10	36
Total	42	55	31	128

$X^2_{\alpha=0.05,\,6} = 9.415;\ 0.10 < p < 0.25$

The Analysis of Variance (ANOVA) – GT2 method (Sokal and Rohlf, 1995:244, 248–249) compares the variances of these measurements with respect to use action and worked material for each sample. Once the statistic is calculated, the upper and lower limits of the variance for each class are calculated and depicted graphically. If the upper and lower limits associated with separate means overlap, they are statistically the same. If they do not overlap, the null hypothesis of no difference can be rejected.

TOOL MOTION OR USE ACTION AND EDGE ANGLE VARIABILITY

Comparison of the GT2-method analyses of the butchery and cutting actions and their associated EU edge angles for the principal time periods suggests considerable variability (Figure 7.7). Significant differences occur in the Solutrean time period, which has the lowest average edge angle, and the Aurignacian, which has a slightly higher average edge angle. The Gravettian and Magdalenian assemblages have higher than average edge angles than the other two time periods and are statistically the same. As expected for scraping and planing activities, the average edge angle is higher than that observed with butchery and cutting activities. The Aurignacian, Gravettian, and Magdalenian variances are all statistically the same, while the Solutrean sample's edge angle is statistically lower. Finally, the burin edge angles for all time periods are statistically the same. Surprisingly, they exhibit a wide range of variability and overlap the ranges of all the time periods' scraping samples and the Gravettian and Magdalenian butchery samples.

When these results are organized by time period and then use action (Figure 7.8), it is evident that edge angles increase within each time period based on use-action, which is an expected pattern.

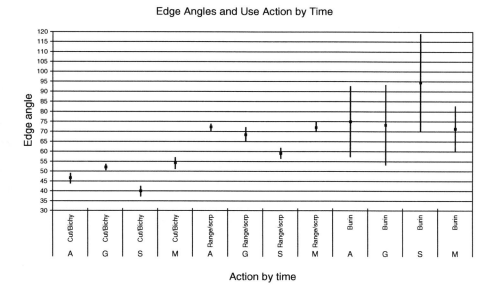

FIGURE 7-7. Edge angle ANOVA by use action and time period.

Edge Angles by Time and Use Action

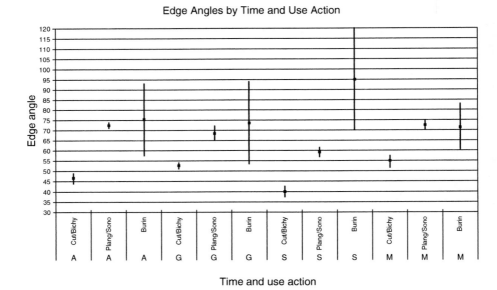

FIGURE 7-8. Edge angle ANOVA by time period and use action.

WORKED MATERIAL AND EDGE ANGLE VARIABILITY

When edge angle variances and worked material hardness are examined with the GT2-method, some patterns are evident (Figure 7.9). As one would expect, the average edge angle measurement increases as worked material hardness increases. High angle edges are preferred because they are stronger than low angle edges and

Edge Angles by Hardness and Time: GT2-method

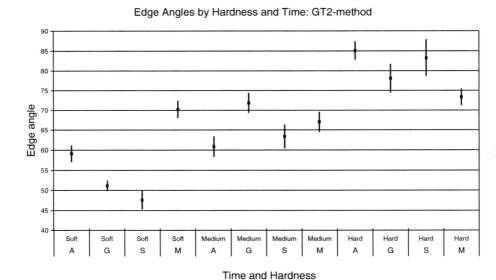

FIGURE 7-9. Edge angle ANOVA by hardness and time period.

hold up better under use; low angle edges are more efficient than higher angle edges for processing soft materials. One therefore expects a higher frequency of lower angle edges where the contact is with softer materials. An interesting exception is the Magdalenian assemblage, which has significantly larger edge angles than the averages of the other time periods, corresponding with the range associated with medium contact materials for all the time periods.

When these results are grouped by time period rather than hardness (Figure 7.10), one notes a significant difference between the average edge angles for the different worked material classes within each time period. The exceptions are the Aurignacian and Magdalenian samples. In the Aurignacian sample, the edge angle variances of the soft and medium hardness categories are statistically the same. In the Magdalenian sample, there is very little variability between the hardness classes, and only the means of the medium and hard categories are statistically different. Also, the average edge angle regardless of material hardness is relatively high.

HAFTING/PREHENSION AND EDGE ANGLE VARIABILITY

The GT2 calculation of variability of EU edge angles for hafted or hand-held tools (Figures 7.11 and 7.12) indicates that hafted tools have EUs with a relatively high average edge angle for each time period. There is a large range of variability within each temporal sample and all of the time periods are statistically the same.

Nearly the opposite is true when hand-held tools and EU edge angles are compared. The Aurignacian is excluded here because only one tool had clear prehension wear. The average edge angle is lower than that observed for the hafted tools, and there is little variability within each sample. While these averages are lower than those seen in the hafted samples, they still fall within the lower range of

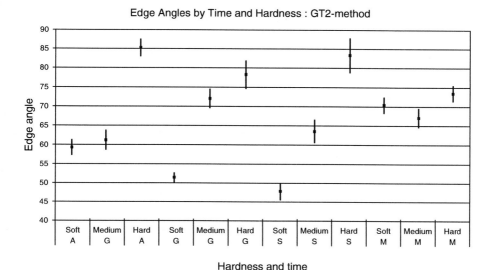

FIGURE 7-10. Edge angle ANOVA by time period and hardness.

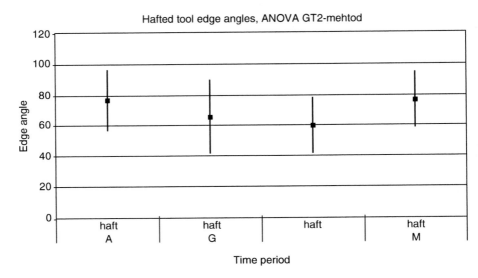

Figure 7-11. Edge angle ANOVA of hafted tools.

the variability plotted for hafted tools for each time period. Each of the hand-held samples is significantly different from the others.

WIDTH/THICKNESS RATIOS

As tools kept and reused over time should show a higher degree of standardization with respect to dimension than expedient tools, the GT2 calculation of variation in the ratio of width to thickness measurements for the principal tools will indicate whether or not tools were curated.

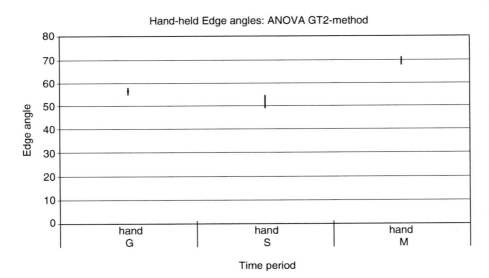

Figure 7-12. Edge angle ANOVA of hand-held tools.

The calculated upper and lower comparison limits for the sample means of each cultural time period (Figure 7.13) indicate that the use-wear assemblages are similar.

These ratios are also temporally compared for hafted and hand-held tools (Figures 7.14 and 7.15). All sample means for the hafted tools exhibit a high amount of variability and all the temporal samples are statistically the same, so the null hypothesis of no difference cannot be rejected. The Aurignacian sample is not included in this comparison because only one tool showed clear evidence of being hafted. A similar situation obtains for hand-held tools. While the range of

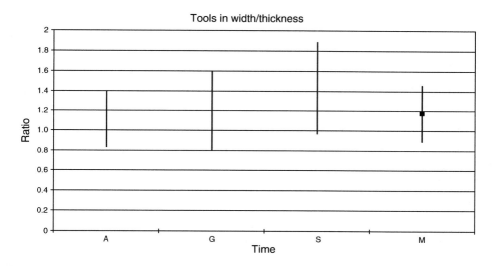

Figure 7-13. Natural log normalized width/thickness ratio ANOVA graph.

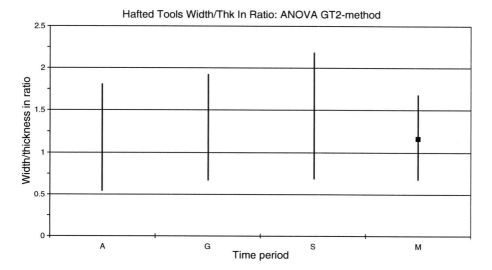

FIGURE 7-14. Natural log normalized width/thickness ratio ANOVA for hafted tools.

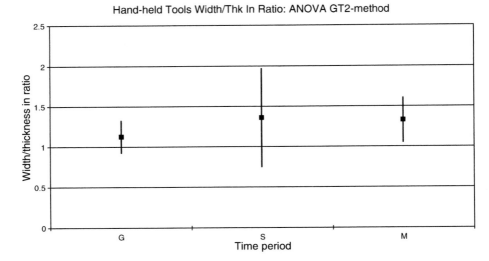

FIGURE 7-15. Natural log normalized width/thickness ANOVA for hand-held tools.

variability is smaller for each period, the null hypothesis is accepted since all of the calculated ranges overlap. Thus, no time period has more standardized hafted or hand-held tools than other time periods.

In another comparison of the width/thickness ratio (non-normalized data), a coefficient of variation (CV) is calculated for each temporal sample (Table 7.6). This is a sample's standard deviation expressed as a percentage of the sample mean; it is useful for comparing samples when they differ appreciably in their means (Sokal and Rohlf, 1995:58). A lower value (percentage) indicates less variability around the mean and therefore represents a more standardized toolkit (Shott, 1986:43) – which suggests curation. The sample displaying the least amount of variability is the Solutrean. The Aurignacian and Magdalenian calculations are essentially the same and higher than the Solutrean result. The highest amount of variability is seen in the Gravettian sample, indicating the lowest degree of standardization and, therefore, the least curation. This is in contrast to the EU analysis, discussed below, which shows that the Gravettian sample is more versatile, and thus more curated.

EMPLOYABLE UNIT AVERAGES

Another comparison aimed at evaluating the degree of curation is the average number of employable units per tool. Tools in a curated toolkit should have a

TABLE 7-6. Log Normalized Width/Thickness Ratio Coefficient of Variation

Time period	N	Mean	S.D.	CV
Aurignacian	23	3.30	1.35	40.91
Gravettian	12	3.63	1.80	49.59
Solutréan	9	4.40	1.27	28.86
Magdalenian	25	3.84	1.59	41.41

higher average number of EUs per tool than an expedient, or more disposable, toolkit since curated tools must be more versatile (Shott, 1986:35). Because the sample sizes vary, a coefficient of variation is calculated for the EU averages and used to compare the assemblages (Table 7.7), with samples having low CVs interpreted as more versatile than those with high CVs (Shott, 1986:43).

The Magdalenian sample has the highest EU coefficient of variation indicating that it is less versatile and thus less curated (Shott, 1986:43). Yet, hafted tools, characteristic of curated toolkits, dominate this assemblage, thus contradicting the EU CV result. One explanation is that the Magdalenian assemblage from Solutré reflects a specialized use that required hafted tools – a need met by making them at the time of use. Additionally, the bulk of the Magdalenian use-wear sample comes from a specific area of the site with exhausted cores and core platform rejuvenation flakes, indicating that tools were manufactured on site. Since these specialized tools needed hafting to be effective, I propose that they were produced on site, placed in hafting elements brought to the site, used and then discarded and replaced with new tools in anticipation of future activities away from Solutré.

The Aurignacian sample has the second highest variation (57.25), suggesting less curation than samples with lower CV scores. This result is unexpected since it counters the chi-square results, which indicated a high frequency of hafted tools – but the problem may be the small size of the Aurignacian hafting sample ($n = 8$).

The Gravettian and Solutréan samples have the lowest coefficients of variation, indicating that these tools served more uses than the Aurignacian and Magdalenian specimens. The higher versatility represents a higher average number of use applications per tool, which I have argued indicates a curated toolkit.

The low CV value associated with the Gravettian assemblage was not expected since it is dominated by blades, has few formal tools, and is dominated by butchery wear. However, the recovered lithic assemblages indicate that little lithic reduction took place on site during the Gravettian time period. It seems that Gravettian groups were arriving at Solutré with a prefabricated toolkit dominated by blades. Therefore, despite a narrow range of activities and a blade-dominated toolkit, which suggest an expedient toolkit, it appears that Gravettian groups were conducting activities at the site with a limited but curated toolkit.

The Solutrean sample has the highest average number of EUs per tool, indicating a more versatile and curated toolkit. This is not surprising, considering the unique nature of Solutrean assemblages compared to the other blade dominated Upper Paleolithic cultures. Bifacial tools are not present in other Western European Upper Paleolithic assemblages. While the two are not culturally related, the Solutrean shares many technological and material characteristics with the Clovis culture

TABLE 7-7. Employable Units' Coefficient of Variation

Time period	N	Mean	S.D.	CV
Aurignacian	40	1.2	0.687	57.25
Gravettian	44	1.36	0.613	45.07
Solutrean	25	1.52	0.714	46.97
Magdalenian	55	0.95	0.591	62.21

W.E. Banks

of North America (ca. 11,500–11,000 B.P.). Clovis assemblages of the Central Plains show evidence of long curation, suitable to mobile populations. It is perhaps not surprising that the Solutréan bifacial assemblage, which dates to the Last Glacial Maximum when high mobility was also necessary, also seems highly curated. Indeed, a number of fragmentary bifacial tools have wear traces indicating use as both projectiles and cutting tools (Figures 7.16 and 7.17) – a pattern commonly seen on early Paleoindian bifaces (Kay, 1996, 1997, 1998, 2000).

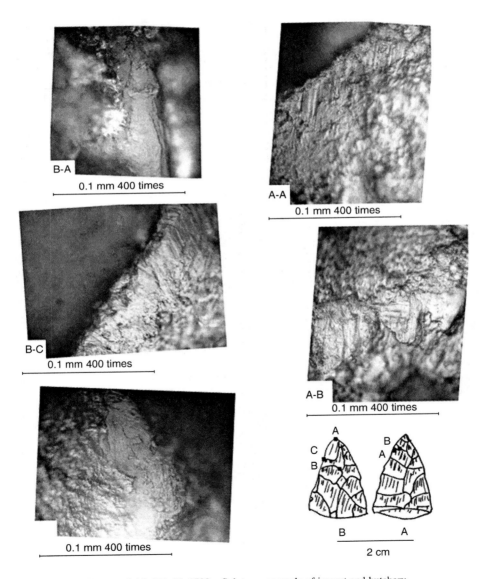

FIGURE 7-16. I11u88–1708 – Solutrean example of impact and butchery.

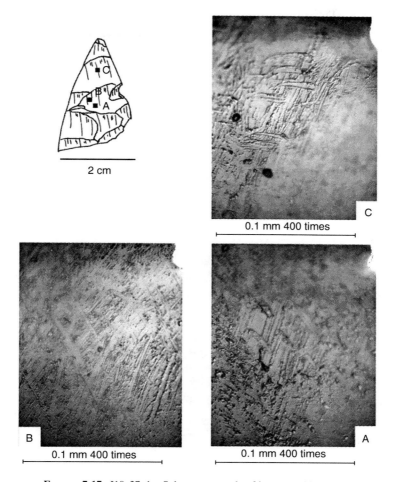

FIGURE 7-17. J10u27–1 – Solutrean example of impact and butchery.

DISCUSSION

After an analysis that moved from a microscopic scale to a human and site-specific scale, we can now shift to a broader perspective and infer human action at an environmental scale. The microscopic analysis of individual tools revealed information about secondary site activities at Solutré as well as changes in the adaptive organization of lithic toolkits over time. The next logical step is to attempt to interpret how the site of Solutré fits within Upper Paleolithic movements across a larger, regional landscape.

The Aurignacian tools show a high frequency of scraping and planing on medium and hard contact materials, and a relatively low occurrence of butchery and cutting on softer contact materials. While the sample exhibiting hafting and prehension wear traces is small, it is likely representative since this time period is relatively lithic poor at Solutré. Relative to the sample, the frequency of tools with hafting use-wear signatures is high. Edge rounding in the Aurignacian assemblage is minor, suggesting that while animals were clearly being killed and processed at the site, other activities were taking place, primarily the preparation or repair of bone/antler hafting elements.

Combier and White (2002), using traditional macroscopic methods of examination, conclude that Aurignacian groups occupied Solutré for brief periods, arriving with prepared toolkits geared towards hunting and processing. On the contrary, the microscopic use-wear data indicate that Aurignacian groups lived in the region immediately surrounding Solutré, typically arriving at the site in anticipation of the horse herds that passed immediately southeast during migration. This pattern of arriving on site before migration resembles the situation evident during the Magdalenian period at Verberie (Enloe, 2000a, 2000b). Subsequent to their arrival, Aurignacian groups likely prepared the hunting and processing components of their toolkit to await the game. The presence of crested blades, core platform rejuvenation flakes, and hearth features all support such a finding. These use-wear and lithic reduction signatures may also represent activities subsequent to kill events, but I think this is less likely. While many Aurignacian tools were hafted, thus indicating curation and possible logistic mobility, most exhibit polishes with only minor or moderate rounding over the edges used. Such a pattern is not expected for the versatile, extensively used, and curated toolkits of highly mobile peoples. Because Aurignacian toolkits contain bone, and sometimes antler, armatures, and many hafting elements were of bone or antler, the high frequency of hard contact material wear traces supports this hypothesis.

The Gravettian sample is markedly different – dominated by unretouched and retouched blades used in butchery and kill activities, many with polishes that are moderately to well rounded over tool edges. The evidence of polish and the low EU coefficients of variation indicate that the Gravettian toolkits were highly versatile and thus curated. The use-wear results show a significantly high frequency of butchery and cutting wear, a significantly low frequency of scraping and planing activities, and little evidence of the working of hard contact materials. This sample is also marked by a high number of hand-held tools and few hafted tools. Finally, it is associated with a high edge angle average for these animal-processing activities. Many of these tools are retouched, a pattern that would be typical if groups arrived on site with a narrow range of anticipated activities and a restricted toolkit that necessitated frequent tool rejuvenation. These data indicate that Gravettian groups were logistically mobile, lived in the region around Solutré, and arrived on site with toolkits geared towards the killing and processing of game animals. They arrived with a prepared toolkit and used it intensively over a short time. While they could obtain tool stone within a radius of several kilometers, they probably had no time to make the journey necessary to refurbish their toolkits.

These use-wear results support the Combier's (2002) conclusions that the Gravettian groups operated within a relatively restricted region, as well as the general conclusions of Combier and Montet-White (2002) concerning Gravettian occupations at Solutré.

The Solutrean sample is markedly different from the previous Upper Paleolithic samples, with no significant variation in tool actions and little evidence of hard contact material processing. Evidence of many tool types and abundant retouched tools, especially bifacially retouched pieces, suggests a curated assemblage. The EU coefficient of variation calculations supports this interpretation. I would argue that these groups were residentially mobile, exploited a wider territory than Gravettain populations and occupied Solutré when the season and opportunity were right. The presence of laurel leaf projectile points made from crystal support this conclusion, since a group needed a larger territory to gain access to such exotic raw materials. The significantly low edge angles associated with tools used in cutting and scraping activities indicate that Solutrean groups used Solutré soon after they had produced new tools and refurbished their toolkits. Solutrean groups likely arrived in the Mâconnais region before the arrival of migratory game animals, refurbished their toolkits, and then moved to Solutré to procure and process game. The use-wear data support the proposal of Combier and Montet-White (2002) that Solutrean groups were highly mobile and likely occupied Solutré for longer periods of time than groups did in earlier time periods.

The Magdalenian sample is different from the others. It is characterized by a diverse toolkit and a low curation signature and yet has many hafted tools, which seemingly contradicts notions of expediency. Furthermore, the sample shows a high average edge angle for cutting activities, a feature typical of versatile and curated toolkits, but a low frequency of butchery wear and work on soft contact materials and a high frequency of burin actions and contact with hard contact materials – a pattern that seems to indicate on-site camp activities or activities not associated with the processing of dispatched game. Magdalenian tools appear to be highly specialized, and it is likely that this specialization required that they be hafted. Thus, the curation signature related to hafting and the high frequency of work on medium and hard contact materials is likely the result of creating, hafting, and using specialized tools and not related to curation or residential mobility requiring a curated toolkit.

These data suggest that Magdalenian populations were residentially mobile and covered a wide area in their seasonal movements, a pattern proposed by Combier and Montet-White (2002). An alternative explanation is that Magdalenian groups were logistically organized and had base camps nearby. While they may have used a large region including areas around and west of Mâcon, as well as uplands in the Jura Mountains to the east, special purpose groups may have intensively exploited Solutré during brief visits while the larger population occupied seasonal base camps nearby. The fact that the Magdalenian lithic assemblages have prepared cores that were brought to the site, possibly to produce tools needed to replace exhausted ones, supports this interpretation.

CONCLUSION

The interpretations derived from the use-wear analysis of a set of Upper Paleolithic tool assemblages at Solutré vary in some ways from interpretations by Combier (2002) and Combier and Montet-White (2002) that employ traditional formal analysis at a macroscopic scale. For the Aurignacian period especially, the interpretation of life at Solutré changes from brief occupations by highly mobile groups ranging across the region to seasonal exploitation of the site by groups residing in the surrounding territory. Interpretations of the Gravettian and Solutrean assemblages based on morphology and use-wear converge, while use-wear analysis provides a plausible, more detailed alternative to the Magdalenian scenario.

These results suggest that use-wear studies are capable of refining our ability to understand the myriad of behaviors that make up ordinary daily life across the millennia. They begin at a scale well below our level of conventional awareness, in a landscape that only a microscope can reveal, characterized by subtle patterns of wear across the surfaces of artifacts. Once microscopic examinations of artifacts are complete, the scale of analysis is adjusted to the familiar perspective of the artifact assemblage, where temporal changes in secondary site activities and toolkit organization can be identified through a combination of traditional morphological analysis and statistical verification. The analytical scale is expanded one last time to consider the wider environment – this time, above and beyond the consciousness of individuals. In this chapter, this last view relates to how different Upper Paleolithic cultural groups moved about the regional landscape and how the site at Solutré was incorporated into these different settlement/subsistence systems. Such shifts in scale and increases in interpretative resolution would not have been possible without high-power use-wear methods. It is clear, therefore, that our understanding of prehistoric human behavior can dramatically increase when we view lithic tools as landscapes scarred by human action rather than simply as objects of human production.

ACKNOWLEDGEMENTS   I would like to thank Marvin Kay for allowing me the use of his microscope and facilities at the University of Arkansas to perform this analysis. I thank Tod Bevitt for creating Figure 7.1. Janice McLean's expertise was crucial for identifying the raw material used to make the drill.

REFERENCES

Banks, W.E., 2004, Toolkit Structure and Site Use: Results of a High-Power Use-Wear Analysis of Lithic Assemblages from Solutré (Saône-et-Loire), France. Unpublished Ph.D. dissertation, Department of Anthropology, University of Kansas, Lawrence.
Banks, W.E., and Kay, M., 2003, High-Resolution Casts for Lithic Use-Wear Analysis. *Lithic Technology* 28:27–34.
Combier, J., 2002, Le problème des déplacements humains, le territoire des chasseurs de Solutré. In *Solutre: 1968–1998*, edited by J. Combier and A. Montet-White, pp. 247–252. Mémoire 30, Société Préhistorique Française, Paris.
Combier, J., and Montet-White, A. 2002, Conclusion. In *Solutre: 1968–1998*, edited by J. Combier and A. Montet-White, pp. 267–274. Mémoire 30, Société Préhistorique Française, Paris.
Enloe, J.G., 2000a, Le Magdalénien du Bassin parisien au Tardilgaciaire: la chasse aux rennes compare à celle d'autres espèces. *Mémoire de la Société Préhistorique Française* 28:39–45.
Enloe, J.G., 2000b, Chasse au Cheval dans le Bassin Parisien. *La Recherche* 332:20–22.
Hoffman, R., and Gross, L., 1970, Reflected-Light Differential-Interference Microscopy: Principles, Use and Image Interpretation. *Journal of Microscopy* 91:149–172.

Kay, M., 1996, Microwear Analysis of Some Clovis and Experimental Chipped Stone Tools. In *Stone Tools: Theoretical Insights into Human Prehistory*, edited by G. H. Odell, pp. 315–344. Plenum Press, New York.

Kay, M., 1997, Imprints of Ancient Tool Use at Monte Verde. In *Monte Verde: A Late Pleistocene Settlement in Chile. Volume II: The Archaeological Findings*, edited by T.E. Dillehay, pp. 649–660. Smithsonian Institution Press, Washington, DC.

Kay, M., 1998, Scratchin' the Surface: Stone Artifact Microwear Evaluation. In *Wilson-Leonard, An 11,000-year Archeological Record of Hunter–Gatherers in Central Texas, Volume III: Artifacts and Special Artifact Studies*, edited by M. B. Collins, pp. 744–794. Studies in Archeology 31, Texas Archeological Research Laboratory, University of Texas at Austin.

Kay, M., 2000, Use-Wear Analysis. In *The 1999 Excavations at the Big Eddy Site (23CE426)*, edited by Neal H. Lopinot, Jack H. Ray, and Michael D. Conner, pp. 177–220. Special Publication No. 3. Center for Archeological Research, Southwest Missouri State University, Springfield.

Montet-White, A., 2002, Les Outillages des Chasseurs de Solutré. In *Solutre: 1968–1998*, edited by J. Combier and A. Montet-White, pp. 225–241. Mémoire 30, Société Préhistorique Française, Paris.

Schlanger, N., 1990, Techniques as Human Action: Two Perspectives. *Archaeological Review from Cambridge* 9:18–26.

Shott, M., 1986, Technological Organization and Settlement Mobility: An Ethnographic Examination. *Journal of Anthropological Research* 42:15–51.

Sokal, R.R., and Rohlf, F.J., 1995, *Biometry: The Principles and Practice of Statistics in Biological Research* (Third Edition). W.H. Freeman and Company, New York.

Thomas, D.H., 1986, *Refiguring Anthropology: First Principles of Probability & Statistics* (Second Edition). Waveland Press, Prospect Heights, IL.

CHAPTER 8

Scale and Archaeological Evaluations: What are We Looking For?

GILL HEY

INTRODUCTION

It is axiomatic that archaeological investigations rely on scaling up. We examine residues, mere traces, of past activity and attempt to say something meaningful about the totality of the events they represent. More pertinently to the theme of this paper, as a rule we sample these residues and make a prediction about the character and extent of archaeological remains from which we interpret past events. Whether we sample individual sites or large landscapes, most archaeological endeavor entails only examining a part of the whole, and this has always been the case.

Today, the majority of archaeological excavations in the UK take place within the framework of development and its attendant planning legislation, and decisions on whether to undertake excavations in advance of development are usually based upon some sort of an evaluation of the presence/absence and significance of archaeological remains on a site. This may be just a "rule of thumb" assessment of the likely presence of sites, a formal and in-depth desk-based appraisal or a more detailed non-intrusive or intrusive evaluation: fieldwalking, geophysical survey or machine trenching. Whatever the technique of assessment, a curator or development-control officer has to scale up, to decide from a small amount of evidence what this represents in terms of the totality of the remains on the site. A decision must then be taken about whether further investigation is required.

The background to this paper was a study by Oxford Archaeology which looked at twelve major infrastructure projects in southern England that were subsequently excavated, in order to assess the success of the evaluations undertaken for predicting archaeological remains and providing a suitable basis for making decisions about further appropriate levels of work on these sites (Hey and Lacey,

GILL HEY ● Oxford Archaeology

2001). The project, known as Planarch, was jointly funded by English Heritage and the European Union as part of its European Regional Development fund, which considers spatial planning (the Interregional IIC programme). It was initiated by Kent County Council and followed an earlier study undertaken by Southampton University (Champion et al., 1995).

The Planarch study suggests that archaeologists have allowed their preconceptions of the past to dominate sampling strategies. Not only that, a trench-eye view has restricted our archaeological vision and limited the scope of our fieldwork. As a result, we tend to find what we expect to find, unless we come across the unexpected in the course of other work.

An unthinking use of statistical approaches to sampling archaeological sites may additionally have reinforced this attitude. Recognizing the difficulties involved in detecting sites by survey methods, a number of authors have pointed out problems and suggested remedies (e.g., Nance and Ball, 1986; Wobst, 1983) and in particular in the British context have suggested that archaeologists should focus much more clearly on the sites that they wish to identify and develop strategies to locate these more effectively (Orton, 2000:115–147). This may be appropriate if we are looking for something specific or can accurately predict what is there, but this is seldom the case. As a result there has been a tendency to develop sampling strategies to locate the remains that are anticipated, thus creating an in-built bias towards finding those sites. In addition, when estimating appropriate sample sizes there has been a tendency to model sites as solid blocks which, of course, they are not. Archaeological statisticians have warned of precisely these drawbacks (e.g., Shennan, 1988:323–8; Orton, 2000:120–2), but their cautions have seldom been heeded. More commonly, however, archaeologists have paid little attention to mathematical modeling of evaluation methods and have adopted a suite of strategies as a matter of custom, with little thought as to how this might be affecting perceptions of past human activity.

Equally worrying is that the debate surrounding the methods of evaluating areas of potential archaeological interest has focused almost entirely on finding "sites", by which we generally mean occupation areas or monuments. Human activity is, of course, much more wide ranging than this. Given theoretical concerns about understanding human agency and how people used the wider landscape and conceptualized the space around them, which have been part of mainstream archaeological theory for well over a decade (e.g., Barrett, 1993; Tilley, 1994), it is surprising that modern fieldwork has failed to grasp the challenge of seeking physical evidence for some of the events undertaken on this wider stage. Should we not be aspiring to capture a more complete record of the traces of past human activities and an understanding of what lay in the spaces between "sites"?

Over recent years, major infrastructure projects in southern Britain have entailed more work than ever before, involving archaeological operations sometimes on an enormous scale. This means that much larger areas than previously have been exposed with care and observed by archaeologists, and it has been possible to assess how successful the evaluation techniques that were used really were.

THE STUDY

The Projects

The Planarch project provided the opportunity to examine the evaluation techniques employed on eleven infrastructure projects in Kent and Essex, in addition to a large project in Oxfordshire, in order to compare predictions and results. The sites were chosen to be representative of archaeological projects in southern Britain; they covered a wide range of topographies and geologies and yielded a variety of periods and types of archaeology (Table 8.1). They also covered a very large area, with 240 ha in total having been investigated archaeologically, partly as formal excavation and partly as watching briefs where prior work suggested low archaeological potential. All the sites had been evaluated using methods that are commonly employed in Britain, some of which have become industry standards, and all had been completed in terms of their fieldwork. An important element of the study was also to model by computer simulations the effects of using alternative trenching strategies (percentages and arrays) upon the archaeological sites revealed in the extensive investigations that were undertaken.

A wide range of evaluation techniques had been employed on these projects including desk-based assessment (e.g., examination of records of earlier discoveries on the site and nearby, air photography, documentary sources and historic mapping), non-intrusive field survey methods (fieldwalking and geophysical survey of various kinds) and intrusive field survey methods (test pits, boreholes and machine trenches) before they had been extensively stripped and either excavated or examined as part of watching briefs.

The Study Methodology

The detail of the methods used during the course of the study can be found in the published report (Hey and Lacey, 2001:6–13). In summary, site drawings such as fieldwalking plots, interpretations of geophysical surveys, test-pit locations, evaluation trench plans, excavation and watching-brief plans were scanned and all were prepared in a GIS format in AutoCAD 2000$^{©}$ using AutoCAD MAP$^{©}$. Different levels of data for individual sites were prepared on separate overlays so that results could be compared. In particular, survey drawings could be overlain on the final site plans to compare the results with "ground truth". On the basis of the data gathered, survey reports and interviews, a series of questions was applied to each evaluation technique used on these projects for each period represented on the site to test the effectiveness of the methods. This was not just for judging the presence or absence of remains, but also for getting relevant information on site layout, date and state of preservation.

Computer simulations were made of a range of forms and sample sizes of machine trenches, focusing on those most commonly used in the UK and adjacent European countries. The simulation trenches were placed randomly over the site areas, taking into account their general overall shape but without any archaeological

TABLE 8-1. Key characteristics of the sites that formed part of the Planarch study

Site	Size (ha)	Development type	Recent land use	Topography	Geology (main type)	Sub-soils	Average depth of overburden	Archaeological remains present
Thurnham	4.4	Railway	Arable	Knoll at foot of Downs	Clay		0.35 m	Neolithic/Bronze Age; Iron Age; Roman
Northumberland Bottom	30	Railway	Arable	Slopes of dry valleys	Chalk	Colluvium-partial	0.4 m	Neolithic/Bronze Age; Iron Age; Roman; medieval
White Horse Stone	12.4	Railway	Arable	Dry valleys and spurs	Chalk	Colluvium	1 m	Neolithic/Bronze Age; Iron Age; Roman; medieval
Tutt Hill	8.5	Railway	Arable and pasture	Side of low hill	Sand	Colluvium- partial	0.55 m	Neolithic/Bronze Age; Iron Age
Westhawk Farm	30	Housing	Arable	Gently sloping	Clay	Colluvium	0.4 m	Neolithic/Bronze Age; Roman; medieval
Thanet Way	10	Road	Arable	Edge of ridge	Chalk	Colluvium-partial	0.5 m	Neolithic/Bronze Age; Iron Age; Roman; early medieval; medieval
Ramsgate Harbour Approach	4	Road	Arable	Dry valley	Brickearth	Colluvium	0.4 m	Neolithic/Bronze Age; Iron Age; early medieval
Whitfield to Eastry Bypass	1	Road	Arable and pasture	Low ridge	Chalk		0.3 m	Neolithic/Bronze Age; Iron Age; early medieval
Tesco, Manston Road, Ramsgate	1.07	Supermarket	Arable (latterly a car park)	Edge of downland	Brickearth		0.5 m	Neolithic/Bronze Age; early medieval; medieval
Elms Farm	11.3	Housing	Pasture	Floodplain	Gravel	Alluvium	0.3 m	Neolithic/Bronze Age; Iron Age; Roman
Stansted Long-term Car Park	7.8	Car park	Arable	Gently sloping plateau	Clay		0.35 m	Neolithic/Bronze Age; Iron Age; Roman; medieval
Yarnton	120	Mineral extraction	Arable	River terraces and floodplain	Gravel	Alluvium-partial	0.45 m	Neolithic/Bronze Age; Iron Age; Roman; early medieval; medieval

Total =240.47 ha

remains being visible, and a series of experiments was set up to assess the probable success rate likely to accrue from using the different proportions and arrays, and also the degree of variability that might be expected in the results.

How successfully did these predictive tools fare when compared with the reality of the total site plan, and to what degree did the scale of the activity assist or impair an understanding of the character of the sites?

The Results

Each evaluation technique provided a different level of information about archaeology at a number of different scales (Figure 8.1), demonstrating not only why the choice of method for each project is difficult but also why it is so important to tailor techniques for individual site conditions.

Desk-based assessments proved to be only poor to moderately good at evaluating the archaeological sites in this study, although they did provide a valuable overview of the project areas at this stage, enabling the examination of a study area encircling the development site as well as the site itself, and involving the consideration of many sources of information about site conditions, previous investigations and local and regional settlement patterns. Fieldwalking fared little better than desk-based assessment. Sites that were finds poor, for example those of the early medieval period, were usually missed by these methods, but fieldwalking was one of the most successful techniques for locating Neolithic and Bronze Age settlements. The small-scale and scattered nature of occupation features of these periods was not easily found by other evaluation methods but flint tools and associated debris very often survived in the ploughsoil. Sites that had been completely ploughed away and were only represented by dispersed artifacts in the cultivation

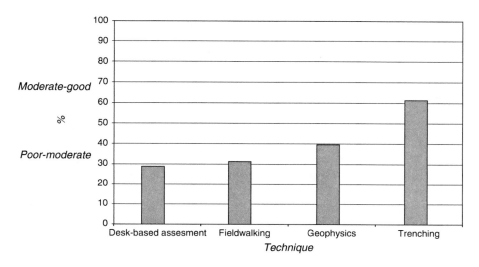

FIGURE 8-1. Success of different archaeological techniques for all periods.

horizon would be identified by few other means. Geophysical survey (usually magnetometer survey in this study) was a more successful method of evaluation and proved very effective at revealing the extent and character of the layout of sites, but its successful application depends on suitable ground conditions and geology, and the presence of features of a reasonable size with magnetically-enhanced fills. For this reason, Roman sites were good subjects for geophysical survey, but even here, stripping sometimes revealed important features which were not visible on the surveys – for example a small temple made up of shallow slots and small postholes at the Westhawk Farm settlement in Kent (Linford and David, 2001:80–1; Booth et al., In Press).

Machine trenching was the most successful evaluation technique when aggregated for all periods present on the sites within the study. It is the most commonly employed method of field assessment in England (Darvill and Russell, 2002:32–4) and the fact that it alone provided moderately good results shows that there are sound reasons for its application. Figure 8.1 shows the results for the evaluation techniques actually employed on the projects in the study and, on average, a 2.4% sample of the sites had been trenched by machine. This is a similar proportion to the 2% evaluation trenching commonly applied in the UK. There were, however, two significant variables in the success of evaluation trenching: the chance positioning of trenches and the type and period of remains present on the archaeological sites.

CHANCE POSITIONING OF TRENCHES

There is a very strong element of chance present during evaluation trenching, and the experiments undertaken using simulated trenches suggest that a variation of between 1% and 1.5% can be expected within sample fractions of between 2% and 10% (Hey and Lacey, 2001: 45–48, and Table 7). Whilst this may be an acceptable figure when using sample sizes of over 5%, it can have a significant impact on the effectiveness of less intensive evaluations. Some random trench simulations at the common 2% sample size produced proportions of archaeology lower than 0.8% of that present. Such results would probably lead to no further work on these sites, all of which contained important archaeological remains. Variability should also be greater for smaller sites comprising more scattered features than for the more substantial settlements present on the projects within the study (cf. Shennan, 1988:310–312).

PERIOD AND TYPE OF REMAINS

Period and type of remains present on the sites was the single greatest variable in the success of the evaluation techniques examined in this study. This can be seen on Figure 8.2 where the relative success of machine trenching for uncovering remains of Roman, Iron Age and medieval date is apparent. The likelihood of detecting Neolithic and Bronze Age features was much less certain and results for early medieval settlement were poor.

The White Horse Stone site in Kent revealed an Iron Age settlement as well as important remains of the Neolithic period, including one of the few Neolithic

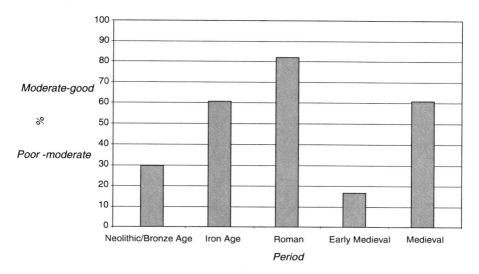

FIGURE 8-2. Success of machine trenching by period.

longhouses ever recovered in southern Britain (Hayden, In Press). Experiments using simulated trenches showed that the Iron Age remains were significantly easier to detect than those of Neolithic date, and in one of the simulations even a 10% trenching regime placed randomly on the site missed the Neolithic building. It is unsurprisingly that the actual 2.1% machine-trenched sample used on this site failed to locate this structure.

The poor results of machine trenching for detecting Neolithic and Bronze Age sites are even more alarming when it is borne in mind that these sites included funerary and ceremonial remains such as ring ditches and ditched enclosures which are much easier to detect than settlement features. Not only are such features relatively large in size, they often have soils which are magnetically enhanced making them comparatively easy to see in geophysical surveys. Although settlement and other types of features were not separated in the study, it is apparent that occupation features would seldom have been detected.

These conclusions are reinforced by the poor results of all evaluation techniques for locating early medieval settlement sites. Such sites usually comprise scattered post-built structures and sunken-featured buildings and are seldom finds rich. Sunken-featured buildings can be backfilled with material that is detectable in geophysical survey, but otherwise the study showed that it was very easy to trench or fieldwalk across and within an early medieval settlement and not recognize its existence – for example, the 3.2% trenching undertaken on the Whitfield to Eastry Bypass. This reinforces the point that these sites are not solid blocks but contain a good many open spaces. These difficulties have been recognized in other parts of England. In the East Midlands, for example, Lewis et al. (1997:86) highlighted the problems of detecting sites with few finds, friable pottery and timber buildings.

Results for detecting occupation sites of Iron Age, Roman and later medieval periods were much better, especially for those of the Roman period. Such sites tend to comprise more substantial features, were usually more densely occupied and contain more durable artefacts; even a 2% sample often revealed sufficient information to allow decisions to be made about further work. The study showed that increasing the sample size to between 4% and 5% often provided additional useful information about sites of these periods, but beyond that the increase in effectiveness diminished noticeably (Hey and Lacey, 2001:43–44, and Figures 27 and 28). In contrast, as sampling regimes increased to 10% (the maximum assessed by the study) the likelihood of discovering Neolithic and Bronze Age sites continued to improve; early medieval sites were still very difficult to find.

WHAT ARE WE MISSING?

A significant concern that arises from the results of the Planarch study is that the comparative success of the evaluation techniques for finding Roman and some Iron Age and medieval sites may be engendering false confidence in these methodologies. The outcome is that we continue uncritically to employ the techniques that encounter the types of remains that we expect to find, unless chance intervenes. Widespread stripping which has accompanied the projects which formed part of the study, and evidence from other sizeable projects, suggests that we are much less successful than we think. The scale of evaluation work and its narrow focus leads us consistently to miss certain feature types, remains of particular periods and a range of activities of all periods. Even on easily detected Roman sites, small and insubstantial structures can be missed, such as the small Roman temple at Westhawk Farm, Kent, mentioned above. If this structure had been isolated it may never have been found.

Feature and Site Types

It is well recognized that evaluation methods are poor at detecting small features, even when they are in groups. Over recent years in southern Britain, two early Neolithic houses have been discovered unexpectedly in areas that had already been evaluated; that at White Horse Stone in Kent has already been referred to and the other was found at Yarnton in the Upper Thames Valley and dated to ca. 3,800 cal BC (Figure 8.3; Hey et al., In Preparation). Yarnton is a good example of a large site that was thoroughly evaluated, with desk-based assessments, fieldwalking, magnetometer survey, test pitting and machine trenching having been undertaken, but which revealed a number of unexpected and important remains when overburden was stripped.

It is very easy to see why the Neolithic structure had been missed. It was made up of a number of small, shallow features, mainly individual postholes in the ground, which yielded very few artefacts. It could not be seen in the magnetometer survey (Figure 8.3) and neither could the numerous Neolithic pits and a number of

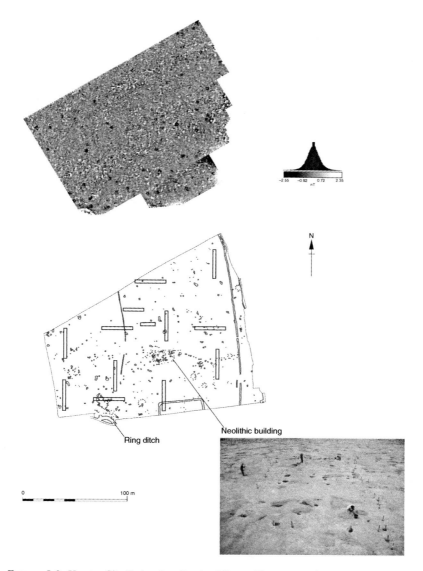

FIGURE 8-3. Yarnton Site 7, showing site plan 2% trenching array and magnetometer survey.

small, circular Bronze Age buildings that were also present. The only feature visible in this survey was the edge of a ring ditch in the south-west corner. Figure 8.3 also shows the 2% trench array that was actually used in the evaluation and which missed the structure.

Size and significance are not the same thing. Structures of this early date have been sought with little success in southern England, and their absence has occasioned debate about the nature of early Neolithic settlement in the region (e.g., Cooney 1997). The discovery of the Yarnton building and that at White Horse

Stone, already discussed, makes a genuine contribution to the understanding of early Neolithic settlement in England. The possibility that we may be consistently missing such remains is a serious issue.

Figure 8.4 shows one of the 18 Bronze Age buildings uncovered at Yarnton that were not found during evaluation. This particular example was discovered with pits, a waterhole and other settlement features, in an area that was chosen for examination specifically to test the apparent absence of remains suggested by the evaluation. The difficulties of discovering early medieval settlements have already been discussed. We think such sites are rare, but is this true?

Burials can be as difficult to detect as small settlement features, especially when they are unmarked in any way, unaccompanied and situated away from settlement. They can be excavated and backfilled very quickly and are seldom discovered by geophysical survey (David, 1994:16–9). This is a problem that relates to burials of all periods. Anglo-Saxon burials at Monkton on the Thanet Way in Kent were only anticipated because of discoveries in the adjacent area; they were not visible in the geophysical survey or the limited evaluation trenching (Bennett and Williams, 1997). A small and unusual Iron Age cemetery came to light unexpectedly during machining for gravel extraction to the south-east of a middle Iron Age settlement at Yarnton that was, by good fortune, being excavated by archaeologists at the time (Hey et al., 1999). The burials were crouched in shallow graves and were unaccompanied. They may form part of a funerary tradition that is more common than we think but which is seldom detected by our evaluation methods.

FIGURE 8-4. A Bronze Age building on the Yarnton floodplain.

Neolithic and Bronze Age funerary remains, as represented by barrows or funerary enclosures, are often detected from the air and by geophysical survey, and can also be found in machine-dug trenches. The relative ease with which such remains are discovered, however, may lead us to believe that this form of burial was universal. Widespread striping over 15 ha on the Thames floodplain at Yarnton revealed a number of single, unmarked Neolithic and Bronze Age inhumation and cremation burials (Hey et al., In Preparation). How many individuals were buried in this way whom we have never found? The cremations are of considerable interest, as not all are complete and some are mixed with cremated animal bone and other artifacts. Investigation of these remains allows a much more complex pattern of burial practices to emerge for these periods, but their recovery relies on chance or widespread stripping of sites for other reasons. We can also be misled into thinking that Neolithic and Bronze Age cemeteries comprise only the visible barrow remains, whereas it is increasingly apparent that they include a whole range of other features both within cemetery areas, but also beyond. An alignment of small pits and associated burials discovered on the Thanet Way in Kent lay beyond what would conventionally be described as the cemetery (Bennett and Williams, 1997:262–4) and might, in other circumstances, not have been examined archaeologically.

Range of Activities of All Periods

The results of the evaluation techniques that have been addressed so far have been expressed in terms of their success in finding what we define as ''sites''. But people did not just inhabit houses and the area immediately outside them, they inhabited landscapes. They herded animals, they collected water and they prepared food. About 30 m away from the Bronze Age settlement at Yarnton was a waterhole that not only added to the range of settlement features and indicated a degree of permanence of settlement, but also provided information about the surrounding landscape, indicating grassland grazed by domesticated animals over a wide area. Several waterholes dating from the early to the late Bronze Age (ca. 2000–800 BC) were discovered unexpectedly during widespread stripping on the Yarnton floodplain, which furnished excellent environmental data for their period of use. They also provided evidence of deliberate deposition and ritual activity, and yielded a range of artifacts that would have decayed on ordinary settlement sites. Wooden and bark bowls and tools made of organic materials had survived. A bowl from Yarnton was found in a deliberately placed deposit of worked wood, including a log ladder, from which a fox skull and deer skull were also recovered. Another waterhole contained the right distal humerus of an adult human that had been worn smooth and had a notch cut in one end. Similar deposits have been discovered in other parts of southern England – for example, a human skull fragment worked into a perforated disc or roundel, found in a waterhole at the Reading Business Park (Boyle, 2004), and a wooden plough ard thought to have been specially placed in a river channel at the Eton Rowing Course excavations (Allen, 2000:94 and Plate 17). These objects represent an entire class of deposit that only emerge during widespread stripping.

Waterholes of all periods provide excellent evidence of the changing environment and land-use practices through time. They show how people cultivated their fields, coppiced the woodland and collected food from it. In addition, widespread stripping can reveal evidence of how people moved across the landscape to meet family and neighbors and exchange animals and objects with others. Trackways and occasionally roads, causeways and bridges can be revealed. In other words such work can reveal a good deal about the significant proportion of the time that people spent away from their domestic space or from monuments. Some of these activities were attended with some ceremony. A limestone causeway exposed at Yarnton had not only been constructed of several tons of stone brought from a source over 4 km away and was laid down on foundation deposits, but feasting debris was found upon it, including a large and significant number of the right limbs of cattle (Mulville, In Press) (Figure 8.5). Capturing this aspect of the inhabited landscape is much more difficult than detecting "sites", but in terms of furthering our understanding of the past it is of considerable importance.

CONCLUSIONS

The Planarch study suggests that the evaluation techniques that we use are designed to target those things that we expect and that are relatively easy to find. Thus we tend to reinforce our preconceptions about the frequency and character of sites of certain periods, such as those of the Iron Age or Romano-British periods. Conversely, we believe that certain other sites, such as Neolithic and Bronze Age settlements, are extremely rare. However, we are not demonstrating that this is true, we are merely showing that the scale of our evaluation work is insufficient to find them. The process of sampling and interpreting what the results represent tends to lead to predictions based on preconceptions and to a bias in the archaeological record in which certain site and activity types are poorly represented and ill understood.

This is not a statistical problem but an outcome of the way in which we view the past. The things that we seek to find are essentially random and we do not know what they are or where they are. Sites exist at a multiplicity of scales and are infinitely variable in terms of their dispositions and component parts. Devising more reliable statistical methods to discover them may be impractical.

Of equal concern is the range of small-scale activities conducted away from settlement sites of all periods that is emerging as a result of large-scale stripping. These have seldom been actively sought and would only be recovered in evaluation by chance, but are providing important new information about the activities that people undertook during the course of their lives. Trench size, even small excavation size, is not the scale at which people operated and relying on a snapshot of settlement is not adequate if we are going to advance our understanding of the past.

It is time to move beyond simplistic definitions of sites and rigid sampling strategies designed to detect and examine these. Problem-orientated evaluation strategies, designed specifically for the circumstances of individual projects and grounded in sound research frameworks are essential ingredients if we are to be

FIGURE 8-5. The middle Iron Age limestone causeway on Yarnton floodplain.

more imaginative about predicting past human activity. Formal and appropriately funded excavations are an essential element of archaeological fieldwork. If, however, we are to recover the more ephemeral traces of the past and the truly unexpected, we must be more courageous in our attempts to examine areas over a large scale, even where little or no remains have come to light during field evaluation. Routine examination of sites after they have been stripped and allocation of limited resources would enable a record to be made of the most important discoveries. The results would add immeasurably to our understanding of the diversity and complexity of life at earlier times.

ACKNOWLEDGEMENTS   I would like to acknowledge the work of Mark Lacey (then of the Oxford Archaeological Unit) who did most of the technical work associated with creating digital images of the sites within the study and simulating different archaeological evaluation techniques upon them. The project evaluating archaeological decision-making and sampling strategies project was initiated by John Williams of Kent County Council, who enthusiastically supported this study and provided much invaluable advice and personal knowledge about development control. Other people who made a positive contribution to the Planarch study include staff of Kent County Council, Essex County Council, English Heritage, Rail Link Engineering and many individuals who ran the projects that were part of the study. Clive Orton kindly commented upon statistical aspects of the project. I have also had many useful conversations with colleagues, and would especially like to thank Richard Bradley.

The patient encouragement of Gary Lock was vital in enabling me to create a written article from a paper given at TAG 2000.

REFERENCES

Allen, T., 2000, Eton Rowing Course at Dorney Lake. The Burial Traditions. In *Tarmac Papers* 4: 65–106.

Barrett, J., 1993, *Fragments from Antiquity: an Archaeology of Social Life in Britain 2900–1200 BC*. Blackwell, Oxford.

Bennett, P., and Williams, J., 1997, Monkton. *Current Archaeology* 151:258–64.

Booth, P., Bingham, A., and Lawrence, S., In Press, *The Roman Roadside Settlement at Westhawk Farm, Ashford, Kent: Excavations 1998–9*. Thames Valley Landscapes Monograph, Oxford.

Boyle, A., 2004, Worked Bone Assemblage. In *Green Park (Reading Business Park)*, edited by E. Brossler, R. Early and C. Allen, pp. 99–100. Thames Valley Landscapes Monograph 19, Oxford.

Champion, T., Shennan, S., and Cuming, P., 1995, *Planning for the Past Volume 3: Decision-making and Field Methods in Archaeological Evaluation*. English Heritage, Kent.

Cooney, G., 1997, Images of Settlement and the Landscape in the Neolithic. In *Neolithic Landscapes*, edited by P. Topping, pp. 23–31. Oxbow Monograph 86, Oxford.

Darvill, T., and Russell, B., 2002, *Archaeology after PPG16: Archaeological Investigations in England 1990–1999*. Bournemouth University School of Conservation Sciences. Research Report 10, Bournemouth and London.

David, A., 1994, The Role of Geophysical Survey in Early Medieval Archaeology. *Anglo-Saxon Studies in Archaeology and History* 7:1–26.

Hayden, C., In Press, The Prehistoric Landscape at White Horse Stone, Boxley, Kent, *CTRL Integrated Site Report Series*, Archaeology Data Service.

Hey, G., and Lacey, M., 2001, *Evaluation of Archaeological Decision-making Processes and Sampling Strategies*. Oxford Archaeological Unit Monograph, Oxford.

Hey, G., Bayliss, A., and Boyle, A., 1999, Iron Age Inhumation Burials at Yarnton, Oxfordshire. *Antiquity* 73:551–62.

Hey, G., Bell, C., and Dennis, C., In Preparation, *Yarnton Neolithic and Bronze Age Settlement and Landscape*. Thames Valley Landscapes Monograph, Oxford.

Lewis, C., Mitchell-Fox, P., and Dyer, C., 1997, *Village, Hamlet and Field: Changing Medieval Settlements in Central England*, Manchester University Press, Manchester.

Linford, N., and David, A., 2001, Study of Geophysical Surveys. In *Evaluation of Archaeological Decision-making Processes and Sampling Strategies*, edited by G. Hey and M. Lacey, Appendix 2. Oxford Archaeological Unit Monograph, Oxford.

Mulville, J., In Press, The Animal Bone. In *Yarnton Iron Age and Roman Settlement and Landscape*. Thames Valley Landscapes Monograph, Oxford.

Nance, J.D., and Ball, B.F., 1986, No Surprises? The Reliability and Validity of Test Pit Sampling. *American Antiquity* 51:457–83.

Shennan, S., 1988, *Quantifying Archaeology*. Edinburgh University Press, Edinburgh.

Orton, C., 2000, *Sampling in Archaeology*. Cambridge University Press, Cambridge.

Tilley, C., 1994, *A Phenomenology of Landscape: Places, Paths and Monuments*, Berg, Oxford.

Wobst, W. M., 1983, We Can't See the Forest for the Trees: Sampling and the Shapes of Archaeological Distributions. In *Archaeological Hammers and Theories*, edited by J.A. Moore and A.S. Keene, pp. 37–85. Academic Press, New York.

CHAPTER 9

Scale, Model Complexity, and Understanding: Simulation of Settlement Processes in the Glenwood Locality of Southwestern Iowa, 1976 and 2000

LARRY J. ZIMMERMAN AND JOE ALAN ARTZ

One archaeology cant is that greater understanding comes with more data and better analytical tools. Supposedly, the better our culture history of an area, the better our understanding of the cultural processes operating there. Intuitively, this bit of received wisdom, repeated often in the conclusions of numerous archaeology conference papers, seems obvious, but is it true?

We contend that it is not always so simple. Although more data and better tools might make for better culture history, they do not always lead to greater under-standing, particularly of culture processes. The reason is a matter of scale.

Scale is defined here as the ratio between the size of something and *a representation of it*. By constructing a representation, we build a model of some reality, such as an artifact, feature, or event. Models are abstractions containing what are understood or believed to be the salient features of that reality. A scale of 1:100 is fundamentally the same as a scale of 1:10. Some level of detail is lost at 1:100, but the underlying structure of the model is the same. If the level of detail known about the reality being modeled increases, is the model automatically improved? If more detail is visible in the model, does that make the model more real? Not necessarily, if the principles used to construct the model remain un-changed. Does understanding increase if better analytical tools are applied to the

LARRY J. ZIMMERMAN • Department of Anthropology, Indiana University, Purdue University, Indian-apolis, and Eiteljorg Museum, Indianapolis   JOE ALAN ARTZ • Office of the State Archaeologist, University of Iowa

model? Not if the structure of the model is an inappropriate or flawed representation to start with.

Nearly a quarter-century ago, Zimmerman (1977) modeled and simulated locational decision-making processes of a horticultural, earthlodge-dwelling cultural complex in southwestern Iowa using a primitive form of geographic information systems (GIS). Recently, Artz et al. (2000) reassessed his simulation using more sophisticated, GIS-based data. A comparison of the two studies illustrates the relationship between spatial scale, model sophistication, and understanding.

GIS AND THE GLENWOOD VARIANT

The Glenwood variant of the Nebraska phase of the Central Plains tradition has been written about since the early 1900s, and has been the focus of intensive work by both amateur and professional archaeologists. It comprises a unique complex of Central Plains tradition earthlodges located directly opposite the mouth of the Platte River in the rugged Loess Hills of western Iowa (Figure 9.1).

Early descriptions of Nebraska phase settlement by Wedel (1959:560–562, 566), Strong (1935), and others suggested that sites consisted of straggling lines of house pits, rarely in groups, with a few isolated houses. Wood (1969) and Krause (1970), however, reported the occurrence of lodges in clusters, leading Gradwohl (1969:2, 135) to contend that the existence of a dispersed form of settlement was an archaeological mental construct rather than a spatial reality. Anderson and Zimmerman (1976) contributed to this debate by reexamining the distribution of

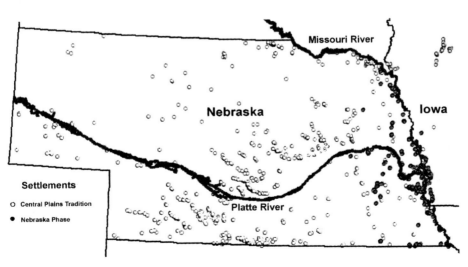

FIGURE 9-1. Location of documented Central Plains tradition sites in Nebraska and Iowa. The Upper Republican, Smoky Hill, and Nebraska phases of this tradition also extend south into Kansas, but digital data for Kansas sites was not available. Site locations in Iowa and Nebraska were provided by the Office of the State Archaeologist, University of Iowa, Iowa City, Iowa, and the Nebraska State Historical Society, Lincoln, Nebraska.

Glenwood locality earthlodges in Mills County, Iowa. They noted two forms of settlement: the dispersed variety, with isolated lodges strung along ridgelines; and the nucleated form, with clusters of lodges on hillslopes and stream terraces. They agreed with Gradwohl that previous studies overemphasized the dispersed form and they offered a model based on climate change to account for both forms of settlement.

Zimmerman (1977) used this model as the core of a computer simulation of Glenwood settlement to see if patterns of lodge location like those noticed in Glenwood and other Central Plains tradition localities could be generated. His goals were:

1. To account for the variability previously noted in the Central Plains tradition settlement patterns of the Glenwood locality;
2. To understand to some degree the processes by which inhabitants of the locality might have made locational decisions; and
3. To operationalize and test the implication of a number of assumptions about or reconstructions of Central Plains tradition culture for settlement patterns (Zimmerman, 1977:41).

An algorithm with ten factors or "rules" governing behavior of the system drove the simulation. The algorithm outlined the key variables from the Anderson–Zimmerman model including preferred settlement location, population change, kinship system, and residence patterns. Response to climatic stress, a key variable in the system, was operationalized through the allocation of land based on concepts of environmental carrying capacity.

To simulate population, Zimmerman employed a Monte Carlo (i.e., stochastic) model that allowed population growth according to predetermined "rules" specified by tables of marriage age, first parturition, and mortality. To simulate residence patterns, he accepted the commonly held idea that Central Plains peoples were matricentric, as horticulturalists tend to be, and as the Caddoan-speaking descendants of the Central Plains tradition were. He defined a notion of "proximal matrilocality" in which the bride and her husband choose to build a residence as close as possible to the bride's parents, if arable land is available.

Zimmerman (1977:79) wrote, "Since the focus of this model is ultimately the location of earthlodges, the rules by which locational decisions were made . . . must be the most precisely analyzed segment of the settlement system." He believed that ideally these rules should be inferred from a statistical analysis of known lodge distributions. Lacking such an analysis, he based the Glenwood I locational rules on a series of assumptions concerning the location of lodges relative to ecological zones (upland prairie, upland forest, floodplains) and elevation.

The simulation program was SIMSCRIPT, a forerunner of today's object-oriented programming languages that, for the time, was quite sophisticated. Zimmerman initialized the system by placing a pioneer population onto locations of known Glenwood lodges. Using a number of simulation runs, he altered the length in simulated years of the run, the size of the founding population, and environmental carrying capacity. Each run generated a map with new lodge locations and population figures.

To test the locations generated, he compared them both visually and statistically to lodge distributions as they were known in 1974. Many runs generated populations, lodge numbers, and lodge locations that were out of line with the known distribution. The run he considered a best fit demonstrated a coefficient of dispersion that was nominally higher than the known distribution.

Zimmerman (1977) noted that proximal matrilocality did indeed generate lodge clusters, and that this might be tested in the archaeological record by looking at dates of lodges in clusters or by conjoining artifacts between lodges within a cluster. The model seemed to indicate that populations at any time within the locality were relatively small, rarely exceeding 100 contemporary individuals. Finally, he inferred that a time span of 100–150 years would likely have been best for the locality. More than that produced vastly more lodges than the 67 known from the published record of the Glenwood locality.

Over the next 20 years, the number of Glenwood locality earthlodges reported increased from 67 to 186 (Billeck, 1993; Green, 1991, 1992). The larger sample size, and the proliferation of digital geospatial data, made possible the kind of spatial analysis of lodge locations that Zimmerman (1977) was unable to undertake. As Hedden (1997) observed, it became feasible to create a GIS with enough specific archaeological and environmental information to model historical processes involved in the origin, expansion, and decline of the Central Plains tradition in western Iowa. Indeed, Perry (1998, 2004) has recently developed a model focusing on diachronic trends that are becoming increasingly apparent in Glenwood settlement patterning.

In 2000, Artz et al. (2000) suggested that Zimmerman's simulation model could be recreated and refined using desktop rather than mainframe computers. They illustrated the feasibility of this concept by running several Visual Basic macros in Excel to recreate the population and demographic modules of Zimmerman's model. We will now consider the second aspect of their "proof of concept," a modeling of lodge locational preferences using ArcView GIS.

DOES INCREASING LEVEL OF DETAIL AUTOMATICALLY IMPROVE A MODEL?

The purpose of this section is to describe the recreation of Zimmerman's original overlay in a modern GIS by Artz et al. (2000). The exercise is instructive for illustrating the effect of scale, or more precisely, of horizontal resolution, on a spatial analysis.

Most of the geospatial base layers that both Artz et al. (2000) and Zimmerman (1977) used were extracts from topographic quadrangle maps produced by the US Geological Survey at a scale of 1:24,000. Zimmerman collected spatial data directly from paper maps by overlaying them with a Mylar grid of 4,000 cells covering an area that measured 5 × 8 miles (8 × 13 km). Cell size was 0.1 × 0.1 mi (161 × 161 m). For each cell, he manually recorded average elevation to the nearest 50 ft and assigned one of five resource types: Missouri River floodplain, hillslope grassland, forest–grassland ecotone, upland forest, and tributary stream bottoms. He defined the bottomland zones topographically. The dominant color of the map for each cell determined grassland versus forest vegetation, with green colors indicating forest, white colors grassland. He classified cells with an equal mixture of both colors as forest/grassland ecotone.

Today, USGS quadrangles are available as digital raster graphics (DRGs) and digital elevation models (DEMs). DRGs are scanned and georeferenced images of the paper maps. Each pixel of the DRG image measures 2.4 m at map scale and has an integer value representing the color of the paper map at that location. DEMs consist of elevation data extracted from the quadrangles and converted to a grid, with each cell assigned an elevation. DEMs are available at horizontal resolutions (cell size) of 10 and 30 m. The Glenwood and Pacific Junction quadrangles that Zimmerman used are available only at 30 m resolution.

Table 9.1 lists the variables Zimmerman chose to digitize to represent the physical environment of the Glenwood locality. The second column states his operational definition of each variable, and the third column is the re-operationalization by Artz et al. (2000) using DRG or DEM data. They captured elevations from the National Elevation Dataset (NED), a nationwide, 30 m DEM. Forest vegetation appears on USGS quadrangles as areas of green. In the DRGs, each pixel is numerically coded for color. They therefore identified forests by isolating the green-coded pixels and expanding them to fill gaps, which result where brown contour lines, blue stream lines, and red and black road symbols cross forested areas. ArcView GIS has several methods for recognizing and filling such gaps.

In his Glenwood I model, Zimmerman classified areas not marked as forest as grassland and cells evenly divided between forest and grassland as "ecotones." In other words, in Glenwood I, a 161-m cell that was 50% forest and 50% grassland was classified as ecotone. To re-operationalize the ecotone class, Artz et al. (2000) assigned forest areas a value of 5 and grasslands a value of 0. They then passed a filter across the vegetation zone that calculated, for each cell, the mean value of all cells within a $161 \times 161\,\text{m}^2$ square. These values ranged from 0 (all grassland) to 5 (all forest). A value of 2.5 represented a case in which the cell's neighborhood was equally divided between the two zones; such cells always occur on the boundary between all-white and all-green areas on the maps and define a zone extending ca. 80 m (1/2 the dimension of a Glenwood I cell) to either side of the zone boundaries. These transitional cells appeared to meet Zimmerman's specification for an ecotone.

Although the intent of this exercise was to re-create Glenwood I's model of the physical environment, Artz et al. (2000) made two exceptions. The first of these involved the differentiation of the two valley bottoms zones. In the Glenwood locality, the foot of the Missouri River bluffs corresponds roughly to the 1,000 ft topographic contour as displayed on 1:24,000 USGS topographic maps. Zimmerman used this elevation as an arbitrary cut-off to differentiate the Missouri Valley and tributary valley zones. This contour, however, makes deep re-entrants into the major tributary valleys of Pony and Keg Creeks, and smaller, but still significant re-entrants into many bluff-edge side valleys. In digitizing the Glenwood environment, Zimmerman reclassified these re-entrants as tributary valleys. To minimize the need for manual reclassification, Artz et al. (2000) used a dataset not available to Zimmerman to re-operationalize the two valley bottom zones: soil surveys created by the Natural Resources Conservation Service (formerly Soil Conservation Service) of

TABLE 9-1. Process Steps Used in 2001 and 2004 to Recreate Zimmerman's (1977) Model of the Physical Environment of the Glenwood Locality

Task	As operationalized in Glenwood I (Zimmerman 1977:59–63)	As operationalized in GIS (Artz et al. 2001 and this paper)
Create grid	Mylar overlay of 7.5 min quads: grid a 5 × 8 mi area into 50 × 80 cells. Each cell is 161 × 161 m.	Clip 30 m DEM from NED
Record elevations	Recorded to nearest 50 ft based on contour lines passing through cell.	Use DEM elevation data
Test the elevation data	Generate contour map with SURFACE II, compare to paper quadrangles.	Generate contours with ArcView Spatial Analyst, compare by overlaying on DRG (digitized 7.5 min quad).
Identify vegetation		
Forest	Cells > 50% green on USGS map (disregarding any other color)	Convert DRG to grid, identify all cells with green colors, expand/shrink to "solidify" cells of other colors that cross green.
Grassland	Cells > 50% white on USGS map (disregarding any other color)	Cells not part of the green zone
Ecotone	Evenly divided white and green	Cells within 0.05 mi (80 m; half a Glenwood 1 cell) of a forest/grassland edge
Separate Missouri River and tributary stream floodplains		
Missouri River floodplain	Elevations < 1,000 ft	"Big Valley soils" from statewide digital soil map
Tributary stream bottomland	Elevations > 1,000 ft	"Trib Valley soils" from statewide digital soil map
Define resource zones		
Missouri River Floodplain	Valley bottom w/elevations < 1,000 ft	Big valley soils
Tributary Valley Bottoms	Valley bottom w/elevations > 1,000 ft	Tributary valley soils
Hillslope Grassland	Nonvalley Grasslands cells	Nonvalley Grassland cells
Oak-Hickory Forest	Nonvalley Forest cells	Nonvalley Forest cells
Forest/grassland Ecotone	Nonvalley Ecotone cells	Nonvalley ecotone cells

the US Department of Agriculture. These surveys are available in digital format for the Glenwood locality, both as vector (polygon) coverage and as 30 m grids. Using these base maps, they classified Zimmerman's Missouri Valley zone as mainly Haynie–Albaton–Onawa and Keg–Salix–Luton soil associations and his tributary bottomland zone as alluvial parent material within the Ida-Hamburg and Monona-Ida soil associations (Nixon 1982).

The second major difference between Glenwood I and its re-operationalization is a matter of scale. By using the DEM and gridded soils data, the spatial resolution increases from a 161 m cell to a 30 m cell, from a total of 4,000 to over 122,000 cells. Figure 9.2a shows the result of the re-operationalized model. To illustrate the contrast, Figure 9.2b shows the same data, this time resampled using nearest neighbor analysis to a cell size of 150 m, near the 161 m resolution of the original model.

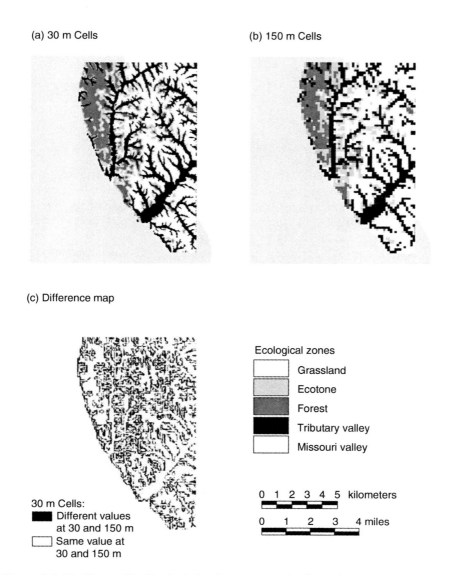

FIGURE 9-2. The Glenwood locality physical environment, operationalized using modern GIS data based on the original, Glenwood I definitions: (a) ecological zones on a 30 m grid; (b) the same zones generalized to a 150 m grid; and (c) difference map showing misclassifications of cells due to generalization.

Although the 30 m data displayed in Figure 9.2a render the landscape in a much more precise fashion, Figures 9.3a and b illustrate that generalizing the data to 150 m does not result in overall information loss. The relative frequency of each class, by area, is virtually identical. At this level of abstraction, a grid of 4,000 cells is as good as a grid of 30 m cells at modeling the overall proportion of each zone.

On the other hand, the 150 m model is not as good as the 30 m model at classifying the landscape at a particular spot. Figure 9.2c shows locations where the value assigned to a 30 m cell is different from that assigned to the overlying 150 m aggregate. As shown in the corresponding histogram (Figure 9.3c), generalization of the data to 150 m results in a loss of the model's ability to accurately represent the environmental context at a finer scale. Specifically, 38% of the 30 m ecotone cells are misrepresented at 150 m, as are 14–23% of the grassland, forest, and tributary valley zones. Only the Missouri Valley zone is correctly classified nearly all the time by the generalization because this zone occupies a large contiguous area where misclassification is nearly impossible. For the model area as a whole, only 14% of the 30 m cells are misclassified at 150 m.

The results of this analysis indicate that simply increasing the scale of the model, in this case from 150 to 30 m cells, does not automatically improve the model's ability to classify broad patterns in the landscape. Even if the 30 m grid is accepted as a more accurate representation of the "reality" being modeled, the 150 m grid still correctly represents that reality for 86% of the model area. Used in a simulation model, the 150 m generalization would probably be appropriate for identifying broadly defined resource zones that were available to the local population.

IS A MORE DETAILED MODEL MORE REAL?

With nearly three times the number of known sites, Artz et al. (2001) concluded that it was appropriate to develop a new set of locational rules inferred from actual lodge site distributions, as Zimmerman (1977) initially envisioned. A wealth of environmental data was available in digital format for this purpose. DEM data, for example, were not only available at a higher resolution than the original model, but could also be used to create derivative layers such as slope and aspect.

Figure 9.4 shows the location of 187 recorded Nebraska phase lodge sites in the Glenwood locality. The pattern that the map reveals is well documented in the archaeological literature of the Nebraska phase. Lodges occur in two locations: on uplands, predominantly along the ridgelines; and on valley bottom terraces and footslopes. Except for a few sites at the foot of the Missouri River bluffs, all lodge sites occur east of the bluff line, in the loess hills, and have never been found away from the bluff footslopes on the Missouri Valley floodplain. Lodges have also never been identified on the relatively broad floodplain of Keg Creek, although undiscovered lodges may be buried in Missouri Valley, Keg Creek, and Pony Creek alluvium (Perry 1978).

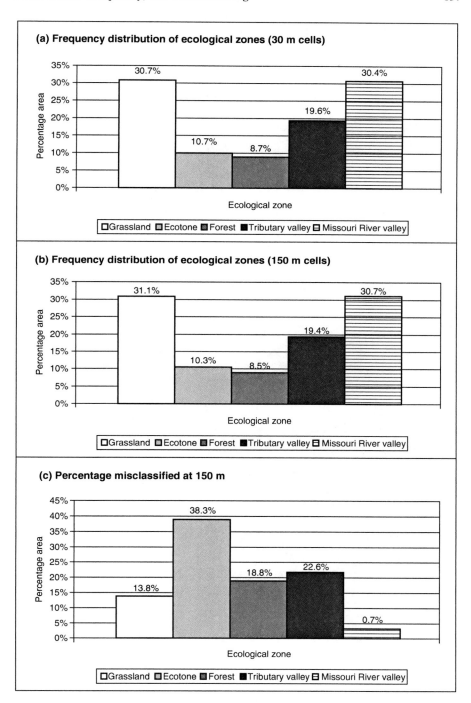

FIGURE 9-3. Histograms comparing the 30 m model to its 150 m generalization: (a) frequency of 30 m cells classified by Glenwood I ecological zone; (b) frequency of 150 m cells classified by ecological zone; and (c) within-zone misclassification of cells due to generalization from 30 to 150 m cells.

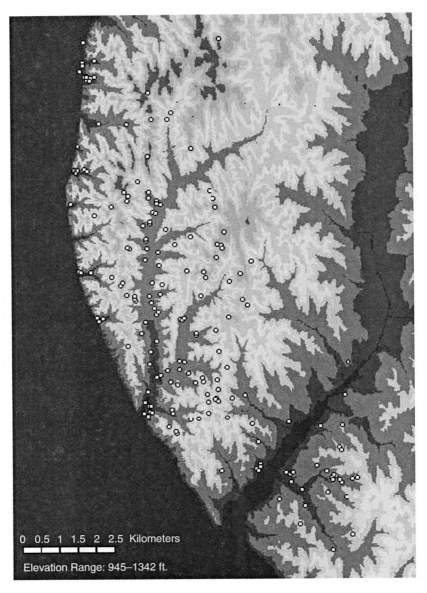

FIGURE 9-4. Location of Nebraska phase lodge sites in Mills County Iowa, displayed on a 30 m National Elevation Dataset DEM of the Glenwood locality. The broad flat Missouri River floodplain in the western part of the locality gives way to dissected, loess-mantled uplands. The two, largest, tributaries cross-cutting the loess hills in the Glenwood locality are, from north to south, Pony Creek and Keg Creek.

The 187 sites are distributed across an area measuring 8 × 14 km, larger than the 8 × 13 km model area defined by Zimmerman (1997). For this area, Artz et al. (2001) examined lodge locations with respect to four variables:

1. Soil parent material, as determined from digitized Natural Resources Conservation Service soil survey maps;
2. Elevation, obtained from 30 m digital elevation models (DEMs) from the National Elevation Dataset (NED);
3. Slope, determined from the NED data; and
4. Aspect (facing direction of slope), also determined from NED data.

We added a fifth variable, distance in meters from the Missouri Valley bluff base, for the present paper. All variables are continuous, except soil parent material, which is a discrete variable with four classes: upland summits, upland slopes, tributary valley floors, and Missouri Valley floor. For analysis, we created nine equal-interval classes for each of the continuous variables.

We used the histogram function in ArcView GIS to count the number of 30 m cells in each class for each variable within the Model Area as a whole. The results are displayed in Figure 9.5 as relative frequency distributions. We then created a second set of frequency distributions, this time counting only cells that contain earthlodge sites.

The Model Area frequency distributions (dashed lines in Figure 9.5) show the distribution of each variable within the project area as a whole. The Lodge Sites Only distributions (solid lines in Figure 9.5) suggest that the inhabitants did not consider all landscape positions equally suitable for lodges. Indeed, the recorded lodge sites are on either loess-derived upland soils or soils of the tributary valleys, with slightly more on the former than the latter (Figure 9.5a). Very few sites occur at elevations below 1,000 ft (elevations on USGS maps are still represented in feet). These areas are on the Missouri floodplain or in the broad lower valley of Keg Creek. Most lodges are between 1,000 and 1,080 ft, an elevation range that includes the valley margins of Keg and Pony Creek and their tributaries and the lower ridge spurs overlooking the valleys. A second mode of lodge site locations occurs on higher ridgelines between 1210 and 1250 ft (Figure 9.5b). Most lodge sites are located within 1,000–3,000 m of the Missouri River bluff base, with very few located farther than 5,000 m (Figure 9.5c).

Within these broadly defined landscape positions, lodge sites tend to be on slopes of intermediate grade (Figure 9.5d). Very few lodges are on the flattest, 0–2% slopes. About 25% occur on slopes between 2% and 6%, and about 65% occur on slopes of 2–14%. Eighteen percent appears to represent a threshold of steepness for lodge site location: the histogram drops abruptly at this value. Most lodge sites are on slopes that face south, southwest, west, and northwest (Figure 9.5e). Fewer sites are located on east and southeast facing slopes, even though these aspects are well represented in the locality as a whole.

To create a preliminary locational model for lodge sites in the Glenwood locality, we assigned to each 30 × 30 m cell a "suitability value" calculated as the mean of within-class relative frequencies for each variable. The results are plotted on Figure 9.6. White pixels are classified as least suitable, and black the most suitable, for lodge locations. The histogram (Figure 9.7) shows suitability rankings for cells that contain lodge sites. Notably, only 40% of the sites are located on "very good" cells, but about 82% are classified as good or very good. The 34 sites classified as "poor" are mainly those appropriately located with respect to

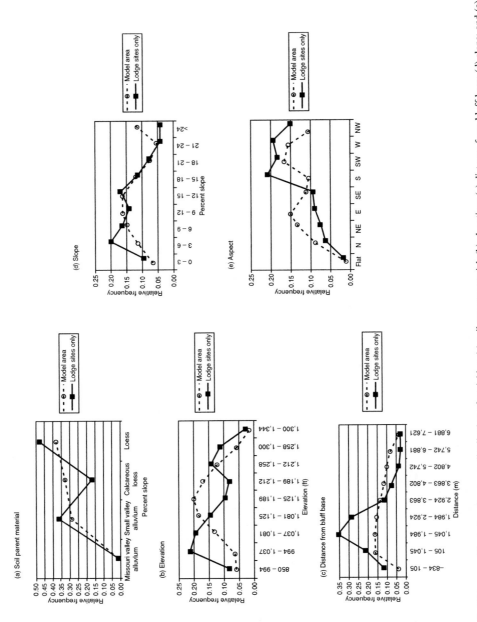

Figure 9-5. Histograms illustrating frequency distribution of variables: (a) soil parent material; (b) elevation; (c) distance from bluff base; (d) slope; and (e) aspect.

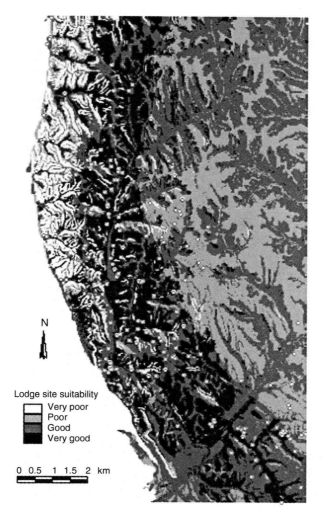

FIGURE 9-6. Map of Glenwood locality showing classification of landscape according to suitability for lodge sites.

aspect and landscape position, but on steeper slopes. Finally, a few sites fall on cells that do not rank highly with respect to any of the variables.

CONCLUSION

Glenwood I was a computer simulation model of Nebraska Phase settlement behavior accomplished in the mid-1970s on a mainframe computer using a primitive version of GIS and object-oriented programming language. As we have seen, the use of higher resolution geospatial data in a modern desktop GIS did not significantly improve the model's representation of the physical environment of

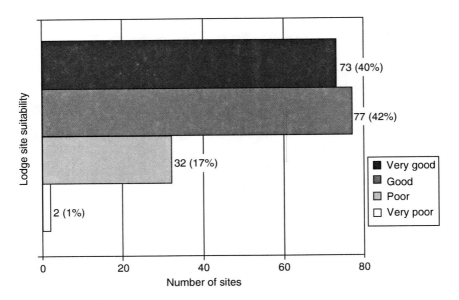

FIGURE 9-7. Histogram of classification of known lodge sites according to modeled lodge site suitability.

the Glenwood locality. Despite differences in the technology used to acquire and manipulate the data, the original model and the present re-operationalization of that model both relied on essentially the same data source: USGS 1:24,000 topographic quadrangles. Whether they acquired them from paper maps or their digital counterparts, Zimmerman (1977) and Artz et al. (2000) had access to the same kinds of environmental data, classified and represented in the same way.

We gained some understanding, however, as our consideration of lodge location moved beyond the constraints of the original model – gains made possible in part by the availability of more data (67 versus 187 known lodge sites) and also by the greater computational power of present-day GIS software, which can quickly generate multiple layers data from a single initial data source. Slope and aspect are examples of derivative layers quickly and routinely generated in current GIS software that were simply too computation-intensive for Zimmerman to consider for Glenwood I in 1977. Furthermore, our reanalysis of the Glenwood data went beyond simply providing more data; it allowed us to create a set of rules for modeling lodge location based on the physical locations of the lodges, rather than on more generalized extrapolations from environmental data. Zimmerman (1977) considered this a desirable goal, but one that was not achievable at the time.

In what might be considered a first step toward "Glenwood 2," we created a model for lodge site locations that favors south-, southwest-, and west-facing slopes of 2–18%, with a slightly higher probability of upland versus bottomland locations. These rules correctly positioned about 80% of the recorded lodge sites. The model can bear considerable refinement, but this is nonetheless an encouraging start.

Simulation modeling of the Nebraska phase in the Glenwood locality is no less difficult now than it was 25 years ago, despite (and perhaps because of) the availability of more archaeological data, more environmental data, and more sophisticated analytical tools. Modeling at an increasingly finer scale (i.e., nearly 1:1), one that approaches reality in terms of numbers of variables, may increase the validity of predicted site locations, but may well defeat an effort to comprehend cultural processes, perhaps because the model can do little to incorporate the cultural meanings of a landscape to its inhabitants. Above and beyond the abilities of computers to manage and manipulate data, good modeling depends – as it always has – on good anthropology to establish the theoretical framework for organizing environmental, archaeological, and cultural data.

Simulation modeling with large data sets and the capacity to manipulate them with powerful computation is seductive, but much depends on the nature of the data manipulation and the questions that drive the model. The risks are clear: researchers unaware of the impact of scalar change may produce fatally flawed models, while researchers who manipulate scale in the quest for new insights, as we did here, may not achieve any greater understanding of cultural processes.

REFERENCES

Anderson, Adrian D., and Zimmerman, Larry J., 1976, Settlement/Subsistence Variability in the Glenwood Locality, Southwestern Iowa. *Plains Anthropologist* 21(72):141–154.

Artz, Joe A., Haury, Cherie E., Hedden, John G., and Zimmerman, Larry J., 2000, From Diaries to Data, From Data to Models: Contributions to Glenwood Locality Archaeology. Paper presented at the 49th Midwest/58th Plains Conference, St. Paul, Minnesota.

Billeck, William T., 1993, Time and Space in the Glenwood Locality: The Nebraska Phase in Western Iowa. Unpublished Ph.D. dissertation, Department of Anthropology, University of Missouri, Columbia.

Gradwohl, David M., 1969, Prehistoric Villages in Eastern Nebraska. *Publications in Anthropology, 4.* Nebraska State Historical Society, Lincoln.

Green, William, 1991, The Paul Rowe Archaeological Collection: A Key to Central Plains Prehistory. *Plains Anthropologist* 36:79–85.

Green, William, editor, 1992, Mills County Archaeology: The Paul Rowe Collection and Southwestern Iowa Prehistory. *Research Papers* (17)5. Office of the State Archaeologist, University of Iowa, Iowa City.

Hedden, John G., 1997, Paper presented at the 55th Annual Plains Conference, Boulder, Colorado.

Krause, Richard, 1970 Aspects of Adaptation Among Upper Republican Subsistence Cultivators. In *Pleistocene and Recent Environments of the Central Great Plains*, edited by Wakefield Dort and J. Knox Jones, pp. 103–116. *Special Publication* 3, Department of Geology, University of Kansas, Lawrence.

Nixon, John R., 1982, *Soil Survey of Mills County, Iowa.* United States Department of Agriculture, Soil Conservation Service, Washington, DC.

Perry, Michael J., 1998, An Archaeological Survey of the Lower Pony Creek Valley: Implications for Glenwood Locality Settlement Pattern. *Central Plains Archaeology* 6:35–56.

Perry, Michael J., 2003, A Pony Creek Settlement Model. *Journal of the Iowa Archaeological Society* 50:129–138.

Strong, William D., 1935, An Introduction to Nebraska Archaeology. *Smithsonian Miscellaneous Collections*, Vol. 93, No. 10. Washington, DC.

Wedel, Waldo R., 1959, An Introduction to Kansas Archeology. *Bureau of American Ethnology, Bulletin 174*. Washington, DC.

Wood, W. Raymond, 1969, Ethnographic Reconstructions. In *Two House Sites in the Central Plains: An Experiment in Archaeology*, edited by W. R. Wood, pp. 102–108. Plains Anthropologist, Memoir 6, Vol 14, Part 2.

Zimmerman, Larry J., 1977, *Prehistoric Locational Behavior: A Computer Simulation*. Report 10, Office of the State Archaeologist of Iowa. Iowa City.

CHAPTER 10

Scale and Its Effects on Understanding Regional Behavioural Systems: An Australian Case Study

MALCOLM RIDGES

THE IMPORTANCE OF SCALE FOR ARCHAEOLOGICAL THEORY

As a concept, scale is important for enabling the ability to specify, explicitly, different perspectives of complex systems. By their very nature, complex systems are composed of many interacting components, each varying continuously across a multitude of measurable contexts. Because of this, there is no simple way of visualising all the patterns and processes within a complex system in a single representation, except for all but the most simple of systems. Consequently, scale is used, arbitrarily, to define the context in which we view and interpret a more manageable portion of a system. In this sense, specifying scale establishes a particular view, or perspective, of a system.

Scale is therefore closely linked to perspective, such that scale is used to provide structure and context for any given perspective, and by extension, a crucial element to situating interpretative statements. If we think about scale this way, it is possible to see how scale is important to archaeology for the way we use it to specify our perspective on the past.

Most commonly, archaeologists are familiar with scale through using it to establish a spatial perspective. At any given map scale, decisions are made about sacrificing complexity to varying degrees in order to capture the most informative spatial structure, for a given theme, at a given level of spatial representation. The map itself is not reality, but captures arbitrary components of spatial reality in order to form a particular perspective of a spatial context. In doing so, each map scale establishes a different perspective on spatial context. Specifying a map scale is

---

MALCOLM RIDGES ● Environment and Conservation, New South Wales

therefore a way specifying, explicitly, a particular perspective in a given spatial context.

The same applies equally to archaeological theory and how it enables different perspectives on the past. Archaeological theories describe behavioural and material reality at various levels of generalisation. Thus, in the same way that maps attempt to capture patterns and processes at arbitrary levels of generalisation of the earth's surface, so to does archaeological theory attempt to capture patterns and processes of the material remains of past human activity at arbitrary levels of generalisation. The importance of scale to archaeological theory therefore extends far beyond what it is normally associated with—maps. Instead, scale is a concept that is important to all statements about archaeological perspective.

In Australia (Lourandos and Ross, 1994), as in other parts of the world (Trigger, 1995), archaeologists have come to accept that no single perspective on the past is sufficient for explaining all the variation observed archaeologically. In the absence of a unified theory of behaviour, many of the general level theories (Schiffer, 1988; Trigger, 1989:20) archaeologists draw upon (either explicitly or implicitly) only refer to various parts of a broader totality of human behaviour. So long as archaeologists adopt a flexible approach to theory, the diversity of theory has come to be seen as a good thing for the discipline.

However, the diversity of perspectives now applied in archaeology potentially presents a problem for interpretation. It is possible to be overwhelmed these days by the multitude of perspectives that can somehow find relevance in any given study (e.g., Dobres and Robb, 2000:9). There is therefore an emerging need for the ability to make explicit statements about the ways different perspectives become relevant in different archaeological contexts.

Many of the features (in both their material sense and as behavioural processes) that archaeologists describe and theorise are subject to the effects of scale by virtue of them having or referring to some sizeable quantity. However, perhaps in trying too hard to employ uniformitarian propositions (Binford, 1983), the influence of scale, and hence specific reference to context, is poorly articulated in many theories. The importance of incorporating scale into theory is highlighted by the attention it has been given in ecology as the discipline comes to terms with addressing such diverse problems as global climate change and responses of individual species to local habitat destruction. As O'Neill and King (1998:5–6) describe:

> These studies... lead to one inescapable conclusion: if you move far enough across scale, the dominant processes change. It is not just that things get bigger or smaller, but the phenomena themselves change.

Despite this, the incorporation of scale into archaeological interpretation is generally under-theorised. The importance of scale for archaeology lies in its necessity for articulating various perspectives on the past, and how these shape the narratives we form. Apart from its common application to describing time and space, scale is applicable to almost any kind of archaeological subject that can be measured or theorised. Consequently, research directed towards investigating processes operating across and within scales, should assist in understanding the way archaeologists employ particular perspectives and theory in different contexts.

Doing so should also lead to more explicit statements about a given perspective and assist in evaluating different interpretations of the past.

AN AUSTRALIAN CASE STUDY

The work reported in this chapter comes from a regional archaeological study conducted in northwest central Queensland, Australia (Figure 10.1). Aboriginal occupation in the region extends back at least 15,000 years (Davidson et al., 1993). These people adopted a hunting and gathering lifestyle that was typical for the arid-zone of Australia (e.g., Gould, 1980). Their population density was very low, and they were highly mobile. Importantly, despite being highly mobile, the

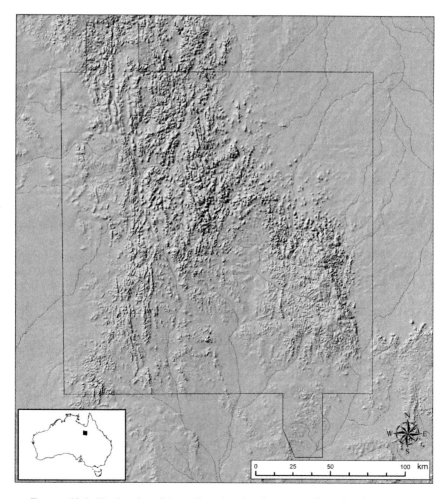

FIGURE 10-1. The location of the study region showing topography and drainage routes.

movement of people related as much to social and economic reasons, as it did subsistence (Roth 1897:132).

Aridity in the region results from low and highly unpredictable rainfall, which occurs predominantly during the summer months in the form of thunderstorms. Evaporation far exceeds precipitation, so that standing water is rare, and there are no rivers in the region that flow continuously. The region demonstrates little relief, varying by only 200 m in elevation. Nonetheless, where relief is appreciable, it is generally abrupt, and although only rarely sufficient to completely hinder the movement of people in any direction, it is enough to have strongly influenced the routes with which people moved throughout the landscape (see Figure 10.1).

In the upland zones, the geology consists of Cambrian and Precambrian sedimentary units that in the west have experienced several phases of uplifting and warping, producing low rugged hills containing complex sequences of metamorphic rocks, many of which are suitable for manufacturing stone tools. Stone tool production is one of the key archaeological features of the region, with artefacts made from quartz, quartzite, chalcedony, chert, silcrete, and metabasalt.

In the east, the upwarping of the sedimentary units produces a low tableland with abrupt mesas at its margins. It is in rockshelters along these mesas that many of the rock-art sites encountered in the region are found (Davidson et al., in press; Ross, 1997). As well as a rich and well preserved archaeological record, the region played host to two kinds of behavioural process that are important for understanding the prehistory of the region: trade and the production of rock-art. Each of these is outlined briefly below.

Roth described in some detail the movement of items into and out of northwest central Queensland. Of these items, the most important were stone axes (Davidson et al., in press), ochre (Jones, 1984), and the narcotic plant *pituri* (Duboisi Hopwoodii) (Watson, 1980). The harvesting of pituri each year facilitated several months of ceremonies and markets at various places throughout the region (Roth 1897:131), and rights to host such events were also an important item of exchange.

It is clear from Roth's writings that there were important distribution centres, from which items entered and left the region, but the specifics of how these items were used within the region is much less clear. Davidson's (1993) work has demonstrated that at least one site, the frequency of axe flakes increased dramatically in the last few thousand years, indicating the expansion of distribution systems. However, the character of this distribution system in spatial terms is unknown except in very broad terms. Subsequently, despite what emerges about the importance of trade from the archaeology and ethnography, how it affected behaviour at the local level was not clear.

The region also contains a diverse assemblage of rock-art about which there is little oral tradition. About 180 sites containing paintings and/or engravings have been recorded in the region. A distinguishing character of the region's rock-art is the prolific occurrence of an anthropomorphic figure (Morwood, 1985). Detailed analysis of these figures showed that they were spatially restricted to the region, and were depicted with stylistic elements that, while adhering to a regional style, potentially encoded additional information about group affiliation (Ross, 1997).

On this basis, Ross argued that the style of anthropomorphic figures reflected a spatial differentiation between social groups.

What therefore emerges about this region is a social system that sort to distinguish itself from its neighbours, but a contrasting economic system that was facilitated by a fluidity of movement. On this basis, it was clear that there were some complex spatial processes evident in the behaviour of people living in the region. Significantly, these spatial processes involved social and economic interactions, so that any approach to understanding them, using spatial patterning of archaeological finds, could not be understood purely from the viewpoint of subsistence and environmental context. Understanding them necessarily involved invoking procedures capable of characterising economic and social spatial relationships along with environmental context.

A MULTI-SCALAR METHODOLOGY

The way archaeologists use scale to obtain different perspectives on the past, was explored in this study through a methodology that involved analysis performed at multiple scales. In the past, studies have emphasised the utility of using data from different scales (Gamble, 1986:26), or have stressed the need to ensure all analysis was performed at a single spatial scale (Lourandos, 1996:15). Rarely has the focus been to perform the analysis at multiple scales.

To explore how scale provided different perspectives on the past, the study focused upon spatial variation in the region's archaeological record. There were several methodological advantages to the use of a spatial framework for investigating the influence of scale:

1. *Diversity of evidence*. For the vast majority of archaeological evidence, location was easier to measure than antiquity, permitting the incorporation of a greater diversity and volume of data.
2. *Control of scale*. With a set of data referenced by location, spatially sub-sampling the dataset simplified exploration of variation due to spatial scale (Mueller, 1975).
3. *Analytical tools*. A geographic information system (GIS) provided a powerful tool for managing and analysing the archaeological dataset (Green, 1990). The utility of the GIS lay in its ability to manipulate the visual display of spatial data, and to provide the analytical tools necessary for describing its spatial relationships.
4. *Ethnographic analogues*. A large volume of detailed anthropological descriptions exists for the spatial component of hunter–gatherer behaviour. In addition, the majority of the archaeological evidence used in the study comprised sites estimated to be of relatively recent antiquity (see Ridges 2003:136), and for the purposes of this study, were assumed to reflect reasonably well the important elements recorded ethnographically.

The choice of a regional focus for investigating the influence of scale was also important since it was at such a scale that the interaction between many of the important components of hunter–gatherer behaviour could be observed. As Gamble (1986:31) noted in his review of the Palaeolithic settlement of Europe, the importance of examining regional hunter–gatherer behaviour was that it encompassed:

> ...the determinant features of the environment, to which groups must adapt, but also the continual process of social reproduction which specifies that the habitat shall be exploited according to the principles of hunter–gatherer formation in order to sustain and reproduce social existence.

Hence, a regional focus permitted the interaction between subsistence, social and economical behaviour to be studied, with the hope that these would produce differences in archaeological pattern at different scales.

Given what was already known about the rock-art of the region, and the importance of trade, this study explored the issue of scale through the spatial analysis of these two key aspects of the region's archaeology. The spatial analysis performed on each of these components was necessarily different. For the analysis of site distributions (used as a surrogate for studying the spatial influence of trade), the approach was to use predictive modelling in order to describe the main characteristics of where sites occur. Such an approach was afforded by the non-site nature of lithic material in the region. In contrast, the analysis of rock-art figures was by necessity a point pattern problem, since rock-art sites occur in the region at discrete locations. Point patterns were investigated using a combination of distribution averages and link analysis. Distribution averages were used to describe trends in the distribution of various features of the rock-art, whereas the link analysis examined the spatial relationships between art sites.

Variation in archaeological pattern due to differences in scale was examined by performing the analysis for both datasets at different spatial and categorical scales. For site distributions, the different scales involved two levels of spatial scale and involved performing the modelling at the region level, along with repeating the modelling for two smaller areas within the region (see Figure 10.2). For the analysis of the rock-art figures, the analysis was performed at a single spatial scale, the whole region, but involved two categorical levels, the distribution of different motif types, and the distribution of design elements of a single motif type (anthropomorphs).

The data used for modelling site distributions came from over a decade of archaeological survey in the region (Davidson, 1993). Additional sources included work undertaken in theses (Drury, 1996; James, 1993; Kippen, 1992), work undertaken for cultural heritage management, and the Queensland archaeological site register. In total, 1,795 locations containing archaeological material were included in the database, and of these, 1,620 contained stone artefacts. For the purposes of describing regional and sub-regional settlement patterns, the results of modelling only those locations that contained stone artefacts and were classified as 'sites', are described here (details of tool type and raw material models are reported in Ridges, 2003). The modelling of these sites was used to examine the main factors influencing the location of activity associated with the manufacture of stone tools and how this changed when the models were recalculated at a different spatial scale.

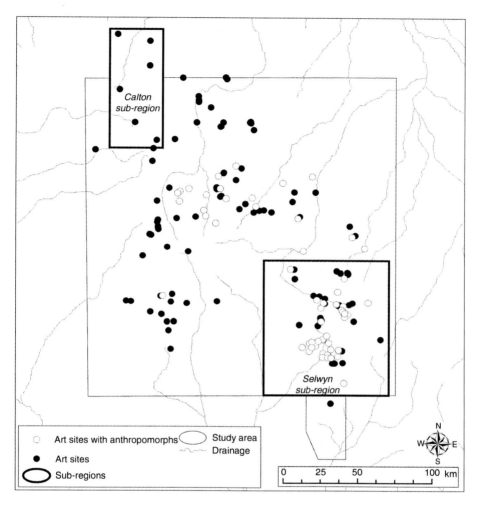

FIGURE 10-2. The location of sub-regions examined in this study.

The rock-art database contained 180 sites, and described a wide range of motif types, including geometric designs such as circles, dots and lines, through to figurative designs such as macropods, bird tracks and hand stencils. In total, 102 different motif types were recognised in the database. Varying levels of recording detail meant that in some instances only the presence or absence of particular designs was available. For others, the recording included a complete census of the figures depicted at the site. All the analysis described here utilised the presence or absence data only. In addition to this data, Ross (1997) had undertaken a detailed study of the distribution and form of anthropomorphic figures where she recorded the presence or absence of 57 design elements of those anthropomorphic figures located within 61 art sites. For the purpose of this study, this data was generalised to the presence or absence of these design elements at each site. Through performing the analysis on both these datasets, it was possible to explore, at the regional scale, variation in the spatial pattern of rock-art depiction at two different classificatory scales.

PREDICTIVE MODELLING RESULTS

The predictive modelling was performed using generalised additive modelling with a binomial family, a special form of logistic regression where the model is derived from non-linear interpolations of the independent variables (MathSoft, 1999). This approach offers a great deal of flexibility in the choice of variables that can be included into the model, whilst maintaining interpretability due to relaxing the need for variable transformation (Ridges 2003:107). For the open sites model, the dependent variable comprised the 1,620 locations that contained stone artefacts, and which were classified as sites, along with 1,795 randomly distributed points, used as pseudoabsences. The independent variables were elevation, slope, aspect, proximity to waterholes, proximity to drainage lines, proximity to drainage lines weighted by stream order, a wetness index, and a vegetation classification of LANDSAT MSS data (see Ridges 2003:124).

Figure 10.3 shows the predicted probability of finding sites containing stone artefacts, produced from the model. The important elements of this model are that the highest probabilities occur along the drainage lines, in the upper parts of the tributaries, mainly in the dissected valleys on the margins of the upland zones (compare Figure 10.1). From examining the amount of variance explained by the independent variables input into the model, it was found that the most important variables were the proximity to waterholes variables and slope. The model therefore indicated that, at the regional level, proximity to water and local terrain were the key factors determining where sites were located. This is largely what would be expected for people subsisting through hunting and gathering in a semi-arid landscape.

However, when the same procedures were repeated on the sub-regions, the character of the models was transformed somewhat in response to the effects of local context. For the site models produced in the Calton and Selwyn sub-regions (see Figure 10.2), the input data included only those sites occurring within each sub-region, and new sets of random points corresponding to the number of archaeological locations recorded in each sub-region. For both sub-regions, the independent variables were the same as for the regional model, except that the resolution of the layers was slightly higher—250 m for the regional models and 100 m for the sub-regions.

Figure 10.4 illustrates the site model for the Calton sub-region, along with terrain and the difference between the sub-regional model and the regional model. The important points to notice about the sub-regional model are the high probability areas along the major creek system in the northwest of the region, and the broad area of high probability throughout the central and northeast areas of the sub-region. For the high probability areas along the creek system in the northwest of the sub-region, it can be seen in Figure 10.4 how there is little difference between

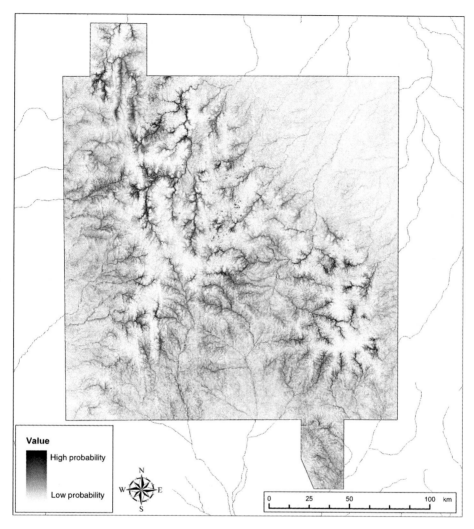

FIGURE 10-3. The regional sites model.

the sub-regional model, and the model derived for the entire region. This was not surprising due to the expectation that this part of the creek system provided the most plentiful and reliable sources of water. In contrast, Figure 10.4 also shows how the areas away from the drainage lines were predicted to have higher probability in the sub-regional model, than that predicted by the regional model.

The difference between the regional and sub-regional models is brought about by the occurrence of numerous local outcrops of a rock type that was used to manufacture stone axes. The Calton sub-region is in effect an intense axe production area, with axes from here being found over much of western Queensland and the Lake Eyre basin. Importantly, this has produced a measurable difference in the pattern of site

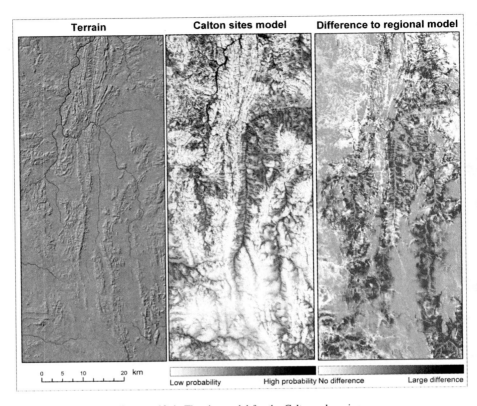

FIGURE 10-4. The site model for the Calton sub-region.

distribution within the sub-region. The result is that sites in the Calton sub-region are drawn away from the drainage lines and onto the plain where the geological outcrops occur, much more so than would be expected by looking at settlement patterns at the regional level only. In this case, behaviour associated with the production of stone axes has produced an identifiable difference in the local settlement pattern.

Repeating the same procedures for the Selwyn sub-region produces the results seen in Figure 10.5. The important point to note in this model is the locally higher values associated with the edge of the dissected plateau, and the lower probabilities predicted for the valleys around the perimeter of the plateau. The significant feature of the Selwyn region is the abundance of art sites located around the perimeter of the plateau. In the Calton sub-region, only six art sites have been recorded, whereas eighty-two art sites have been recorded in the Selwyn sub-region.

The higher predicted probabilities for sites in the sub-region model along the margins of the plateau, again reflects the influence of local context. Whereas there was an identifiable difference in the settlement pattern for mostly economic reasons in the Calton sub-region, in the Selwyn sub-region it is associated instead with what presumably are largely social reasons brought about through the production of rock-art. In the Selwyn case, there is an identifiable shift from the probability for

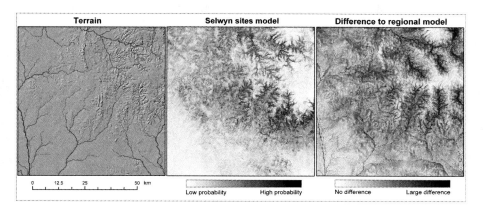

FIGURE 10-5. The site model for the Selwyn sub-region.

sites to be located adjacent to streams, towards areas abutting the base of the dissected plateau where art sites occur. Thus, for the Selwyn sub-region, the context of rock-art production created a modification in settlement pattern that was not well predicted by settlement patterns examined at the regional level.

ROCK-ART RESULTS

The first component of investigating spatial pattern in the region's rock-art assemblage was to examine the distribution of motifs and the anthropomorph design elements (ADEs) measured by Ross (1997). One of the difficulties encountered with this was comparing the 102 individual distributions for the motif types and 57 ADEs. To simplify these comparisons, each of the motifs (in this case considering just three groups of similar motif types) and each ADE are represented by a single point in Figure 10.6. Each point represents the average X and Y co-ordinates of all those sites containing the respective motif group or ADE. The axes in each plot are the respective co-ordinate averages for all art sites, and only those sites containing anthropomorphs, respectively.

In the plots shown in Figure 10.6, a point located near the centre of the axes indicates a distribution that is similar in character to the distribution of all art sites. In contrast, a point that occurs in the upper left-hand corner of the plot indicates a distribution that primarily occurs in the northwest range of the art site distribution. Comparison of the plots indicates that the spatial distribution for the motifs versus ADEs were quite different. For the motif groups, there is a tendency for bars to be located on the northeast margin of the art site distribution, whereas circles and linked arcs tend to occur on its southwest margin. From this it was deduced that there was a southwest to northeast distinction in the distribution of these three major motif groups.

In contrast to the motif groups, the ADE distribution is such that the majority of ADEs cluster around the origin of the plot – that is, they have a distribution that is

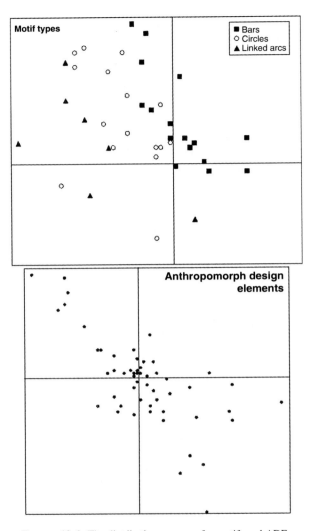

FIGURE 10-6. The distribution averages for motifs and ADEs.

similar to the distribution of sites containing anthropomorphs. However, there are two groups of ADEs that tend to occur in either the northwest or southeast of the anthropomorph site distribution. In this case, the distribution of some ADEs tends to follow a northwest to southeast trend, and which is diametrically opposed to that trend seen for the major motif groups.

The differences in motif versus ADE distributions were examined further through link analysis (see Figure 10.7). The object of this analysis was to examine the location of each site that contained a particular motif or ADE, in relation to all other sites containing the same motif or ADE of interest. This was achieved by using the GIS to construct lines from each art site, to every other art site that

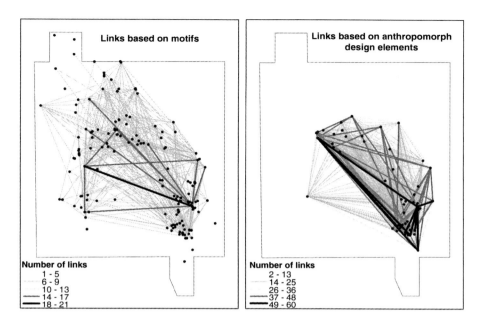

FIGURE 10-7. The link patterns for motifs and ADEs.

contained the same motif or ADE. For the motifs, this resulted in around 15,000 'links' between sites, and around 18,000 'links' between sites for the sites containing anthropomorphs. For any pair of sites, there may be multiple links depending upon the number of motifs or ADEs the two sites had in common. In Figure 10.7, those links involving a larger number of shared motif or ADEs are shaded in a darker grey and represented with a heavier line. To assist interpretation, the links involving fewer motifs or ADEs have been made transparent.

Significantly, the pattern of links for the motif types and the ADEs again demonstrate quite different characteristics. For the motif types, there are fewer links involving a large number of shared motifs, and little perceivable trend in their orientation. In contrast, the ADE links demonstrated a strong northwest–southeast trend, reinforcing the pattern seen in Figure 10.6. The pattern of ADE links indicates that there are many similarities between the design of anthropomorphs depicted in sites in the northwest and southeast of the anthropomorph distribution.

The differences in the spatial pattern seen for motifs and ADEs are significant because of what they reveal about regional social behaviour. In the case of the motif types, the northeast–southwest trend can be related to the drainage divide occurring in the region (see Figure 10.8). As was mentioned above, the drainage lines provided the main routes of travel in the region, and consequently, there is the likelihood that people entering and leaving the region did so from either the northeast or southwest. As many of the motifs found in the region also occur in neighbouring rock-art regions, the pattern seen in the links analysis for motifs may

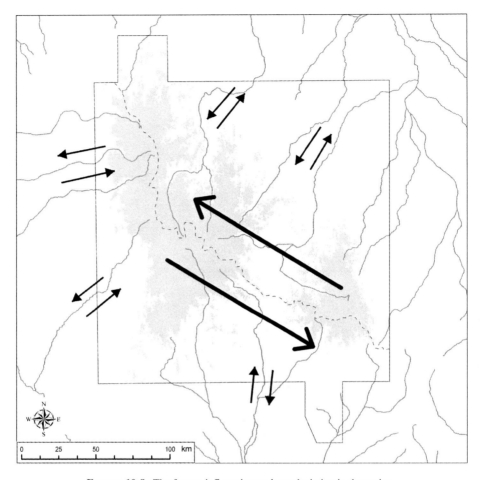

FIGURE 10-8. The factors influencing rock-art depiction in the region.

indicate that the lack of within-region pattern results from the important motif links
occurring at a much broader scale, that is between regions.

In contrast, the northwest–southeast trend seen in the pattern of ADE distribution can be related to the two sets of uplands occurring in the region. The
composition of ADEs at different sites appears to have served as a mechanism for
reaffirming the links between groups of people living in each of the upland areas.
This is consistent with Roth's (1897:42) interpretation that the region was occupied
by a single language group, but containing two sub-populations. It is also consistent
with Ross' (1997) findings that anthropomorphs represent a unique artistic style
seen only in the region, and which most likely was associated with the maintenance
of group identity. In addition, it can be seen from these results that group identity
was also reinforced by the pattern of its distribution within the region. Hence,
despite the single spatial scale of the rock-art data set, it was relatively clear from

this analysis that at the regional scale, quite different processes were operating on two distinct social levels.

DISCUSSION

This study highlighted some of the complexities associated with understanding regional hunter–gatherer behaviour. Importantly, these complexities take on quite different personas depending on the perspective used to examine regional behaviour. For instance, at the regional level, settlement patterns appear to be driven by the requirements of subsisting through hunting and gathering in a semi-arid landscape. However, within that regional trend there remains significant local variation brought about by local context. In these cases, the drivers at a local level can be quite different to those seen at the regional level, even though this only involves minor shifts within the overall characteristics of the regional settlement pattern.

It is also significant that at a single spatial scale, the region, quite contrasting archaeological patterns can be produced at different categorical scales. The analysis of the rock-art data demonstrated this issue by revealing what were likely to be two relatively distinct levels of social behaviour interacting at the regional scale. The way archaeological data are categorised can therefore just as equally produce quite different perspectives of past behaviour as can altering spatial or temporal scale.

However, what is perhaps most important about the findings of this study is that the character of regional hunter–gatherer behaviour is composed of a complex mix of social, economic and subsistence related behaviour, all varying and inter-acting at different scales. This returns us to the first point made in this chapter, which is how scale is important for defining perspective on complex systems. What has been seen here is that regional hunter–gatherer behaviour is a complex system, and understanding it will not only depend on how scale is used to study it from different perspectives, but it also requires the use of different perspectives in order to capture all of its inherent complexity.

Consequently, it can hopefully be seen how scale, and its close association with defining archaeological perspective, is an important theoretical issue. Not so much in terms of the way scale offers new ways of interpreting archaeological pattern, but as a means through which more explicit statements can be made about how different perspectives are defined and related to one another. To date, arch-aeological theory about hunters and gatherers has not dealt with the complexities of variation in regional behaviour to any great degree. Bettinger (1991:3) claims that in part this stems from viewing hunter–gatherers as primitive, and its corollary that therefore they should be understandable in simple, generalised terms. However, as was demonstrated in this study, at the regional level even relatively straightforward processes like hunter–gatherer settlement patterns, can become complex when different scales are brought into play. Thus, the problem is just as likely to be related to the difficulty of understanding complex systems, even if those systems might be comprised of relatively simple processes. It would therefore appear that scale might prove to be an important theoretical issue for more explicit discussions about the complexities of regional behaviour of all kinds, and can hopefully lead to more explicit statements about the way we employ existing archaeological theory in different contexts.

REFERENCES

Bettinger, R.L., 1991, *Hunter–Gatherers: Archaeological and Evolutionary Theory*. Plenum Press, New York.

Binford, L.R., 1983, *Working at Archaeology*. Academic Press, New York.

Davidson, I., 1993, Archaeology of the Selwyn Ranges. In *People of the Stone Age. Hunter-Gatherers and Early Farmers*, edited by G. Burenhult, pp. 210–211. Harper Collins, New York.

Davidson, I., Cook, N., Fischer, M., Ridges, M., Ross, J., and Sutton, S., in press, Archaeology in Another Country: Exchange and Symbols in North West Central Queensland. In *Many Exchanges: Archaeology, History, Community and the Work of Isabel McBryde*, edited by I. Macfarlane, M.-J. Mountain, and R. Paton. Aboriginal History.

Davidson, I., Sutton, S., and Gale, S.J., 1993, The Human Occupation of Cuckadoo 1 Rockshelter, Northwest Central Queensland. In *Sahul in Review: Pleistocene Archaeology in Australia, New Guinea and Island Melanesia*, edited by M.A. Smith, M. Spriggs, and B. Fankhauser, pp. 164–172. Australian National University Press, Canberra.

Dobres, M., and Robb, J., 2000, Agency in Archaeology. Paradigm or Platitude? In *Agency in Archaeology*, edited by M. Dobres and J. Robb, pp. 3–17. Routledge, London.

Drury, T., 1996, An Investigation into the Influence of Geological Landscapes and Land Systems on Stone Artefact Variability in the Selwyn Range, North West Queensland. Unpublished BA (Hons.), University of New England.

Gamble, C., 1986, *The Palaeolthic Settlement of Europe*. Cambridge University Press, Cambridge.

Gould, R.A., 1980, *Living Archaeology*. Cambridge University Press, Cambridge.

Green, S.W., 1990, Approaching Archaeological Space: An Introduction to the Volume. In *Interpreting Space: GIS and Archaeology*, edited by K.M.S. Allen, S.W. Green, and E.B.W. Zubrow, pp. 3–8. Taylor and Francis, London.

James, R.E., 1993, *Stones, Samples and the Stories We Tell*. Unpublished BA (Hons) Thesis, University of New England.

Jones, P., 1984, Red Ochre Expeditions: An Ethnographic and Historical Analysis of Aboriginal Trade. In *The Lake Eyre Basin*, pp. 3–10. Journal of the Anthropological Society of South Australia, Volume 22.

Kippen, K., 1992, An Analysis of Stone Artefacts from Twelve Open Scatters in the Selwyn Range, Northwest Central Queensland. Unpublished B.A. (Hons) Thesis, University of New England.

Lourandos, H., 1996, Change in Australian Prehistory: Scale, Trends and Frameworks of interpretation. In *Australian Archaeology '95: Proceedings of the 1995 Australian Archaeological Association Annual Conference, Volume 6*, edited by S. Ulm, I. Lilley, and A. Ross, pp. 15–21. Anthropology Museum, University of Queensland, St Lucia.

Lourandos, H., and Ross, A., 1994, The Great Intensification Debate: Its History and Place in Australian Archaeology. *Australian Archaeology* 39:54–63.

Mathsoft, 1999, *S-Plus 2000. Guide to Statistics*. Volume 2. Mathsoft, Seattle.

Morwood, M.J., 1985, Facts and Figures: Notes on Rock Art in the Mt Isa Area, Northwest Queensland. *Rock Art Research* 2:140–5.

Mueller, J.W., 1975, Archaeological Research as Cluster Sampling. In *Sampling in Archaeology*, edited by J.W. Mueller, pp. 33–41. University of Arizona Press, Tucson.

O'Neill, R.V., and King, A.W., 1998, Homage to St. Michael; Or Why are there So Many Books on Scale? In *Ecological Scale. Theory and Applications*, edited by D.L. Peterson and V.T. Parker, pp. 3–15. Columbia University Press, New York.

Ridges, M., 2003, Numerous Indications. The Archaeology of Regional Hunter-Gatherer Behaviour in Northwest Central Queensland, Australia. Unpublished Phd Thesis, University of New England.

Ross, J., 1997, Painted Relationships: An Archaeological Analysis of a Distinctive Anthropomorphic Rock Art Motif in Northwest Central Queensland. Unpublished BA (Hons) Thesis, University of New England.

Roth, W.E., 1897, *Ethnological Studies among the North-West Central Queensland Aborigines.* Government Printer, Brisbane.

Schiffer, M.B., 1988, The Structure of Archaeological Theory. *American Antiquity* 53:461–483.

Trigger, B.G., 1989, *A History of Archaeological Thought.* Cambridge University Press, Cambridge.

Trigger, B.G., 1995, Expanding Middle-Range Theory. *Antiquity* 69:449–458.

Watson, P., 1980, The Use of Mulligan River Pituri. *Occasional Papers in Anthropology* 10:25–42.

CHAPTER 11

Custer's Last Battle: Struggling with Scale

RICHARD A. FOX

INTRODUCTION

Increased scale enhances the scope and depth of historical interpretation, paving the way for more accurate constructions of bygone events. Improved interpretation through increased scale also has a corollary; the better the interpretive results, the more strained the defense of cherished beliefs about the past. Few examples in archaeology better illustrate this than Joshua's biblical conquest of the Promised Land – from ca. 1407 BCE to 1400 BCE according to orthodox dating (derived from biblical synchronisms with Near Eastern absolute chronologies, primarily the Egyptian). Yet nothing in Egyptian records speaks of a Conquest, directly or indirectly, nor do the biblical conquest (Joshua) and settlement traditions (Judges) hint at Egyptians in the land. Such silence is rather odd; the Conquest (allegedly) happened during the Late Bronze Age, a period well-known, thanks in no small part to archaeology, as the height of Egyptian power and hegemony in Canaan. Indeed, the Book of Joshua's "conquered cities" (at least those identified) – including Jericho – have yielded to archaeologists hardly a trace of Late Bronze conflict, and some lack altogether traces of settlement at that time (e.g., Stiebing, 1989). And not surprisingly, Canaanite Late Bronze Age settlements are rarely fortified – a sure reflection of Egyptian control.

But for some, preservation of the biblical story is paramount, and all manner of "solutions" have been proposed. Making archaeology fit orthodox Conquest dating is one way. Destruction layers, for example, are ripped from their terminal Middle Bronze Age temporal context (ca. 1550 BCE) and reassigned to the end of Late Bronze I (ca. 1400 BCE) (e.g., Bimson and Livingston, 1987). Such attempts accept the absolute chronology upon which the Holy Land's Bronze and Iron ages (and later) history is built. Others reject it. Rohl (1995), for example, re-invents the Egyptian absolute chronology to validate biblical history. Still others are committed to an historical Conquest, but not its orthodox dating. Using the accepted chronology, they put the Conquest earlier or later. One destination, for example (e.g., Anati, in Stiebing, 1985:58–59), is the terminal Early Bronze Age (just after 2200

RICHARD A. FOX ● University of South Dakota

BCE), a quite attractive destination because, unlike the Late Bronze, it is "Egypt-free" and has plenty of destroyed walled cities (including Jericho).

Of course, none of these "solutions" can explain how walls tumbling to the sound of trumpets, the Red Sea parting, and a day-long stationary sun (not to mention a host of other unusual phenomena) made it into otherwise reliable history. But other snags are unique to each "solution". Rohl's "new chronology" flounders in several ways, including circular reasoning. He argues that Meggido VIII reflects Solomon's wealth (a biblical story). Therefore the accepted chronology must be shuffled to reflect this (and other of Rohl's arguments). The "new chronology" then validates biblical historicity. The Middle Bronze Age "solution" crams the entire Late Bronze into 20 years, a rather insurmountable obstacle at many sites – e.g., the four extensive Late Bronze I building levels at Meggido. And an Early Bronze Conquest extends the Israelite formative period to a thousand years or so, an impossibly long period especially in light of Aharoni's discovery of early Israel's Iron Age I (ca. 1200–1000 BCE) hill country settlement (see, e.g., Finkelstein and Silberman, 2001:105 ff).

The bottom line is such "solutions" to secular archaeology in the Holy Land create more problems than they solve; indeed they create problems far beyond the reach of the would-be "solvers." The vast scale archaeology brings to the ancient biblical world is vexing indeed. Similarly, the scale available in historical archaeology can also vex worldviews – not so much the spiritual, but certainly nationalism and patriotism. Such is sometimes the case for the Custer battle – that famous event of June 25, 1876 on Little Big Horn River in what is now Montana[1].

My historical–archaeological investigations (1983 to 1985) at the Custer battlefield show that Brevet Major General George A. Custer's battalion of 7th US Cavalry troopers entered the fray in good tactical order, but that stability disintegrated, leading to denouement largely amid panic and fear (Fox, 1993, 1996, 1997). While certainly the soldiers were brave – as are all with the courage to enter battle – there was no heroic last stand. Such a view is contrary to the image held by many, if not most – the "last stand" image, the heroic stand against insurmountable odds, the gallant but futile defense to the last man, if not the last bullet. More than anything, "Custer's last stand" is a symbol of white America's

---

[1] Results of Custer's fate – he and all 210 men in his battalion perished – are best known. Less well-known are the valley and Reno-Benteen fights, which, with the Custer fight, make up the Little Big Horn battle. Major Marcus Reno, second-in-command of the 7th Cavalry, initiated fighting by attacking the Indian village located in the valley. Ultimately Reno's battalion was driven away. The soldiers scrambled in confusion out of the valley to high bluffs across the river. There the Reno-Benteen fight began. By chance Reno met Captain Frederick Benteen, then returning with his battalion from a scout upriver. The two battalions consolidated on the bluffs where warriors laid siege throughout June 25th and well into the next day.

Custer's battle took place some four miles north of the Reno-Benteen battlefield. After ordering Reno's attack in the valley, Custer, intending to capture noncombatants, veered to the right and marched north unopposed as the Indians confronted Reno. Warriors belatedly learned of Custer's battalion, by then in pursuit of noncombatants fleeing their village, as they drove Reno to the bluffs. Many left to meet the new threat. Ultimately a numerically superior force of warriors gathered. Most likely it was over in little more than an hour; Custer and all the troopers in his battalion were dead. Indian casualties are difficult to estimate; perhaps forty or fifty warriors died. Though most with Reno and Benteen survived, the Army failed in its objective to remove the Sioux to their reservation.

ethos, and as such it is difficult to overcome (or should I say impossible?). Indeed, over the past decade, my interpretation has provoked various defenses of the last stand image. But, as I show here, such defenses often err in various illogical, sometimes torturous ways. Reactions such as these help illustrate the fine-grained scale available in historical archaeology.

THE CUSTER BATTLE BRIEFLY

Support for a "last stand" exists, at least superficially, in the documentary record. Some Sioux and Northern Cheyenne – Custer's foes on the Little Big Horn – said as much. "I tell no lies about dead men," assured Sitting Bull (in 1877), who continued: "These men who came with [Custer] were as good [as] men who ever fought." Several years afterwards (1881) Low Dog told the same story, "The white warriors stood their ground bravely, and none of them made any attempt to get away." Still later (in 1905), Rain-in-the-Face recounted, "I had always thought that white men were cowards, but I had great respect for them after [the Custer battle]".

These and a few other accounts reflect a human propensity, one put well by a French artillery officer and contemporary of Custer, Ardant du Picq (1946:63). To paraphrase him, the vanquished always console themselves, and the victors never contradict. And those who told such stories had reason not to contradict. While they won, within a year following the Little Big Horn battle their way of life came to an end. Reservation life loomed. Thrust into uncertain times, leaders like Sitting Bull (the people white chroniclers sought out) tended to assuage their listeners. Thus Indian accounts from the decade or so after the battle are by and large complimentary.

But archaeology on Custer's field paints a different picture, one of denouement amid panic and fear. Cartridge cases (spent cartridges) show this best. Operation of a firearm leaves a firing pin mark – called a signature – on the cartridge case. Firing pin signatures vary between individual firearms. These "unique" signatures, plus a record of the exact location of each casing, make it possible to identify individual positions and trace individuals across the battlefield. For the cavalry, unique signatures reveal that some troopers manned skirmish lines on Calhoun Hill (Figure 11.1). The two lines are indicative of tactical stability. Yet this kind of patterning is absent at all other sectors occupied by soldiers. This suggests a breakdown in stability, or tactical disintegration. It appears on archaeological grounds that disintegration began around Calhoun Hill (see Figure 11.1) where soldiers ceased skirmishing, bunched together, and eventually fled into the Keogh sector.

Consistent with this pattern are numerous accounts by Custer battle veterans who in 1876 were lesser lights among their people. Related decades after the battle, when the tribes' lots in life had been settled and with little left to lose, these stories are far more candid. They tell of a loss of cohesion among the troops. Like material remains, the hundreds of Indian eyewitness accounts provide a record of combat behaviors – their own and those of the soldiers they defeated. Indeed, behaviors attendant to flight – panic and fear – are found in numerous Indian descriptions of soldier behavior, often as metaphor. Runs the Enemy, for instance, recalled that the

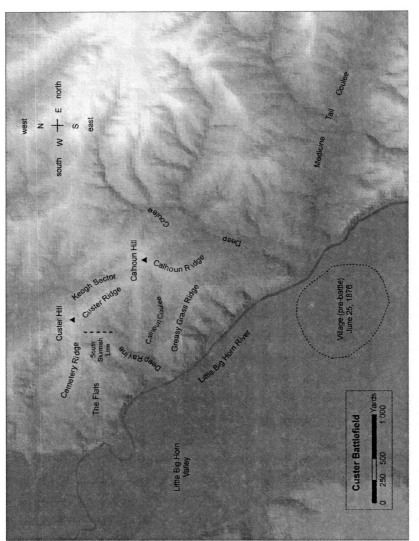

FIGURE 11-1. Custer's 1876 battlefield and vicinity near Hardin, Montana, with features and places identified in the text. For explanations of the customary and Cheyenne directional schemes (i.e. N–S–E–W) also see the text.

rush from Calhoun Hill looked like a "stampede of buffalo." Once in the Keogh
sector, warriors, using clubs, knives and hatchets, jumped among the soldiers. Gall,
Dewey Beard, Moving Robe, and others remembered this. Horned Horse recol-
lected that "it was just like this [fingers intertwined], Indians and white men." Gall
said that the soldiers "threw their [carbines] aside and fought with little guns."
Fleeing soldiers acted as if drunk (Hollow Horn Bear), were shot from behind (Red
Feather) and were jerked from horses (White Bull).

Clearly mayhem had developed. But how? A look at battalion organization is
necessary. Custer's battalion operated in two wings. Capt. Myles Keogh commanded the right wing (companies C, I, L); Capt. George Yates directed the left
wing (companies E and F). Formerly in and around Medicine Tail Coulee, a
seasonal creek which feeds the Little Big Horn, the two wings had reunited at
Calhoun Hill. The right wing stayed there. Company L deployed in skirmish
formation on Calhoun Hill; the remaining two companies held in reserve, probably
in the Keogh sector.

Meanwhile, the left wing moved north along Custer Ridge, then northwesterly
into the Little Big Horn Valley, finally returning to Cemetery Ridge, so-called
because today a national cemetery is situated there.

During this time – as the left wing maneuvered – warrior numbers increased,
first a few, then more and more. Generally ignorant of the left wing movements, the
Indians cautiously infiltrated right wing positions. Fighting remained desultory as
infiltration continued, to which many Indian accounts attest. Nonetheless, warriors
eventually got very close to right wing positions, some threatening the riderless
horses – a strategy reported by Gall, the Hunkpapa Sioux leader.

Threats to the cavalry mounts, and the nearness of warriors, demanded relief.
Capt. Keogh sent one of his reserve companies into Calhoun Coulee, where many
Indians had by now gathered. Wooden Leg recalled this "charge," as he called it,
but did not know that it was Company C, a fact deduced from various lines of
evidence. The company, about 40 strong, sent the antagonists scattering.

What happened next? Red Bird recalled that Lame White Man, a Cheyenne,
rallied the warriors and they attacked Company C. This was the beginning of the
end for Custer's battalion. The company collapsed and fled toward Calhoun Hill.

In response, the men in L Company shifted their skirmish line position, firing
west in order to cover the men from C. Originally the line had faced south, stymieing
the few warriors who had followed the two wings out of Medicine Tail Coulee.
Confusion among the right wing troops emboldened other warriors. These, including
Crazy Horse and Gall, joined in the attack. Soon the panic engulfed L Company. Now,
with both companies broken, the survivors from C and L bunched together (they
gathered in a "bunch" according to Runs the Enemy). Some soldiers fired, leaving
the cluster of casings found by the archaeologists. Then they fled into the Keogh
sector toward Company I, now also under attack – by Two Moon and others.

Warriors followed C and L survivors, and their movements can be tracked by
the signatures on spent cartridges they ejected along the way. By now the entire
right wing had disintegrated. Routed, right wing survivors, with warriors among
them, fled the Keogh sector, rushing toward Custer Hill. The left wing had taken up
this position in response to the right wing collapse. Out of approximately 120 men

in the right wing, about 20 made it to Custer Hill. There they linked up with the 90 or so men in the left wing, which included Custer and his staff. The battalion had been reduced by half – to about 105 men.

There – on Custer Hill – the survivors were surrounded. Though matters had evolved into a desperate situation, officers evidently restored some measure of control. Warriors, moments earlier aggressive and bold, reverted again to stealth tactics, presumably as a result of the restoration in order. The siege – it lasted ''just a few minutes'' according to Hollow Horn Bear – had begun. Two Moon recalled that a trumpeter blew a call whereupon about 45 men – five mounted, the others on foot – rushed from Custer Hill toward the river. The mounted soldiers, as He Dog put it, tried to get away to the south. But they did not make it.

The mounted men probably intended to ride to Reno for help. The major and his three companies had earlier charged toward the southern end of the Indian village, a sprawling camp along the Little Big Horn on its west side. Unknown to Custer, however, warriors had thwarted Reno's battalion (about 130 men), forcing it to the Reno/Benteen battlefield. Upon reaching the bluffs, Reno met Benteen, who also commanded a battalion of three companies. As the two joined up, the warriors – virtually all had responded to Reno's attack – began to learn of Custer's presence. Word of ''the other soldiers'' spread slowly. Individuals and groups began to move downriver, collecting around Custer over time. Eventually more than a thousand warriors reached the Custer Ridge vicinity. Such numbers helped fuel the disintegration process which resulted in a shattered command ensconced on Custer Hill.

The 40 or so pedestrian troopers who rushed from Custer Hill probably intended to divert attention from the five horseman, allowing them to reach Reno. Whatever their intent, the troopers – E Company as we now know – succumbed to panic induced by a heavy Indian attack. Iron Hawk recalled the Sioux charge, one which carried the Indians right into the terrified soldiers. The company disintegrated. Bear Lying Down thought the troopers acted as if drunk. According to Lights, soldiers fired wildly in the air, and warriors wrenched their guns away. The attack caused E Company to ''swerve,'' as one Indian put it, toward a rugged coulee now called Deep Ravine. Many, such as Good Voiced Elk and Standing Bear, recalled that surviving soldiers jumped into the coulee. Once there, the fighting evolved into a hide-and-seek affair as soldiers struggled on their own. The fate that earlier befell C Company had now engulfed Company E.

Meanwhile, the siege at Custer Hill had taken its toll – a grim siege, not the swirling, glorious finale of history. About 60 men had remained behind when E Company rushed from the hill. Of these 60, some fled from time to time toward Deep Ravine, perhaps 20 in all, leaving some 40 to die on Custer Hill, including the general. Indeed, in the aftermath, military observers, Lt. Edward Godfrey included, counted 42 bodies on Custer Hill, mostly identified as men from F Company. Their deaths, and this hill, more than anything have immortalized the Custer battle – ''the last stand'' of history. Yet the last fighting did not occur on Custer Hill. The struggle ended in and around Deep Ravine. Flying Hawk, American Horse and Young Two Moon (not to be confused with his uncle, Two Moon) said exactly that, echoing Respects Nothing, who reported, ''[The soldiers] at Custer Hill were all killed before those were down along the ravine.'' (Ricker 1906).

The Custer battle ended in the tangled brush of Deep Ravine. In all, the battle lasted about 90 minutes; around an hour of subdued exchanges as cautious warriors infiltrated, followed by the dissolution of tactical stability – when "the battle became furious" as Foolish Elk described it. Gall, Crow King and others estimated the "furious" activity at about 30 minutes. Iron Hawk summarized the whole affair. Referring to the transition from stability to disintegration, he said, "Custer's men in the beginning shot straight, but later they shot like drunken men, firing into the ground, into the air, wildly in every way" – until all were killed. And so Custer's last battle ended.

STRUGGLING WITH SCALE

When Custer's last battle ended, the battle over what happened began. Because I reject the "last stand," my ideas have added considerable new fuel to that fire. My synthesis (Fox, 1993) is scalar. It ends with the broad sweep of events that led Custer that day to the killing field. These events, I argued, cannot be fully understood without a detailed understanding of the battle itself. So before I dealt with prebattle events, I built the historical–archaeological interpretation of the actual battle. That construction is rich with history, but it is history mediated (as in the summary above, where I favor Indians accounts that speak of panic, not of unyielding soldiers) by an archaeological foundation. Thus it is that I opened with an archaeological analysis, an analysis that implicated tactical disintegration in the defeat of Custer's battalion. Thus it is not surprising that critics seek to undermine the archaeology of Custer's last fight. In doing so, however, some tend to selectively ignore history or pejoratively dismiss archaeologically generated ideas as "revisionist."

Ignoring History

I pointed out a decade ago in my historical-archaeological synthesis (Fox, 1993:128) that relic collecting has occurred on Custer's field, even citing several episodes. "Last stand" advocates most commonly dismiss the Custer battlefield archaeology by floating the relic collection argument. Over the years, they say, Custer Hill (or whatever sector) has been picked clean, so Fox's conclusion that cartridge case patterning indicates disintegration can be ignored. Mostly this is done in conversation, on websites, and on internet discussion boards, but Larry Sklenar has made a specific point of it. He writes " . . . some investigators attempted to write the definitive account of Custer's defeat, even though parts of the field had been corrupted by *millions* of souvenir hunters" (Sklenar 2000:xiii; emphasis added). Now I doubt "millions" have collected. Nonetheless, so it is that Sklenar, in constructing his Custer battle (basically a "last stand"), issues himself a license to ignore my historical-archaeological synthesis.

Oddly, Sklenar (2000:276), after rejecting our controlled, systematic archaeological surveys (Scott and Fox, 1987; Scott, et al., 1989), proceeds to use poorly reported material remains collected unsystematically in the 1940s and 1950s to support his analysis. But this is just an aside, inexplicable as it is. Like all others who resort to the relic-collecting argument, Sklenar ignores (or misses) the fact that I cite (Fox, 1993:246–247) several eyewitnesses whose observations essentially support the cartridge case patterning uncovered during the 1980s digs. Soldiers helped bury the dead. Observing the aftermath, they too wondered what happened. Some commented on the distribution of cartridge cases. Sgt. John Ryan (1923) wrote of the field in general. He recalled that other than a few cartridge cases beneath Custer, "strangely" he saw none elsewhere (Fox 1993:159). While this is an error – archaeology turned up government cartridge cases in all sectors occupied by troops –something clearly baffled Ryan, who probably expected to see in spent cartridges something like a "last stand."

Lt. Charles DeRudio seemed equally as baffled, telling an 1879 official inquiry that he saw but "few shells...[and on Custer Hill] there were a few shells of our caliber" (Nichols 1983:359–360). Lt. George Wallace, when asked at the same inquiry if he saw government casings at locations other than Calhoun Hill, replied there were "very few" (Nichols 1983:76). Both Wallace and DeRudio, probably to soften the implications of their testimony, allowed that maybe Indians retrieved cartridge cases. Some individuals (unnamed) said the same to Charles Roe, a second Cavalry officer and Custer battle student. But Roe reported that others (also unnamed) did not buy the Indians-collected-them argument. Rather they saw in the patterning what amounts to disintegration. Roe (1927) wrote of their view, "Much fatigued and worn out [certainly a contributing factor in disintegration; see Fox, 1993:267–269], the men may not have been able to fully exert themselves, [this] evidenced from the fact that very few cartridge shells were found."

A few observers actually reported cartridge case counts. A week after the battle, Captain Myles Moylan reported that he saw as many as 40 empty government cartridges on Calhoun Hill (Frost, 1976:246). Three years later Moylan remembered 28 cartridge cases on Calhoun Hill around one man, with scattered shells "between the bodies" (Nichols, 1983:263). As well, Wallace saw on Calhoun Hill piles of 25–30 spent casings at "one or two places" (Nichols, 1983:76). And Private John Dolan (Anonymous, 1992:8) recalled during the summer of 1876 that "some twenty" spent rounds lay near Sergeant Jeremiah Finley, whose body was discovered on Calhoun Ridge. But these numbers are not especially important. What is important is what might be called an "historical pattern"; nobody (to my knowledge) ever reported cartridge case counts for sectors other than Calhoun Hill and Calhoun Ridge. This "pattern" does not at all conflict with the historical observation that tactical stability in Calhoun sectors disintegrated, eventually leading to denouement.

A twist on the relic collection argument is that we know Custer Hill was picked clean because early battlefield superintendents had to salt the field to provide visitors with satisfactory experiences. This is entirely anecdotal. No one to my knowledge has ever produced any evidence. But never mind...note the unfounded assumption – salting took place because Custer Hill got picked clean. But the practice, if such did take place, can be accounted for with another unfounded assumption – namely, salting happened because originally there was little or nothing there. Obviously such exercises lead nowhere. One thing is certain though. If relic hunters picked Custer Hill clean, or otherwise seriously compromised the archaeological record, then they were quite particular. They sure left a lot of spent Indian casings (ammunitions for the many types of breech-loading firearms carried by warriors are easily distinguished from government ammunitions fired by the two weapons troopers carried, the Springfield carbine and Colt revolver).

Revisionist History

Some critics find it convenient to counter my historical archeology synthesis of Custer's last battle by labeling it as politically correct. Michno (1997:285) seems to do this, but with subtlety; he mentions no one by name. Rather there are "those who use the physical record for their own moral agendas" (Michno, 1997:285). So too does David Evans. According to him the historical record "does not require re-engineering by revisionist historians" (Evans, 1999:281). Equipped with this bias, Evans (1999:263–301) constructs his battle. How does he do this? By ignoring "revisionist history", Evans frees the material record from my historical–archaeological synthesis. Now it can be used to suit his purposes. This is fair enough, except that he uses the archaeological record piecemeal, selecting from it only what seems (to him) to support this or that interpretation. Evans' practice is the "handmaiden to history" approach, a view rejected, over the last 40 years or so, by archaeologists and historians involved in shaping historical archaeology as a distinctly independent discipline.

The "handmaiden" approach, as I noted in 1993 (Fox, 1993:9), is inherently faulty because it misuses archaeological data by failing to consider the contextual significance of material remains. Here is an example. Evans (1999:270ff) deploys some soldiers to Greasy Grass Ridge and has them fighting there. Eventually Indian pressure increased sufficiently to cause them to break and run. Yet, as I pointed out in my synthesis (Fox, 1993:99), there is no archaeological evidence for soldiers fighting on this elevation. But it was a warrior stronghold. Several clusters of Indian cartridge cases show this, including the government cases (from captured carbines) found in the clusters (Fox, 1993:99). Evans, who appeals only to his interpretation of documents for this deployment, overlooks the archaeology here. Yet in contrast, for example, he imagines in detail the demise of a single trooper based on six artifacts at another sector – three carbine casings, a Colt casing, a Colt bullet, and a deformed .50 caliber bullet. Selective use of the archaeological record leads only to faulty ideas about the nature of this battle.

Confusing History

Custer Ridge, defined at either end by Calhoun and Custer hills, is the primary directional reference for most battle descriptions. The ridge is oriented roughly northwest–southeast in relation to magnetic north (refer to Figure 11.1). Euro-american descriptions customarily refer to the Custer Hill end as north, Calhoun

Hill is the southern extremity, the Keogh sector is east, while west is the river side of Custer Ridge. But in some Indian accounts north is equivalent to customary east, south to west, east to south, and west to customary north. Ridge orientation makes either usage acceptable (see Fox, 1993:150).

Bob Snelson's (2002) version of Custer's last battle is in part based on a flawed understanding of the Indian directional scheme. Recall my historical–archaeological construction pits Lame White Man against C Company, which made its foray from a reserve position in the Keogh sector. Not so, according to Snelson (2002:70–72). In his version (basically a "last stand" in which panic overcomes the few still alive at the very end), warrior threats caused Custer's five companies to retreat to Calhoun Hill. Two withdrew from near the mouth of Medicine Tail Coulee (MTC), the other three, C Company included, from a ridge next to the coulee but some distance upstream from its mouth. On the way, Custer dropped off C Company (or part of it) at Calhoun Ridge to serve as a rear guard, which Lame White Man soon attacked. In support, Snelson (2002:71) argues:

> The Lame White Man story has Company C charging onto Calhoun Ridge from the *east* via Calhoun Coulee. [But] [t]he Sioux and Cheyenne accounts typically identify north as west and *south as east*. [Therefore] Company C charged up Calhoun Ridge from the south [from the ridge next to MTC] which would have been *east* according to the warrior accounts (emphases added).

Snelson generalizes here. Sioux and Cheyenne accounts do not "typically" use the Indian directional scheme. They are few compared to those that do not. This is not a minor issue. Indeed, only two accounts tell us from whence came the soldiers confronted by Lame White Man. They are Kate Bighead's and Wooden Leg's. But neither simply says – as Snelson has it – that they came generally from the "east". Rather, Bighead's simply says from a ridge (Marquis, 1967:85ff), Wooden Leg's says from the *east end* of a ridge (Marquis, 1931:231). Context in both makes clear that the ridge is the one *where the soldiers were killed* (Marquis, 1931:231–237; Marquis, 1967:87–90). Bighead adds it was the ridge with the soldier memorial monument (Marquis, 1967:89). No ridge in MTC meets these criteria. But Custer Ridge does, and only Custer Ridge. The cavalry unit I identified (Fox, 1993:155ff) as C Company (an identification Snelson accepts) rode off the east end (customary south) of Custer Ridge. By generalizing, Snelson has overlooked or ignored the specifics that defeat his C Company interpretation.

Another overlooked specific is direction. The Bighead and Wooden Leg accounts say the troopers who came off the ridge rode toward the river. How, if they rode off the MTC ridge toward the Little Big Horn, did they end up at Calhoun Ridge? And why ride toward the river, a direction that, in Snelson's scheme, could only take the soldiers into the warriors responsible for the decision to retreat? Snelson's interpretation cannot accommodate these questions.

From Circular Reasoning to Special Pleading

Kate Bighead, also called Antelope, was, like Wooden Leg, a Northern Cheyenne. She was in the village on June 25, 1876. Her account was written by Thomas

Marquis, a Northern Cheyenne Agency physician during the 1920s and 1930s, who must have had direct contact with Bighead. Marquis' (1967:80–96) Bighead story recounts, among other things, how the attack by Lame White Man and group initiated major fighting, following which everything else happened. These two ingredients – a major fight that precipitates all else – make Lame White Man's attack very attractive to "last stand" theorists. So, it is said, Lame White Man's attack was directed toward Custer Hill.

Gregory Michno is among those who use Lame White Man's attack in this way, and one of his star witnesses is Kate Bighead. According to Michno, she watched Lame White Man attack the South Skirmish Line (SSL). The attack, says Michno, began below Custer Hill and against E Company, which rode off the Custer Hill hoping to stem the assault. By Michno's reckoning, the episode began about half an hour after the battle's first exchanges, which took place in the Calhoun vicinity, and which amounted to nothing more than a stalemate (Michno, 1997:195, 198, 200). This interpretation not only precludes tactical disintegration as an impetus for defeat, it also makes room for a "last stand", in Michno's eyes a protracted, nearly two-hour long struggle.

Michno has promoted his argument in two books, *Mystery of E Company* (1994) and *Lakota Noon* (1997). The way Michno does this in *Mystery* represents classic circular reasoning. He correctly observes that the SSL can be seen from the west end of Greasy Grass Ridge (the end that terminates at Deep Ravine). Bighead described Lame White Man's attack. Since that attack occurred on the SSL, she must have been located near the west end of Greasy Grass Ridge. Therefore Kate Bighead saw Lame White Man assault soldiers deployed on the SSL. After all, continues Michno, from this position her description does not fit anything south-east toward the Calhoun sectors (Michno, 1994:109, 273). Of course this kind of "reasoning" works for everyone. Put Bighead where she cannot see the other guy's version, just yours.

Circular reasoning is abandoned in *Lakota Noon*. So too is Greasy Grass Ridge. Nonetheless Bighead remains in a position to see Lame White Man's alleged SSL attack. Michno agrees Bighead used Indian directions (see Figure 11.1) – she said she was *south* (customary west) of Custer Ridge, and it is upon her use of "south" that Michno's (1997:109, 210) reasoning turns. If Bighead stopped south (the river side) of Custer Ridge, then her position, argues Michno (1997:210), "must be [located] *about ninety degrees removed* from both the east and west ends [of Custer Ridge]...and *about midway* between" the two ends (emphases added).

Midway? Ninety degrees removed? What does he mean? How does this locate Bighead? Imagine an isosceles right triangle, the hypotenuse of which is equal in length to the distance between Custer and Calhoun hills (Figure 11.2). Then superimpose the hypotenuse on Custer Ridge. Two corners of the triangle (at the hypotenuse ends) now coincide with Custer and Calhoun hills. The triangle's apex falls at a single point south of Custer Ridge. And the single point is "midway" between the ridge's two ends. Lines drawn from this midway point to Calhoun and Custer hills form a 90° angle, satisfying Michno's "ninety degrees removed" criterion.

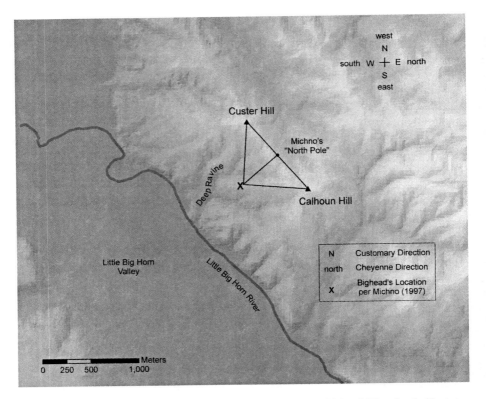

FIGURE 11-2. Michno's (1997) arbitrarily derived location for Kate Bighead. The triangle illustrates Michno's divined "ninety degrees removed" and "midway" criteria. To make the criteria work, Michno subtly "relocates" the North Pole to the position indicated.

The imaginary triangle is of course mine; it nonetheless illustrates Bighead's "position" per Michno. From this location she sees what Michno wants her to see. To do it, though, he forgets that he agrees the Bighead account uses the alternate directional scheme. Suddenly she is looking customary north. When she described a band of soldiers on a "low ridge north of the deep gulch," says Michno (1997: 210–211), she gazed from her "position" across Deep Ravine (a deep gulch) at the so-called SSL (a low ridge).

Of course all this is nonsense, even allowing Michno's slight ambiguity (*about* midway, *about* ninety degrees). Because the account states Bighead was "south" (of what in the account's context is Custer Ridge) means nothing of the sort. Michno's special pleading results in an entirely contrived "position". He in effect repositioned the North Pole to a point (about) midway along Custer Ridge (midway on the hypotenuse). Now all points toward the river are "not-south" except those on a perpendicular that (about) bisects Custer Ridge. Bighead's "south" subtly morphs into *due south*. Then the "ninety degrees removed" dictum arbitrarily selected a single point (the triangle's apex) on the contrived "due south" perpendicular. In the end, Michno determined Bighead's ''position'' using nothing more than an arbitrary contrivance.

The North Pole could, of course, just as easily go at the east end of Custer Ridge, or even the west end. Indeed, it can go anywhere on Custer Ridge. Thus an infinite number of ''due south'' perpendiculars are possible, from which an infinite number of triangle types of various dimensions can be created. Put the North Pole at Calhoun Hill, for example, and use a scalene triangle of proper dimensions, and Bighead is in position to see Lame White Man attack at Calhoun Coulee. But of course that will not work either. The North Pole must remain in the Arctic – at such an enormous distance that *all points* on the river side of Custer Ridge are *south*. Bighead could have been anywhere between Custer Ridge and the river, if she was there at all.

What of Bighead's whereabouts during the battle? Her story is in the first-person, and purports to be an eyewitness report of the battle, beginning to end. This (an eyewitness story) is very unlikely for several reasons. First, certainly Marquis' Bighead account violates the caveat that eyewitnesses see but little beyond their narrow field of vision. Imagine seeing the whole thing through the higher terrain, commotion, dust, and gun smoke.

Second, the eyewitness caveat makes it likely the story is an oral history. Indeed, it so resembles Marquis' (1931) Wooden Leg-battle-story that it smacks of a Northern Cheyenne oral thread. Marquis may be involved too, although if so just how remains a matter of speculation. Possibly he inserted ''Bighead the eyewitness'' into oral history to make it more genuine for his white readers. Maybe Marquis added material from his numerous interviews to make it a complete story.

Lastly, descriptions of battle events in the Bighead story also signal oral history. They are referenced exclusively to battlefield topographic features (''North of the deep gulch,'' ''south of the ridge,'' and so on), not Bighead's (alleged) positions. Remove her entirely from the story, and the narrative is not affected in the slightest. With or without her, Bighead's battle sequence in the Bighead account is consistent with the historical–archaeological synthesis (1) Lame White Man's attack, (2) Calhoun Hill (Bighead's ''east end''), (3) Keogh sector (''north side''), and finally (4) Custer Hill (''west end'') where ''the remaining soldiers collected'' (Marquis, 1967:87–89). Michno makes Lame White Man's attack available for his SSL version only by plucking it from its narrative context, and of course after summarily dismissing archaeological patterning consistent with that context.

Michno (1994:64, 1997:xi, 223, 258) realizes the limitations on eyewitness perspectives, that Bighead's account is based on oral history, and that it may reflect more than a bit of Marquis. He even understands – quite well actually – that ''I did,'' ''I saw,'' and so on, can be inserted into oral history (Michno, 1997:223–224). Still, he blithely treats Bighead literally, as if she did in fact circumnavigate the field, stopping here and there, observing this and that – seeing all from battle's-start to battle's-end (Michno, 1994:275, 1997:210). Why Michno did not conclude that there are no assurances Bighead was even on the battlefield during the battle is perplexing. Even had she watched, Bighead could not have seen it all, throwing into question just what she did and did not observe. Until these kinds of problems are resolved Bighead cannot be used as an eyewitness. These considerations simply render moot Michno's ''Bighead location'' exercises, not to mention all such exercises.

In the end, the oral history recounted in the Bighead story is consistent with archaeological patterning, with white observers like DeRudio and Wallace who saw in the cartridge cases a patterning similar to that discovered archaeologically, and, importantly, with other Indian accounts that describe the flow of battle, two of which are Red Bird's (also known as Little Wolf) and Young Two Moon's testimonies.

Incredulity, Divination, and Doubt

Accounts left by Red Bird and Young Two Moon (not to mention others; see Fox, 1993:143–161), both Northern Cheyenne veterans of the battle, support the archaeo-logical conclusion that tactical disintegration began in the Calhoun sectors. Their accounts are compelling for at least two reasons; both are keyed to intelligible sketch maps, and each is from an independent source – Walter Camp (1918), who interviewed Red Bird, and Walter Campbell (n.d.b: 8–11; nom de plume Stanley Vestal; see also Wells, 1989:10), who interviewed Young Two Moon. The two Custer battle veterans clearly refer to (1) the initial decisive attack (that spawned disintegration), (2) the location of that attack – the Calhoun sectors, and (3) its results – a flow of battle from the Calhoun sectors northerly into the Keogh sector, and ultimately to the Custer Hill environs. Furthermore, (4) both unambiguously name Lame White Man (also known as Walking White, a Southern Cheyenne who married into the Northern Cheyenne) as a principle in this attack.

Now, this confluence of archaeological and historical data does not fit well with ''last stand'' advocates, including Michno. He frees Red Bird's and Young Two Moon's accounts from archaeology by invoking the relic collection argument (Michno, 1997:285). But the two accounts still remain troublingly close to the archaeological conclusions about Custer's last battle. So Michno is compelled to submit them to his two-prong historical ''analysis.'' The first prong attempts to discredit Red Bird and Young Two Moon by generating doubt, arguing from incredulity and creating ambiquity. The second attempts to rehabilitate the two witnesses.

DISCREDITING HISTORY

To discredit Red Bird, Michno employs several tactics. Because Camp reported that Flying By (a Minneconjou veteran of the battle) did not understand his (Camp's) map, we must wonder, says Michno, about Red Bird's map-reading abilities. We must wonder too because Red Bird told George Bird Grinnell that he did not see all of the battle. But generating doubt gets us nowhere, for the tactic is easily turned. For example, and as Michno (1997:211) correctly notes (but promptly ignores), Red Bird told Camp (1918) ''I was there.'' Perhaps then we should wonder if ''I was there'' means the part Red Bird *did* witness was Lame White Man's foray. Simi-larly, Camp had the sagacity to sense Flying By's cartographic deficiencies. We might then wonder why he said nothing about Red Bird's map-reading. Could it be that Red Bird had no trouble?

Red Bird, says Michno, also informed Thomas Marquis (the Northern Cheyenne Agency physician). But, he adds, Marquis would never have written that Lame White Man attacked just below Custer Hill if Red Bird said it came in the Calhoun sectors. And, offers Michno (1994:271), compare Marquis, who received from Red Bird direct on-field information, with Camp's report which is just "a few sentences... based on two letters on a paper map...". How can Camp's Red Bird be right in the face of this! But Michno's argument from incredulity is manufactured. The fact is, we currently have no idea what Red Bird told Marquis, or how Marquis used Red Bird's information, if at all.

Indeed, nowhere have I found where Marquis (or anybody else) says he was on the battlefield with Red Bird, and Michno does not cite his claim. He seems to just divine it, evidently from the earlier of two books by Marquis titled *Wooden Leg* (1931). In it, Marquis (1931:ix) names his Indian sources, including Red Bird. Michno evidently assumes that means the two visited the battlefield together, and then transfers his assumption to Marquis' (1976) later book, *Keep the Last Bullet for Yourself* (written in the mid-1930s, but not published until 1976).

The latter is the book upon which Michno relies for his Red Bird–Lame White Man argument. But neither book states, or even remotely implies, that the two ever visited the battlefield together (nor do any of Marquis' writings). Furthermore, nowhere in *Bullet* does Marquis name (or otherwise identify) Red Bird as an informant (actually few are named; although Marquis certainly interviewed battle participants, the battle story in *Bullet* is his interpretation without support). Marquis does not put Red Bird on the battlefield with him (or anybody for that matter), nor does he credit Red Bird with even the remotest thing about the issue at hand (Lame White Man's attack). In fact, although Red Bird appears four times as part of the *Bullet* narrative, each time but briefly, Marquis does not quote or paraphrase Red Bird on anything. What is fact, however, is an eyewitness account given by Red Bird to Walter Camp exists, and it is thoroughly unambiguous – Red Bird clearly says Lame White Man assaulted soldiers on Calhoun Ridge. This makes Michno's machinations all the more ridiculous.

Regarding Campbell's Young Two Moon interview, Michno (1994:271) writes in *Mystery* that "where [Lame White Man's] attack might have occurred is uncertain". If Michno means precisely where, he is right enough, but is nonetheless disingenuous. Says Michno, "our only clue" other than a symbol "apparently" putting Lame White Man near Calhoun Hill is "first charge, side of hill" (Michno, 1994:271). Not so. In fact, the "symbol" to which Michno refers (#1 on Campbell's sketch) does not "apparently" locate Lame White Man; it unambiguously puts him well south of Custer Hill, at or near Calhoun Hill. Furthermore, Michno fails to mention that Young Two Moon's text-aided map clearly carries Lame White Man's warriors from #1 (near Calhoun Hill), through the Keogh sector, then beyond to abreast of Custer Hill. That, of course, makes it rather certain that the affair did not occur where Michno needs it.

This is the same for *Lakota Noon*. Here, though, the "ambiguity strategy" is dropped in favor of generating more doubt. Grinnell's Cheyennes, says Michno, named several warriors who fought around Calhoun Hill, but never mentioned Lame White Man (Michno, 1997:211). That is correct, but one Grinnell informant was Young Two Moon, who did indeed mention Lame White Man to Campbell. Apparently we are to discard Campbell because the younger Two Moon did not mention Lame White Man to Grinnell. If we apply this strategy wholesale to all Indian accounts, much of the native record, if not most, will have to be jettisoned altogether.

REHABILITATING HISTORY

In *Mystery*, Michno seems to sense that in Red Bird and Young Two Moon he opposes high quality evidence. After trying to discredit them, he quickly launches into an apologetic about why we should listen to the two after all – we should not, says Michno, selectively use or discard testimony. Sounds like the high road here, but it is not to be. Instead, Michno tries to make Red Bird and Young Two Moon work for him. Maybe, he says, their statements are not opposed to my (Michno's) "last stand" story. The two witnesses, recognizes Michno, surely do start Lame White Man's attack well south (customary) of the South Skirmish Line. Maybe then all we need to do is adjust the axis of his assault – maybe it came from the southern environs, not the west as traditionally supposed. Maybe, opines Michno, that is the essence of Red Bird's statement and Young Two Moon's map (Michno, 1994:271).

Red Bird's axis of attack (per Camp) is L-shaped, beginning on Calhoun Ridge, turning customary north at Calhoun Hill and running north into the Keogh sector. Michno's shifted axis is a short straight line that runs directly from the western terminus of Greasy Grass Ridge to the South Skirmish Line. It not only shortens Red Bird's route, but clips off the Calhoun Ridge, Calhoun Hill and Keogh portions (without letting the reader know). Young Two Moon's axis is also "L" shaped, running north along Custer ridge to Custer Hill, then westerly to somewhere below Custer Hill. Michno's axis clips off the Custer Hill-to-below Custer Hill leg. So in actuality Michno does not just shift axes, he distorts them, thereby masking the flow of battle clearly described by the two informants. These "shifts" are facilitated by not divulging the nature of Red Bird's and Young Two Moon's axes of attack.

Michno rationalizes his "axis shift" this way. The bulk of the evidence (i.e., his interpretations of the evidence) all but demands it. Therefore Campbell and Camp likely missed Young Two Moon's and Red Bird's meanings. Meanings could very well have become confused when the two warriors' terrain perceptions clashed with the maps. After a lot of "may have's, "could be's, and "may be's, an "axis shift" seemingly becomes reality. In this way Michno concludes that his version – Lame White Man and his contingent initiated their attack at the South Skirmish Line sector – becomes "increasingly sustainable" (Michno, 1994:273).

Of course the "axis shift" is founded on sand. It boils down to this kind of thinking. Michno knows his South Skirmish Line episode is right; the bulk of the evidence proves it (at least the way he interprets it). So Red Bird and Young Two Moon – after all, they were there – must have seen it. But that is not what they reported. Therefore their testimonies must have got mixed up in the recording. The axis is what was misunderstood. Adjust for that and the two, says Michno, actually saw Lame White Man at the South Skirmish Line. Meanwhile, the archaeological patterning is brushed aside courtesy of the "relic collecting" argument (Michno, 1997:285).

CONCLUSION

Elbert Hubbard was a storyteller. His vision of Custer's last battle measures the romance of that famous confrontation. Writing in 1915, his "last stand" came down to endurance. Surrounded, General Custer realized how serious matters had become. In desperation, he dispatched a message to General Terry, pleading for help. Then came noon "and buzzards began to gather in the azure", wrote Hubbard. The "blistering hot" afternoon dragged on; the sun sank. "Custer warned his men that sleep was death." Dawn came. Daylight found Terry struggling to make it in time. Finally, Custer and his men ran out of ammunition. Then the Indians closed in and it was over. Sadly, Terry had fallen an hour or two short (Hubbard, 1974:118–121).

To my knowledge serious students of Custer's last battle have in their writings neither subscribed to Hubbard's fantasy, or something like it, nor exhibited his breathtakingly simplistic grasp (Hubbard's literary bent notwithstanding) of the subject – including the authors herein criticized. Certainly their constructions, especially Michno's, are comparatively quite detailed, more so than I can adequately convey in the space limitations here. But perhaps restricted space creates the opposite impression, and/or an impression that I have attempted to discredit the whole of each author's work by singling out a weakness here and there. While, for example, inaccurately locating Lame White Man's attack does indeed weaken a "last stand," that is not my intent. Rather I have illustrated how, at the very least, responses to the refined scale available in historical archaeology can be at times rather strained.

The main trend among "Custer's last stand" defenders is to cite relic collecting in order to reject the patterning discovered (using firing pin signature analysis) in government cartridge cases. That practice, of course, requires overlooking documentary evidence that clearly supports the stability/disintegration pattern. The evidence consists of (1) white observers who clearly stated they saw few cartridge cases beyond the Calhoun sectors, and (2) the "historical pattern" – accounts given by whites that speak of spent casing numbers at sectors other than two in the Calhoun area are nonexistent.

But there is something more. The archaeology helps make sense of the historical record. Equipped with archaeological knowledge, for instance, I recognized that the Bighead account does not use customary reckoning. Adjusting for that, her account fits the material pattern. But in this case, as I have shown, Michno dismisses archaeology, and that leads to the rather curious practice of relocating the North Pole to, using alternate directions, "position" his witness, and then shifting to the customary scheme so she can look in the right direction. It is tempting to see such reasoning as a measure – perhaps the polar opposites of a long, long continuum? – of the analytical power the refined scale historical archaeology wields in the pursuit of understanding our past.

ACKNOWLEDGEMENTS   The Custer Battlefield Historical and Museum Association funded the work upon which this article is based. Thanks to the Association. And, thanks to the editors for the invitation to contribute and for their editorial input. Brian Molyneaux's creative GIS applications resulted in the figures.

REFERENCES

Anonymous, 1992 [1876], That Fatal Day. In *First-hand Accounts of the Battle of the Little Big Horn*, edited by Karen L. Daniels and E. Elden Davis, pp. 7–9. Powder River Press, Howell, Minnesota. (Originally published in the *St. Paul (Minnesota) Dispatch*, July 19, 1876).

Bimson, John, and Livingston, David, 1987, Redating the Exodus. *Biblical Archaeology Review* 13(5):40–53, 66–68.

Camp, Walter, 1918, Interview with Little Wolf (Red Bird), August 26, 1918. Hammer Collection, Box 3, Folder 1, Lilly Library, Indiana University, Bloomington.

du Picq, Ardant, 1946, *Battle Studies*. Military Service Publishing Company, Harrisburg, Pennsylvania.

Evans, David C., 1999, *Custer's Last Fight: The Story of the Battle of the Little Big Horn*. Upton and Sons, El Segundo, California.

Finklestein, Israel, and Silberman, Neil A., 2001, *The Bible Unearthed; Archaeology's New Vision of Ancient Israel and the Origin of its Sacred Texts*. Simon and Schuster, New York.

Fox, Richard A., 1993, *Archaeology, History, and Custer's Last Battle: The Little Big Horn Reexamined*. University of Oklahoma Press, Norman.

Fox, Richard A., 1996, West River History: The Indian Village on Little Bighorn River, June 25–26, 1876. In *Legacy: New Perspectives on the Battle of the Little Bighorn*, edited by Charles E. Rankin, pp. 139–165. Montana Historical Society Press, Helena.

Fox, Richard A., 1997, The Art and Archaeology of Custer's Last Battle. In *The Cultural Life of Images: Visual Representation in Archaeology*, edited by Brian Leigh Molyneaux, pp. 159–183. Routledge, London.

Frost, Lawrence A., 1976, *General Custer's Libbie*. Superior Publishing Company, Seattle.

Hubbard, Elbert, 1974 [1915], The Custer Battle. *The Teepee Book* 1:106–122. In two volumes, edited by J.M. Carroll. Sol Lewis, New York. (Reprinted from the June 1915 *Teepee Book* 1[6]).

Marquis, Thomas, 1931, *Wooden Leg: A Warrior who Fought Custer*. University of Nebraska Press, Lincoln.

Marquis, Thomas, 1967, She Watched Custer's Last Battle. In *Custer on the Little Bighorn*, pp. 80–96. Dr. Marquis Custer Publications, Lodi, CA.

Marquis, Thomas, 1976, *Keep the Last Bullet for Yourself: The True Story of Custer's Last Stand*. Reference Publications, Algonac, Michigan.

Michno, Gregory, 1994, *The Mystery of E Troop: Custer's Gray Horse Company at the Little Bighorn*. Mountain Press Publishing Company, Missoula, Montana.

Michno, Gregory, 1997, *Lakota Noon: The Indian Narrative of Custer's Defeat*. Mountain Press Publishing Company, Missoula, Montana.

Nichols, Ronald H., 1983, *Reno Court of Inquiry*. Costa Mesa, California, privately published [in three volumes; third volume publication date is 1984].

Ricker, Eli S., 1906, *Interview with Respects Nothing, November 9*. Ricker Collection, Series 2, Box 6, Reel 5, Tablet 29. Nebraska State Historical Society, Lincoln.

Roe, Charles F., 1927, General Roe's Narrative. In *Custer's Last Battle*, edited by Robert Bruce, pp. 8–18. National Highway Association, New York.

Rohl, David M., 1995, *Pharaohs and Kings: A Biblical Quest*. Crown Publishers, New York.

Ryan, John M., 1923, One of Custer's Sergeants tells Story of Eno's Part in Fight on Little Big Horn. *Hardin (Montana) Tribune*, June 22 (Supplement). Also *Billings Gazette*, June 25 [same title].

Scott, Douglas D., and Fox, Richard A., 1987, *Archaeological Insights into the Custer Battle*. University of Oklahoma Press, Norman.

Scott, Douglas D., Fox, Richard A., Connor, Melissa, M., and Harmon, D. 1989, *Archaeological Perspectives on the Battle of the Little Bighorn*. University of Oklahoma Press, Norman.

Sklenar, Larry, 2000, *To Hell with Honor: Custer and the Little Bighorn*. University of Oklahoma Press, Norman.

Snelson, Bob, 2002, *Death of a Myth*. Snelsonbooks, Florence, Colorado.

Stiebing, William S., 1985, Should the Exodus and Israelite Settlement be Redated? *Biblical Archaeology Review* 11(4):58–69.

Stiebing, William S., 1989, *Out of the Desert: Archaeology and the Exodus/Conquest Narratives*. Prometheus Books, Buffalo, New York.

INTERPRETING SCALE: TOWARDS NEW METHODOLOGIES AND UNDERSTANDINGS

CHAPTER 12

Temporal Scales and Archaeological Landscapes from the Eastern Desert of Australia and Intermontane North America

SIMON J. HOLDAWAY AND
LUANN WANDSNIDER

INTRODUCTION

Time gets much less attention than space in discussions of archaeological scale. This may seem strange in a primarily historical discipline for which the demonstration of human antiquity is something of a defining moment (Grayson, 1983). Part of the reason may lie in the nature of time. Time unfolds along a continuum, and the way observers perceive time depends on their location and the scales they adopt. Compare the contemporary Western experience of earth time, for example, with time at the scale of the universe. A person traveling at the speed of light would experience a different time (Hawking, 1998; Ramenofsky, 1998) than the person caught up in the linear progression of our planet-bound life. Of course, archaeologists rarely deal with quantum time, but the example serves to remind us that time is not an absolute dimension. Archaeologists create their own conceptual units for measuring time. They project these units at different scales and choose their own observation points, dividing the continuum of time into arbitrary packages that relate in some way to specific research goals (Ramenofsky, 1998).

Few archaeologists have grappled explicitly with scale issues. Crumley (1979) and Marquardt (1992; see also Crumley and Marquardt, 1987) emphasize that social and economic processes may each resolve best at different spatial scales. Stein

SIMON J. HOLDAWAY ● University of Auckland, LUANN WANDSNIDER ● University of Nebraska-Lincoln

(1993) attempts to reconcile the vastly different temporal scales of geology and archaeology. Most recently, Dobres (2000; see also Lock and Molyneaux, this volume) differentiates between the phenomenological scales at which events contributing to archaeological deposits unfold (i.e., activities, behaviors, and practices) and the interpretative scales of archaeological reasoning (i.e., generalized, theoretically informed). The former are comprehensible in what Binford (1981) refers to as "ethnographic time" and what Stein (1993) calls "human time"; the latter are timeless or time-free.

Dobres contrasts phenomenological and interpretative scales with the analytic scales that researchers use. The choice depends on their research interests (see also Crumley, 1979; Marquardt, 1992) and on the nature of archaeological deposits. As her focus is primarily on agency at individual and collective levels, she emphasizes the phenomenological scale, but she insists that phenomenological, interpretative, and analytical scales have no necessary relationship. Thus, when pursuing such interpretative goals as agency, archaeologists are not limited to one particular scale of phenomena. Nor, according to a close reading of Dobres, are they limited by the nature of the archaeological record, as the scale at which they view the material record is not related to any particular phenomenological scale of agency.

In this chapter, we explicitly focus on archaeological temporal scale, by which we mean both the temporal structure of the phenomenon we study, i.e., the archaeological deposit, and the scales of measurement and interpretation we bring to that phenomenon. Temporal structure refers to (1) the grain, resolution, or microstratigraphic acuity and (2) the extent or scope of phenomena represented in archaeological deposits, observations and interpretations. Grain (Binford, 1980; O'Neill and King, 1998:7), resolution (Behrensmeyer, et al., 2000; Ramenofsky and Steffen, 1998:4–5; Stein, 1993:2) and microstratigraphic acuity (Schindel, 1982) refer to the smallest resolvable temporal interval in an observation set. Extent (O'Neill and King, 1998:7) and scope (Schindel, 1982) refer to the total expanse of time represented in an observation set (see also inclusiveness – Ramenofsky and Steffen, 1998:4–5). To these, Schindel (1982) adds (3) temporal sequence completeness, as many deposits are records of depositional gaps as well as accumulations.

Ecologists O'Neill and King (1998:7) offer important observations on how scale of observation and measurement affect the effective grain and extent of deposits. They note, for instance, that the sampling frequency in time influences the grain of observation, a relationship described elsewhere as the *Nyquist principle*. Similarly, the time span of a particular measurement necessarily influences grain. The practice of calculating means for some span of time necessarily coarsens the grain while subsampling a sequence reduces its extent. In archaeology, both behavior and geological processes contribute to grain (resolution), extent (scope), and completeness of sequences. Measurement practices further affect these aspects of temporal scale.

While Dobres argues that there is no necessary relationship between phenomenological, interpretative, and analytical scales, we follow geoarchaeologists, geomorphologists, paleontologists, and ecologists in emphasizing that the nature of archaeological deposits very much determines the analytical scale – and therefore the range of interpretative scales (see Murray, 2003; Stein, 1993:5; Stern, 1993, 1994; Stern, et al., 2002). Thus while the archaeological record may potentially be viewed at a variety of different scales from a range of different view points, issues of compatibility between data, analysis and interpretation cannot be ignored. We begin with this point, using it as the basis for a critique of the recent and current hunter–gatherer literature and drawing on our current work from western New South Wales, Australia, and southwest Wyoming, USA. We argue that neither of the current interpretative approaches to the hunter–gatherer archaeological record, ethnoarchaeological models or insights derived from behavioral ecology, deal adequately with the temporality of the record. Integrating the temporality of data and interpretation suggests to us a third way, whereby we can use explanations developed by viewing the archaeological record at a variety of scales to create a rich historical tapestry of past human behavioral variability.

TEMPORAL SCALE IN ARCHAEOLOGY

Measuring time in a number of different ways frees the archaeologist to search for processes operating at different temporal scales (Fletcher, 1992). However, this liberty brings with it the responsibility of ensuring that the scale of explanation meshes with both the scale of observation and the temporal scale of archaeological deposits. Unfortunately, the "Tyranny of Familiar Things", to use Plog's (1974) phrase, means that it is easy to adopt a common sense approach and see archaeological materials as the products of daily living. From this point of view, the archaeologist simply assumes that both behavior and deposition occur at the same temporal scale as that experienced at the "ethnographic" (Binford, 1981) or "human scale" (Stein, 1993, 2001), i.e., at intervals consistent with the life of the observer (Wandsnider, 2003). In almost every instance, however, the processes operating to create archaeological assemblages reflect a scale that is likely to be many times longer than that of daily living, an observation made by Binford (1981) in his discussion of the Pompeii premise (see also Foley, 1981). This frequently creates a disjuncture between the scale of observation and the scale of interpretation.

Recognition of this disjuncture dates at least from the 1980s with a seminal paper by Bailey (1983). Since that time, case studies and theoretical statements have appeared under the title "time perspectivism" (e.g., Bailey, 1981, 1987; Fletcher, 1992; Murray, 1997, 1999, 2003; Stern, 1993, 1994, Stern, et al., 2002). Despite this attention, there remains in archaeology a void between the scales at which theoretical models are constructed and the scales of the units adopted to collect and aggregate data used in evaluating these models.

In the search for interpretative models, archaeologists frequently appear as itinerant foragers, willing to scour other disciplines for theoretical resources. The pickings seem so much richer in the ethnographic, historical, and ecological literature. Nowhere is this truer than in hunter–gatherer studies where, as we argue below, ethnography (either current or of the recent past), ecology (in the form of evolutionary ecology), and forms of evolutionary theory now underpin most hunter–gatherer studies conducted in North America and Australia. To the "Tyranny of Material Things" can be added versions of Alcock's (1993) "Tyranny of Historical Records", Wobst's (1978) "Tyranny of the Ethnographic Record", and a yet to be articulated "Tyranny of Ecological Models". While all these sources – historical records, ethnographic records, ecological models – are rich in detail, thereby contrasting with the apparent poverty of the archaeological record, their richness emphasizes the short-term over the long-term, multitemporal historical record, the very attributes that make the archaeological record so fascinating to study!

In what follows, we argue that all three sets of models (i.e., involving lifeways ethnography, historical documents and ecology) are useful for interpreting hunter–gatherer behavior only if history is ignored and time is characterized as flat, an observation made by Bailey (1983:170) when referring to structural functional models. Change, when it occurs, is punctuated, involving the transition from one stable state to another. We therefore find this characterization of human history most unlikely and suspect that it flows from a lack of consideration of temporal scale.

TEMPORAL SCALES AND
HUNTER–GATHERER RESEARCH

Archaeologists have conducted research on deposits created by hunter–gatherers at a variety of temporal scales reflecting the operation of the various tyrannies noted above. While archaeological hunter–gatherer research is richer than we can portray here, we recognize two distinct modes of analysis and interpretation using two different temporal scales.

"Pompeii" Deposits and Functional Interpretation

The first mode of temporal scales relies on, or attempts to warrant, the assumption that the deposits under study may be interpreted according to the "human scale" (Stein, 1993), as though they represent "Pompeii" deposits, i.e., fine grain or fine resolution deposits preserving "frozen-moments" or short duration events in time. Most archaeologists working in Australia and North America recognize that some, probably most, deposits represent a form of palimpsest, but this assessment rarely affects their interpretations.

Because many researchers in Australia rely on ethnographic analogy as a source of models for interpreting archaeological materials, the formational history of the record they are interpreting becomes polarized. They consider sites as either *in situ* or mixed, the behavioral equivalent of single ethnographically conceived campsites or a jumble of material from multiple occupations. In effect, by using ethnography in these situations, they need not distinguish between the phenomenological, interpretative, and analytical scales Dobres discusses – beyond the mixed versus intact dichotomy – since interpretation can only exist at one (ethnographic) temporal scale.

In North America, researchers have largely abandoned ethnographic analogy per se, instead substituting settlement components of Binford's (1980) model that relates structure of resources, hunter–gatherer mobility and settlement. However, as discussed below, the use of Binford's insights as direct analogs for the past has led North American archaeologists to the same interpretative dilemmas that their antipodean colleagues have reached.

In Australia, an unequal distribution of resources related to seasonal fluctuations in the environment has long formed the mechanism for explaining why people in the past performed different economic functions at the same places within a landscape (e.g., Thomson, 1939; Allen, 1972). In the arid zone, archaeologists generally assume that the most critical resource is water. Ethnographic case studies (e.g., Cane, 1984; Gould, 1969) suggest that during times of rain, populations disperse to exploit resources in regions where water sources are ephemeral. As the rains depart and the country enters into drought conditions, people retreat to more permanent water sources and exploit the resources around these locations. Archaeologists have used these observations as the basis for explanations of the distribution of archaeological sites (e.g., Allen, 1972; White and Peterson, 1969; Ross, 1984; Ross, et al., 1992; Smith, 1989, 1993, 1996; Veth, 1993; Williams, 1987). According to the model, those sites located away from sources of permanent water should show relatively few artifacts with little evidence for maintenance activities, while those closer to more permanent water should have more abundant artifacts and show a greater range of materials and artifacts, reflecting occupation by larger groups for longer periods (e.g., Veth, 1993:71).

Thus, in arid Australia, changes in water availability become the means by which archaeologists can assess intersite assemblage variability. They use different artifact assemblages to infer different activities practiced at particular locations, hence permitting the identification of site types (i.e., where type refers to function, Veth, 1993:80). Then they link these site types together in an ethnographically familiar, synthetic settlement system. The task of the archaeologist becomes one of measuring the temporal duration over which this system existed, together with its spatial extent. When they find similar sets of artifacts existing over extended periods, they can assume that the settlement/subsistence system has remained unchanged since occupation of the region began.

On a worldwide scale, the late occurrence of broad-spectrum changes in the Australian hunter–gatherer economies is well known. Changes elsewhere labeled as the broad-spectrum revolution occur from the mid to late Holocene in Australia, apparently unconnected with significant environmental change (Edwards and O'Connell, 1995). In the arid zone, the exploitation of grass seeds becomes important (Smith, 1986) and population increases, although there is debate about whether increasing numbers of people were the trigger for (e.g., Smith, 1989), or a consequence of (e.g., Veth, 1989), the late Holocene changes. Either way, the assumption is that people adapted to the Australian arid zone by implementing a series of technological and social solutions and, consequently, producing a characteristic settlement pattern.

Our concern with the application of such models to Australia centers on the utility of ethnographic models in the interpretation of long-term historically derived archaeological records. The problem is that functionalist interpretations of artifacts have changed over recent years. Ethnoarchaeological studies have shown, for example, that discard behavior is much more important than function in determining the spatial association of artifacts (Wandsnider, 1996). Ethnohistoric, ethnoarchaeological and experimental studies also report little relationship between artifact form and function (e.g., Hayden, 1979). In Australia, as elsewhere, similar artifact forms appear to have had a range of functions in the past while, conversely, a range of different artifact morphologies had single functions (e.g., Kamminga, 1982).

The implications of these studies for the identifications of site types seem clear: if assemblages do not represent tool kits, if the spatial association of artifacts reflects discard behavior rather than the existence of activity areas, the inference of a single or limited range of functions for a site must be viewed with skepticism. Following on from this, the inability to determine site function must call into question the nature of the Australian settlement pattern reconstructions, particularly the substantive transferal of ethnographically derived, short-term (i.e., seasonal) mobility models to explain long-term accumulations of artifacts.

In contrast, several factors have contributed to the demise in North America of an explicit ethnographic reconstructive orientation. First, starting especially in the late 1970s, a number of researchers critiqued the practice of reconstructing the past using ethnographic units. Wobst (1978) called attention to the abnormal sample that ethnography provides and to the ethnographic practice of normalizing important variation. Dunnell (1980) heavily criticized some of the early New Archaeologists for their reliance upon ethnographic concepts and units. In his analysis of the behavioral archaeology program, Binford (1981) argued, echoing Clarke (1973), that archaeological deposits refer to another order of reality, something attributable to an interpretative unit, a cultural system operating over the medium- and long term, as opposed to an empirical unit, such as an ethnographic group.

Second, the experience of North American archaeologists with the archaeological record made it very clear that simple application of ethnographic models – those dealing with the articulation of functional settlement units – to archaeological deposits was flawed (Ramenofsky and Steffen, 1998:9). Instead, they began to talk of land use, by which they attempted to explain archaeological patterning in the long term. Thomas' (1973, 1975) and Bettinger's (1977) attempts to generate expectations for the archaeological record if Great Basin locations were utilized in the distant past, as documented by Steward for the Shoshone recent past, are only two such examples (see also Dancey, 1973; Jones, 1984).

Third was the publication of Binford's (1980) ''Willow Smoke and Dog's Tails''. Binford described and explained patterned variation in hunter–gatherer mobility and settlement according to the spatial and temporal structure of critical resources. He offered a conceptual schema to help understand some of the principle sources of variation seen in hunter–gatherer mobility and settlement. He distinguished between foragers, employing residential mobility to move consumers between patches of low abundance resources, and collectors, whose mobility is tethered to stores and who employ logistical mobility to provision consumers from widely dispersed, seasonally superabundant patches. To aid his discussion, he offered a typology of sites.

From all of these sources followed a reconfiguration of the ethnographic analogical arguments so widely seen in Australian applications. For example, archaeologists discussed the degree to which their evidence indicated forager or collector adaptations (e.g., Sanger, 1996) or the degree to which one could use their evidence to stipulate these adaptations (e.g., Cowan, 1999). In other applications, archaeologists relied on the site types (residential camps, field camps, stations, caches, and locations) that Binford had identified as created through different deployments of residential and logistical mobility (see Simms, 1992 for an elaboration of this contention). Such applications confused the substantive content of Binford's forager–collector contribution with its conceptual content. For this reason, they committed exactly the same sins already detailed above for the Australian case.

Palimpsest Deposits and "Strategic" Interpretations

As Dunnell (1980) notes, one of the major research foci of the New Archaeology was the nature of the archaeological record, how it formed, and how we could interpret it. In the early 1980s, the "Pompeii premise" debate between Binford (1981) and Schiffer (1985) addressed the interpretative implications of the time-averaged nature of archaeological deposits. In contrast to "Pompeii" assemblages, Binford discussed "palimpsest deposits," that is, coarse-grain or -resolution deposits representing the accumulation of materials over decades if not hundreds of years. He and Foley (1981) argued that with such assemblages, the ethnographic time of daily living was masked by stronger patterns introduced by the longer-term operation of human settlement and mobility patterns. Furthermore, both authors contended that processes unfolding in archaeological rather than ethnographic time were the rightful objects of archaeological study.

Beginning in the 1990s, North American archaeological literature on hunter–gatherers reflected the dual impact of the thinking articulated by Binford (1981) and Foley (1981) as well as the influence of optimal foraging theory and behavioral ecological research (e.g., Torrence, 1989; Bettinger, 1991). Archaeologists described past hunter–gatherer behavior using the concept of "strategies" similar in form to the analytical evolutionary stable strategies (ESS) of evolutionary ecology. They undertook studies that recognized mobility strategies (e.g., Amick, 1996; Bamforth and Becker, 2000; Smith and McNees, 1999), technological and land use strategies (e.g., Cowan, 1999), reproductive strategies (e.g., Bettinger, 1993), and subsistence strategies (e.g., Dering, 1999; Stafford, et al., 2000).

Australian archaeologists were obviously aware of these theoretical developments in North America. In recent years, numbers of studies have sought to define strategies following Binford and other North American authors rather than constructing functional settlement patterns. Hiscock, for instance, has considered both technology (e.g., Hiscock, 1996) and assemblage composition (e.g., Hiscock, 1994) from the viewpoint of behavioral ecology in an attempt to explain changes in mid to late Holocene stone artifact assemblages in Australia. In the former study, he cites changing strategies as the reason for differences in the degree of bipolar flaking present in sites in the north of Australia. In the later study, he explains the presence of a range of new artifact forms (adze bits, backed blades and seed grinding gear) as adaptations to the risks involved in moving into new, particularly arid, environments in the mid-Holocene. McNiven (1994) has also used North American studies in his attempt to relate increases in the frequency of certain tool types and the presence of exotic raw materials to the changes in mobility strategy evidenced by Late Pleistocene sites in southwest Tasmania (but see Holdaway, 2000, 2004).

Both the Australian and North American studies use strategies as "problem-solving processes that are responsive to conditions created by the interplay between humans and their social and natural environment" (Nelson, 1991:58). The "problem" to be solved, sometimes unstated, is usually related to minimizing risk, optimizing stone tool resources, maximizing reproductive success and so on – in other words, the grist of optimal foraging and behavioral ecology.

The second important research emphasis, launched by the New Archaeology in the 1970s but largely unexploited until much later, is middle range research. This endeavor links archaeological material with the interpretation of cultural dynamics and makes possible the strategic interpretations discussed above. For example, Amick (1996) and Bamforth and Becker (2000) rely on the reductive nature of chipped stone technology and various reasonable stipulations derived thereof to offer expectations for archaeological assemblages formed because of different configurations of Paleoindian mobility. Dering (1999) and Stafford et al. (2000) rely on plant community ecology (productivity, diversity, abundance, rebound rates) to situate their interpretations of Archaic age subsistence strategies in west Texas and southern Illinois, respectively. In Australia, Cosgrove and Allen (2001) use the behavior of Bennetts Wallaby together with paleoenvironment reconstruction and faunal analysis to understand prey choice and processing patterns. Important in all these applications are two things: the emphasis on variation and its explanation as the differential implementation of strategies; and the consequences such strategies, as defined, have for the differential deposition of artifacts with different use-lives and temporalities.[1]

How compatible are "strategic" interpretive units with the palimpsest nature of archaeological deposits resulting from hunter–gatherers? At face value, they appear very compatible. These "strategies" only become recognizable because of repeated behaviors resulting in the patterned deposition of artifacts. Indeed, for the archaeological record to register these strategies, these behaviors must have been consistent over decades if not centuries.

However, such patterning also suggests great stability in aspects (i.e., the common mundane, or the rare, or both) of land use organization, at least for periods extending to decades and more. Given our current understanding of hunter–gatherer land use and organization, can we expect this kind of intra- or inter-generational stability or is it the product of the application of concepts ill-suited to modeling

---

[1] It is important to note that some archaeologists simultaneously pursue both approaches. Cowan (1999) attempts to recognize different subsistence and land use strategies in terms of different lithic technological strategies for Archaic and Woodland western New York. He relies on sophisticated analyses of chipped stone assemblages and explicitly considers the possibility that the patterning he documents may relate to the convolution of multiple disparate strategies. For unknown reasons, however, something compels him to translate his interpretations of past subsistence and land use into the settlement system lexicon described above for Australian hunter–gatherers, rather than offering it in terms of "strategies."

change? The problem shows clearly in Australia, truly the continent of hunter–gatherers. Since it had neither agriculture nor complex society, Australia always lacked clear indicators of major changes in either settlement patterns or adaptive strategies. As discussed above, the Holocene apparently had only one major change, sometime around 5,000 BP, which produced various phenomena that some archaeologists have linked together with a theory of intensification (the Australian equivalent of the broad spectrum revolution [Lourandos, 1997]). They explain this change in a variety of ways, some of the more popular in recent years based on social rather than demographic change. Yet, regardless of the theoretical background they adopt, their explanations as a whole have the same all or nothing quality. When they detect change, they characterize it as instantaneous and total. The shift seems mechanical – as if history did not exist in the movement from one stable system to another. To us this seems an unlikely situation either in the prehistory of Australia or elsewhere. "Strategies" are strategies in metaphor only. They are abstractions from innumerable individual strategic (the word as commonly used) acts pursued by members of one or more constantly changing ethnic groups. Rather than modeling continuity, we should be using the archaeological record to resolve historical change, since archaeology alone is able to address this question.

TEMPORAL STRUCTURE AND PLACE HISTORY INTERPRETATIONS

Archaeological sites in the arid zones of Australia and North America, like archaeological sites anywhere, are places where artifacts and sediments accumulate. In both these regions, surface exposures of artifacts are either lag deposits or simple accumulations. In the arid zone of western New South Wales, Australia, artifact accumulations were buried until relatively recently. Their modern day exposure can be securely associated with 19th century grazing activity when European pastoralists introduced cloven hoof domestic livestock to an environment that had until then been the domain of marsupials (Fanning 1999, 2002). The resulting vegetation loss and topsoil erosion is hard to comprehend. Literally millions of stone artifacts today lay exposed over thousands upon thousands of hectares. Although exposure has sometimes resulted in hopelessly mixed hydraulic jumbles, more often it has been gentler, resulting in the loss of vertical integrity but largely retaining horizontal position (Fanning and Holdaway, 2001a). In effect, then, erosion has excavated large regions, producing the types of exposures that archaeologists excavating traditionally would take a generation to achieve (Holdaway et al., 2000).

In the Wyoming Basin of intermountain North America, there are both deeply buried deposits and surface deposits. Not surprisingly, the topographic landform and vegetative cover contemporary with occupations in antiquity contributes to their present day form, with sites exposed on terraces, buried in swales and along slopes, and exposed or buried in dune fields (see, Eckerle, 1997; Ebert, 1992 for discussion). In the Wyoming Basin proper, it appears that surface deposits represent only a small portion of the subsurface assemblage. For example, dense artifact accumulations in the Seedskadee project area are one-to-two orders of magnitude less than excavated deposits from the same area. Yet, the same kinds of artifacts appear in both surface and subsurface assemblages, suggesting that surface assemblages are a representative sample of the near surface buried assemblages. Features, of course, are much better preserved and documented in excavated contexts.

Studying both extensive lag (interior Australia) and accumulated (Wyoming Basin) deposits forces us to recognize that our archaeological sites are time-transgressive in nature, with different temporal structures (*sensu* Murray, 2003), i.e., grain (or resolution), extent (or scope) and depositional gaps. That is, they encourage a third mode of analysis and interpretation beyond the functional interpretation of ''Pompeii'' deposits and the simple strategic interpretation of palimpsest deposits. These assemblages have not accumulated as the result of a single ''occupation'' – or more correctly, given the lagging or accumulation processes, there is no visible stratification to support the interpretation of assemblages as ''living floors''. Instead, these assemblages reflect repeated use of a place, with contributions from all the artifact-producing activities that have occurred there. Thus, it may be more profitable, and perhaps more accurate, to visualize the site as a record of deposition as opposed to one of function. Since vertical integrity was either never present or has been lost, there is no reason to think of spatial association as analogous to functional association. Similarly, since the artifacts represent the discard from many events, it is easy to imagine assemblages accumulating as the result of several different behavioral strategies.

In developing ways to interpret records such as this, archaeologists often adopted Binford's (1980) concept of foragers and collectors and his discussion of site types. Because the archaeological record is time-averaged, however, assemblage site types do not relate specifically to either foragers or collectors. Here, Binford's discussion of the Mask site (Binford, 1978) becomes important. As described, the Mask site consists of artifacts relating to a number of activities at a location that ''functioned'' as a hunting lookout. However, the ''function'' of the artifact sets has little apparent relationship to the ''function'' for which the site was occupied. Instead, Binford stresses the complex relationship between identifications of site function and the activities that lead to the incorporation of artifacts into the archaeological record. The way archaeologists determine site function, as with the categorization of artifacts, depends on which of the activities evident at the site they give precedence. Archaeological sites do not form a record of the activities that occurred at a location, but are formed instead by the act of artifact discard at a location.

The palimpsest nature of time-averaged archaeological deposits compels us to reject their categorization as single functional entities. Binford's discussion of foragers and collectors (1980) is of little use if one understands it as a means of obtaining prehistoric settlement patterns through the identification of site types. Nor is it useful to think of assemblages as resulting from the operation of a single strategy. Time-averaged deposits do not link together as though the operation of a single set of integrated activities produced them (Stern, 1994). Instead, we see in Binford's writings how to understand the nature of artifact deposition as the product of a number of settlement patterns or as the outcome of a variety of resource gathering strategies. As Binford (1982) showed, depending on where a site fits into a particular strategy, discard rates for different types of artifacts will vary. However, a single location may change its place and role in a strategy through time. One settlement system may overlay another as resource availability changes. Therefore, artifacts from one location are not the products of either a single synchronic settlement system or a single strategic system. Rather, they represent the cumulation of discard events over the entire history of uses of that place. We emphasize this crucial point in our work because there is no possibility of stratigraphically distinguishing different "occupations." The material products of all activities that occurred at one place in the landscape create a palimpsest. Therefore, we do not attempt to isolate individual occupations or depositional events because we see the relative complexity of the assemblage composition as an indicator of the complex history of place use. Of course, resource availability may not diminish at some locations, leading people in the past to use such places in much the same way over significant periods. However, given the vast time spans often represented in archaeological deposits, we suspect this to be the exception rather than the rule. At any rate, rather than assuming redundancy, and therefore continually seeking to synthesize a single strategy or settlement system to exclude all variability, we prefer to make investigating assemblage variability the goal of our research.

Environmental Variability

The environments with which we deal are highly variable and interpretable at a variety of temporal scales. In Australia, for instance, the stratigraphic sequence between the late Pleistocene and the late Holocene one of us has investigated has long periods of erosion separated by much shorter periods of deposition or surface stability (Fanning and Holdaway, 2001b). Archaeological materials therefore appear only on these depositional or stable surfaces. One period of surface stability occurred during the last 2,000 years before European settlement. We have dated many heat retainer hearths to this time. Despite the geological stability, however, the hearth dates tell of a fluctuating human presence. During one period of around two hundred to three hundred years, which may correlate with an increase in temperature known worldwide as the Medieval Climatic Anomaly, occupation appears to have ceased. Both before and after this gap in occupation, hearths were constructed but analysis of the radiocarbon results shows that hearth construction was occasional, occurring every few decades (Holdaway et al., 2002). Based on the location of the dated hearths, there is little evidence that the occupants at any one time were aware of those who had occupied the valley previously. Hearths with different age estimates, for instance, are side by side with no evidence of reuse. Therefore, hearth construction is discontinuous over two millennia, continuous at the scale of centuries within single millennia, and discontinuous again at the scale of decades. The history of place use at this location is one of desert-swapping and variability – change that is visible only if sufficient time passes for a patterned archaeological record to accumulate and if the archaeologist explores this variability at multiple scales.

Similarly, in the Wyoming Basin, Smith and McNees (1999) document clear evidence for persistent places (Schlanger, 1992), i.e., places with Archaic-age slab-lined pits visited repeatedly over a period of hundreds of years as demonstrated through chronometric dating. During the same period, at other locations in the basin, contributors to Larson and Francis (1997) point to the presence of pit houses, suggesting dedicated and deliberate time-transgressive use at these locations. At still other locations in the basin, especially in contemporary-dune fields with recent assemblages, both surface and subsurface archaeological records document place use with no evidence of anticipated return. Spatial contiguity in stratified artifact distributions (Dewar and McBride, 1992) indicates subsequent returns (as at the multiple multicomponent sites documented through cultural resource compliance activities in the basin, e.g., Taliaferro, Smith and Creasman, 1988). There is little evidence, however, that those who returned to particular locations were aware of previous occupations. The very high proportion of the chipped stone debris resulting from biface reduction, even though tool-quality cobbles are often (but not always) widely available, points to both planned greater mobility and planned short occupations (as per arguments offered by Kelly, 1988; see also Bamforth and Becker, 2000). At this point, the data seem to point to the practice of desert-hopping by Archaic and Late Prehistoric populations, with repeated movement throughout and, according to Smith's (1999) analysis of obsidian source–distance relationships, just outside the basin proper.

Assemblage Variability

Thus, those who assume that they can apply single settlement systems or single strategies to interpret the archaeological records of foragers and collectors are failing to consider environmental variability. Variability in strategies, rather than continuity, provides the key to unlocking the history of place use. Take a curated artifact. Its place of use may vary during its use life as it is transported from location to location (Kuhn, 1994; Shott, 1996). Eventually the tool will wear out and be deposited in a site. Clearly, in such a case, one cannot treat locations of use and location of deposition as though they were one in the same. There is an argument that a closer relationship between function and location of deposition exists for tools with short use lives. However, this ignores both the general lack of specificity of tool function and form and the specific results of Binford's Mask site research, as discussed above. There may be many different kinds of short-term activities represented at a site and yet these activities may have little relation to site function.

These problems reduce the utility of function as an organizing concept with which to understand the distribution of artifactual material across a landscape. The alternative is to see assemblage composition not in synchronic functional terms, but as the result of a series of discard events distributed through time (Shott, 2003). Certainly, artifacts served purposes but the users may or may not have carried out these purposes at the places they abandoned them (Binford, 1979). Archaeologists have spent a great deal of time showing that there is little casual association between the functions an artifact performed and the location of its discard. Instead of concentrating on the function of artifacts, we suggest that it is more profitable to concentrate on their discard. Barring post depositional changes, we can be sure that the places we find artifacts are the places where they were abandoned. Thus, the association between location and discard is much more secure than the association between location and use.

What we need is an understanding of the significance of the association between location and discard. Here we suggest a return to the notion of time provided in the example of the deposition of a curated artifact discussed above. People make some artifacts for use over time, and they carry and use them in a variety of different locations. They discard such artifacts when they are no longer capable of fulfilling a particular set of functions – when they are worn out. The place where discard occurs depends on where the user is at the time the artifact wears out. Seen from this perspective, discard has a temporal quality. In the simplest formulation of this model – an idealized scenario that does not account for the life history of all curated artifacts – discard will occur most often where the people using curated artifacts spend the most time. If they use these artifacts for the same length of time at each place, the expended artifacts will accumulate uniformly across space. If, however, they use them in proportion to the amount of time they spend at one location, they will discard more expended curated artifacts over time at these locations.

In addition, the notion of temporality need not rest solely with curated artifacts (Holdaway, et al., 2000, 2004; Shiner, et al., 2005). Economic decisions based on optimality models may also relate to time rather than function. In stone artifact analysis, for instance, one may interpret choice in such variables as raw material and degree of core reduction in similar ways. Since cores of different materials tended to travel from location to location before discard, one may infer occupation duration from the degree to which reduction debris at a site is local or imported. During fleeting occupations, people would tend to transport materials to a site rather than seek out and use local materials (Elston, 1990). Limited use of this material would result in minimal discard, perhaps the occasional abandonment of an expended tool or the discard of resharpening flakes. In contrast, during prolonged occupations, they would make much greater use of local material. With less need to conserve imported tools and raw materials, they would tend to use them up, creating more reduction debris – if for no other reason than continued occupation at one location limited the chance to visit more distant sources (Elston, 1990).

Accumulation as History

From a temporal perspective, an artifact assemblage at a site preserves a history of the use of that site. Since desertic hunter–gatherers were most often mobile, it is most unlikely that locations had continuous use. As Binford demonstrated, hunter–gatherer strategies, or forager and collector modes, reflect the nature of the environment, particularly the degree to which people may have repeatedly used a place.

It follows that a site's artifact assemblage records not the discard from single events but the accumulation from all events within one stratigraphic division.

The interpretation of assemblages from a temporal perspective permits an understanding of the sum of all activities at a particular locality in the past. From this perspective, we are not interested in isolating single events from the mix that occurred through time. Nor are we interested in averaging the events or determining which event was most common. The pattern comes from the outflow from all discard events. It is the complexity, or otherwise, of the assemblage at a particular location that is of interest as an expression of the history of the use of place.

Certainly, archaeologists will still be able to tell something about the range of activities performed at a particular location in the past and this knowledge will be of considerable interest. However, of more significance will be the sum of the activities that accumulated at this place through time. As discussed above, synchronic functional assessments of settlement pattern fail because they cannot deal with a dynamic past that was in a constant state of flux. Studies that emphasize strategies do not fare any better. Archaeology needs to outgrow a functionalist, ahistoric anthropology. The search for living floors and the "cautionary tale" of ethno-archaeological studies demonstrate a concern for identifying the material manifestation of events as the sole basis for inference about the past. However, such studies ignore human variability. Why should we expect the archaeological record representing events distributed across hundreds or even thousands of years to mimic short duration events? Gamble (1999:68) identifies "flagship" (read "those with the best information content") sites as those with pristine artifacts, presumably, where accumulation time is short and deposition rapid. We disagree. Pattern in the archaeological record comes from the accumulation owed to multiple events. In other words, the power of assemblage analysis comes from the analysis of assemblage variation, and multiple events create this variation. We will learn relatively little by studying the archaeological manifestation of single events. Living floors, even if we could regularly identify them, will tell us little about the past because they sample time at only one point. Pattern is much more significant if it is the result of the accumulation of artifacts due to time-transgressive behavior.

DISCUSSION

The temporal structure of deposits and the temporality we can infer from the artifactual record permits the assessment of multiple patterns understandable at a variety of temporal scales. Understanding human environment interaction therefore becomes a matter of relating the tempo and mode of artifact accumulation with the tempo and mode of physical and social environmental change (Fletcher, 1992). Three observations follow.

First, we see this time perspectivism approach as a new way of dealing with landscape and the interpretation of the strategies critiqued above. It is not that we need to individually resolve the multiple strategies that have produced assemblages. Rather the analysis of assemblage variation provides the means to determine place use histories, and, from there we can approach the interpretation of various strategies pursued in the past. We have therefore shifted the search for strategies from analyses aimed at defining synchronic moments in the past to patterns of variation generated through time. Previous approaches to either settlement pattern research or to the isolation of strategies often required limited artifact analysis. In many settlement pattern studies, artifact assemblages are little more than Stone Age visiting cards (Isaac, 1981) – markers of the use of a location in the past but little else. In such studies, site type identification does not require much artifact analysis. Sometimes, the presence of a few artifact types will do.

Alternatively, in the search for strategies, some archaeologists have turned attention to single classes of artifact (in North America, point types are most common). We suspect that the Stone Age visiting cards left by prehistoric peoples have produced distributions of sites across many landscapes in different continents that appear largely similar. What these visiting cards hide, however, are assemblages that record a huge variety of depositional histories with complex patterns of human–environment interactions. In the search for strategies, the artifact analyses are more complex, since they involve considerations of optimality through such factors as design or raw material acquisition, but they are ultimately limited in their facility for revealing historical variation. Strategies are absolute. They can change completely or not at all. Modeling the archaeological record as the product of functioning systems seems to promote an unchanging past. In contrast, investigating the temporal nature of the archaeological record allows us to begin to model the complexities of human environmental interactions.

Second, one of the questions that remains unanswered is whether the patterns attributed to the operation of strategies are apparent at a variety of different temporal scales. If they are not, and we suspect that this is likely to be the case in many situations, it begs the question of how we should interpret the patterns we are able to identify. What ''strategies'' are observable only over the long-term, and how should we differentiate them from ''strategies'' observable at shorter temporal scales? From studies of historical change may come a clearer understanding of the behavioral regularities from which ''strategies'' are abstracted. Questions concerning the temporal scale at which any patterns emerge rarely appear in either the Australian or North American literature, yet they remain of fundamental import if one is to meet concerns about the lack of match between the scales of interpretation and observation.

Third, understood from a temporal perspective, the challenge becomes how to assemble multiple, individual place use histories so as to understand the patterned use of space over the long term not by groups of individuals belonging to particular ethnic groups, nor by groups reducible to single structural poses or strategies. The material record of past behavior produces its own form of history. We can seek explanation for this history by analyzing the material remains at a variety of temporal scales. The patterns we see are the product of human behavior but not isolatable into units familiar to students of short-term ethnography or at least ethnography as it is currently written (Murray, 1997). Historical continuities exist in material culture but these continuities do not necessarily correlate with what people think either about the material culture or about themselves. As one of us has been able to show (Wandsnider, 1998), two different ethnic groups, each leaving behind markedly different material records reflecting markedly different settlement patterns and distinct behavioral strategies, can use a single place. Place use is the constant here. The history of use of place is no more or less valid because two different ethnic groups used a single location. Group ethnicity provides one way of dividing the material record into classes for analysis, and the nature of their economic pursuits forms another, but these are not the only possible analytical units nor are they oftentimes obtainable. As historical archaeologists have been able to show (e.g., Lightfoot, 1995; Lightfoot, et al., 1998), the ethnic identity of the people who used and abandoned artifacts is much less interesting than the fact that the artifacts were used and abandoned at a particular place and time.

CONCLUSION

Thirty years ago, Plog (1973, 1974) urged archaeologists to move beyond synchronic interpretations of a diachronic archaeological record. Research on the nature of the archaeological record during the 1970s and 1980s highlighted its temporal structure and the multiple temporal scales at which one might productively approach it, adding another dimension to Plog's critique. Archaeologists have begun to move beyond functional interpretation of hunter–gatherer deposits to interpretations of stable strategies. The next step, we suggest, is to consider formationally informed accumulation and place histories, sensitive to temporal structure, as the lens through which a variety of strategies, operating at a variety of tempos, become evident.

ACKNOWLEDGEMENTS   A version of this paper was given at an SAA symposium in 2001 organized by Amber Johnson and Lewis Binford. Harry Allen, Peter Bleed, Angela Close, Mathew Dooley, Don Grayson, Thegn Ladefoged, and Julie Stein provided comments on earlier drafts. The paper was completed while one of us (SH) was a visiting scholar at the Department of Anthropology, University of Washington.

REFERENCES

Allen, H., 1972, *Where the Crow Flies Backwards*. PhD dissertation, University of Sydney, Sydney.

Amick, D.C., 1996, Regional Patterns of Folsom Mobility and Land Use in the American Southwest. *World Archaeology* 27:411–426.

Alcock, S.E., 1993, *Graecia Capta: The Landscapes of Roman Greece*. Cambridge University Press, Cambridge.

Bailey, G., 1981, Concepts, Timescales and Explanations in Economic Prehistory. In *Economic Archaeology: Towards an Integration of Ecological and Social Approaches*, edited by A. Sheridan and G. Bailey, pp. 97–117. BAR 96, Oxford.

Bailey, G.N., 1983, Concepts of Time in Quaternary Prehistory. *Annual Review of Anthropology* 12:165–192.

Bailey, G.N., 1987, Breaking the Time Barrier. *Archaeological Review from Cambridge* 6:5–20.

Bamforth, D.B., and Becker, M.S., 2000, Core/Biface Ratios, Mobility, Refitting, and Arifact Use-Lives: A Paleoindian Example. *Plains Anthropologist* 45:273–290.

Behrensmeyer, A., Kidwell, S., and Gastaldo, R., 2000, Taphonomy and Paleobiology. *Paleobiology* 26:103–147.

Bettinger, R., 1977, Aboriginal Human Ecology in Owens Valley: Prehistoric Change in the Great Basin. *American Antiquity* 42:3–17.

Bettinger, R., 1991, *Hunter–Gatherers Archaeological and Evolutionary Theory.* Plenum Press, New York.

Bettinger, R., 1993, Doing Great Basin Archaeology Recently: Coping with Variability. *Journal of Archaeological Research* 1:43–66.

Binford, L., 1978, Dimensional Analysis of Behavior and Site Structure: Learning from an Eskimo Hunting Stand. *American Antiquity* 43:330–361.

Binford, L., 1979, Organization and Formation Processes: Looking at Curated Technologies. *Journal of Anthropological Research* 35:255–273.

Binford, L., 1980, Willow Smoke and Dogs' Tails: Hunter–Gatherer Settlement Systems and Archaeological Site Formation. *American Antiquity* 45:4–20.

Binford, L., 1981, Behavioral Archaeology and the "Pompeii Premise". *Journal of Anthropological Research* 37:195–208.

Binford, L.R., 1982, The Archaeology of Place. *Journal of Anthropological Archaeology* 1:5–31.

Cane, S., 1984, *Desert Camps: A Case Study of Stone Artefacts and Aboriginal Behaviour in the Western Desert.* PhD dissertation, Department of Prehistory, Research School of Pacific Studies, Australian National University, Canberra.

Clarke, D.L., 1973, Archaeology and the Loss of Innocence. *Antiquity* 46:6–18.

Cosgrove, R., and Allen, J., 2001, Prey Choice and Hunting Strategy in the Late Pleistocene: Evidence from Southwest Tasmania. In *Histories of Old Ages Essays in Honour of Rhys Jones,* edited by A. Anderson, I. Lilley and S. O'Connor, pp. 397–429. Pandanus Books, Canberra.

Cowan, F.L., 1999, Making Sense of Flake Scatters: Lithic Technological Strategies and Mobility. *American Antiquity* 64:593–607.

Crumley, C.L., 1979, Three Locational Models: An Epistomological Assessment for Anthropology and Archaeology. *Advances in Archaeological Method and Theory* 2:143–173.

Crumley, C.L., and Marquardt, W.H., editors, 1987, *Regional Dynamics: Burgundian Landscapes in Historical Perspective.* Academic Press, San Diego.

Dancey, W.S., 1973, *Prehistoric Land Use and Settlement Patterns in the Priest Rapids Area, Washington.* PhD dissertation, University of Washington, Seattle.

Dering, P., 1999, Earth-Oven Plant Processing in Archaic Period Economies: An Example from a Semi-Arid Savannah in South-Central North America. *American Antiquity* 64:659–674.

Dewar, R.E., and McBride, K.A., 1992, Remnant Settlement Patterns. In *Space, Time, and Archaeological Landscapes,* edited by J. Rossignol and L. Wandsnider, pp. 227–256. Plenum, New York.

Dobres, M-A., 2000, *Technology and Social Agency: Outlining a Practice Framework for Archaeology.* B. Blackwell, Oxford.

Dunnell, R.C., 1980, Evolutionary Theory and Archaeology. *Advances in Archaeological Method and Theory* 3:38–99.

Ebert, J.I., 1992, *Distributional Archaeology.* University of New Mexico Press, Albuquerque.

Eckerle, W.P., 1997, Eolian Geoarchaeology of the Wyoming Basin: Changing Environments and Archaic Subsistence Strategies in the Holocene. In *Changing Perspectives of the Archaic on the Northwest Plains and Rocky Mountains,* edited by M.L. Larson, and J.E. Francis, pp. 139–167. University of South Dakota Press, Vermillion.

Edwards, D., and O'Connell, J., 1995, Broad Spectrum Diets in Arid Australia. *Antiquity* 69:769–783.

Elston, R.G., 1990, A Cost–Benefit Model of Lithic Assemblage Variability. In *The Archaeology of James Creek Shelter,* edited by R.G. Elston and E.E. Budy, pp. 153–164. University of Utah Anthropological Papers 115, Salt Lake City.

Fanning, P., 1999, Recent Landscape History in Arid Western New South Wales, Australia: A Model for Regional Change. *Geomorphology* 29:191–209.

Fanning, P., 2002, *Beyond The Divide: A New Geoarchaeology Of Aboriginal Stone Artefact Scatters In Western NSW, Australia.* PhD dissertation, Graduate School of the Environment, Division of Environmental and Life Sciences, Macquarie University.

Fanning, P., and Holdaway, S., 2001a, Temporal Limits to the Archaeological Record in Arid Western NSW, Australia: Lessons from OSL and Radiocarbon Dating of Hearths and Sediments. In *Australasian Connections and New Directions: Proceedings of the 7th Australasian Archaeometry Conference*, edited by M. Jones and P. Sheppard, pp. 85–104. Research in Anthropology and Linguistics 5, Department of Anthropology, University of Auckland, Auckland.

Fanning, P., and Holdaway, S., 2001b, Stone Artifact Scatters in Western NSW, Australia: Geomorphic Controls on Artifact Size. *Geoarchaeology* 16:667–686.

Fletcher, R., 1992, Time Perspectivism, Annales, and the Potential of Archaeology. In *Archaeology, Annales, and Ethnohistory*, edited by A.B. Knapp, pp. 35–50. Cambridge University Press, Cambridge.

Foley, R.A., 1981, A Model of Regional Archaeological Structure. *Proceedings of the Prehistoric Society* 47:1–17.

Gamble, C., 1999, *The Palaeolithic Societies of Europe*. Cambridge University Press, Cambridge.

Grayson, D.K., 1983, *The Establishment of Human Antiquity*. Academic Press, New York.

Gould, R., 1969, *Yiwara: Foragers of the Australian Desert*. Scribner, New York.

Hawking, S.W., 1998, *A Brief History of Time*. Bantam Press, London.

Hayden, B., 1979, *Palaeolithic Reflections: Lithic Technology and Ethnographic Excavation Among Australian Aborigines*. Australian Institute of Aboriginal Studies, Canberra.

Hiscock, P., 1994, Technological Responses to Risk in Holocene Australia. *Journal of World Prehistory* 8:267–292.

Hiscock, P., 1996, Mobility and Technology in the Kakadu Coastal Wetlands. *Bulletin of the Indo-Pacific Prehistory Association* 15:151–157.

Holdaway, S., 2000, Economic Approaches to Stone Artefact Raw Material Variation. In *Australian Archaeologist: Collected Papers in Honour of Jim Allen*, edited by A. Anderson and T. Murray, pp. 217–230. Coombs Academic Publishing, The Australian National University, Canberra.

Holdaway, S., 2004, Continuity and Change. An Investigation of the Flaked Stone Artefacts from the Pleistocene Deposits at Bone Cave South West Tasmania, Australia. Report of the Southern Forest Archaeological Project Volume 2, Archaeology Program, School of Historical and European Studies, La Trobe University, Melbourne.

Holdaway, S., Fanning, P., and Witter, D., 2000, Prehistoric Aboriginal Occupation of the Rangelands: Interpreting the Surface Archaeological Record of Far Western New South Wales, Australia. *Rangelands* 22:44–57.

Holdaway, S., Fanning, P., Witter, D., Jones, J., Nicholls, G., and Shiner, J., 2002, Variability in the Chronology of Late Holocene Occupation on the Arid Margin of Southeastern Australia. *Journal of Archaeological Science* 29:351–363.

Holdaway, S., Shiner, J., and Fanning, P., 2004, Hunter–Gatherers and the Archaeology of the Long Term: An Analysis of Surface, Stone Artefact Scatters from Sturt National Park, New South Wales, Australia. *Asian Perspectives* 43(1):34–72.

Isaac, G.L., 1981, Stone Age Visiting Cards: Approaches to the Study of Early Land Use Patterns. In *Patterns of the Past Studies in Honour of Favid Clarke,* edited by I. Hodder, G. Isaac and N. Hammond, pp. 131–155. Cambridge University Press, Cambridge.

Jones, G.T., 1984, *Prehistoric Land Use in the Steens Mountain Area, Southeastern Oregon*. PhD dissertation. University of Washington, Seattle.

Kamminga, J., 1982, *Over the Edge: Functional Analysis of Australian Stone Tools*. Occasional Papers in Anthropology, Number 12, Anthropology Museum, University of Queensland, St Lucia, Queensland.

Kelly, R.L., 1988, The Three Sides of a Biface. *American Antiquity* 53:717–734.

Kuhn, S.L., 1994, A Formal Approach to the Design and Assembly of Mobile Toolkits. *American Antiquity* 59:426–442.

Larson, M.L., and Francis, J.E., 1997, *Changing Perspectives of the Archaic on the Northwest Plains and Rocky Mountains*. University of South Dakota, Vermillion.

Lightfoot, K.G., 1995, Culture Contact Studies: Redefining the Relationship Between Prehistoric and Historical Archaeology. *American Antiquity*, 60:199–217.

Lightfoot, K.G., Martinez, A., and Schiff, A.M., 1998, Daily Practice and Material Culture in Pluralistic Social Settings: An Archaeological Study of Culture Change and Persistence from Fort Ross, California. *American Antiquity*, 63:199–222.

Lourandos, H., 1997, *Continent of Hunter–Gatherers: New Perspectives in Australian Prehistory.* Cambridge University Press, Cambridge.

Marquardt, W.H., 1992, Dialectical Archaeology. *Archaeological Method and Theory* 4:101–140.

McNiven, I., 1994, Technological Organization and Settlement in Southwest Tasmania after the Glacial Maximum. *Antiquity* 68:75–82.

Murray, T., 1997, Dynamic Modelling and New Social Theory of the Mid- to Long-Term. In *Time, Process and Structured Transformation in Archaeology,* edited by S.E. van der Leeuw and J. McGlade, pp. 449–463. Routledge, London.

Murray, T., 1999, A Return to the 'Pompeii Premise'. In *Time and Archaeology*, edited by T. Murray, pp. 8–27. Routledge, London.

Murray, T., 2004, Archbishop Ussher and Archaeological Time. In *The Archaeologist as Detective: The Leo Klejn Festschrift,* edited by L. Vishnyatsky, pp. 204–215. Folio Press, St. Petersburg.

Nelson, M.C., 1991, The Study of Technological Organization. *Archaeological Method and Theory* 3:57–100.

O'Neill, R.V., and King, A.W., 1998, Homage to St. Michael; or, Why Are There So Many Books on Scale? In *Ecological Scale: Theory and Applications,* edited by D.L. Peterson and V.T. Parker, pp. 3–16. Columbia University Press, New York.

Plog, F.T., 1973, Diachronic Anthropology. In *Research and Theory in Current Anthropology,* edited by C. Redman, pp. 181–198. John Wiley and Sons, New York.

Plog, F., 1974, *The Study of Prehistoric Change.* Academic Press, New York.

Ramenofsky, A.F., 1998, The Illusion of Time. In *Unit Issues in Archaeology,* edited by A.F. Ramenofsky and A. Steffen, pp. 74–84. University of Utah Press, Salt Lake City.

Ramenofsky, A.F. and A. Steffen, 1998, Units as Tools of Measurement. In *Unit Issues in Archaeology,* edited by A.F. Ramenofsky and A. Steffen, pp. 3–17. University of Utah Press, Salt Lake City.

Ross, A., 1984, *If There Were Water: Prehistoric Settlement Patterns in the Victorian Mallee.* PhD dissertation, School of Earth Sciences, Macquarie University, Sydney.

Ross, A., Donnelly, T., and Wasson, R., 1992, The Peopling of the Arid Zone: Human Environment Interactions. In *The Naïve Lands: Prehistory and Environmental Change in Australia and the Southwest Pacific,* edited by J. Dodson, pp. 76–114. Longman Cheshire, Melbourne.

Sanger, D., 1996, Testing the Models: Hunter–Gatherer Use of Space in the Gulf of Maine, USA. *World Archaeology* 27:512–526.

Schiffer, M.B., 1985, Is There a "Pompeii Premise" in Archaeology? *Journal of Anthropological Research* 41:18–41.

Schindel, D.E., 1982, Resolution Analysis: A New Approach to the Gaps in the Fossil Record. *Paleobiology* 8:340–353.

Schlanger, S., 1992, Persistent Places. In *Space, Time, and Archaeological Landscapes,* edited by J. Rossignol and L. Wandsnider, pp. 91–112. Plenum, New York.

Shiner, J., Holdaway, S., Allen, H., and Fanning, P., 2005, Understanding Stone Artefact Assemblage Variability in Late Holocene Contexts in Western New South Wales, Australia: Burkes Cave, Stud Creek and Fowlers Gap. In *Rocking The Boat: New Approaches To Stone Artefact Reduction, Use And Classification In Australia,* edited by C. Clarkson and L. Lamb, pp. 67–80. British Archaeological Reports, International Monograph Series. Archaeopress, Oxford.

Shott, M., 1996, An Exegesis of the Curation Concept. *Journal of Anthropological Research* 52:259–280.

Shott, M., 2003, Size as a Factor in Middle Palaeolithic Assemblage Variation in the Old World: a North American Perspective. In *Lithic Analysis at the Millennium,* edited by N. Moloney and M. Shott, pp. 137–149. Archtype, London.

Simms, S., 1992, Ethnoarchaeology: Obnoxious Spectator, Trivial Pursuit, or the Keys to a Time Machine? In *Quandries and Quests: Visions of Archaeology's Future,* edited by L. Wandsnider, pp. 186–198. Volume 20. Center for Archaeological Investigation, Southern Illinois University, Carbondale.

Smith, C.S., 1999, Obsidian Use in Wyoming and the Concept of Curation. *Plains Anthropologist* 44:271–291.

Smith, C.S., and Creasman, S.D., 1988, *The Taliaferro Site: 5000 Years of Prehistory in Southwest Wyoming.* Cultural Resources Series No. 6. US Bureau of Land Management.

Smith, C.S., and McNees, L.M., 1999, Facilities and Hunter-gatherer Long-term Land Use Patterns: An Example from Southwest Wyoming. *American Antiquity* 64:117–136.

Smith, M.A., 1986, The Antiquity of Seed Grinding in Arid Australia. *Archaeology in Oceania* 21:29–39.

Smith, M.A., 1989, The Case for a Resident Human Population in the Central Australian Ranges During Full Glacial Aridity. *Archaeology in Oceania* 24:93–105.

Smith, M.A., 1993, Biogeography, Human Ecology and Prehistory in the Sandridge Deserts. *Australian Archaeology* 37:35–49.

Smith, M.A., 1996, Prehistory and Human Ecology in Central Australia: An Archaeological Perspective. In *Exploring Central Australia: Society, the Environment and the 1894 Horn Expedition*, edited by S.R. Morton and D.J. Mulvaney, pp. 61–73. Surrey Beatty and Sons, Chipping Norton.

Stafford, C.R., Richards, R.L., and Anslinger, C.M., 2000, The Bluegrass Fauna and Changes in Middle Holocene Hunter–gatherer Foraging in the Southern Midwest. *American Antiquity* 65:317–336.

Stein, J.K., 1993, Scale in Archaeology, Geosciences, and Geoarchaeology. In *Effects of Scale on Archaeological and Geoscientific Perspectives*, edited by J.K. Stein and A.R. Linse, pp. 1–10. Geological Society of America, Boulder, Colorado.

Stein, J.K., 2001, Archaeological Sediments in Cultural Environments. In *Sediments in Archaeological Context*, edited by J.K. Stein and W.R. Farrand, pp. 1–28. University of Utah Press, Salt Lake City.

Stern, N., 1993, The Structure of the Lower Pleistocene Archaeological Record. *Current Anthropology*, 34:201–225.

Stern, N., 1994, The Implications of Time-Averaging for Reconstructing the Land-Use Patterns of Early Tool-Using Hominids. *Journal of Human Evolution* 27:89–105.

Stern, N., Porch, N., and McDougall, I., 2002, FxJj43: A Window into a 1.5-Million-Year-Old Palaeo-landscape in the Okote Member of the Koobi Fora Formation, Northern Kenya. *Geoarchaeology* 17:349–392.

Torrence, R., 1989, Tools as Optimal Solutions. In *Time, Energy and Stone Tools*, edited by R. Torrence, pp. 1–6. Cambridge University Press, Cambridge.

Thomas, D.H., 1973, An Empirical Test for Steward's Model of Great Basin Settlement Patterns. *American Antiquity* 38:155–176.

Thomas, D.H., 1975, Nonsite Sampling in Archaeology: Up the Creek Without a Site? In *Sampling in Archaeology*, edited by J.W. Mueller, pp. 61–81. University of Arizona, Tucson.

Thomson, D.F., 1939, The Seasonal Factor in Human Culture Illustrated from the Life of a Contemporary Nomadic Group. *Proceedings of the Prehistoric Society* 5:209–221.

Veth, P., 1989, Islands in the Interior: A Model for the Colonisation of Australia's Arid Zone. *Archaeology in Oceania* 24:81–92.

Veth, P., 1993, *Islands in the Interior: The Dynamics of Prehistoric Adaptations within the Arid Zone of Australia*. International Monographs in Prehistory, Archaeological Series 3. Ann Arbor.

Wandsnider, L., 1996, Describing and Comparing Archaeological Spatial Structures. *Journal of Archaeological Method and Theory* 3:319–384.

Wandsnider, L., 1998, Landscape Element Configuration, Lifespace, and Occupation History: Ethno-archaeological Observations and Archaeological Applications. In *Surface Archaeology*, edited by A.P. Sullivan III, pp. 21–39. University of New Mexico Press, Albuquerque.

Wandsnider, L., 2003, Solving the Puzzle of the Archaeological Labyrinth: Time Perspectivism in Mediterranean Surface Archaeology. In *Side-by-Side,* edited by S. Alcock and J. Cherry, pp. 49–62. Oxbow Press, Oxford.

White, C., and Peterson, N., 1969, Ethnographic Interpretations of the Prehistory of Western Arnhem Land. *Southwestern Journal of Anthropology* 25:45–67.

Williams, E., 1987, Complex Hunter–Gatherers: A View from Australia. *Antiquity* 61:310–321.

Wobst, H.M., 1978, The Archaeo-Ethnology of Hunter-gatherers or the Tyranny of the Ethnographic Record in Archaeology. *American Antiquity* 43:303–309.

CHAPTER 13

Large Scale, Long Duration and Broad Perceptions: Scale Issues in Historic Landscape Characterisation

GRAHAM FAIRCLOUGH

INTRODUCTION

Historic Landscape Characterisation (HLC) is a method of landscape-scale interpretation and analysis of the historic environment that has been developed over the last 10 years for archaeological resource management purposes by English Heritage and English local government (Aldred and Fairclough, 2003; Clark et al., 2004; English Heritage, 2004; Fairclough, 2002).

This chapter examines how HLC confronts scale in several guises. The HLC method is GIS-based, which immediately introduces simple issues of spatial scale at three levels: input, output and interpretation. Issues of scale related to geographic size (''map scale'') are fairly mechanical, however, and relatively easily resolved. HLC also confronts more challenging scale issues: some also concerned with spatial scale, but most with other scales such as temporal, perceptual or social. Some concern even more interesting questions such as scales of use, application and objectives. These issues can be divided into two groups – first, categories of scale – space, time and perception – that *define* the HLC method; and second, less central and more unusual, types of scale issues that mainly arise *from* HLC projects. First, however, a short description of HLC is needed.

HISTORIC LANDSCAPE
CHARACTERISATION (HLC)

HLC is an archaeological resource management (ARM) tool that was invented in England (UK) during the 1990s (Herring 1998; Fairclough 1999; Fairclough et al.,

1999; Fairclough and Macinnes, 2003; Clark et al., 2004). It arose as a response to debates about whether a selective list – a Register – of landscapes of historic importance should be compiled. This was (and still is) a very problematic concept, but it is also a scale-dependent issue, because traditional methods of designation and protection used successfully for monuments and buildings cannot be expected to work at the scale of whole landscapes.

Apart from that scale-related objection (and other philosophical reservations – i.e., definition, how to treat "living", semi-natural, heritage), there remained the issue of selectivity. Which landscapes are not historic? Everywhere has historic and cultural character of some description. Landscape is valuable because it is a part of life everywhere. Early drafts of the European Landscape Convention included a European list, but the adopted version withdrew from a selective approach in favour of a more comprehensive and democratic approach, recognising local distinctiveness and aiming to promote the sustainable management of landscape everywhere (Council of Europe, 2000, 2002). The Convention thus tailors its objectives, holistic or integrated, to the scale of the resource in question, in this case the whole landscape of Europe.

In England, and in Scotland (Dixon and Hingley, 2002; Macinnes, 2002), unlike in Wales (Cadw et al., 1998, 2001), the heritage agencies did not adopt the Register approach, but set off in a different direction, similar to that used by landscape architects and landscape ecologists using landscape character assessment (Countryside Agency and Scottish Natural Heritage, 2002). In England, the result was a programme of GIS-based countywide HLC projects (Fairclough, 2003a, 2003b). There is a sizeable literature now on the HLC method itself (see bibliographies in, for example, Aldred and Fairclough, 2003; Fairclough, 2002, 2003b; Clark, et al., 2004) and this chapter is not the place for a further detailed description. Various methods are in use because of rapid evolution since the first HLC was carried out in Cornwall in 1994 (Herring, 1998), but they all share common principles, including those related to scale.

HLC considers "landscape" to be mainly a product of perception, not the same as the environment. It is "imagined" from its material components, notably all those derived from the past. It recognises many ways of perceiving landscapes – those of different experts (e.g., historians, ecologists, architects, art historians or agronomists), of the public, of personal and collective views, of economic viewpoints. It adopts as its main guide the perspective of archaeologists (in the broadest sense, that is the study of all types of material culture to understand both past and present), in the knowledge that this single viewpoint must eventually be integrated with the others.

The principles and methods of HLC sit within the European Landscape Convention's general definition: "an area, as perceived by people, whose character is the result of the action and interaction of natural and/or human factors" (Council of Europe 2000 Article 1). To flesh out this subtle and comprehensive definition, whose every word is significant (but most notably perhaps "perceived" and "action"), a set of principles based on English HLC were drawn up for use as one of the frameworks of an EU Culture 2000 network, European Pathways to the Cultural Landscape (EPCL), (Clarke et al., 2003; EPCL, 2002–2004; Ermischer, 2002):

1. the present-day landscape is the main object of study and protection – the present that survives in (and makes) the past, landscape as material culture – the reference to scale here is time-scale;
2. "time-depth" is the most important characteristic of landscape, treating landscape as a matter of history rather than geography – here scale also concerns the range of interdisciplinary work needed;
3. a concern with area not point data, with landscape not sites, with spatial scale directing HLC very firmly towards small scales (i.e., large areas), not large scales (i.e., small areas);
4. all aspects of the landscape, no matter how modern, ordinary or unattractive are part of landscape character, not just "special" areas – this introduces scales measured in terms of relevance, topicality and value;
5. semi-natural and living features (e.g., woodland, land cover or hedges) are as much a part of landscape character as are archaeological features or buildings: bio-diversity is cultural – here, scale is concerned with the degree and extent of human agency and intervention, (not, as in views of landscape focussed on "wilderness", untouched nature, with its presence or absence);
6. a characterisation of landscape is a matter of interpretation not record, perception not facts: "landscape" is an idea not a thing, although con-structed by our minds and emotions from the combination of physical objects – here the scale issues are those of objectivity/subjectivity, top-down/bottom-up approaches, and the range of views on the question of the reality and usefulness (or otherwise) of facts and data; and finally,
7. peoples' views, perceptions and opinions are an important aspect of land-scape characterisation.

At some stage, HLC-derived perception should be laid alongside public per-ceptions; how to do this introduces further very under-explored issues of scale.

Most of this chapter is written with the latest most advanced HLC projects in mind, and a short description of their method might help the reader. The method uses GIS to allow the subjective definition of areas of land as GIS polygons to which attribute data is attached. The polygons are defined to capture blocks of land which mainly have a single predominant character derived from historic processes (e.g., type of field pattern, woodland, industrial uses etc). These usually absorb minor variations, a conscious reduction of complexity – that is, they are a general-isation of historic landscape character that is dictated by a project's scale and its range of objectives. The attributes recorded for each polygon can record subsidiary as well as predominant characteristics. The polygon net allows the attribute data to be used for classification, and comparative and thematic analysis on a wide range of fronts, and at several levels from county to parish. Polygon attributes also recordwhat we know and can infer about earlier periods of landscape history, sometimes derived from historic maps but preferably from current maps and air photography.

There are other methods of studying the landscape and its past, of course. HLC is distinguished from landscape archaeology and history by its particular way of using GIS, its multiple and variable output scales (and to an extent input scales), its aim of creating area-based generalisations rather than detail for specific sites and features, and by its concern for the semi-natural and non-site components of landscape. It recognises time-depth in two ways, through the different dates of parts of the palimpsest of the surviving landscape, and through identifying relict features from earlier times. HLC also differs from some landscape approaches in adopting a primarily archaeologists', rather than historians', mentality. In a sense, it regards landscape as being mainly prehistoric (or rather a-historic) whatever its date, since even historic maps are debatable and selective documents.

HLC has rather more in common with landscape assessment by landscape architects, in that they use the same landscape-scale and present-day perspectives. It nevertheless differs from that sub-discipline in its focus on the vertical viewpoint (maps, air photographs, studying the land as an object), rather than on the more horizontal and topographically informed perspective necessarily employed by landscape architects. HLC achieves its three-dimensions by adopting the extra vertical dimension of time and "stratification", like landscape assessment studying the present top layer of the land but doing so with an in-built recognition of deep time, looking beyond the past few well-documented centuries. It also avoids seeing the landscape as either timeless or naturally determined, an interest in *process* that brings it closer to landscape ecology than to landscape assessment.

SCALES THAT DEFINE HLC

Space

This is the most obvious area where scale is a critical issue in HLC. HLC is highly scale-conscious and, as indicated, differs from many other types of landscape study. In large measure this is because it adopts a scale of data reference, data input, analysis and interpretation that is very different to most landscape assessment, and of a different nature entirely to site-based archaeology. HLC uses a small (large area) scale – in English terms a county scale (which, in such a small country, is somewhere below sub-regional). The study area of each HLC project is usually a whole county, a block of territory normally in the range of ca. $2,500–5,000\,km^2$. This extensive scale of work was partly chosen for pragmatic reasons, partly the institutional arrangement of British archaeological resource management. More importantly, however, it was also selected as a scale that could maintain a sensible overview, so that the whole landscape could be characterised without being caught up in very local or site-based detail.

It also filled a gap in archaeological resource management, that is, the coverage of the historic environment in Sites and Monument Records (SMRs). There are any number of parish or similar scale archaeological landscape surveys (and landscape histories) and a number of national frameworks such as the models of Oliver Rackham (1986), Jan Thirsk (1987) and Brian Roberts and Stuart Wrathmell (2000, 2002, itself using a distinctive scale of settled nucleus to dispersion). Between these two scales of the local, large scale, effectively "big site" work, of landscape archaeology, and the high level small scale national frameworks, there were very few tested or accepted archaeological or historical methodologies that could be used within ARM at intermediate (e.g., sub-regional) scales. Those that did exist were overviews of site-based archaeology, not landscape as such but regional histories, essays based on the use of site-based knowledge to inform a regional narrative.

The sub-regional level of English county councils offers us a chance to step onto a middle rung of a ladder of understanding that climbs from local landscape, village and site levels to national (and European or world) scales. It is important to emphasise that none of the sets of information or interpretation on this ladder can operate too far up or down from the level at which their data was captured and their perceptions formed. A common misunderstanding among archaeologists and historians using the English Heritage Settlement Atlas (Roberts and Wrathmell, 2000) for the first time was that it was "wrong" because its nationally based insights (and in particular its boundaries) cannot always be validated or seen at more local level. This was not its purpose, however – it was designed to be valid as a national perspective, hence its use of national data sets and scales. Whilst HLC hard copy output maps, for example, are often at a scale of broadly 1:100,000, those of the Atlas are published at scales of 1:1,200,000 and 1:2,000,000 (Roberts and Wrathmell, 2000). The Atlas' insights work at national level; but they need modification and more detailing at larger, local, scales, below that of counties. Nor would they work at a smaller scale – they would be too detailed for a European or world map, for example.

HLC's products have the same sensitivity to scale of use. The capture of both data and interpretations takes place usually at a large scale of 1:7,500 to 1:10,000, but assumptions about what is significant is informed by much smaller scale, for example at 1:25,000. Blocks of ancient woodland, for example, which are small (less than 1–3 ha for example) or relatively minor in context (a tiny percentage of an area otherwise characterised by, for example, enclosed fields) will not be included in HLC because at the county-scale (or "landscape-scale") it is not significant. The crucial point of HLC is that it is not an attempt to map the "real world" (the environment), but to capture a particular interpretation of it (the "landscape") at a particular chosen scale that works for particular uses. The Settlement Atlas shows a similar result using a national level (scale) of selection and omission, and of interpretation. Its authors point out that: "All maps represent a compromise between the scale of the base-map, the data to be depicted and the nature of the graphics used" (Roberts and Wrathmell, 2000:19)

The intention is to produce a picture, a model, of the world or of our interpretation of the world, that has a validity at the national scale but not necessarily also at all larger scales. Were HLC to be carried out for a single parish, a higher level of detail would be required.

Time

If spatial scale is a relatively straightforward issue for HLC (though still not always understood by those not familiar with HLC), time-scales are a little less easy to explain. The relationship between scale and detail is fairly obvious, and the zooming-in/zooming-out of representation and understanding is quite widely appreciated, not least through photographic sequences showing the whole planet to individual buildings that we see routinely in the opening credits of Hollywood films. Time is a different type of scale, however. For this discussion, it might be useful to identify two aspects:

1. *sequence,* i.e., chronology, for example between (in HLC terms, broadly speaking) 12,000 years ago and today, with additional questions of whether to divide this span equally or unequally into years, centuries or other longer epochs (see for example the seven "eras" defined for Lincoln by Stocker, 2003); and
2. *resolution,* i.e., whether to look at personal or collective time, or the diurnal, seasonal or long rhythms of the landscape.

Some landscape assessment operates at diurnal or seasonal scales. The environment's appearance (if not, perhaps, its fundamental character) changes on this time-scale, as weather, light, temperature or crop conditions affect the manner of how people perceive landscape. This can be predominantly in terms of visual or other sensual experience, but also more physically. The obvious archaeological example is crop marks, being both seasonal (i.e., when they appear) and diurnal (i.e., when they can be seen – light and cloud cover issues, not to mention practical issues such as the right place at the right time). Some landscapes therefore operate at this type of time-scale, though it is rare for landscape assessment to operate at scales larger than season. On the other hand, the field observations made by landscape architects are, of course, affected by daily and intraday issues which best practice recognises (Countryside Agency and Scottish Natural Heritage, 2002). HLC however, being desk-based or map-based, rarely reaches this far down the time-scale. Its scale is more long-term, because, like archaeology as a whole, it studies long-term change over thousands of years.

HLC's concern with broad social processes, and with human agency at the collective level over the long-term, (the effect on landscape of groups of people operating over generations rather than the impact of individuals that, for example, landscape history might study), also leads it to deal with long time-scales. This is the equivalent to the small scales used spatially: HLC allies large areas with long duration. HLC's place on the scale of time could well be described as "timescape-scale" by analogy with the shorthand term "landscape-scale". In practice, of course, there is a distinction reminiscent of that between input and output spatial scales. The actions in the past whose material traces HLC observes when creating landscape character may well be the product of very short time-spans (perhaps even days or hours), repeated annually in the case of farming, for example, but short moments nevertheless. The time-scale on which HLC operates, however, takes sequences of events as a single whole, just as it takes blocks of fields, for example, as a single spatial entity.

Because of this, HLC at first glance can appear to be divided into episodes or time slices. This tends to be a characteristic of landscape archaeology, which often subdivides the palimpsest of visible or buried archaeology at the large scale into periods ("Bronze Age", or "first millennium" or 20th century). This is not a strictly accurate way of perceiving the HLC method, however. HLC often attaches attributes to its polygons based on time-slices, most commonly anchored to historic map editions (e.g., 18th century county maps, mid-19th century OS (cadastral) first edition maps, Dyson-Bruce, 2002). This approach, for example, can give rise to describing certain field systems as being pre-18th century on the basis of the date of the first map to show them, even though other knowledge about the past and about landscape evolution, (for example the framework produced by the Atlas, or extrapolation from other data such as parish or estate models form documentary research, or inferences from morphology) would suggest a medieval or even earlier date. The more self-consciously archaeological HLCs (as opposed to more document-led HLCs) do not base their interpretation and extrapolation only on historic maps. In effect they regard landscape, even quite recent landscape, as being effectively prehistoric in the detailed and very literal sense of a thing or process without documents, whether it is what we normally call "prehistoric" in date or not (perhaps, the French *proto-historique* might be more useful.)

Time-layering in HLC is not a data-collecting and analytical tool, because ultimately just as landscape is a seamless whole geographically, so too is it seamless chronologically. The whole of the past resides in the present, seen or unseen, known or awaiting discovery. The aim of HLC is to capture the past within the single layer of the present. Through filters such as landscape legibility, appropriate spatial scale, relevance or contribution to landscape character, it condenses time into a single layer – which is, in the strict sense, the only landscape we can ever have, the product of our perception today, in the here-and-now.

This concertina-effect, condensing all time (or its main manifestations given the sequential time scale that HLC adopts) into one layer, is central to HLC. It could be argued that this creates a new type of time-scale, even a new "time", one in which all periods are represented simultaneously.

Perception

Landscape is a common heritage to a much greater extent than perhaps any other aspect of heritage, historic environment or bio-diversity. This is partly an issue of perception, because landscape is ubiquitous, on the doorstep so to speak. There is a more fundamental underlying issue, however, which is that everyone has their "own" landscape, or usually several, whereas people do not always feel direct ownership or access to significant historic buildings or archaeological sites, or even to the means of understanding all aspects of their significance. Landscape is generally common, common*place* even, and it is normally closely personal. As a consequence, there is a long spectrum of perception and ways of valuing every single piece of land. There is, in effect, a scale of perception. Where on that scale expert views of landscape (and specifically for this discussion, HLC) sit is not always obvious, and never a given. It cannot be a quantitative scale, like spatial scales, nor automatically ordered like time-scales. It has no "natural" sequence – some might place "expert" at one end, "popular" or "lay" at the opposite; others might scale it from collective to personal, or national to local; others again might symbolise it as a circle of points, with, for example, archaeology, ecology, aesthetics, social, economic or architectural at the points that are not opposite ends of a spectrum but in a more rounded relationship (see the many circular charts that have been published to try to explain "What is Landscape" e.g., Countryside Agency and Scottish Natural Heritage, 2002:7).

If putting the many different types of perception of value (English Heritage 1997) into a single scale is not possible, this need not prevent us from seeing the issue as one of scale. HLC adopts one scale in particular, and (unsurprisingly given its origins) this is that of the archaeologically informed expert view. It aspires, however, to capture broader community perceptions, and its objective is eventual integration with perception scales of landscape analysis based on, for example, the ideas of landscape ecologists or landscape architects. These of course operate at different points on the scale, providing different definitions and descriptions of landscape whose integration will be the perceptual equivalent of the concertina time-scale, the past-in-the-present scale referred to earlier (Palang and Fry, 2003).

Because each expert world-view can modify the others, the process of integration will create an iterative cycle, a spiral of never-ending provisionality. More importantly, however, these types of perception are only the tip of a very large iceberg, because there are so many different ways of seeing, at one extreme as many as there are individual people, but certainly as many as there are different nucleated communities of place, or different dispersed communities of interest. Traditional approaches to heritage management (the identification and protection of the best examples of each type of building or archaeological site) tend, by virtue of being generic and thematic, to produce selections at national or regional level. In contrast, characterisation's approach (as in HLC) is to push to the fore distinctiveness at a more local level, in a sub-regional context, and to locate itself in terms of perception as "place" not "special interest". This debate about scales of perceptions, and about multiple ways of valuing, whilst by no means new, is not yet resolved, and this chapter can do little more than raise the desirability of developing ways to articulate the various scales on which HLC and ARM need to operate.

SCALE ISSUES THAT ARISE FROM HLC

Scales of Selectivity

The level of detail that HLC adopts is to some extent simply a product of spatial scale and size. Cadastral maps (such as the British Ordnance Survey maps and Street Plans) exaggerate the width of roads to highlight them against the background of the rest of the world that is depicted – thus, on 1:50,000 Ordnance Survey maps, road widths are depicted at much smaller scale. The most recent digitised edition of these large scale maps enhance roads even further so that roadside features (e.g., wayside crosses) mapped on previous editions suddenly appear (or rather disappear) as if they lie underneath the road, which in the real world they do not, but in the map world might do. HLC does something similar, in selecting certain attributes of a block of land (e.g., its 80% coverage of ancient woodland)

while ignoring others (e.g., its 5% of settlement, or 15% of fields). It does not –
paradoxically to many – incorporate information about individual archaeological
sites such as hillforts or long barrows, or about buildings such as churches and
farms, even though most people agree that these are critical components of the
landscape and its character. These fall beyond HLC's scale "catchment". Their
contribution to landscape character needs to be captured more locally at point scale,
or through generalised narratives.

No hard and fast rules exist for HLC decisions on what to exclude or include as
practice remains consciously subjective and interpretative, and above all, contextual. There is a certain circularity in this decision: HLC has adopted a certain scale
("county scale") and therefore can only use data sets that work at that scale. This
treatment of scale privileges end-user functionality (i.e., the sort of information
needed by land managers) and overview; it focuses on output not input scales.

Scales of Detail and Generalisation

The scale of detail (or its opposite in this context, generalisation) is connected with
other spatial scales, but is a very much broader issue. It returns to the earlier
discussion about the different national, regional and local scales of landscape
interpretation, which requires at county scale a high level of generality. But the
issue is more fundamental to the aims and purpose of HLC. The HLC method
could have been devised to operate at regional or national scale, and it would have
emerged looking very different. Conversely, it could have been established on a
parish-by-parish basis, using methods of landscape archaeology supported by documentary evidence to produce "real" maps of the past. The development of HLC,
however, was governed by two main factors. The first was a need for relatively
rapid overall coverage of very large areas, and therefore a level of generalisation
was an essential choice. The second factor, most importantly, was the need for
generalised overviews to give strategic input into archaeological resource management. These were largely non-existent in the early 1990s, as ARM principally
worked at the tactical level with site specific data which, if not comprehensive,
was at least commonplace and widely available through SMRs. The main criterion
for this aspect of HLC, therefore, was to produce generalised, and therefore if
necessary superficial, overviews of a whole county's landscape to act as the
framework for later more local or detailed work and to provide strategic guidance.
This was a trade-off of depth against breadth, justified by the strategy's objective.
The decision to produce overviews and generalisations (a choice of one type of
scale) determined another such choice, that of spatial scale.

At the extreme ends of the detail/general scale, HLC perhaps ceases in the
conventional sense to be a scaled-down map of the world, in the manner of OS
mapping, an excavation plan, a building survey or a mapped artefact distribution.
It starts instead to become an interpretative view that belongs on a different scale
entirely to that of linear scales. The switch over from point data (at whatever scale)
to generalised area "data" (and not in the sense of simply depicting site extent
and boundaries but in the more complex sense of an interpretative construct

rather than pure data, if such ever exists) moves HLC into a different category. This may be how HLC and its related methods can begin to capture public and personal perceptions in a significant way. It can also start to capture the values and benefits – the "affordances" – that people see in and take from their landscapes, the understanding of which is as essential a prerequisite for sustainable landscape management as is a better understanding of history and archaeology.

Subjective and Interpretative Scales

HLC projects and their GIS databases are also linked to issues of subjectivity, which can also usefully be viewed in scalar terms. The HLC approach can be placed on a scale concerned with how interpretations and understanding are created. At one extreme are hard scientific views of the world that sees everything as ultimately quantifiable. In terms of "landscape" or "environment", some schools of ecology move towards this extreme, just as did landscape assessment in the 1970s before it withdrew from that particular *cul-de-sac* and found the more fruitful qualitative road that it currently travels along (Countryside Agency and Scottish National Heritage, 2002). At the other extreme is a view of landscape that is almost entirely associative, that identifies landscape character in terms of painters' and writers' perception, as places that merely anchor historical events or reflect their landscape designers' creativity, or which flow from personal memories and collective identity. Most landscape practitioners now accept that landscape can and should as much as possible occupy all of this scale, from objective recording to subjective appreciation. As with linear scale at county level, the HLC method puts itself in the middle ranges of this spectrum. HLC is the subjective interpretation of material objects, recorded as objectively (or rather as transparently and repeatedly) as possible, but analysed by subjective interpretation (e.g., fields of a particular shape, size or context, for example, are interpreted as being probably late medieval assarts).

When a completed HLC is either enriched by more local survey or subjected to, for example, parish-size analysis, its position on this scale slides towards objectivity and scientifically rigorous proof. When it moves in the opposite direction (towards smaller scale regional outputs, i.e., increased levels of generalisation) the subjective quotient rises as broad extrapolations are made from a few known area-related "facts" to wider interpretations and assumptions. Additionally, and perhaps paradoxically, smaller scale regional overviews may well be the scale at which to capture community and cultural perception and identity, whilst personal associations and the capture of affordances will probably require work at local scales.

Scales of Applications, Affordances and Management

An appropriate point to close this chapter is with the practical applications of HLC that define it as a tool for helping to manage environmental change rather than as an academic exercise per se. These raise rather simpler scale issues, again referring to the input/output distinction. As a method of understanding based on small-scale, broad-brush generalisation, HLC is most effective as a strategic management tool, for which it sets an overall picture of how the landscape and its character deserves to be managed. It is more difficult to use it to determine more local management priorities and probably misleading (or impossible) to use it at a very site-specific level. This is not to say that components of landscape (e.g., "sites") do not need study and management in their own right, but that landscape and heritage management operate simultaneously on many scales, and the scales may not always be perfectly harmonised. Some sites are priorities for management of their archaeological deposits but do not register strongly at the landscape scale; many landscape components do not need micro-management as long as their general contribution to character is safeguarded.

An HLC GIS provides a net of polygons that are currently defined by largely historical and archaeological attributes such as field morphology, change through time, the character of land use, or the nature of settlement. This net can be used, however, to translate site-data into landscape-scale interpretation. Recent, still experimental, work is exploring how this might apply to architectural attributes of landscape, notably farmsteads. Early signs are that the grain of HLC for farmstead character, for example, will be smaller-scale than the building-specific, or even thematic, approaches of most architectural research or conservation work.

A further use of the polygon net, to return to an earlier theme, is to capture local personal and community perception of landscape. It remains to be seen which scale issues will need to be confronted. It can be predicted that some aspects of public perception will be extremely localised, and capable of being recorded as point data – memories of individual childhood picnic-fields, views in paintings, birth places, field names and family place nicknames for example. But others may be highly generalised and abstract, perhaps also regional in spatial scale, and unanchored in conventional temporal scales ("timeless", "olden days" – before your memory of what your grandparents told you). There will also increasingly be "introduced" associations from film and TV, bringing national and global scales to bear on an essentially local context, but also perhaps through recycling (e.g., recolouring) of historic film footage changing people's perceptions of temporal scales.

CONCLUSION

Many of the ways in which characterisation such as HLC interacts with scale are not particularly difficult or problematic. It is simply necessary for those using character-based tools for heritage and archaeological resource management to appreciate that all their work sits at a particular place on a larger scale, and that there is more than one type of scale. The "band" in which they operate might be a relatively narrow part of any particular scale – as in HLC's size scale, broadly mid-level on the long gradation from local to international. It can be wide – at least in aspiration – for example, in the aim of capturing the full range of perspectives and value-systems that people of all types and backgrounds invest in (with our current example) landscape. It can have a concertina effect, as in looking at long-term time as part of a present-day temporal palimpsest. It may appear straightforward to know where any piece of work is located on these scales, but a lack of awareness of the full potential range of the scale would be restrictive. The confrontation with scale – that is making conscious choices about scale and being aware of the implications – is also necessary in order to identify future directions of work and the essential interfaces that need to be built with other disciplines (e.g., between archaeology and landscape ecology, Palang and Fry, 2003). Finally, because characterisation is a search for context (the way that a building or an archaeological site fits into a wider spatial or thematic context, the way that a local area is contextualised regionally, and how national or European frameworks overarch all), it always needs to confront scale in all its forms, and to be explicitly and theoretically aware of the context of its own methods in terms of many different types of scale.

REFERENCES

Aldred, O., and Fairclough, G.J., 2003, *Historic Landscape Characterisation: Taking Stock of the Method – The National HLC Method Review*. English Heritage and Somerset County Council, London. Also at: http://www.english-heritage.org.uk/characterisation (accessed 6th December 2004).

Cadw, Countryside Council for Wales and ICOMOS-UK, 1998, *Register of Landscapes of Outstanding Historic Interest in Wales*. Cadw, Cardiff.

Cadw, Countryside Council for Wales and ICOMOS-UK, 2001, *Register of Landscapes of Special Historic Interest in Wales*. Cadw, Cardiff.

Clark, J., Darlington, J., and Fairclough, G.J., editors, 2003, *Pathways to Europe's Landscape*. EPCL/EU, Heide.

Clark, J., Darlington, J., and Fairclough, G.J., 2004, *Using Historic Landcsape Characterisation*. English Heritage and Lancashire County Council, Preston. Also at: http://www.english-heritage.org.uk/characterisation (accessed 29th November 2004).

Council of Europe, 2000, *European Landscape Convention*, Strasbourg: European Treaty Series No. 176. Council of Europe. Online: http://www.coe.int/t/e/Cultural_Co-operation/Environment/Landscape (accessed 29th November 2004).

Council of Europe, 2002, The European Landscape Convention. In *Naturopa* 98. Strasbourg: Council of Europe.

Countryside Agency and Scottish Natural Heritage, 2002, *Landscape Character Assessment: Guidance for England and Scotland*. Cheltenham, Countryside Agency, CAX 84. Online: http://www.ccnetwork.org.uk (accessed 29th November 2004).

Dixon, P., and Hingley, R., 2002, Historic land-use assessment in Scotland. In *Europe's Cultural Landscape: Archaeologists and the Management of Change*, edited by G.J. Fairclough and S.J. Rippon, pp. 85–88. Europae Archaeologiae Consilium and English Heritage, Brussels and London.

Dyson-Bruce, L., 2002, Historic Landscape Assessment – the East of England experience. In *Archaeological Informatics: Pushing the Envelope. Computer Applications and Quantitative Methods in Archaeology, Proceedings of the 29th Conference, Gotland, April 2001*, edited by G. Burenhult, BAR International Series 1016, pp. 35–42. Archaeopress, Oxford.

English Heritage, 1997, Sustaining the Historic Environment. English Heritage, London.

English Heritage, 2004, Promoting Characterisation: Landscape. Online: http://www.english-heritage.org.uk/characterisation (accessed 29th November 2004).

European Pathways to the Cultural Landscape, 2002–2004, The Culture 2000 Network. Online: http://www.pcl-eu.de/(accessed 29th November 2004)

Ermischer, G., 2002, Spessart goes Europe: The Historic Landscape Characterisation of a German Upland Region. In *Europe's Cultural Landscape: Archaeologists and the Management of Change*, edited by G.J. Fairclough and S.J. Rippon, pp. 157–168. Europae Archaeologiae Consilium and English Heritage, Brussels and London.

Fairclough, G.J., 1999, Protecting Time and Space: Understanding Historic Landscape for Conservation in England. In *The Archaeology and Anthropology of Landscape: Shaping Your Landscape*, edited by P.J. Ucko and Layton, R., pp. 119–134. Proceedings of the World Archaeology Congress, New Delhi, 1994, One World Archaeology, Volume 30. Routledge, London.

Fairclough, G.J., 2002, Cultural Landscape, Computers and Characterisation. In *Archaeological Informatics: Pushing the Envelope*. Computer Applications and Quantitative Methods in Archaeology, Proceedings of the 29th Conference, Gotland, April 2001, edited by G. Burenhult, pp. 277–294. BAR International Series 1016, Archaeopress, Oxford.

Fairclough, G.J., 2003a, The Character of the Historic Environment – Heritage Protection and the sustainable management of change. In *Von Nutzen und Nachteil der Demkmalplfelge für das Leben* 70:103–109. Tag fürDenkmalpflege. Jahrestagung der Vereinigung der Landesdenkmalpfleger in der Bundesrepublik Deutschland vom 17–21 Juni 2002 in Wiesbaden (Arbeitsheft 4 des Landesamtes für Denkmalpflege Hessen). Wiesbaden.

Fairclough, G.J., 2003b, The Long Chain: Archaeology, Historical Landscape Characterization and Time Depth in the Landscape. In *Landscape Interfaces: Cultural Heritage in Changing Landscapes*, edited by H. Palang and G. Fry, pp. 295–317. Landscape Series 1. Kluwer Academic Publishers, Dordrecht.

Fairclough, G.J., Lambrick, G., and McNab A., 1999, *Yesterday's World, Tomorrow's Landscape (The English Heritage Historic Landscape Project 1992–94)*. English Heritage, London.

Fairclough, G.J., and Macinnes, L., 2003, *Understanding Historic Landscape Character. Topic Paper 5, Landscape Character Assessment Guidance for England and Scotland*. Countryside Agency, Scottish Natural Heritage, Historic Scotland and English Heritage. Online: http://www/ccnetwork.org.uk (accessed 29th November 2004).

Fairclough, G.J., and Rippon, S.J., editors, 2002, *Europe's Cultural Landscape: Archaeologists and the Management of Change*. Europae Archaeologiae Consilium and English Heritage, Brussels and London.

Herring, P., 1998, *Cornwall's Historic Landscape: Presenting a Method of Historic Landscape Character Assessment*. Cornwall Archaeology Unit (Cornwall County Council) and English Heritage, Truro.

Jones, M.J., Stocker, D., Vince, A., with Herridge, J., 2003, *The City by the Pool: Assessing the Archaeology of the City of Lincoln*. Lincoln Archaeological Studies 10. Oxbow Books, Oxford.

Macinnes, L., 2002, Examples of Current National Approaches – Scotland. In *Europe's Cultural Landscape: Archaeologists and the Management of Change*, edited by G.J. Fairclough and S.J. Rippon, pp. 171–174. Europae Archaeologiae Consilium and English Heritage, Brussels and London.

Palang, H., and Fry, G., editors, 2003, *Landscape Interfaces: Cultural Heritage in Changing Landscapes*. Landscape Series 1. Kluwer Academic Publishers, Dordrecht.

Rackham, O., 1986, *The History of the Countryside*. Dent, London.

Roberts, B.K., and Wrathmell, S., 2000, *An Atlas of Rural Settlement in England*. English Heritage, London.

Roberts, B.K., and Wrathmell, S., 2002, *Region and Place, Rural Settlement in England*. English Heritage, London.

Thirsk, J., 1987, *England's Agricultural Regions and Agrarian History, 1500–1750*. Studies in Economic and Social History. Macmillan, London.

CHAPTER 14

Multiscalar Approaches to Settlement Pattern Analysis

Andrew Bevan and James Conolly

INTRODUCTION

The increasing popularity of Geographic Information Systems/Science (GIS) in archaeology can be linked to the development of user-friendly software and corresponding improvements in spatial data handling techniques. As a result, GIS is deployed commonly as an organisational tool, but rather less attention has been paid to important developments in spatial statistics that can help make sense of such datasets. Perhaps the most important new developments all relate to the issue of scale, with respect to: (i) the problems encountered when combining datasets collected at different resolutions (e.g., Gotway and Young, 2002); (ii) the scale-related biases inherent in aggregate analytical units (e.g., the Modifiable Areal Unit Problem: Openshaw, 1996; Harris this volume); (iii) or techniques for multiscalar pattern recognition.

Here, we focus on the last of these three areas. Our paper reviews existing statistical approaches to settlement patterning in archaeology, explores in detail one useful multiscalar method – Ripley's K function – and suggests both the problems and potential of such techniques when interpreting the particular evidence provided by landscape survey. We draw on case studies from the Kythera Island Project (KIP), a multidisciplinary initiative designed to study the cultural and environmental history of the island of Kythera, Greece (Broodbank, 1999). From the project's onset in 1998, GIS has been used to store, manage, and analyse a wide variety of KIP research contributions, including the results of intensive archaeological survey, geoarchaeology, botany, historical geography and archival studies (Bevan and Conolly, 2004).

Andrew Bevan ● University College London
James Conolly ● Trent University

SPATIAL STATISTICS AND SETTLEMENT
PATTERNS

Settlement analysis in archaeology seeks to build up from the static spatial distribution of material culture and anthropogenic modifications visible in the contemporary landscape to an understanding of the dynamic cultural and environmental processes of human settlement systems.

With the obvious exception of phenomenological approaches, most studies of settlement and landscape accept that there is a need to adopt an empirical approach to pursuing this goal, even if in so-doing, many then fail to embed their conclusions within a wider inferential framework. Standard quantitative methods tend to explore either: (i) correlations between settlement (or other zones of human activity) and social or environmental variables (e.g., "predictive modelling"), or; (ii) the degree to which new settlements or households are located in physical relation to existing ones (we might call this "neighbourhood dependence"). The traditional tools used by archaeologists include, respectively, linear or logistic regression and nearest neighbour or quadrat analysis, but each of these raises methodological problems. The first two have the capacity to mislead in contexts where spatial dependence can be shown to exist (i.e., most geographic contexts: Fotheringham et al., 2002:162–166), and the last two are insufficient for detecting multiscalar spatial patterns. Here we concentrate on the latter, but the need to integrate these approaches is raised again in discussion at the end.

Settlement distributions are often described in terms of their configuration vis-a-vis three idealized states – namely random, regular, or clustered – but rarely do these states occur so clearly in practice (van Andel et al., 1986). In reality, settlement patterns are more complex, and measures such of these need to be contextually sensitive to the fact that the scale of analysis can change what appears to be a nucleated or centralized pattern, to one better described as dispersed. A regular or uniform pattern between contemporaneous sites has been taken to reflect a form of competition between settlements, the existence of site catchments or both (Hodder and Orton, 1976:54–85), sometimes because of demographic growth from an initial random distribution (Perles 2000:132–147). Clustering of sites may result from a number of factors, although localized distribution of resources and the emergence of polities or regional centres have often been highlighted (Roberts, 1996:15–37; Ladefoged and Pearson 2000). In contrast, random distributions have usually been treated as the statistical null-hypothesis, though several commentators provide good examples of how apparent random distributions in fact can be conditioned by selected environmental, biological, and social variables (Maschner and Stein, 1995; Woodman 2000; Daniel 2001). Indeed, a problem we will return to later is that point pattern analysis implicitly assumes spatial isotropy (i.e., invariance by rotation) and homogeneity despite the fact that actual human landscapes offer both topographically dependent movement environments and spatially heterogeneous natural resources (water, soils, etc.).

The favoured technique of archaeologists for detecting clustered or uniform distributions is nearest neighbour analysis. Clark and Evans (1954) first explored the utility of this method for ecological purposes, and it was soon being used to understand settlement patterning (Dacey, 1960; Haggett, 1965). Its application to archaeological settlement pattern analysis followed some time later (Hodder and Hassall, 1971; Hodder, 1972; Whallon, 1973; Washburn, 1974; Hodder and Orton, 1976), continued in the 1980s and 1990s, and the technique retains its prominence today both in general textbooks (e.g., Wheatley and Gillings 2002) and culturally specific studies (e.g., Ladefoged and Pearson 2000; Perles 2001:134–138).

Clark and Evan's nearest neighbour coefficient is probably popular in the archaeological community for two reasons: (i) it is straightforward to calculate, and; (ii) it provides an easily interpretable coefficient. However, nearest neighbour analysis was not designed to detect spatial patterning at anything but the 1st nearest neighbour. Increasing the nearest neighbour measurement to the 2nd, 3rd...nth neighbour may detect clustering at different scales, but the statistical validation of patterning then becomes difficult (Hodder and Orton, 1976:41). Nearest neighbour analysis is also significantly influenced by the size of the area to be analyzed, with regular, random, or clustered distributions arising being dependent on the amount of surrounding area included in the analysis (Hodder and Orton, 1976:41). While there are workarounds for these problems, the technique remains a relatively coarse ruler with which to measure point distribution patterns.

In particular, the focus on 1st neighbour distances may overlook more complex, multiscalar, spatial patterns. Consider, for example, the point patterns in Figure 14.1. The left panel shows a hypothetical distribution of 56 sites. A single order nearest neighbour analysis applied to the 56 points in the left panel would detect the presence of clusters, and a K-means statistic could be employed to show that the optimum number of clusters was likely to be 8 (Blankholm, 1990:65). However, neither of these analyses would be able to identify the fact that there is also a higher-order scale producing three clusters. Furthermore, if we include the finer artefact-scale resolution represented on the right panel (rather than just an approximation of the centre of the artefact distribution), then clustering can be shown to exist at three different spatial scales: (i) artefacts forming sites (clusters i–x); (ii) sites forming primary clusters (clusters 1–8); and (iii) primary clusters forming secondary clusters (clusters A–C).

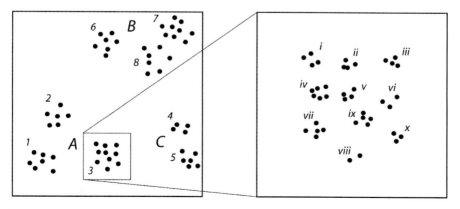

FIGURE 14-1. Multiscalar point patterns.

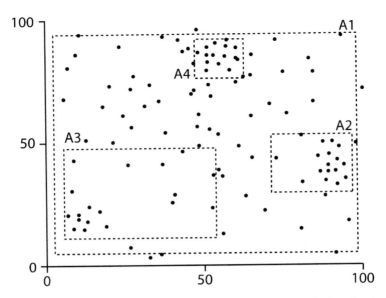

FIGURE 14-2. The influence of study area size on the detection and characterization of patterns (after Goreaud and Pélissier 2000: 15).

Another major problem with nearest-neighbour analysis is the effect the size of the study area has on the detection of patterning. For example, Figure 14.2 shows how adjusting the scale of analysis has a major influence on the homogeneity, intensity and clustering tendencies of point distributions. In the entire study area, A1, the pattern is homogenous with a clustered structure (i.e., clustering occurs relatively evenly) so that a frequency distribution of nearest neighbour values would be normally distributed. At smaller scales, for example in area A2, the pattern is heterogeneous with a strong left to right gradient. A neighbourhood density function would be positively skewed with a bimodal tendency. Area A3 is similarly heterogeneous, although its density value is significantly lower than A2. Area A4 has a high intensity and homogenous distribution, although here it is far more regular than seen elsewhere.

These two scalar issues – one related to analytical resolution, the other related to analytical area – although presented in abstract, are very real when attempting to make sense of settlement distributions, given that the latter may show a variety of characteristics depending on the resolution and the shape of the study area. The fact that GIS-led approaches to the collection and management of archaeological survey data are able to store data at several different scales within the same environment (e.g., artefacts, sites and regions) underlines the need for spatially sensitive approaches to the analysis of distribution patterns. Moreover, the dichotomy created by nearest neighbour analyses, dispersion vs. nucleation, is useful only at a very general level. Measures that take into account the intensity of settlement, its homogeneity, and the scale at which it is clustered or dispersed are clearly superior.

We therefore propose the use of a broader range of statistical approaches to point patterning, including methods that are inherently multiscalar such as Ripley's

K-function that we consider in some detail. Ripley's K-function (Ripley, 1976; 1997; 1981) was designed to identify the relative aggregation and segregation of point data at different spatial scales. It is defined for a process of intensity λ, where $\lambda K(r)$ is the expected number of neighbours in a circle of radius r at an arbitrary point in the distribution (Pélissier and Goreaud 2001:101). The K-distribution is a cumulative frequency distribution of average point intensity at set intervals of r. Significance intervals are generated by Monte Carlo simulation of random distributions of the points, and a 95% confidence interval can usually be obtained within 1,000–5,000 iterations (Manly, 1991). These estimates can be compared with the observed values of K to provide a statistically robust measure of cluster size and cluster distance in the dataset. We use an edge effect correction method proposed by Goreaud and Pélissier (1999). For clarity of presentation, the cumulative K distribution is usually transformed to $L(r) = \sqrt{K(r)/\pi}\text{-}r$, where the expectation under randomness $(L(r)=0)$ is a horizontal line. $L(r) < 0$ means that there are fewer than expected neighbours at distance r, suggesting a regular pattern, and $L(r) > 0$, means that there are more neighbours at distance r, indicating a clustered pattern (Pélissier and Goreaud 2001:102).

RESEARCH CONTEXT

Our broad area of interest is human settlement in Mediterranean landscapes, particularly the Aegean. The Aegean was first colonized by late Pleistocene pre-modern humans, possesses the earliest farming communities in Europe and, during the Bronze Age, was the setting for some of Europe's first complex societies. It saw the rise of the Greek Classical *polis*-states, and was subsequently entangled in the geopolitics of the Roman, Byzantine, Ottoman, Venetian and British empires. In the 19–20th century it was brought under the umbrella of the modern Greek nation state, and most recently, in the 21st century, it is part of an emerging European super-state. The impacts of these events on Aegean rural landscape history have been the subject of an enviable breadth of intensive survey projects that have provided high-resolution data on long-term dynamics of Aegean settlement systems (e.g., Broodbank, 1999; Cherry et al., 1991; van Andel et al., 1986; Bintliff and Snodgrass, 1985; Renfrew & Wagstaff, 1982, to name but a few). The Aegean is of obvious importance for archaeologists interested in long-term patterns and processes of human social and cultural evolution, mobility and population dynamics, settlement systems and ecology.

In this study, our largest unit of analysis is the island of Kythera, which lies approximately 15 km from Cape Malea on the southern tip of the Peloponnese (Figure 14.3). Its geographical location between two distinctive and influential regions, the Greek mainland and Crete, has been instrumental in shaping a distinctive Kytherian history. The island's role within, and contribution to, wider (early Aegean, eastern and/or central Mediterranean, and later pan-European) social and economic networks was one of the several thematic issues underlying the establishment of the Kythera Island Project (KIP) in 1998 (Broodbank, 1999). One way to explore the relationship between on- and off-island processes is to consider the

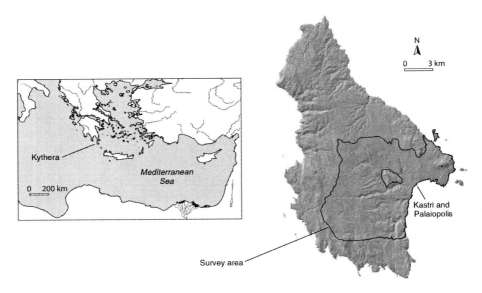

FIGURE 14-3. Kythera and the KIP survey area.

island's settlement patterns, particularly for cycles of nucleation and dispersion. Such cycles have been documented in other areas of the Aegean, notably on Melos (Renfrew and Wagstaff, 1982), Kea (Cherry et al., 1991:474) and in the southern Argolid, and interpreted as strategic responses to the expansion and contraction of inter-regional trade and exchange. Although such information does not offer a simple ruler to measure the islands and islanders' relationship to (political) economic cycles, it can offer insight into how the island settlement and demographic structure responded to broader trends in Aegean social and political history.

While our interest in exploring settlement patterning reflects this broader concern with Aegean rural landscape history, our purpose here is primarily methodological. Previous work by both of us (Bevan 2002; Bevan and Conolly 2004; and Conolly 2000) have highlighted the influence of analytical scale on constructing meaning from the archaeological record and this paper offers a further contribution to this endeavour by assessing critically the statistical tools available for quantifying nucleation/dispersal phenomena. We hope that this will provide a sound analytical platform upon which further, more holistic analysis of the Kythera material may proceed, and will also be of considerable use to others who wish to makes sense of such landscape patterning at different spatial scales.

THE KIP DATA SET

Intensive archaeological survey between 1998 and 2001 has documented the location and chronology of nearly 200 previously unknown prehistoric, Classical, Roman, Medieval and Venetian settlements across a study area covering about one third of the island. More comprehensive information about the fieldwork can be found in Broodbank (1999) and Blackman (1999, 2000, 2001, 2002). For the purposes of this paper, we restrict ourselves to analysis of settlement distributions from four chronological periods in the island's history. The first study considers the real spatial complexities behind an obvious feature of the recent Greek landscape, nucleation of settlement into villages. The second study then moves on to consider the additional issues raised in attempting to make sense of a settlement landscape identified purely by archaeological survey, specifically for Kythera in the Second Palace Period ("Neopalatial", ca. 1700–1450 BC). Some additional challenges – both temporal and multivariate – facing the analysis of spatial pattern in a survey context are then introduced briefly with respect to two further chronological periods on Kythera, the Early Bronze Age (ca. 3100–2000 BC) and the Classical (ca. 480–323 BC). Our intention is thereby to explore the viability of point pattern analysis under conditions of increasing methodological complexity.

RESULTS AND INTERPRETATION

Modern Buildings and Villages

Our first case study draws on a relatively modern dataset, primarily based on the Greek Army's mapping of standing buildings and villages identifiable on aerial photographs of Kythera from the 1960s (see Bevan et al., 2004). This data has been checked in the field by KIP and is relatively comprehensive (though isolated field houses were often missed). Here we examine this phenomena in two stages, beginning with ca. 9,000 individual buildings and then considering ca. 80 larger-scale "village" clusters (Figure 14.4).

We can calculate a Clark and Evans R statistic of 0.12–0.33 (depending on whether we use a mean or median nearest neighbour value) for the spatial aggregation of individual buildings on the island, suggesting a highly clustered pattern. Indeed this is confirmed if we calculate a modified Ripley's K ($L(r)$) function. It exhibits a large positive deviation from the upper confidence interval, even at the largest distance examined (e.g., 5 km). This indicates clustering at all scales, but more importantly, the existence of a heterogeneous pattern which is being driven by more than one type of underlying process (Figure 14.5) – indeed we might logically point to the known differences between the cultural factors influencing the spacing of buildings within villages (e.g., community values, shared resources) and those effecting the position of the more isolated fieldhouses (e.g., deliberate spacing between land holdings). This kind of result is problematic because the heavy clustering in certain areas hinders correct interpretation of smaller-scale spatial structure in others.

One way to get round this problem is to analyse village and non-village areas separately. Similarly, we can step up a typological level and consider the distribution of villages represented as single points. Such analysis will be approximate because defining which building clusters constitute "villages" is often subjective (it might be made less so by calculating a K means statistic but this may cross-cut alternative political, administrative or economic definitions of "a village"). Total

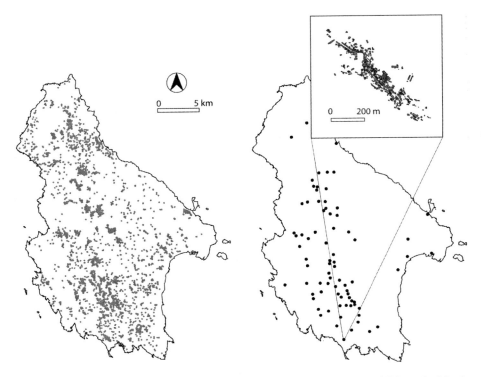

FIGURE 14-4. The distribution of extant buildings (left) and principal villages (right) on the island. The top right window is a close up plan of the village of Chora as an example of the original detail of the dataset.

estimates for the island can vary from 60 to 80 distinct communities, even in the 20th century, and here we use a relatively maximal estimate. An R-statistic of 0.74–0.84 (mean and median) suggests a slightly clustered village pattern, reflecting the fact that many settlements concentrate in inland areas next to the more suitable agricultural land. Figure 14.6 plots the complete frequency distribution of nearest

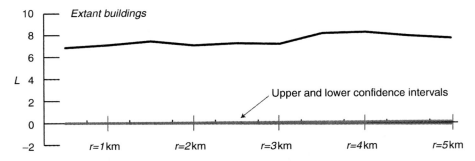

FIGURE 14-5. The modified K-distribution (L) for extant buildings. The K-distribution (dark line) sits well above the (grey) line marking a clustered distribution (at $p<0.1$). Note that the upper and lower boundaries are not ready distinguishable in this chart because of the scale of the y-axis.

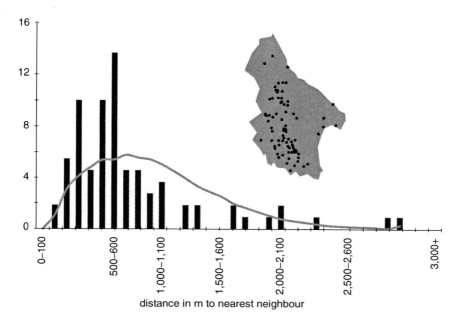

FIGURE 14-6. The frequency distribution of nearest neighbour distances in 100 m bins. The grey line represents an expected distribution derived from 1,000 × 80 iterations.

neighbour distances. Expected values (the grey line) were estimated by Monte Carlo simulation (i.e. from the average of a 1,000 sets, each n=80). Again, the observed pattern suggests that small inter-village distances (300–400 m and 500–700 m are more frequent than we might expect from a random distribution (significant at $p < 0.001$, Kolmogorov–Smirnov one-sample test).

We can then narrow our focus to just the inland area where most villages cluster. This is useful not least because in environmental terms, this region is relatively homogenous, with similar topography, water resources and access to preferred soils. Here the spatial distribution of villages is more regular and we get an $R = 1.26$ or 1.31 (mean/median), for the minimum convex polygon of the inland villages. A Ripley's L plot (Figure 14.7) also indicates a greater than expected regularity at smaller scales (statistically significant up to ca. 300 m radius), but in addition, shows that at larger scales, the pattern is not noticeably different from a random one. This suggests that in this more consistent resource environment, communities shared out the available space more evenly and establish clearer individual catchments, probably linked to the spatial organisation of in-field land holdings, refuse disposal and local political identity.

The Second Palace Period

The previous example was chosen because it dealt with standing buildings and an extant settlement pattern (though one with some time depth). However, for most prehistoric and many historic settlement distributions, the only viable technique for

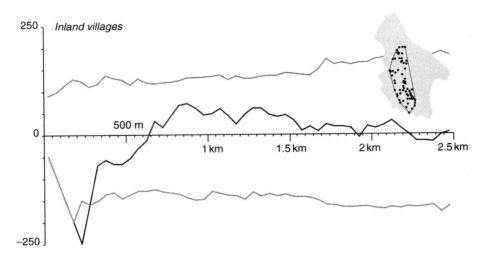

FIGURE 14-7. The modified K-distribution (L) for the principal villages in the inland area (as defined by the minimum convex polygon as shown). The K-distribution (dark line) sits within the upper (clustered) and lower (regular) boundaries with the exception of the range 150–300 m range (thus suggesting that at this scale there is a more regular spacing of villages than is statistically expected).

accessing regional scale information of this kind is intensive surface survey. Traditional extensive reconnaissance and site recording are usually incompatible with useful point pattern analysis (except for comparing very large or prominent sites such as tells), because their coverage areas (and intensity of search) are difficult to define and because they clearly miss so much of the actual site distribution. Modern intensive survey produces far more amenable results, not only because it is concerned with expressing accurate coverage intensity, but also because, under the right conditions (geomorphological and environmental), it can hope to recover a more comprehensive impression of past settlement landscapes. Even so, survey only produces proxy data (surface artefact scatters) for actual patterns of habitation and land use: we will therefore first explore a relatively simple, well-dated dataset—the Second Palace ("Neopalatial", ca. 1700–1450 BC) Period sites (Figure 14.8) – before briefly considering examples in which the problems of using such proxy data are more severe. KIP has been able to document ca. 100 Second Palace sites, comprising one major port zone focused on Kastri, and beyond it, a countryside covered quite densely in small scatters (nearly 2 per km²). For a variety of reasons, these rural scatters appear to be the permanent or semi-permanent dwellings of 1–2 families engaged in agricultural subsistence (we could call them "farmsteads": see Bevan 2002 for a preliminary analysis). They can all be quite closely dated to within a couple of centuries of each other (if not less) and therefore most are likely to have been contemporary habitations.

This settlement pattern is therefore a relatively simple case because it repre-sents a comparatively shallow temporal palimpsest and comprises a limited set of site types and sizes. Even so, in order to explore the spatial distribution effectively, we must exclude the influence of the major port site of Kastri. This is because we infer that there are two separate groups of processes dictating settlement patterning

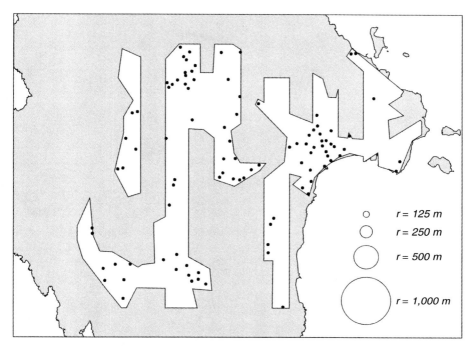

FIGURE 14-8. The distribution of Second Palace Period sites within the survey area.

in the Second Palace Period: one group generating the distribution of rural house-holds in the hinterland of the island, and another group of processes accounting for the pattern in the vicinity of Kastri. The real influence of the clustering at Kastri becomes clear if we consider the likely distribution of actual people across the landscape as suggested by site size. If, for example, we weight the sites according to their relative size, randomly placing one point within each site scatter area for every 0.5 ha of scatter (this threshold is arbitrary, but for our purposes here, we might think of them as crudely equivalent to notional nuclear households), then we produce a more realistic model of the likely spatial distribution of the Second Palace population. Almost all rural sites continue to be represented by a single point but the port centre (which consists of several large adjacent scatters) is represented by many more. If we run a Ripley's K function on this data, it shows a huge positive deviation from the confidence interval (Figure 14.9), again indicat-ing significant heterogeneity.

In contrast, if we exclude the Kastri zone as representing a separate phenom-enon, we are left with a more homogenous settlement landscape, at least in terms of the theoretical population represented by each point in the analysis. We can estimate a Clark and Evans R-value of 0.85/0.91 (mean/median, where the expected values are estimated from 1,000 random sets, distributed only within the intensively surveyed area, and not the Kastri zone), which is not significantly different from a random pattern. We can also look at this across the full frequency distribution of nearest neighbour values. Previous analysis, based on the site data available in 2001

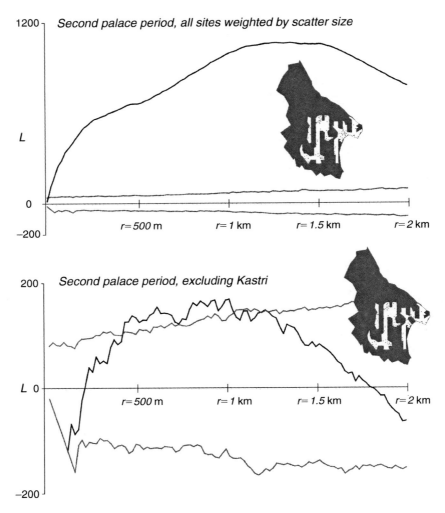

FIGURE 14-9. The modified *K*-distribution (*L*) for all Second Palace Period sites (upper), and Second Palace Period sites, excluding Kastri (lower).

suggested certain site spacings were more common than might be expected (e.g., ca. 300 m apart: Bevan 2002:227–231). However, while these small site spacings remain highly prominent after the dataset has been augmented by further field study (adding ca. 20 extra sites), it is less clear that the pattern departs from one that might be expected by random placement. A Ripley's modified *K* function (Figure 14.9) suggests only a limited tendency towards regular spacing at smaller scales (significant at $p=0.05$, but not at $p=0.01$), and apparently random from $r=200$ to 500 m. From $r=500$ m to $r=1,000$ m, sites cluster into statistically significant groups ($p<0.01$), reflecting the exploitation of broadly preferred eco-zones, including two basins and a well-watered plateau.

PROSPECTS

Aspects of the analysis above have already suggested that a major problem in applying K-functions and related multiscalar techniques to real settlement patterns is an underlying assumption of homogeneity; more precisely, such techniques assume that there is a single stochastic process behind the observed point distribution. A typical case is the distribution created by a pure Poisson process, but there are real world examples as well (such as wind-dispersion of seedlings from parent trees or forest stand thinning: Goreaud and Pélissier 2000:27). However, in archaeological cases, we deal with a bewildering variety of heterogeneity, for example of both natural environments and of site sizes, functions and dates. Furthermore, archaeological datasets exist in anisotropic spaces (e.g., as-a-crow-flies distances rarely reflect the nature of movement across real landscapes). In contrast, point pattern analysis tends to rely on Euclidean distance measures, and while this may be an acceptable proxy at smaller scales, it becomes more problematic the greater are the distances involved.

The last of these concerns may in the future be addressed by developing more terrain sensitive ways of creating inter-point distance matrices (e.g., cost surface analysis, though not without its own problems: Douglas, 1994). This final section considers three types of heterogeneous problem in greater detail: (i) landscape variability; (ii) imperfect chronological resolution, and; (iii) variation in site size or function. Possible responses to these problems are suggested.

Landscapes vary across space in terms of their provision of water resources, soils, rainfall, solar irradiation, etc. The degree of spatial heterogeneity will itself also vary between landscapes, with highly localized heterogeneity being a defining feature of Mediterranean environments (Horden and Purcell 2000). In terms of settlement patterns, this is unfortunate because ideally, we would want to be able to distinguish static locational preferences (e.g., driven by favoured soils) from dynamic processes such as the budding of satellite settlements from parent ones. However, there are several possible solutions:

1. Deduce a study area where the influence of environment on site location is relatively homogeneous (e.g., similar slopes, soils, access to water, etc.) and only consider point patterns within this zone (for an ecological example of such an approach: Goreaud and Pélissier, 1999:435–8).
2. Define such an homogeneous study area using more formal statistical methods such as an analysis of the local density function (Fotheringham et al., 2002:138–146).
3. Weight the intensity of random points so they follow the apparent locational preferences of observed sites. This could be done by allocating random points (during Monte Carlo simulation) according to a site location probability surface (e.g., derived from predictive modelling) so that the resulting probability distribution broadly matches the observed one.

If we turn to the question of chronology, the EBA data from Kythera is a good example of a "temporally fuzzy" settlement pattern. A KIP sample of 60+ sites at a density of nearly 1.5/km^2 represents in Aegean EBA terms a superb dataset and

Ripley's K analysis suggest sites have a tendency to cluster significantly at $r=500$ m, with clustering maintained to about $r=1250$ m (Figure 14.10). However, it is extremely unlikely that all of these sites were in use contemporaneously or continuously throughout the ca. 1,000 year duration of the EBA. Finer chronological resolution will be possible in the future (fabric analysis can often distinguish three EBA sub-phases: Kiriatzi 2003), but the degree of resolution will necessarily vary from site to site. A related problem is one of continuity of occupation: Whitelaw (2000:147–150) is persuasive in suggesting that in the EBA Aegean, occupation may often have been episodic rather than continuous within any given phase. Given these difficulties, EBA settlement pattern analysis is often extremely suspect, and the clustering is more likely to be a reflection of repeated occupation of favourable environments for small-scale subsistence farming, rather than any larger-scale social process.

These problems emphasize the need to find formal methods to incorporate temporal uncertainty into our pattern analysis. Not only do we have to consider distributions that have been "dated" to our period of interest with varying degrees of diagnostic certainty (both at the scale of individual artefacts and for the overall dating of sites), but we also have to contend with the possibility that individual sites may have been discontinuously occupied throughout the finest chronological divisions we can achieve and therefore may not be contemporary landscape phenomena. On a practical level, these problems benefit from a min–max approach in which analysis is run (i) on the sample of definite sites only, and (ii) on all possible sites in the phase. If there are indications that clustering/regularity persists in each of these cases then the pattern can be considered a robust one. Similarly, one response to the possibility of discontinuous settlement is to perturbate the site distribution artificially for any given chronological phase by arbitrarily excluding a certain number of points — again, if clustering or regularity persists despite repeated minor alterations of this kind (the process is a kind of internal Monte Carlo test and is necessarily laborious) then it can be interpreted with greater confidence.

The KIP Classical sites are a good instance of the problems of categorical heterogeneity. We not only have sites and settlement clusters of varying sizes, but also of varying functions, that preliminary analysis suggests probably include a major port, permanent farmsteads, temporary shelters, sanctuaries, kiln sites and metallurgical areas. We might consider the spatial relationships between any one or two of these categories, but the results (Figure 14.10) become meaningless the more functionally mixed the dataset becomes, except to show some possible heterogeneity (in that the observed pattern barely comes down within the confidence interval at large distances) and that from about $r=250$ m there is strong clustering of (diverse) activity areas. The key is therefore to compare like with like, reducing analysis to consider only one or two categories (K-function analysis can be extend to consider bivariate spatial relationships). In methodological terms this means careful assessment of function on a site by site basis (e.g., "villas" in a Roman landscape). Likewise, even for a relatively continuous variable such as site size, physical (population), economic (permanent market) or political (formal municipal status) thresholds sometimes exist that can guide sub-classification.

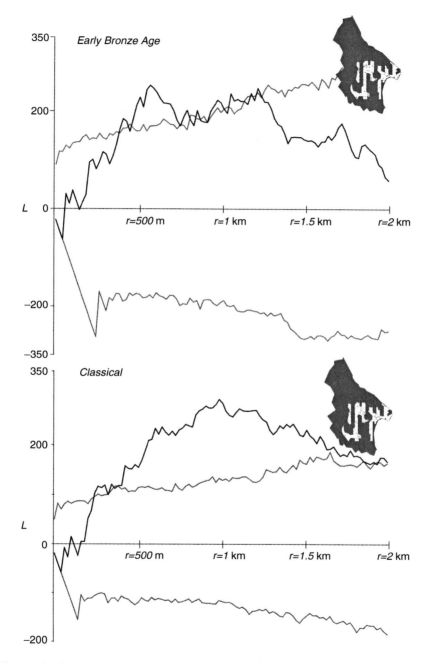

FIGURE 14-10. The modified K-distribution (L) for EBA sites (upper) and Classical sites (lower).

CONCLUSIONS

This paper has emphasized the highly reflexive approach necessary for the correct identification and interpretation of the processes behind settlement patterns. In our opinion, the key challenges are: (i) to define a sample/study area and its levels of search intensity appropriately (correcting for or exploring "edge effects" statistically where necessary); (ii) to assess and sub-divide site size, function and date range (analysing comparable features only and/or arbitrating uncertain cases statistically); (iii) to account for the resource structure of the landscape (either by only considering environmental homogenous sub-regions or by factoring resource preferences into the significance-testing stage of analysis), and (iv) to use techniques of analysis that are sensitive to detecting patterns at different spatial scales. The latter in particular is an area increasingly well-explored in other disciplines, but as yet with minimal impact on archaeological practice. There remains some value in Clark and Evan's nearest neighbour function for identifying relationships between sites at one scale of analysis, but it may fail to detect larger-scale patterning. More critically, the dichotomy it encourages between "nucleated" and "dispersed" is at best an overly simplistic model and, at worst, bears little relationship to the reality of settlement organization, which at different scales can show both nucleated and dispersed components. In our Kytheran case study, there is obviously further work to be done, but even with the existing dataset, we have shown that using a combination of Monte Carlo testing, frequency distributions, local density mappings and Ripley's K-function allows a more sensitive assessment of multiscalar patters and therefore a more critical evaluation of the processes underlying settlement distributions.

ACKNOWLEDGMENTS   Our thanks to the many people involved in KIP and in particular, to Cyprian Broodbank and Evangelia Kiriatzi (KIP co-directors) for help and advice at many stages. François Goreaud and Clive Orton also offered valuable help and advice. This research was conducted at the Institute of Archaeology, University College London, and Bevan's contribution was made possible by a Leverhulme Trust Research Grant. This paper uses KIP data that was current in mid-2003. Site characterization and lab-based analyses are on-going and thus our overall interpretations are provisional.

REFERENCES

Bevan, A. 2002, The Rural Landscape of Neopalatial Kythera: A GIS Perspective. *Journal of Mediterranean Archaeology* 15.2:217–256.

Bevan, A., Frederick, C., and Krahtopoulou, N., 2004, A Digital Mediterranean Countryside: GIS Approaches to the Spatial Structure of the Post-Medieval Landscape on Kythera (Greece). *Archaeologia E Calcolatori* 14:217–236.

Bevan, A., and Conolly, J., 2004, GIS, Archaeological Survey and Landscape Archaeology on the Island of Kythera, Greece. *Journal of Field Archaeology* 29:123–138.

Bintliff, J., and Snodgrass, A., 1985, The Cambridge/Bradford Boeotia Expedition: The First Four Years. *Journal of Field Archaeology* 12:123–161.

Blackman, D., 1999, Kythera, *Archaeological Reports for 1998–1999* [British School at Athens] 45:20–21.

Blackman, D., 2000, Kythera. *Archaeological Reports for 1999–2000* [British School at Athens] 46:22–24.

Blackman, D., 2001, Kythera. *Archaeological Reports for 2000–2001* [British School at Athens] 47:20–21.

Blackman, D., 2002, Kythera. *Archaeological Reports for 2001–2002* [British School at Athens] 48:16–17.

Blankholm, H.P., 1990, *Intrasite Spatial Analysis in Theory and Practice.* Aarhus, Arhus University Press.

Broodbank, C., 1999, Kythera Survey: Preliminary Report on the 1998 Season. *British School at Athens* 94:191–214.

Cherry, J., Davis, J.L., and Mantzourani, E., editors, 1991, *Landscape Archaeology as Long-Term History: Northern Keos in the Cycladic Islands.* Monumenta Archaeologica, Volume 16. Los Angeles.

Clark, P.J., and Evans, F.C., 1954, Distance to Nearest Neighbour as a Measure of Spatial Relationships in Populations. *Ecology* 35:444–453.

Conolly, J. 2000, Çatalhöyük and the Archaeological 'Object'. In *Methodology At Çatalhöyük*, edited by Ian Hodder, pp. 51–56. Mcdonald Institute of Archaeological Research Monographs, Cambridge.

Dacey, M.F., 1960, The Spacing of River Towns. *Annals of the Association of American Geographers* 50:59–61.

Daniel, I.R. (2001), Stone Raw Material Availability and Early Archaic Settlement in the Southeastern United States. *American Antiquity*, 66(2):237–265.

Douglas, D.H., 1994 Least Cost Path in GIS Using an Accumulated Cost Surface and Slope Lines. *Cartographica* 31(3):37–51.

Fotheringham, S.A., Brunsdon, C., and Charlton, M. 2002, *Quantitative Geography: Perspectives on Spatial Data Analysis.* Sage, London.

Goreaud, F., and Pélissier, R., 1999, On Explicit Formulas of Edge Correction for Ripley's *K*-Function. *Journal of Vegetation Science* 10:433–38.

Goreaud, F., and Pélissier, R. 2000, Spatial Structure Analysis of Heterogeneous Point Patterns: Examples of Application to Forest Stands. *ADS in ADE-4 Topic Documentation* 8.1:1–49.

Gotway, C.A., and Young, L.J., 2002, Combining Incompatible Spatial Data. *Journal of the American Statistical Association.* 97:632–648.

Haggett, P., 1965, *Locational Analysis in Human Geography.* E. Arnold, London.

Hodder, I., 1972, Locational Models and the Study of Romano-British Settlement. In *Models in Archaeology*, edited by D.L. Clarke, pp. 887–909. Metheun, London.

Hodder, I., and Hassall. M., 1971, The Non-Random Spacing in Romano-British Walled Towns. *Man* 6:391–407.

Hodder, I., and Orton, C., 1979, *Spatial Analysis in Archaeology.* Second Edition. Cambridge University Press, Cambridge.

Horden, P., and Purcell, N., 2000, *The Corrupting Sea: A Study of Mediterranean History.* Blackwell, Oxford.

Kiriatzi, E., 2003, Sherds, Fabrics and Clay Sources: Reconstructing the Ceramic Landscapes of Prehistoric Kythera, In METRON: Measuring the Aegean Bronze Age, edited by R. Laffineur and K. Foster, pp. 123–129. Liege, University of Liege.

Ladefoged, T., and Pearson, R., 2000, Fortified Castles on Okinawa Island during the Gusuku Period, AD 1200–1600. *Antiquity* 74:404–412.

Manly, B.F.J., 1991, *Randomization and Monte Carlo Methods in Biology.* Chapman and Hall, London.

Maschner, H.D.G., and Stein, J.W., 1995, Multivariate Approaches to Site Location on the Northwest Coast of North America. *Antiquity* 69(262):61–73.

Openshaw, S., 1996, Developing GIS-Relevant Zone-Based Spatial Analysis Methods. In *Spatial Analysis: Modelling in a GIS Environment*, edited by P. Longley and M. Batty, pp. 55–73. Geoinformation International, London.

Pélissier, R., and Goreaud, F., 2001, A Practical Approach to the Study of Spatial Structure In Simple Cases of Heterogeneous Vegetation. *Journal of Vegetation Science* 12:99–108.

Perles, C., 2001, *The Early Neolithic in Greece.* Cambridge University Press, Cambridge.

Renfrew, C., and Wagstaff, M., editors, 1982, *An Island Polity: The Archaeology of Exploitation in Melos.* Cambridge University Press, Cambridge.

Ripley, B.D., 1976, The Second-Order Analysis of Stationary Point Processes. *Journal of Applied Probability* 13:255–266.

Ripley, B.D., 1977, Modelling Spatial Patterns. *Journal of the Royal Statistical Society* 2:172–212.

Ripley, B.D., 1981. *Spatial Statistics.* John Wiley and Sons, New York.

Roberts, B.K., 1996, *Landscapes of Settlement: Prehistory to the Present.* Routledge, London.

van Andel, T.H., Runnels, C.N., and Pope, K., 1986, Five Thousand Years of Land Use and Abuse in the Southern Argolid, Greece. *Hesperia* 55:103–128.

van Andel, T.H., and Runnels, C.N., The Evolution of Settlement in the Southern Argolid, Greece: An Economic Explanation. *Hesperia* 56 (1987), 303–334.

Washburn, D. K., 1974, Spatial Analysis of Occupation Floors II: The Application of Nearest Neighbor Analysis. *American Antiquity* 39:16–34.

Whallon, R., 1973, Spatial Analysis of Occupation Floors I: The Application of Nearest Neighbor Analysis of Variance. *American Antiquity* 38:266–278.

Wheatley, D., and Gillings, M., 2002, *Spatial Technology and Archaeology: The Archaeological Applications of GIS.* Taylor & Francis, London.

Whitelaw, T., 2000, Settlement Instability and Landscape Degradation in the Southern Aegean in the Third Millennium BC, In *Landscape and Landuse in Postglacial Greece. Sheffield Studies in Aegean Archaeology, Volume 3,* edited by P. Halstead and C. Frederick, pp. 135–161. Sheffield Academic Press, Sheffield.

Woodman, P.E., 2000, A Predictive Model for Mesolithic Site Location on Islay using Logistic Regression and GIS. In *Hunter–Gatherer Landscape Archaeology: The Southern Hebrides Mesolithic Project 1988–98. Vol. 2: Archaeological Fieldwork on Colonsay, Computer Modelling, Experimental Archaeology, and Final Interpretations,* edited by S. Mithen, pp. 445–464. Mcdonald Institute for Archaeological Research, Cambridge.

CHAPTER 15

Grain, Extent, and Intensity: The Components of Scale in Archaeological Survey

Oskar Burger and Lawrence C. Todd

INTRODUCTION

Archaeological entities, processes and explanations are bound by metaphysical concepts of time and space. So we may expect chronological and spatial revisions to be followed by profound disciplinary consequences. But, the very great importance of time and space measurement scales has often led the archaeologist to confuse the scales used for measurement with that which is being measured. (Clarke, 1973:13)

Most [archaeologists] must content themselves with finding some percentage of the sites in their chosen regions – all the major ceremonial centers, perhaps most of the larger villages, and some undetermined fraction of the tiny hamlets and seasonal camps. If you ask them whether or not they have an adequate sample, either they say ''I hope so,'' or they shrug and say ''I don't know.'' Both answers are correct. They do hope so, and they don't know. (Flannery, 1976:131–132)

Regional survey is the primary method through which archaeologists investigate large-scale prehistoric patterns. The first settlement pattern surveys investigated cultural processes existing at scales beyond those captured by excavation. For example, highly influential studies such as Gordon Willey's surveys of Virú Valley, Peru (Willey, 1953), endeavored to identify large-scale sociopolitical patterns in the distributions of sites and their inferred function within a settlement pattern. Large-scale regional frameworks have since become fundamental to archaeological investigation (Ammerman, 1981; Binford, 1964; Dunnell and Dancey, 1983; Schiffer, et al., 1978) and are essential for understanding the impacts of large-scale processes of contemporary land use and development on the archaeological record.

Oskar Burger ● University of New Mexico   Lawrence C. Todd ● Greybull River Sustainable Landscape Ecology, Meeteetse, Wyoming, USA

The scales selected for the research design of an archaeological survey will in many ways determine the characteristics of the patterns inferred (Banning 2002; Dunnell and Dancey 1983; Hodder and Orton 1976). Scale is a concept closely tied to issues of sampling and requires explicit methodological attention for two reasons: (a) the bounds of large-scale processes and patterns are normally beyond the area directly observed by an archaeological survey; and (b) much small-scale information passes through the gaps between pedestrian surveyors (Burger et al. 2004). While such challenges are frequently acknowledged (Ebert 1992; Willey 1953), the methodological answers have proven difficult to develop. As a result, the opening quotes by Clarke and Flannery are just as relevant today as they were thirty years ago. In this chapter, we suggest that the archaeological record be investigated at multiple scales. We focus on methodological tools that ground issues of scale for quantitative analysis and present an approach to sampling that allows archaeologists to analyze the nature of changes in artifact densities that occur as a result of changes in spatial scale and observer intensity.

Archaeological survey has changed over the years with the ever-present goals of improving accuracy and efficiency. Global positioning systems (GPS) have become extremely common field devices. The application of remote-sensing and the powerful capabilities of geographic information systems (GIS) technology have also opened numerous new avenues of analysis, the full potentials of which are far from realized. However, simply applying GIS technology to existing archaeological data sets does not solve the problems of scale as many suspect it can. While numerous innovations have taken place in archaeology, survey methodologies have remained rather tradition-bound (see Wiens 1989 for a discussion of the same trend in field ecology).

One recent development that has improved our ability to investigate the nature of archaeological regions and prehistoric landuse is distributional or siteless survey (Dunnell and Dancey 1983; Ebert 1992; Ebert and Kohler 1988; Foley 1981; Thomas 1975). In these surveys, artifact distributions are continuous populations bounded by a defined space as opposed to a series of artificially divided units or "sites," which makes them amenable to documentation at a range of scales. While the techniques below are relevant to any consideration of sampling the surface record they are especially designed for furthering the aims of the distributional approach.

Ecological Approaches to Scale

Many of the scale-related challenges faced by ecologists, and the tools developed to address them, are relevant to archaeology. Archaeologists and ecologists both deal with palimpsest records of historical processes. In the same way that many different human activities and taphonomic processes create overlapping records in archaeology, a similar suite of processes related to climate, geology, and human land use affect the properties of plant communities and other ecological systems. Both fields study systems open to influence from outside variables. Both conduct research that requires inferring of process from pattern. And fundamentally, both must face issues of scale when linking small-scale observations to largescale processes. In plant ecology specifically, recently developed sampling designs that consider scale greatly improve the accuracy of plant species samples (Stohlgren, et al., 1998). These sampling designs also improve the analysis of spatial distributions and plant community structure. Because plants and artifacts share "small unit size in relation to a very large spatial context, and also ... a patchy distribution," methods that lead to accurate plant community samples can also be applicable to archaeological survey (Foley, 1981:174).

An increased emphasis on scale in ecology during the late 1980s was described as "a paradigm shift based on scale" in relation to symposia at the annual Ecological Society of America meetings (Golley 1989:65), and it continues to be a major issue. This awareness of scale has made its way into archaeology as well (e.g., Stein, 1993; Wandsnider, 1998). While Hodder and Orton (1976) showed that archaeological patterns may change with the size of the sampling frame, ecology provides a key additional point, that as the scale of observation changes, so do the relevant processes. At local scales, predator and prey populations often have a negative correlation, suggesting a cyclical relationship of prey abundance that increases until the predator population grows to the point that the prey become exhausted. At larger scales, predator and prey populations are positively correlated, suggesting that both respond to a similar set of background ecological variables at one scale and to population dynamics at another (O'Neill and King, 1998; Schneider, 2001b). In a like manner, while climate largely determines the spatial distribution of net primary productivity (NPP) at continental scales, the primary influences within regions are aspect and soils (O'Neill and King, 1998). Both predator/prey dynamics and the distribution of NPP are relevant to our understanding of the past to some degree but the investigation of the nature of artifact distributions across regions also brings a number of unique but analogous scale-dependent issues that require direct archaeological investigation.

Perhaps the most important realization regarding the effects of scale is that resolution strongly influences the perception of patterning (Church, 1996; Levin, 1992; O'Neill and King, 1998; Wiens, 1989). "We can no longer ... cling to the belief that the scale on which we view systems does not affect what we see ... " (Wiens, 1999:371). Following from this is the methodological correlate that there is no best scale of observation (Gardner, 1998; Levin, 1992; Schneider, 1994, 1998). The combination of these two notions forms the basis of our recent investigations into archaeological survey method on the Oglala National Grassland in northwestern Nebraska. Borrowing techniques from landscape ecology offers new avenues for documenting and analyzing the patterns generated by archaeological survey.

To illustrate our perspective, we present some initial results of our surveys on the Oglala National Grassland. We adopted the Modified-Whittaker multiscale sampling plot, originally developed for plant species surveys (Stohlgren, et al., 1998; Stohlgren, et al., 1995), and found its design to be highly applicable in archaeology. We also used the multiscale layout of the Modified-Whittaker for experiments investigating the properties of the surface record to explore the degree to which intensity of observation is an additional aspect of scale relevant to survey and sampling design.

TERMS OF SCALE FOR
ARCHAEOLOGICAL SURVEY

Grain, Extent, and Intensity

Scale has multiple meanings and applications in the literature (Schneider, 2002; see contributors to Peterson and Parker, 1998). This simply means that it fits correctly in a variety of circumstances, depending largely on context. We explore one variant in particular because it is quantitative, widely applicable, and especially relevant for the specific concerns of scale in archaeological survey. Schnieder (2002) defines scale as "the extent relative to the grain of a variable indexed by time or space." This definition applies to both the tools of measurement and that being measured or described. The *extent* is the area surveyed, and the *grain* is the size of the sample unit (Figure 15.1). Surveys will not detect patterns that are finer in scale than the grain of the sample (Wiens, 1989, 1990). The extent of a survey also defines the population of artifacts being sampled. Grain and extent are generally thought of as variables imposed by the researcher (Milne 1992), but in archaeological survey the extent is often (but not always) a project-specific restraint leaving grain as the

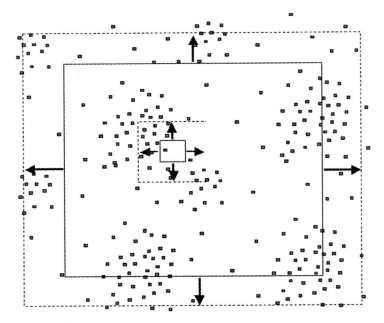

FIGURE 15-1. Grain relative to extent in the sampling of an artifact distribution. As extent (outer square) increases, the diversity of the total sample increases. As grain increases (smaller square) variance within the sample becomes averaged-out and small-scale patterning may be lost. (Modified from Wiens 1989, Figure 1).

primary variable for experimental or methodological manipulation, although it is usually not specified.

The off-site or distributional approaches noted above are fundamentally concerned with issues of grain. Questions about the appropriate lower limits of survey resolution generated by distributional archaeology suggest that, as a basic unit of observation, artifacts rather than sites may be the more appropriate. Operationally, this means that the grain of a distributional archaeological survey is at the artifact scale (mm-cm^2) rather than the site scale (m^2-ha). Clearly such differences in observational grain entail a number of methodological considerations that are of fundamental concern here.

The investigation of the surface record and experiments aimed at identifying relationships between method, process, and scale benefit from the use of controlled and defined sample units (Dunnell and Dancey, 1983). However, most pedestrian surveys lack specified grains or sample units. The width of a surveyor's field of vision is not an appropriate measure of grain because it is highly variable. Material properties such as mean size or density are difficult to quantify for most surveys and even closely spaced transect widths may miss significant amounts of material (Burger, et al., 2004; Wandsnider and Camilli, 1992). These issues are less important when the goal is the discovery of artifacts, but when certain phases of the survey are geared toward parameter estimation, methodological evaluation, or any specific experiment, spatial control and knowledge of sample properties become much more important. The grain is generally too spatially variable among even highly controlled pedestrian survey transects for use in the quantification of the effects of scale. In addition, transect spacing defines the intensity of coverage rather than a value for a minimum unit of observation. For example, if a hypothetical survey covered 20 km^2 with 30 m transects, the grain and the extant would be the same value, 20 km^2. Alternatively, there are methodological tools for investigating the record at multiple grains, using block surveys with discrete boundaries that enable the manipulation of the grain/extent relationship. We discuss one of these, the Modified-Whittaker multiscale sampling plot, below.

The third element of scale is, as the discussion above implies, *intensity* of observation. In the example above, the 30 m transect describes the intensity used to survey the 20 km^2 area, but it does not describe the grain. In most archaeological surveys, intensity is equivalent to transect width, which is guided by the assumption that the narrower the transect, the greater the intensity and the more accurate the sample. Even relatively narrow transects, however, may disproportionately overlook low-density scatters and isolated finds (Wandsnider and Camilli, 1992), and it is likely that all surveys overlook material (Banning, 2002:62). Because intensity influences the number of artifacts found per unit of area, it must be considered when investigating the role of scale and impressions of spatial structure within archaeological distributions.

Our suggested definition for scale may seem to counter common usages of the term. For instance, an archaeologist might describe a process as existing at the "scale of a settlement pattern" and discuss the challenge of linking artifact-scale observations to large-scale behavioral inference. However, such articulations are still ratios of the extent to the grain as long as the statement "artifact-scale" implies the range of sizes (from smallest to largest) present within a population of artifacts – in this case, the range of spatial extents between the smallest and the largest areas likely to figure in a past culture's land use strategy.

In a more general sense, scale is also important in the relation between the properties of data and the resolution of their interpretation (Stein, 1993). Moreover, the scale implies by an interpretive model should agree with the scale provided by the data under analysis. Kelly (1999:112) warns that "fine-grained questions cannot be asked of a coarse-grained record...." Because most archaeological situations are coarse-grained, or the "product of a qualitatively different set of time scales than is living behavior" (Ebert, 1992:25), differences in scale may not be intuitively obvious. Therefore, archaeologists need tools for explicitly relating the scale of the record to the scales of interpretation brought to it.

Multiscale Analysis

Multiscale analysis occurs when the "variance in a measured quantity, or the relation of two measured quantities, is computed at a series of different scales" (Schneider, 2002:738). This generally refers to any analysis of change that occurs because of changes in scale. Numerous mathematical techniques are available for conducting multiscale analysis (e.g., Gardner, 1998; King, et al., 1991; Levin and Buttel, 1986; O'Neill and King, 1998; Schneider, 1994, 1998, 2001b, 2002; Schneider, et al., 1997; Webster and Oliver, 2001), but many are computationally dense or require detailed knowledge of the links between pattern and process. We apply two of the more straightforward of these techniques, calculating scope and spatial allometry, to our survey data below.

EXPERIMENTS WITH MULTISCALE SAMPLING ON THE OGLALA NATIONAL GRASSLAND

Solving scale problems requires the systematic evaluation of multiple grains and extents (Wiens, 1989, 2001). The first step in accomplishing this is the appropriate sampling method. The Modified-Whittaker multiscale sampling plot gathers observations at the spatial scales of 1, 10, 100, and 1,000 m^2 (Figure 15.2). This sampling design has greatly improved the accuracy of plant species surveys conducted by rangeland ecologists while also enhancing their ability to analyze community structures at landscape levels (Stohlgren, et al., 1995; 1997; 1998). Previous plant survey techniques, which are quite similar to archaeological transects, failed to accurately represent rare plant species (those composing less than 1% of the cover) and consequently over-represented the significance of dominant species. In a similar manner, Wandsnider and Camilli, (1992) demonstrated that archaeological transect surveys consistently over-represent high-density clusters of artifacts and miss disproportionately large portions of low-density and isolated material. The similarity in methodological bias inherent in the traditional approaches of both

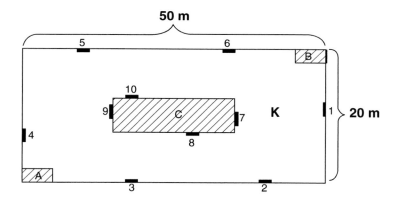

FIGURE 15-2. The Modified-Whittaker nested sampling plot. The subplots numbered 1–10 are 0.5 × 2.0 m (1 m²), the A and B plots are 2 × 5 m (10 m²), and the C plot is 5 × 20 m (100 m²). The outer boundary of the plot, K, is 20 × 50 m (1,000 m²). The incremental increases in area give the Modified-Whittaker its multiscale sampling capability.

fields motivated us to experiment with this method by surveying ten Modified-Whittaker plots on the Oglala National Grassland during the summers of 1999–2001 (Burger, et al., 2004).

The archaeological record of our study area is predominantly a palimpsest (as with *all* archaeological deposits) of chipped stone artifacts (primarily small, unmodified pieces of debitage) on a geomorphologically active landscape. Several material types are found and the chronological sequence represented, evidenced by temporally diagnostic projectile points, spans the full range of the chronology for the Great Plains from Paleoindian to Late Prehistoric. Fire-cracked rock is occasionally found but is relatively rare and one locality revealed a few small fragments of pottery. Structures have not been observed but hearths are occasionally found in the vertical cuts along prominent drainages.

Each Modified-Whittaker plot was covered with "nested" observer intensities in order to evaluate the effects of different methods on the accuracy of observations gathered on the same surface. Observation intensity can be investigated as a change in scale because the nature of the patterns we infer from survey data are constrained and perhaps determined by issues as mundane as transect width. The basic findings of our experiments with multiscale sampling provide some background for our perspective on the investigation of scale issues. Note, however, that lessons learned from a 1,000 m² plot may only apply heuristically to much larger spatial extents where qualitatively distinct issues may arise.

One of the first questions our survey experiments sought to answer was – how does observer intensity affect the accuracy of the archaeological document? The archaeological document is the subset of information actually observed and recorded when sampling the archaeological record (Wandsnider and Camilli, 1992). Accuracy is the "deviation between actual and measured", that is, between the archaeological document and the archaeological record (Wandsnider and Camilli, 1992:171). Archaeologists generally lack the ability to address the question "what did we miss?" during a survey. Answering the "what we missed" question

required intensive coverage of the ground surface compared to conventional standards because we needed a measure of what was actually on the surface in order to
determine how much was overlooked by coarser-grained methods. This is equivalent to attempting to quantify the difference between the sample and the target
population, a necessary goal for all evaluations of methodological accuracy.

We first covered the entire 1,000 m^2 of the Modified-Whittaker plot in a
walking survey. For transect spacing, the rule was that each crew member had to
be able to touch the shoulder of the person next to them, resulting in an average
spacing of 70 cm. During this survey we marked the location of each artifact with a
red pin flag and then conducted a rather intensive recording process, documenting
over 20 observations on each pin-flagged item. Additional items observed while
recording were marked and recorded with a blue pin flag, distinguishing them from
the systematic discoveries (after Wandsnider and Camilli, 1992).

We hypothesized that once the red (systematic) and blue (nonsystematic)
discoveries were combined, the resulting document would approximate the total
population of surface artifacts, so we could use it to evaluate the accuracy of other
transect samples of the same ground surface. As we needed an observer intensity
greater than that provided by the 70 cm walking survey in order to evaluate the
accuracy of the first survey, a second crew conducted a crawl survey, moving
shoulder to shoulder over subplots 1–10, A, B, and C (Figures 15.2 and 15.3).

Comparing the results of these two survey intensities over ten plots has yielded
some interesting results. Since the crawl survey sampled a subset of the area
covered by the walking survey, we compared only this subset, adding together the
blue and red flag discoveries. There were no blue-flagged discoveries during the

Figure 15-3. The crawling survey is used to cover the ten 1 m^2 subplots, two 10 m^2 subplots, and the
100 m^2 C subplot for a total area crawled of 130 m^2. In comparison, the walking survey covers the entire
1000 m^2 K plot.

crawl surveys, indicating that crawling does indeed capture the total population of surface items (or very nearly so). Most notably, the crawl survey recovered on average 362% more artifacts than the walking survey (Burger, et al., 2004). Such a drastic increase has implications for calculating the artifact-scale accuracy of surveys conducted at standard transect widths of 10–30 m. This also relates directly to issues of scale. The number of items missed by a survey will increase as transect spacing widens.

In addition to discovery, surveys need to enhance our understandings of artifact distributions. The region we study is a hunter-gatherer landscape and most of the behaviors in the past were "small-scale" activities (Ebert and Kohler, 1988; Yellen, 1977). Failing to evaluate the difference between the scales of the sample and the target population greatly obscures the accuracy of any resulting impression of past land use. Fine-scale subsamples such as those provided by crawling the subplots of the Modified-Whittaker can therefore yield more precise estimates of chipped stone densities, and this may lead to a better understanding of the cultural and natural variables that have altered them.

The phenomenal increase in items discovered by the crawl survey dramatically changed our perspective on archaeological survey methods. We knew, as all archaeologists do, that transect surveys miss some materials, but the combined findings of the magnitude of overlooked artifacts and the multiscale capabilities of the Midified-Whittaker method convinced us that some changes to conventional survey wisdom might be worth considering.

TECHNIQUES FOR ANALYZING SCALE

Here we present three techniques for grappling with issues of scale, analytically and conceptually: space–time diagrams, scope, and spatial allometry. Each of these techniques evaluates scalar properties of multiscale samples and variables produced by methods such as the Modified-Whittaker are used to gather multiscale samples.

Space–Time Diagrams

Space–time diagrams are useful graphical tools for both heuristic and analytical needs when representing scale relationships (Figure 15.4). The first space–time diagram was the work of Steele (1978), a marine biologist interested in the relationships of phytoplankton, zooplankton, and fish distributions across time and space. Subsequent applications of such diagrams identify scale-dependent properties relating pattern and process, for example, showing that the population densities of marine fish were influenced by movement at some scales and mortality at others (Schneider, 2002).

Space–time diagrams can be very useful for describing scalar relationships in archaeology as well. Scalar differences frequently exist between behavioral records and the archaeological evidence (Figure 15.4a). Yet the taphonomic pro-

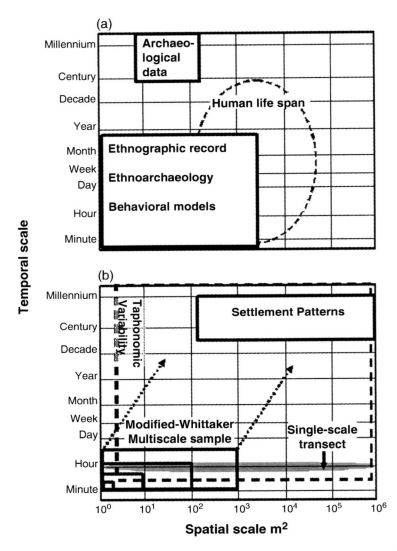

FIGURE 15-4. Space–time diagrams for landscape phenomena commonly studied by archaeologists and two methods used to study them. (a) In most archaeological situations a tremendous temporal and spatial gap exists between the resolution provided by archaeological data and the evidence used to inform them. Archaeological data typically exist beyond the time scale of a human life. (b) The dotted-line rectangle represents the range in variability of taphonomic influences on landscape patterning. The nested spatial samples of the Modified-Whittaker plot ensure stronger inferences to larger scales as indicated by the dotted-line arrows. While single-scale methods do not provide samples that can be quantified in terms of resolution, they can be thought of as a long linear extension of contiguous quadrats. The use of single-scale transects combined with multiscale sampling should generate highly informative samples. If the parameters of a specific settlement pattern were known or inferred, the gap between it and the sampling method could actually be quantified with this diagram. Note that in both diagrams the axes are log transformed.

cesses that arrange, modify, and accumulate cultural materials act at scales that encompass most of the prehistoric social phenomena archaeologists investigate (Figure 15.4b). The ability to infer the nature of these processes (social and taphonomic) at scales larger than what was directly observed may therefore be improved with multiscale sampling methods (Figure 15.4b, dotted lines), as discussed above.

To maximize the information return and efficiency of archaeological survey, we may want to consider using combinations of single-scale discovery methods and multiscale methods. For example, it may be appropriate to cover a large area in widely spaced transects (≥ 5 m) and evaluate the precision of the survey with finer-grained plots such as the Modified-Whittaker. Using space–time diagrams, we can identify any scale issues that might affect a particular project or subject, visualize differences in scalar coverage in interdisciplinary collaborations, or represent relationships between the scope of survey projects and the impacts of contemporary land use.

Scope

Scale is quantified as a ratio of large to small. Cartographic scales, for example, have values such as 1:24,000, which relate a distance on the earth to the scaled measure of that distance on a much smaller piece of paper. This same concept can be extended to any sampling design, measurement device, instrument, or spatially referenced variable (Schneider, 2001a, 2002). When scale is the ratio measure of the extent to the grain, this calculation is the ''scope'' of the variable (Schneider, 2002; Wiens, 2001). Because scope is calculated by dividing a small scale into a large scale, scope is dimensionless (the units cancel) and is therefore widely applicable for describing issues of scale. For example, the scope of a meter stick is 1 m/1 mm $= 10^3$ (Schneider, 2002).

The spatial extents for the grains of the Modified-Whittaker plot and the extent of the surveyed area are in Table 15.1. The calculations of the actual scopes of the grains and extents of our survey demonstrate how scope is determined: the area for each frame is simply divided by the area of the unit being related to it. The larger the scope, the greater is the degree of scale-up required to bridge the gap from small to large. Scope is useful for comparing projects, experiments, or studies with respect to scale (Schneider, 2001c). Furthermore, scope is a necessary of spatial allometry, a technique derived from scaling theory that can be used to understand how a variable of interest changes as a function of grain.

Spatial Allometry

Archaeologists can use spatial allometry to investigate the influence of spatial scale and/or observer intensity on the rate of artifact discovery, which is one of the factors determining sample size, and for analyzing assemblage diversity. In our sample plots, we use spatial allometry to investigate how artifact density scales with area.

TABLE 15-1. Scope Calculations for Multiscale Samples on the Oglala National Grassland.

Numbered subplots = 1 m^2
Subplots A and B = 10 m^2
Subplot C = 100 m^2
K plot = 1,000 m^2
Area crawled = 130 m^2 = 1–10, A, B, C
Area walked = 1,000 m^2 = K plot
Grassland Region = 418 ha

Unit	Frame	Scope
1 Subplot	K plot	1,000
Subplots 1–10	K plot	100
Area crawled	K plot	7.7
Area walked	Grassland region	4,180
All plots	Grassland region	418

In spatial allometry, some quantity of interest is scaled against area. This is done by setting one scope equal to another that is raised to an exponent β (Schneider, 2002).

$$\left(\frac{Q(M)}{Q(M_o)}\right) = \left(\frac{M}{M_o}\right)^{\beta}$$

$Q(M)$ is one measured quantity (such as chipped stone density) that is set equal to another quantity M (such as area). The scaling exponent, β, evens out any lack of perfect similarity between the two variables. If β is equal to 1, then the relationship is isometric (Schneider, et al., 1997:132). If it is not equal to 1, it is allometric (Schneider, et al., 1997:132). Most applications of allometric scaling relate rates or processes to properties of differing magnitudes and it has been used in many contexts (Schneider, 1998, 2001a; Schneider, et al., 1997; see also Brown, et al., 2004; Peters, 1983):

$$\left(\frac{Q(M_{big})}{Q(M_{small})}\right) = \left(\frac{M_{big}}{M_{small}}\right)^{\beta}$$

The rate of change of a quantity $Q(M)$ can be equated to another quantity such as the size of the sampling frame used to measure it, M. In relating artifact density to area, artifact density is the quantity that changes with respect to M. A common application of this approach is the measurement of ocean coastlines, which, because of their fractal dimensions, are essentially infinite in length (Pennycuick and Kline, 1986). Scaling functions can correct for differences in various lengths of the same coastline obtained by different measurement methods (Pennycuick and Kline, 1986). Many common scaling relationships could be deciphered with this approach, such as volume scaling with length to the power of 3 ($V = L^3$).

Landscape ecologists have looked at a variety of factors that scale allometrically with area, such as percent bare ground or species richness (e.g., Milne, 1992).

In a like manner, archaeologists can investigate the relationships between area and artifact density. This is a means of understanding the properties of the surface record by systematically investigating changes in grain and extent. For example, the chipped stone densities from the Modified-Whittaker surveys can be scaled with area by equating the largest and smallest sample grains provided by the plot to the number of flakes found at each grain (although any two grains could be investigated in this way).

$$\left(\frac{Q(M)}{Q(M_{ref})}\right) = \left(\frac{M}{M_{ref}}\right)^{\beta}$$

$$\left(\frac{92.8cs}{0.03cs}\right) = \left(\frac{(1000\,m^2)}{(1\,m^2)}\right)^{\beta}$$

For the data from our surveys, the $1\,m^2$ subplot is used as the reference value (M_{ref}) because it simplifies the math to have the value of 1 in the denominator. To solve for β, take the natural log of each side of the equation:

$$\beta = \ln(92.8/0.03)/\ln(1{,}000) = 1.16$$

In this case the value of β is a little larger than 1, which means that for the combined sample of our ten 0.1 ha plots, the relationship between area and artifact density is supra-linear: the rate of artifact discovery is proportionately greater as area increases. A fourfold increase in area within the scope of this relationship (1–1,000 m) causes chipped stone density to increase by a factor of 4.99 because $4^{1.16} = 4.99$, but a twofold increase in area leads to an increase in artifact encounter by a factor of 2.23. This equation, $CS = A^{1.16}$, estimates the magnitude of increase in discovery for a given grain within the scope of the calculation, not the number of artifacts found. In this way it can be used to compare rates of discovery and the area to density relationship. For the crawling survey, the chipped stone found at 1 m and 100 m leads to $\beta = 0.77$ (17.8 flakes at 100 m and 0.5 flakes at 1 m). Thus, a four-fold increase in the area crawled leads to an increase in chipped stone encountered by a factor of 2.91 ($4^{0.77} = 2.91$). The difference in the value of β indicates that the observational intensity can determine the scalar relationship between artifact density and area for a survey. Furthermore, this leads to a quantified measure of this difference that is a widely applicable means of comparison. The scale of observation can strongly influence perception of regional patterning (Figure 15.5). Within areas of similar surface context and culture history, this approach may also serve as a crude measure of spatial heterogeneity in that a perfectly homogenous distribution would necessarily have an exponent of 1 if sampled at a high level of accuracy. An important caveat here is that both the values for the scaling exponents are close to 1 and hence both scaling relationship may be close to isometric. However, the values of the exponents from walking and crawling are significantly different from each other, which demonstrates that the two high-resolution samples provoke fundamentally different impressions of the surface record.

The difference in rate of artifact encounter is counter-intuitive in one respect. The walking survey encounters new artifacts at a faster rate than the crawling

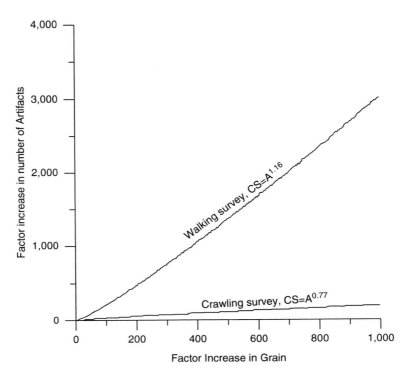

FIGURE 15-5. Curves generated from spatially allometry of area and chipped stone density. The walking survey encounters new artifacts at a rate much faster than the crawl survey even though the crawl survey finds more artifacts per unit area, which is an issue of scale. These two high resolution samples lead to very different impressions of the surface record.

survey even though the crawling survey finds many more artifacts per unit area (Figure 15.5). This indicates that the probability of encountering an artifact within a defined space is differentially affected by changes in transect width. Because the crawl survey finds essentially everything on the surface, it is less affected by changes in grain. For the walking survey, artifacts are more likely to be missed in smaller areas. As the grain increases, the number of artifacts in that area increases as well and the walking survey is more likely to make a discovery of the larger population. This artificially accelerates the rate of encounter as area increases. The probability of missing any given artifact within 1 m^2 is much greater than the probability of missing the artifact population within 100 m^2, thus demonstrating that assemblage diversity and sample size are strongly influenced by methodological decisions of scale.

Multiscale sampling leads to new directions in quantitative techniques for analyzing artifact distributions. Allometric scaling of density with area can be used to analyze the effects of scale on sample parameters. For chipped stone especially, the area-density relationship is highly variable, and our future applications will divide the sample into strata by topographic location and artifact class for comparative analysis. While the application used here considered only the number of artifacts per unit of area, we could divide a diverse sample into classes such as material type in order to compare their distributions across spatial scales (Ebert, 1992).

A further application of allometric scaling is for the analysis of assemblage diversity. The comparison of measures of diversity between samples from different locations is a challenging task whether one analyzes plant community structure or the composition of an artifact assemblage. The major difficulty with such comparisons is that the primary determinant of the number of types present is sample size (Ricklefs and Miller, 2000). As the sample increases, the probability of encountering rare variants increases. Grain, extent, and intensity determine the size of the sample; consequently, projects that have varied in any of these measures need to account for these differences to achieve reliable comparative analysis. The number of types per unit area can be analyzed with spatial allometry just as artifact density was, above. In this regard, overall assemblage diversity and the relative abundances of each type within the assemblage can be compared.

This approach could be especially useful for understanding the effects of scale on surfaces with relatively large numbers of artifact classes. In regions such as Mesoamerica, diagnostic ceramic types lead to highly diverse assemblages and the relative abundances of these types carry major interpretive weight (e.g., Sanders, et al., 1979). Intra-site samples used to derive population densities and times of occupations could benefit from plotting the rate of accumulation for the diagnostic ceramic types relative to the entire sample. Different types will accumulate at different rates. Furthermore, as Leonard (1987) suggests, asymptotic curves may indicate that a representative sample has been obtained and the researcher can use this as a tool to assess whether or not all classes of artifacts in a heterogeneously distributed population have been adequately sampled.

INVESTIGATING THE NATURE OF THE
SURFACE RECORD BY CONSIDERING
MULTIPLE SCALES

The Modified-Whittaker is not a discovery technique for archaeological survey. While there is a tendency to emphasize discovery in the design and interpretation of most surveys, many researchers seek to investigate the distributional properties of surface artifacts and the processes that act upon them (Banning, 2002; Dunnell and Dancey, 1983; Ebert and Kohler, 1988; Foley, 1981; Hodder and Orton, 1976; Schiffer, et al., 1978; Yellen, 1996). An important aspect of this for research and management is the development of methodological tools for identifying the degree of blurring, distorting, or destruction of the record caused by different post-deposition variables. Such experimentally based approaches require accurate samples in order to understand the crucial scales at which certain processes influence archaeological patterns. For instance, in a recent evaluation of the effects of large herbivore grazing, we divided potential scopes of impact into three ranges (Figure 15.6). The first of these is the microscale, which we define as artifact movements of less than 1 m on seasonal or annual time intervals that are caused by factors such as single

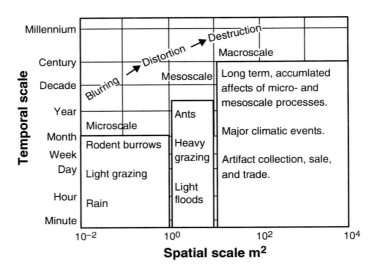

FIGURE 15-6. Space–time diagram depicting the impacts of various agents that are important to consider in both research and management.

seasons of grazing, hail storms, extreme winds, and plant roots. Such movement blurs archaeological patterning. Mesoscale impacts range from 1 to 10 m; they are caused by such processes as multiple seasons of grazing, harvester ants, or localized erosion. They may begin to distort or destroy archaeological patterns. Macroscale movements are subdivided into five levels: macro1 (10–100 m); macro2 (100–1,000 m); macro3 (1–10 km); macro4 (10–100 km); and macro5 (greater than 100 km). Over time, processes that act seasonally or annually at the micro- or mesoscales can lead to macroscale disturbance. This includes artifact collection! Understanding how these processes act is an important domain of research for interpreting archaeological patterns and is needed to effectively manage archaeological landscapes.

This study is part of an ongoing attempt to provide a framework that more tightly integrates research and management concerns with other biotic and abiotic components of the landscape. During this project we became increasingly aware of the range of agents that were constantly active at multiple scales in our study region. Small animal foraging behaviors cause small-scale impacts that can distort and potentially destroy archaeological distributions over the long term. Rodent burrowing may result in a continual cycling of sediment that severely distorts vertical stratigraphy. Harvester ants will scour over 80 m^2 of ground surface for mound building materials that often include artifacts (Burris, 2004; Schoville and Todd, 2001). While many of these agents may have minor impacts over short periods of time, sustained impacts, such as grazing, may be severe (Figure 15.6). Grazing is of course linked to other variables that influence artifact visibility, movement, and collection. For example, we found that artifact movement was microscale for moderate grazing intensities over a single season; however, in an intensively grazed plot placed immediately adjacent to a water tank, the maximum movement was mesoscale – over 2 m in a single season, caused in part by a severe rainstorm and the disturbed earth near the water tank. All such variables are important concerns for interpretations of prehistoric behaviors and for managing the archaeological record as a limited, diminishing, and highly valuable resource.

DISCUSSION

The systematic misrepresentation of surface distributions that results from conventional discovery-based methods prevents surveys from addressing the range of scales that existed within prehistoric land use strategies. Thus far we have identified three critical elements of scale in archaeological survey design: grain, extent, and observational intensity. We also need to consider "intersite space" in our samples (Dunnell and Dancey, 1983; Ebert and Kohler, 1988; Foley, 1981; Thomas, 1975). The use of nested-intensity designs such as the Modified-Whittaker will improve the accuracy and comparability of samples, as a strategy of sub-sampling for augmenting single-scale (discover-based) methods that, by definition, prevent the identification of scale problems. They are valuable experimental tools because they allow archaeologists to investigate how survey intensity influences sample accuracy. For most archaeological concerns, understanding the relationship between the sample and the target population is a fundamental first step to building accurate interpretations and developing useful management protocols.

Integrating this Approach with Others

Because the intensity of sampling and the area sampled influence the number of artifact classes documented, a strategy that holds these two variables constant will improve our ability to evaluate and compare regions. As mentioned above, we emphasize evaluative aspects of survey that focus on the nature of the surface record rather than discovery alone, but both are necessary for systematic coverage that measures up to distributional approaches to survey. The use of coarse-grained transects to record artifact clusters is an effective means of discovery, while crawl surveys of the subplots within the Modified-Whittaker plot obtain highly accurate systematic subsamples within a consistent framework. Extreme levels of experimental control are too costly for all phases of survey, but are certainly useful for filling in the gaps left by discovery-based (i.e., coarse-grained) methods and for quality control. While our survey was developed for a hunter–gatherer landscape in an arid geomorphologically active setting, all survey situations could benefit from multiple intensities and multiple spatial scales in the sampling design. For example, if a large region had been previously surveyed in 20 m transects, the results of that survey could be used to select locations for more intensive evaluation. Covering as little as 1% of this hypothetical region with the Modified-Whittaker plot would greatly increase the information return, comparability, methodological control, and awareness for the rate of change in its distributional properties.

There is much to be gained from considering multiple scales of reference in archaeological interpretation and analysis. The resilience of an interpretation may be directly proportional to the number of spatial and temporal perspectives that support it.

CONCLUSION

> If we study a system at an inappropriate scale, we may not detect its actual dynamics and patterns but may instead identify patterns that are artifacts of scale. Because we are clever at devising explanations of what we see, we may think we understand the system when we have not even observed it correctly. (Wiens, 1989:390)

Any field that must explain complex phenomena must also consider scale. The perspective outlined here connects archaeology to other fields in the use of basic conceptual and methodological tools that address scalar issues. Achieving a precise and applicable set of techniques for scale in archaeology will have the advantages of increasing understanding for the formational histories of landscapes, allow for more accurate interpretations of prehistoric land use, and improve our ability to assess contemporary human impacts on the landscape. In the absence of attention to scalar issues, creative, yet erroneous conclusions may be easily reached regarding the causal linkages between pattern and process. With current trends of investigating the dynamics of whole landscapes (Banning, 2002), the need to bridge scalar gaps will continue to be a fundamental aspect of archaeological research.

We have presented a series of tools for dealing with scalar issues, some more widely applicable than others. Perhaps the most relevant of the techniques presented are multiscale sampling, the concept of scope, and the use of space–time diagrams. These tools are useful for depicting scalar relationships between models, methods, instruments, taphonomic processes, and cultural variables. Spatial allometry demonstrates the degree to which observer intensity can influence the parameters of the sample. Clearly, the naïve and overly optimistic notion of ''100 % survey coverage'' should be purged from archaeological survey jargon.

The use of multiscale analysis supports a variety of techniques that archaeologists could potentially use to: (1) compare different archaeological surveys; (2) quantitatively describe the properties of the surface record; (3) analyze the distributional behavior of different classes of artifacts within a landscape sample; and (4) develop heuristic and quantitative techniques for confronting problems of scale in archaeology.

Looking at the archaeological record through just one pane of a window is potentially misleading. Varying the window size and the closeness of our gaze allows us not only to be able to identify what we miss with certain vantages, but also to see how our impressions of world are affected by conventional wisdoms. This may lead to uncomfortable realizations about our prevailing interpretations of the archaeological record, but it may also lead to refreshing, more accurate, and more holistic, interpretations of a complex material record and its more interesting behavioral origins.

ACKNOWLEDGEMENTS   We greatly appreciate the patience and hard work of the Colorado State University field school students from 1999 to 2001 who made these studies possible. Tom Stohlgren has provided invaluable guidance on issues of sampling, scale, and measures of diversity. Doug Stephens, the USDA archaeologist on the Oglala during our surveys, was tremendously supportive and provided valuable insight, encouragement, and understanding throughout the project. David Schnieder was generous with advice and reprints for the development of this approach to scale in archaeology. Michael Anderson provided valuable consultation on ecological techniques of spatial analysis. Much of this work would not have been possible without the time and effort of Paul Burnett, Kristi Burnett, Becky Thomas, David Rapson, and Linda Anderson. Ann Ramenofsky and Judson Finley made valuable comments on early drafts of this manuscript. Paul Burnett commented on multiple versions. We thank Luann Wandsnider for putting us in touch with the editors of this volume and for providing valuable correspondence during our survey project. Any errors in judgment or reasoning are, of course, our own responsibility.

REFERENCES

Ammerman, A. J., 1981, Surveys and Archaeological Research. *Annual Review of Anthropology* 10:63–88.

Banning, E. B., 2002, *Archaeological Survey*. Kluwer Academic, New York.

Binford, L. R., 1964, A Consideration of Archaeological Research Design. *American Antiquity* 29(4):425–441.

Burger, O., Todd, L. C., Burnett, P., Stohlgren, T. J., and Stephens, D., 2004, Multi-scale and Nested-Intensity Sampling Techniques for Archaeological Survey. *Journal of Field Archaeology* 29 (3 and 4): 409–422.

Burris, L. E., 2004, *Harvester Ant Mounds: Utility for Small Object Detection in Archaeological Survey*. Unpublished MA Thesis, Department of Anthropology, Colorado State University, Fort Collins.

Brown, J. H., Gillooly, J. F., Allen, A. P., Savage, V. M., and West, G. B., 2004, Toward a Metabolic Theory of Ecology. *Ecology* 85(7):1771–1789.

Church, M., 1996, Space, Time and the Mountain - How Do We Order What We See? In *The Scientific Nature of Geomorphology: Proceedings of the 27th Binghampton Symposium in Geomorphology*, edited by C. E. Thorn, pp. 147–170. John Wiley and Sons, Hoboken, New Jersey.

Clarke, D. L., 1973, Archaeology: The Loss of Innocence. *Antiquity* 47:6–18.

Dunnell, R. C., and Dancey, W. S., 1983, The Siteless Survey: A Regional Scale Data Collection Strategy. In *Advances in Archaeological Method and Theory*, edited by M. B. Schiffer, pp. 267–287. Volume 5. Academic Press, New York.

Ebert, J. I., 1992, *Distributional Archaeology*. University of New Mexico Press, Albuquerque.

Ebert, J. I., and Kohler, T. A., 1988, The Theoretical Basis of Archaeological Predictive Modeling and a Consideration of Appropriate Data-Collection Methods. In *Quantifying the Present and Predicting the Past: Theory, Method, and Application of Archaeological Predictive Modeling*, edited by L. Sebastian, pp. 91–172. US Bureau of Land Management, Denver.

Flannery, K. V., 1976, Sampling at the Regional Level. In *The Early Mesoamerican Village*, edited by K. V. Flannery, pp. 131–136. Academic Press, New York.

Foley, R. A., 1981, Off-Site Archaeology: An Alternative for the Short-Sited. In *Patterns of the Past: Essays in Honor of David L. Clarke*, edited by N. Hammond, pp. 157–183. Cambridge University Press, Cambridge.

Gardner, R. H., 1998, Pattern, Process, and the Analysis of Spatial Scales. In *Ecological Scale: Theory and Application*, edited by D. L. Peterson and V. T. Parker, pp. 17–34. Columbia University Press, New York.

Golley, F., 1989, Paradigm Shift: Editor's Comment. *Landscape Ecology* 3:65–66.

Hodder, I., and Orton, C., 1976, *Spatial Anaylsis in Archaeology*. Cambridge University Press, Cambridge.

Kelly, R. L., 1999, Thinking About Prehistory. In *Models for the Millennium: Great Basin Anthropology Today*, edited by C. Beck, pp. 111–117. University of Utah Press, Salt Lake City.

King, A. W., Johnson, A.R., and O'Neill, R.V., 1991, Transmutation and Functional Representation of Heterogeneous Landsapes. *Landscape Ecology* 5(4):239–253.

Leonard, R. D., 1987, Incremental Sampling in Artifact Analysis. *Journal of Field Archaeology* 14(4):498–500.

Levin, S. A., 1992, The Problem of Pattern and Scale in Ecology. *Ecology* 73(6):1943–1967.

Levin, S. A., and Buttel, L., 1986, *Measures of Patchiness in Ecological Systems*. Publication ERC-130. Ecosystem Research Center, Cornell University, Ithaca.

Milne, B. T., 1992, Spatial Aggregation and Neutral Models in Fractal Landscapes. *American Naturalist* 139:32–57.

O'Neill, R. V., and King, A. W., 1998, Homage to St. Michael; or, Why Are There So Many Books on Scale? In *Ecological Scale: Theory and Application*, edited by D. L. Peterson and V. T. Parker, pp. 3–16. Columbia University Press, New York.

Pennycuick, C. J., and Kline, N. C., 1986, Units of Measurement for Fractal Extent, Applied to the Coastal Distribution of Bald Eagle Nests in the Aleutian Islands. *Oecologia* 68:254–258.

Peters, R. H., 1983, *The Ecological Implications of Body Size*. Cambridge University Press, Cambridge.

Peterson, David. L., and Parker V. Thomas, 1998, *Ecological Scale: Theory and Application*. Columbia University Press, New York.

Ricklefs, R. E., and Miller, G. L., 2000, *Ecology*. Fourth Edition. W. H. Freeman and Company, New York.

Sanders, W. T., Parsons, J. R., and Santley, R. S., 1979, *The Basin of Mexico: The Ecological Processes in the Evolution of a Civilization*. Academic Press, New York.

Schiffer, M. B., Sullivan, A. P., and Klinger, T. C., 1978, The Design of Archaeological Surveys. *World Archaeology* 10:1–28.

Schneider, D. C., 1994, *Quantitative Ecology: Spatial and Temporal Scaling*. Academic Press, San Diego.

Schneider, D. C., 1998, Applied Scaling Theory. In *Ecological Scale: Theory and Application*, edited by D. L. Peterson and V. T. Parker, pp. 253–269. Columbia University Press, New York.

Schneider, D. C., 2001a, The Rise of the Concept of Scale in Ecology. *BioScience* 51(7):545–553.

Schneider, D. C., 2001b, Scale, Concept and Effects of. In *Encyclopedia of Biodiversity*, edited by S. A. Levin, pp. 245–254. Volume 5. Academic Press, San Diego.

Schneider, D. C., 2001c, Spatial Allometry: Theory and Application to Experimental and Natural Ecosystems. In *Scaling Relations in Experimental Ecology*, edited by J. E. Petersen, pp. 113–156. Columbia University Press, New York.

Schneider, D. C., 2002, Scaling Theory: Application to Marine Ornithology. *Ecosystems* 5:736–748.

Schneider, D. C., Walters, R., Thrush, S., and Dayton, P., 1997, Scale-Up of Ecological Experiments: Density Variation in the Mobile Bivalve Macomona liliana. *Journal of Experimental Marine Biology and Ecology* 216:129–152.

Schoville, B. J., and Todd, L. C., 2001, Harvester Ants and the Archaeological Record: Formational Dynamics and Interpretive Potentials. Paper presented at the 59th Annual Plains Anthropological Conference, Lincoln, Nebraska.

Steele, J. H., 1978, Some Comments on Plankton Patches. In *Spatial Pattern in Plankton Communities*, edited by J. H. Steele, pp. 11–20. Plenum Press, New York.

Stein, J. K., 1993, Scale in Archaeology, Geosciences, and Geoarchaeology. In *Effects of Scale on Archaeological and Geoscientific Perspectives*, edited by A. R. Linse, pp. 1–10. Special Paper No. 283. Geological Society of America, Boulder.

Stohlgren, T. J., Falkner, M. B., and Schell, L. D., 1995, A Modified-Whittaker Nested Vegetation Sampling Method. *Vegetatio* 117:113–121.

Stohlgren, T. J., Chong, G. W., Kalkhan, M. A., and Schell, L. D., 1997, Multiscale Sampling of Plant Diversity: Effects of Minimum Mapping Unit Size. *Ecological Applications* 7:1064–1074.

Stohlgren, T. J., Bull, K. A., and Otsuki, Y., 1998, Comparison of Rangeland Vegetation Sampling Techniques in the Central Grasslands. *Journal of Range Management* 51:164–172.

Thomas, D. H., 1975, Nonsite Sampling in Archaeology: Up the Creek Without a Site? In *Sampling in Archaeology*, edited by J. W. Mueller, pp. 61–81. University of Arizona Press, Tuscon.

Wandsnider, L., 1998, Regional Scale Processes and Archaeological Landscape Units. In *Unit Issues in Archaeology,* edited by A. Steffen, pp. 87–102. University of Utah Press, Salt Lake City.

Wandsnider, L., and Camilli, E., 1992, The Character of Surface Archaeological Deposits and Its Influence on Survey Accuracy. *Journal of Field Archaeology* 19:169–188.

Webster, R., and Oliver, M. A., 2001, *Geostatistics for Environmental Scientists. Statistics in Practice.* John Wiley and Sons, Ltd, West Sussex, England.

Wiens, J. A., 1989, Spatial Scaling in Ecology. *Functional Ecology* 3:385–397.

Wiens, J. A., 1990, On the Use of 'Grain' and 'Grain-Size' in Ecology. *Functional Ecology* 4:720.

Wiens, J. A., 1999, The Science and Practice of Landscape Ecology. In *Landscape Ecological Analysis*, edited by R. H. Gardner, pp. 371–383. Springer-Verlag, Berlin.

Wiens, J. A., 2001, Understanding the Problem of Scale in Experimental Ecology. In *Scaling Relations in Experimental Ecology*, edited by J. E. Petersen, pp. 61–88. Columbia University Press, New York.

Willey, G. R., 1953, *Prehistoric Settlement Patterns in the Virú Valley, Perú*. Bureau of American Ethnology Bulletin No. 155. Smithsonian Institution, Washington DC.

Yellen, J. E., 1996, Behavioral and Taphonomic Patterning at Katanda 9: a Middle Stone Age Site, Kivu Province, Zaire. *Journal of Archaeological Science* 23:915–932.

Yellen, J. E., 1977, *Archaeological Approaches to the Present: Models for Reconstructing the Past.* Academic Press, New York.

CHAPTER 16

Persons and Landscapes: Shifting Scales of Landscape Archaeology

Vuk Trifković

INTRODUCTION

Although archaeology has long been an explicitly spatial discipline, it is only recently with the introduction of phenomenological-based approaches that space has been acknowledged as more than a mere backdrop for human action. Sometimes referred to as an ''archaeology of practice'', these recent approaches emphasise that places can only acquire significance in relation to people's bodies, movements and practices. Examples of the archaeology of practice are abundant, being both influential and well rehearsed; there is no need to repeat them here (Barrett, 1994; Thomas, 1996; Tilley, 1994). Even so, I would argue that this concept is not without its drawbacks.

There is no doubt that ideas focusing on practice, agency, dwelling and the body brought about by such theoretical innovation are welcome but the problem is that the archaeology of practice has ventured far from its original intentions. The resulting criticism can be simplified into two main problem areas:

1. The articulation of agency and individual action; and
2. The inadequate relationship between representational and non-discursive meaning.

Fundamental to both of these areas is the issue of scale. The articulation of individual action and agency is an issue of balancing the individual against the social, as is the relationship between representational and non-discursive meaning. In one of the most concise critiques of the archaeology of practice, Hodder (1999) identifies a stubborn reaction against any discourse or framework of meaning outside that of practice that inevitably impoverishes the archaeology of practice. He is right to emphasize the need to connect non-discursive practices with the external, but historically specific, framework of representational meaning (Hodder, 1999:137), an approach that is explored in this paper.

Vuk Trifković • University of Oxford

One recent attempt to rectify, rather than just criticise, the problematic aspects of the archaeology of practice is through new ways of treating the body, the *somatization* of archaeology (Meskell, 1996). Proponents of somatization argue that with the body conceptualised as the central axis of archaeological inquiry we can engender agency and move towards the reconstitution of embodied actors at a specific point in the past. We would also be in a better position to resolve the troubled, scale dependent relationship between the individual and the group, as neither can exists without the other and ultimately neither without bodies. Finally, it is argued, somatization enables stronger links between embodied agents and the context, both symbolic and environmental, within which they operate. Whether one agrees or not with such interpretative attempts, it is clear that such an approach may be able to situate certain persons and their physical bodies not just in their wider context, but in the flux of grand scale frameworks of meaning that were surrounding a specific person inhabiting a specific body.

Apart from the arguments that practical examples of the somatization of archaeology have only been made possible either through using the insights of textual evidence (Treherne, 1995; Meskell, 1996) or through extraordinary conditions of preservation (Öetzi, for example, in Hodder 2000), I would suggest that there are other, more substantial, problems with this approach. Arguments in favour of the somatization of archaeology are closely integrated with the criticism of landscape archaeology for forgoing bodies and embodied actors in favour of monuments, landscapes and larger social entities. Unfortunately, the converse is also true, for while focusing on embodied agents in their historical context, they have ignored the landscapes surrounding them. For example, Treherne (1995) discusses the landscape implications of new forms of burial monuments and their locations in a single sentence, while landscape is not even an issue in Meskell's work. Even Last's (1998) explorations of fine scale deposition and the orientation of different individuals within the Barnack barrow in Cambridgeshire are confined to the boundaries of the monument. While the exploration of historically situated and embodied agents is obviously a laudable enterprise, a full sense of agency is never achieved in these accounts because they provide no information about the links between persons and the landscapes they have inhabited. In fact, there is no concept of these reconstructed persons being situated in any spatial or environmental locale, let alone the exploration of the mutually defining relationships between spaces, agents and their bodies, operating within locales. Instead we appear to have finely crafted individuals floating in an empty black void of history.

This situation is untenable for two main reasons. First, there can be no appropriate account of the body and embodiment without consideration of the mutually defining relationship between embodied agents and the landscapes surrounding them. Second, as bodies and persons are the locus in which practices meet long term contexts, I do not believe we can adequately articulate non-discursive, quotidian practices with long-term historical contexts and pervasive frameworks of meaning, as argued for by Hodder (2000) or Treherne (1995), without considering the articulation between landscapes and embodied actors.

The problems that arise from this tension are as much to do with scale and perspective, as being the result of what Meskell emphatically labels "the seduction of social constructivism'' (Meskell, 1998). The emergence and relative success of both an archaeology of practice and the concomitant attempt to somatize archaeology reflect the overwhelming conditions and the burning questions of contemporary society. This is a tale of two perspectives. The first is global, a perspective of landscape and environment dominant in the archaeology of practice and seemingly suitable for a shrinking, boundless, global world (Harvey 2000). The second, which has experienced a more rapid rise, is the most micro-scale of all, the bodily perspective developed in the context of the bold rise of ''radical individualism'', the proclaimed ''death of society'' (Cohen, 1994) and the general post-modern endemic loss of confidence resulting in the emergence of the body as an irreducible basis for understanding. Once again, very little attempt has been made to integrate these two perspectives, the global and the molecular, and to recognize these as different scales of the same approach (Harvey 2000:15). Yet, the integration of the two is recognised as crucial. Harvey (2000), for example, pins the hopes of society overall on the activist discourse that attempts to connect different scales, such as a rising global discourse of human rights refracted through an issue of the most intimate scale, that of the control of the female body. The same can be argued for archaeology, so that the archaeology of practice and approaches to embodiment become complementary rather than opposed schools of thought, with differences mainly attributed to the different perspectives and operational scales adopted in each case.

I am clearly not the first nor the last to address the most fundamental question of the social sciences, if not of the whole intellectual enterprise: how to articulate subject and object, how to operate on more than one scale without privileging any particular one. My thinking is grounded in the work of Latour (1993) and Deleuze and Guattari (2002) and their identification of the need to affirm the uniqueness and singularity of things through tracing the connections between entities and the effects of those connections. To do this we first need to disentangle the two poles, body and personhood on one hand and landscape on the other, and then re-territorialize them in a new way through the creation of new connections between bodies and landscape – thus rendering the two as hybrid, mixed, mutually defining and above all unique and specific. To achieve this goal I intend to use two concepts: first that of taskscapes, defined by Ingold (2000) as the landscape embodied through agency, a concept that may help link actors with their spatial context. The second is the metaphor of distributed objects and persons (Gell, 1998; Strathern, 1988) that could replace relatively simplistic definitions of individuals, and enable a stronger connection between embodied agents and the spatial context in which they operate.

My arguments concerning taskscapes and their relationship to agency, practice and process have all been detailed elsewhere (Trifković, 2005); here I wish to concentrate on the limits of the concept of taskscapes. Ingold states (2000:163) that there is no need to draw the boundaries of the taskscape around the limits of the animate, arguing that taskscapes have to be extended beyond the scope of human action, at least to other animate objects. The question of animate and inanimate, of dynamic and static is, after all, a question of scale, for if we observed landscape over a long enough period of time, the inanimate would appear animate: trees would grow, mountains would move and oceans swell and retreat. I see enormous potential for the exploration of taskscapes beyond the limits of the animate. Coupled with the rhizomatic connectivity between agents, bodies, tasks, objects and places, taskscapes, and thus indirectly the concrete effects of practice, agency and process, can be explored not just on the landscape level, but whenever tasks are indexed, be it to bodies, places or objects. It is this property of taskscapes that is explored archaeologically below.

If we are to avoid the proliferation of "faceless" blobs (Tringham, 1991) in our prehistoric narratives and understand the mutually defining relationships between places and the embodied agents that inhabit them we need to expand the limits of taskscapes. We need taskscapes that are not just collapsed onto the landscape, but ones that are mapped onto bodies through marks, scars, shapes and pathologies, material bodies transforming and transformed, constructing and constructed by the environment around them as much as by their actions within that environment. This may bring out the difference between individual bodies reflecting different biographies, relations and identities, which become even more interesting against the backdrop of changing long-term trajectories into the past. It is maybe because of its apparent banality that this approach has remained overlooked. It seems puzzling that both anthropology and archaeology are engaged in a discussion of abstract concepts such as identity, gender or personhood, and yet a relatively simple idea such as the fact that bodies are shaped by their activities in the landscape is seldom considered. For example, Astuti (1995 and 1998) whose colourful Madagascan Vezo ethnography illustrates the importance of the mutually defining relationship between places, the tasks that are ongoing there, and the bodies of the people conducting the tasks, states that the treatment of the Vezo bodily construction and its relation to activities within the landscape is only discussed because of its relevance to the way the Vezo deal with the tension between the sexes and gender. Material culture derives its significance and importance not merely through its physical properties, but from its location, and/or its manner of procurement. Objects can have strong links with the places they are from or associated with in some other way, and they can permanently imply those places and taskscapes that they are connected with. Objects can imply places not just by virtue of their origin but through the association between their function and use and the places where those activities are or were ongoing.

TOWARDS A CONNECTED METHODOLOGY

The theoretical introduction above has one relevant conclusion: if we are to explore the mutually defining relationship between people and landscapes we need a methodology that will engender the fusion of regional and intra-site data and then examine the relationships between entities operating at different scales. As argued above, since taskscapes are inherently present in material objects and agents' bodies, and since persons and objects are dispersed through the landscape, we need to develop an analytical environment in which it is possible to slide between the macro and micropoles of inquiry. This must entail landscape analysis that works at both scales, at the very least establishing and revealing the relationships between objects, persons and places, and preferably being able to analyse those connections. The most suitable tool for such an endeavour would be an Object Orientated GIS (Tschan, 1999) although here I re-create aspects of the Object Oriented paradigm using tools more readily available in the conventional computing toolbox. The proposed strategy consists of several complementary levels of exploration:

1. a scale based approach to visibility studies;
2. the taskscapes of material objects including intra-site spatial patterning and the taskscapes represented by objects; and
3. the integration of intra-site and inter-site perspectives.

The first part of such an analysis, which we could call a general landscape analysis, involves an abstract exploration of the most general landscape properties: an investigation of abstract properties describing the general structure of a space. To use Cartesian terminology this level of analysis aims to describe the properties of space as a neutral container. Such abstract structural properties of landscape can be discovered by various characterisation techniques based around the cumulative analyses of visibility and accessibility that will result in the identification of important and visually prominent locations, the isolation of bounded landscape zones, and the assessment of relative accessibility for the whole of the case study area. This type of analysis can be performed at the macroscale only.

The analysis of taskscapes indexed in material objects involves two parallel directions of investigation. The first comprises the relatively straightforward investigation of the intra-site spatial configuration of objects, graves and other features. Such an analysis is easily conducted within a conventional GIS and can be integrated with the larger scale landscape analysis without much controversy. The second analytical theme consists of the investigation of distributed objects and their taskscapes as captured in intra-site data. Although this part of the approach may be considered esoteric, hard to achieve or even unnecessary, I would argue that it can provide answers if, and only if, the questions are phrased appropriately. The culmination of such a connected analysis would be in making the relationships established through the second theme explicit, analysing these relationships and presenting them as a coherent narrative. Such an approach needs to allow for the constant shift of scale between data of various resolutions and needs a methodology for tracing the links and connections between the often disparate elements within the analysis.

The Macroscale – The Quality Of Vision

The example of landscape scale analysis presented here is based on visibility, a currently popular aspect of GIS usage in archaeology. One of the problems of standard visibility analysis is that it explores the quantitative and not the qualitative characteristics of vision. Attempts to refine the investigation of visibility have centred on a qualitative understanding of vision, often through the exploration of factors that are intrinsically scale dependent. The main thrust of this has been attempts to integrate measures of distance and direction of vistas into GIS based visibility analysis, emanating from the seminal work of Higuchi (1983), a Japanese gardener and landscape researcher. From Higuchi's highly sophisticated analysis of visibility, the obvious has been taken, that distance and direction directly influence the quality of vision. Wheatley and Gillings (2000:14) were the first within archaeology to act upon this, and apart from introducing the concept of the quality of vision, they have also provided a simple algorithm integrating Higuchi's ideas of the impact of distance and directionality into the calculation of viewsheds. Following Higuchi, Wheatley and Gillings (2000:18) have proposed that the field of vision can be divided into distance and/or quality of vision ranges, the exact number and definition of which depends on the size of the object observed and the level of detail that is sought. Missing from Wheatley and Gillings' algorithm, however, is its application to cumulative visibility explorations, a routine which I have written to take the usual parameters for visibility studies and calculate cumulative viewsheds for each user-defined distance/quality range (called Higuchi Total Visibility; details in Trifković, 2005). Although various distance ranges could be experimented with, I have decided to use three: short range includes everything that is closer than 300 metres; mid range stretches between 300 m and 3 km; and anything over 3 km is deemed to be in the long range.

This cumulative approach to the quality of vision engenders something of a spectometry of vision, determining both the frequency and quality of visibility. Underlying this is the idea that places could be landmarks at different scales, and this analysis is primarily aimed at exploring how frequently each location is seen at different levels of visual quality. Higuchi Total Visibility analysis, therefore, can be used to assess the potential for locations being a landmark at different quality/distance scales. Also, cumulative Higuchi analysis will show the changing distribution of the three main levels of the quality of vision within a landscape, hopefully revealing scale related differences in the topography on which those distributions are based. More explicitly, the distribution of the visibility in each range may reveal some properties of the topography of that level, possibly isolating landscape zones of various scales.

The study area is the Iron Gates, a series of gorges and vales in the Carpathian Mountains through which the River Danube runs for some 130 km. Due to an extensive dam building project the area has undergone an intense period of surveying and archaeological scrutiny, albeit in the 1960s and 1970s, and has remained an exception in Balkan archaeology as one of the few regions where a systematic archaeological survey has been conducted. A central question of the archaeology of the Iron Gates is the problem of the relationship between the Neolithic and Mesolithic elements within the sites on the right bank, specifically Lepenski Vir, Vlasac and Padina, which are broadly dated to between 10000 and 5500 BC (for a recent summary see Borić, 2002). For this analysis, topographic data from the vicinity of the three principal sites has been captured digitally and explored in a conventional GIS, raster-based environment, aiming to reveal the embedded structure of the area's visual configuration.

Long range Higuchi Total Visibility, Figure 16.1, shows the distribution of all vistas that are at least 3 km away from the corresponding observation points. Comparison of this with total visibility per se (Trifković, 2005, Figure 26) displays a statistically significant fit, implying that long range visibility accounts for most of the total visibility and if a location is to have a high visibility ranking, it has to be

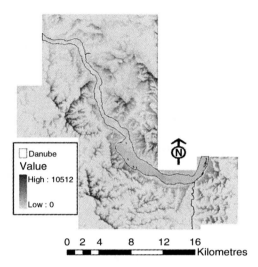

FIGURE 16-1. Higuchi Total Visibility long range (>3 km).

recurrently seen from far away. In turn this indicates that the locations ranking highly in Total Visibility usually have a poor quality of vision, that is, they are usually seen just as distant contours on the horizon rather than close-up, in detail.

Mid range Higuchi Total Visibility, defined as visibility between 300 m and 3 km, shows a slightly different pattern (Figure 16.2). The correlation with Total Visibility per se is lower and the visibility seems to be more evenly distributed.

Compared to the overall elevation (Trifković, 2005, Figure 30), the mid range Higuchi Total Visibility is noticeably skewed towards the lower range, i.e., lower

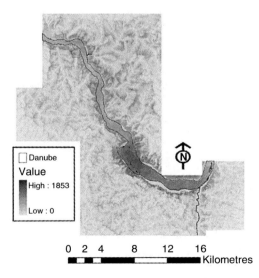

FIGURE 16-2. Higuchi Total Visibility mid range, (300–3,000 m).

than 100 m OD, making a slight recovery at higher elevations. On balance this result indicates two possibilities. First it shows important landmarks within the mid range quality of vision, that is, those places that would be more frequently seen well. It is conceivable that these landmarks would be more impressive and be comprehended more fully as a result of being seen well and more often, unlike the frequently, but poorly, seen long range peaks and ridges that form just a hazy backdrop to a vista. Second, Higuchi mid-range Total Visibility reveals medium range landscape units; for example, the Gorge itself, which appears to be one such unit bounded within the range of medium visibility, as are some of the larger tributary river valleys.

The most drastic difference from Total Visibility per se is that of short-range visibility, less than 300 m (Figure 16.3). This result portrays an entirely different set of factors at play as, naturally, the area seen in short range is not large but what is seen is comprehended very well including the details of objects observed. In addition, the tightly bounded zone of visibility in the short range means that olfactory, auditory or even tactile sensory input could be felt more strongly. Such zones coincide mainly with the sides and bottoms of the hinterland valleys surrounded by the high mountains. Movement through these spaces meant there was eventually some land seen in the distance but that one was immersed in a highly sensory-charged zone with the steep sides of the valley being very well seen and fully perceived through other senses (Figure 16.4).

The Microscale – Connecting With People

The landscape analysis described briefly so far would not accomplish the agenda set out in the introduction, i.e., exploring the mutually defining links between landscapes, objects and persons. Although these increasingly refined landscape characterisation tools have enabled us to calculate sophisticated measurements of

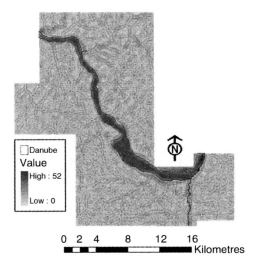

FIGURE 16-3. Short range Higuchi Total Visibility (<300 m).

FIGURE 16-4. Higuchi ranges: Note how the long range is obscured.

the distribution of visibility and the importance of the landmarks, if such analyses are not connected to specific agents and their bodies, these techniques will remain glorified binary viewsheds. The reconstruction of taskscapes will be in danger of becoming merely a new buzzword for conventional site catchment analysis. The challenge, then, is to connect the results of landscape scale analysis to inquiry at the micro-, somatic- or bodily scale. Innovative landscape inquiry, however, well thought through, cannot be found in landscape characterisation alone, but its power lies in the ability to make landscape analysis relevant and directly connected to analysis at the bodily scale. Only at the microscale can we begin to explore the intersection of long-term processes and short term agencies, of the interactions between people creating landscapes and the landscapes shaping the people. At the same time, microscale analysis can only make sense if the persons and their bodies and biographies are set within the context of the landscape, not just considered within the safe confines of the intra-site record. The challenge becomes how to achieve this without prioritising either approach.

Faced with this predicament, it is not enough merely to shift the scale of analysis and approach the issue of mutual relationships exclusively from the perspective of objects and individual bodies; the shift needs to be as much concep-tual as it is methodological. One way of exploring this is to trace taskscapes in the arrangement and the properties of objects and human remains recovered during excavation. In order to accomplish this I intend to shift scale but also to shift focus and look at fundamentally spatial questions through the prism of the remains of individual bodies from the site of Vlasac (Srejović and Letica, 1978) together with the objects and structures associated with them. The aim is to discover the funda-mental patterns of taskscapes that are inculcated in those objects and persons and the method involves exploding the biography of each person onto the wider landscape to trace taskscapes through the arrangement and properties of objects, structures and graves. This approach will be demonstrated through the case-study of two graves:

SITTING GRAVES AND VISIBILITY

Many sites within Iron Gates Gorge have at least one so-called sitting, or a la turca, grave, for example grave 17 from Vlasac, that of a 29–35 year old male (Figure 16.5). The body was arranged in a typical a la turca position, with the skull and rib cage collapsed in a heap leaning against a broken stone construction as if in a conical grave or niche cut into stone. On the left side of the skull was an oval depression, probably a result of a strong blow to the head. Apart from the mild spondylosis apparent on one of the vertebrae, there was no other pathological evidence.

To begin exploring the landscape connections of this grave, a binary viewshed from the grave can be compared with viewsheds from other points within the site including other graves. Although the structure of grave 17's visible area shows many similarities with the characteristics of visibility from the site overall, it is clear that the extent of visibility over the Danube is significantly higher. This means that accidentally or not, the location of grave 17 presides over the Danube; it appears to have been strategically placed to maximise the visible area of the Danube. This implies a topographic relationship with the Danube suggesting an attachment to place manifested through links with the river that must be understood as the pivotal axis of the Gorge. In addition, it also suggests that a certain class of people, older adults, have through long periods of acting in this landscape presumably developed links not just to the Gorge as a whole, but to specific aspects of it, particularly the

FIGURE 16-5. Plan of Graves 17 and 16 from Vlasac (from Srejović and Letica, 1978).

river. It also indicates that there may have been such a thing as significant landmarks in the symbolic constellation of the prehistoric inhabitants of the Iron Gates, and that one mode of engagement with place and landmarks, perhaps confined only to the older men, was the gaze. This is reassuring for visibility-based methods of analysis and certainly supports the idea that the significance of isolated landmarks is based on them being seen.

OFFSET GRAVES AND ALIGNMENTS ON TRESKAVAC

The smallest and probably the most controversial group of graves at Vlasac are those with offset orientations that are perpendicular to the river. Spatially defined groups of graves have been characterised by their orientation, in this case towards the north-northwest. This group only includes two, or perhaps three graves, the most prominent of which is grave 79, that of an adult woman with a very interesting biographical pattern (Figure 16.6). The bodily position and orientation is by no means unusual: a complete skeletal inhumation extended on its back with both arms positioned in the pelvic area. Even though grave goods were absent, materials such as ochre, red limestone and cyprinidae teeth, all linked to fertility and apotropaic powers, were found in copious amounts. Ochre and red limestone were painted around the pelvic area, cyprinidae teeth were sprinkled around the head and pelvic area and a block of red limestone was found in the grave.

Perhaps the reason for this burial treatment is to be found in the woman's severe pathological problems. Those which have left their mark on the skeleton are severe spondylosis and spondyloarthrosis of the spine and extremely serious arthrosis of the elbow, hip and knee. These combined ailments must have almost certainly rendered her if not entirely invalid, then certainly heavily dependent on others. The exact origin of these ailments is not known, but isotopic analysis suggests that the

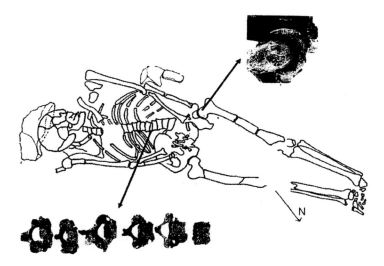

FIGURE 16-6. Grave 79, an adult woman with hip and spinal column deformations (from Srejović and Letica, 1978).

ailments could have been caused by repetitive strain and possibly incurred through activities practiced along the river (Trifković, 2005).

Unfortunately such a dramatic pattern is not replicated in other graves although what appears to be significant is that all of these graves are aligned on the cliff of Treskavac, the consistently outstanding landmark identified in the visibility analyses and in the long distance view in particular (Figure 16.7). More remarkable, perhaps, is the fact that Treskavac itself is barely perceptible from the site of Vlasac, only the topmost part of this impressive cliff being visible beyond the conical hill 314 (Figure 16.8).

It seems, therefore, that this group of graves is mirroring the same trend as that identified in another group of graves aligned in a different direction, to the east. These burials display rich and sometimes dramatic biographies aligned on unusual landscape features (Trifković, 2005). Grave 79 is the most dramatic example of this trend, and perhaps it is not surprising, therefore, that it is spatially connected to the most dramatic landmark in the Upper Gorge. An interesting implication for visibility-based landscape analysis is that the graves are oriented on the most dominant landmark in the Gorge, the cliff of Treskavac, even though it is barely visible from the site of Vlasac itself.

This brief discussion of Vlasac has attempted to reveal several, primarily spatial, trends at the site that highlight the relationship between the persons buried there and the material culture and landscape that surrounded them. The two illustrations indicate that the people buried with unusual alignments and bodily treatments tend to have a richer spectrum of biographical indices. It is precisely

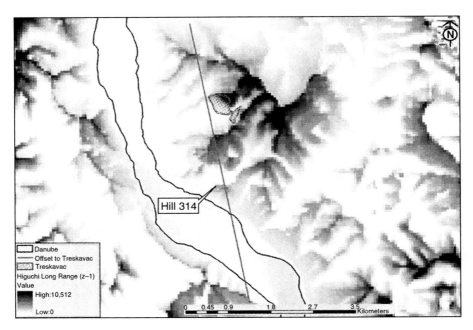

FIGURE 16-7. The long range viewshed from Vlasac showing the cliff of Treskavac, and the alignment from grave 79.

FIGURE 16-8. Treskavac as viewed from Vlasac.

such graves that tend to invoke an explicit topophilia with the Danube and the landmarks dominant in the area where activities such as fishing were conducted. These two are just the most extreme examples; a similar argument can be extended to other graves with an offset alignment and complex biographical indices. What is intriguing is the potential link between the dominant landmarks and the somewhat troubled biographies of these people. This association with individuals suffering from serious ailments can be interpreted as the invocation of powerful places and the forces vested in them at times of dramatic breakdown in the everyday pattern of existence. Normally, the bond between personal identity, well-being and the river or landmarks associated with riverine activities was important, but not overwhelmingly so, and it usually remained obviated. It is in these unusual burials, often accompanied by other apotropaic interventions (the application of ochre, cyprinidae teeth, ancestral secondary burials), that these links with powerful places were made explicit. If this was indeed the case, it would fit well within an apparent preoccupation with the apotropaic, a dominant trend in early prehistoric Iron Gates (Borić, 2002).

CONCLUSION

During the 1990s landscape archaeology went though somewhat of a renaissance with spatial questions shifting from an afterthought to the focus of much archaeological analysis (Tilley, 1994). Theoretically, landscape archaeology became the testing ground for many new ideas and it seemed to be offering an integral and holistic perspective on the past. Today, I would argue, there is a lingering doubt about whether landscape archaeology has fulfilled its promise. If the sub-discipline is to move forward it must confront the fundamental question of how to include culturally determined agents into landscape inquiry and not merely express an interest in articulating the two. I believe that the crux of this issue is re-thinking the relationship between the two scales, the environment and the agents who operate within it. In order not to treat people as little more than uniform and abstract templates we need to connect new perspectives on personhood with landscape inquiry and understand the mutually defining relationship between the two scales. More specifically, the theoretical approach demonstrated above has attempted to fuse the perspective of the global (macroscale, landscape, long term processes and temporalities) with the local (microscale, bodily, specific, individual). I have tried to do so through harnessing the two similar concepts of taskscapes and distributed objects as traced through the exploration of the connections between spatial properties of the landscape and the contextual analysis of the arrangement of artefacts, archaeological structures and human remains. These two theoretical tools, which share a similar intellectual background, are different expressions of the same ontological stance that privileges relations instead of essences, therefore providing for the connections between global and local perspectives. GIS provides for such a solution through a platform on which the intra-site analysis of each burial and archaeological features can interact with the large-scale landscape matrix. The importance of GIS goes beyond its data management capabilities – it directly confronts the theoretical challenge to operationalise the concepts that will allow us to see the global in the local, and the local in the global. This has been demonstrated here through the use of taskscapes and the theory of dividuality enabled by the role of a GIS expanded from merely allowing the juxtaposition of the two scales to generating ideas for new analyses which are themselves multiscalar.

REFERENCES

Astuti, R., 1995, *People of the Sea: Identity and Descent among the Vezo of Madagascar*. Cambridge, Cambridge University Press.

Astuti, R., 1998, "It's a boy, It's a girl!": Reflections on Sex and Gender in Madagascar and Beyond. In *Bodies and Persons: Comparative Perspectives from Africa and Melanesia*, edited by M. Lambek and A. Strathern, pp. 29–52. Cambridge, Cambridge University Press.

Barrett, J., 1994, *Fragments from Antiquity: an Archaeology of Social Life in Britain, 2900–1200 BC*. Oxford, Blackwell.

Borić, D., 2002, The Lepenski Vir Conundrum: Reinterpretation of the Mesolithic and Neolithic Sequences in the Danube Gorges. *Antiquity* 76:1026–39.

Cohen, A.P., 1994, *Self Consciousness: an Alternative Anthropology of Identity*. London, Routledge.

Deleuze, G., and Guattari, F., 2002 (1984), *A Thousand Plateaus*. London, Continuum International Publishing Group – Mansell.

Gell, A., 1998, *Art and Agency: the Anthropological Theory*. Oxford, Clarendon Press.

Harvey, D., 2000, *Spaces of Hope*. Edinburgh, Edinburgh University Press.

Higuchi, T., 1983, *The Visual and Spatial Structure of Landscapes*. Cambridge, MIT Press.

Hodder, I., 1999, *The Archaeological Process: an Introduction*. Oxford, Blackwells.

Hodder, I., 2000, Agency and Individuals in Long-term Processes. In *Agency in Archaeology*, edited by M.A. Dobres and J. Robb, pp. 21–33. London, Routledge.

Ingold, T., 2000, *The Perception of the Environment: Essays in Livelihood, Dwelling and Skill*. London, Routledge.

Last, J., 1998, Books of Life: Biography and Memory in a Bronze Age Barrow. *Oxford Journal of Archaeology* 17(1):45–53.

Latour, B., 1993, *We Have Never Been Modern*. London, Harvester Wheatsheaf.

Meskell, L., 1996, The Somatization of Archaeology. *Norwegian Archaeological Review* 29:1–17.

Meskell, L., 1998, The Irresistible Body and the Seduction of Archaeology. In *Changing Bodies, Changing Meanings: Studies on the Human Body in Antiquity*, edited by D. Monserrat, pp. 139–161. London, Routledge.

Srejović, D., and Letica, Z., 1978, V*lasac: Mezolitsko Naselje u Djerdapu*. Beograd, Srpska Akademija Nauka i Umetnosti.

Strathern, M., 1988, *The Gender of the Gift: Problems with Women and Problems with Society in Melanesia*. Berkeley, University of California Press.

Thomas, J., 1996, *Time, Culture and Identity*. Cambridge, Cambridge University Press.

Treherne, P., 1995, The Warrior's Beauty: the Masculine Body and Self-identity in Bronze-Age Europe. *Journal of European Archaeology* 3 (1):105–144.

Tilley, C., 1994, *A Phenomenology of Landscape: Places, Paths and Monuments*. Oxford, Berg.

Trifković, V., 2005, *The Construction of Space in Early Holocene Iron Gates*. Oxford: Unpublished D.Phil thesis, University of Oxford.

Tringham, R., 1991, Households with Faces: the Challenge of Gender in Prehistoric Architectural Remains. In *Engendering Archaeology: Women and Prehistory*, edited by J. Gero and M. Conkey, pp. 93–131. Oxford, Blackwell.

Tschan, A., 1999, An Introduction to Object-Oriented GIS in Archaeology. In *New Techniques for Old Times. CAA 1998*, edited by J. Bareceló, I.Briz, and A.Vila, pp. 303–316. BAR International Series 757.

Wheatley, D., and Gillings, M., 2000, Vision, Perception and GIS: Developing Enriched Approaches to the Study of Archaeological Visibility. In *Beyond the Map: Archaeology and Spatial Technologies*, edited by Gary Lock, pp. 1–27. Oxford, IOS Press.

Index